MW00983549

The Structure and Interpretation of Quantum Mechanics

The Structure and Interpretation of *Quantum Mechanics*

R. I. G. HUGHES

Harvard University Press
Cambridge, Massachusetts, and London, England

Printed in the United States of America
Third printing, 1994

First Harvard University Press paperback edition, 1992

Library of Congress Cataloging in Publication Data

Hughes, R. I. G.
The structure and interpretation of quantum mechanics/
R. I. G. Hughes
p. cm.
Bibliography: p.
Includes index.
ISBN 0-674-84391-6 (alk. paper) (cloth)
ISBN 0-674-84392-4 (paper)
1. Quantum theory. 2. Physics—Philosophy. I. Title.
QC174.12.H82 1989
530.1′2—dc19 88-16551
CIP

To Nicholas and Catharine
(a.k.a. Nick and Kate)

Contents

Preface

I take it to be an unassailable truth that what Taoism, Confucianism, Zen Buddhism, and the writings of Carlos Castaneda have in common, they have in common with quantum mechanics. As truths go, however, this one isn't very illuminating. Quantum mechanics, one of the two great and revolutionary theories of physics to appear during the first thirty years of this century, is essentially a mathematical theory; one will gain little genuine insight into it without some awareness of the mathematical models it employs.

That is one of the two beliefs which have guided the writing of this book. The other is that the requisite mathematical knowledge is not, after all, fearsomely difficult to acquire. In fact, one kind of reader I have in mind is the reader who, while not seized by paralysis at the sight of a mathematical formula, does not happen to have a working knowledge of vector-space theory. In this respect the book is self-contained; the mathematical background it assumes is that of high school mathematics, and the additional mathematics needed, the mathematics of vector spaces, is presented in Chapters 1 and 5.

Another kind of reader has taken physics courses, and solved textbook problems in quantum mechanics, but, like most of us, continues to find the theory deeply mysterious. Perhaps rashly, this reader hopes that a philosophical account will clarify matters. Between these two ideal types there is, if not a continuous spectrum, at least a considerable diversity of readers to whom the book will prove accessible.

In presenting the mathematics, the strategy I have used is to treat finitely dimensional spaces, particularly two-dimensional spaces, in some detail, and then to indicate in general terms how the same ideas are applied in the infinitely dimensional case. Correspondingly, the quantum-mechanical quantities I deal with are usually spin components, rather than position and momentum. It turns out that most of the problematic features of quantum theory can be presented in terms of the behavior of the spin-$\frac{1}{2}$ particle, whose representation requires no more than the two-dimensional space $\mathbb{C}^2$.

The first half of the book not only sets out the mathematics of vector spaces; it also shows how elegantly these structures can model a probabilistic world. But if, as quantum mechanics suggests, the world they represent is the actual world, then we face deep problems of interpretation. Defying as it does any "natural" interpretation, whether in terms of causal processes or of systems and their properties, quantum theory challenges some of our most basic metaphysical assumptions.

These issues of interpretation are the subject of the second half of the book (Chapters 6–10). Most of the well-known problems are aired—like those of Schrödinger's cat, the two-slit experiment, and the EPR correlations—but certain topics, such as hidden-variable theories, get very scanty treatment, and others, like the Pauli exclusion principle, are not mentioned at all. I confine myself to orthodox (nonrelativistic) quantum mechanics; I do not discuss, for example, Dirac's relativistic account of the hydrogen atom, nor do I deal with quantum field theories. This book is in no sense an encyclopedia of the interpretation of quantum theory.

Both my exposition of the structure of the theory and the positive suggestions I make concerning its interpretation are, in the broadest sense, quantum-logical. My account of the theory's structure is essentially that given by John von Neumann and by George Mackey. The interpretation I lean to, and which I call the "quantum event interpretation," is in many respects consonant with that advocated by Jeffrey Bub, by William Demopoulos, and by Allen Stairs. The general account of physical theories which acts as a backdrop to these specific discussions of quantum theory is the semantic view associated with Patrick Suppes and Bas van Fraassen: theories are seen as supplying models for the phenomena they deal with.

Having thus outlined my program and declared my allegiances, I leave the reader to decide whether to proceed further, or to open another beer, or both.

* * *

Among those to whom I owe thanks are Malcolm McMillan and M. H. L. Pryce of the University of British Columbia, in whose physics classes I learned about quantum mechanics; I hope that in the pages that follow they can recognize the beautiful theory that they taught me. For what I learned when I came to teach courses myself I owe a debt to my students at the University of British Columbia, at the University of Toronto, at Princeton, and at Yale. Allen Poteshman, in particular, read most of the manuscript in his senior year at Yale and would return to me weekly, politely drawing my attention to obscurities, fallacies, and simple errors of fact. Roger Cooke, Michael Keane, and W. Moran have kindly allowed me to reprint their "elementary proof" of Gleason's theorem, and my commentary on it has been much improved by Roger Cooke's suggestions. For detailed comments on a late draft of the book I am also indebted to Jon Jarrett, while for specific advice, encouragement, and appropriate reproof I would like to thank Steven Savitt, Michael Feld, Clark Glymour, David Malament, and Lee Smolin.

Sections of the book were written in railway carriages, airport lounges, and theatrical dressing rooms, but for more tranquil environments I am grateful to Sue Hughes and Paul Schleicher, to Susan Brison, and to Margot Livesey, in whose houses whole chapters took shape. The final manuscript was typed up swiftly and accurately by Caroline Curtis, and the diagrams elegantly rendered by Mike Leone; Patricia Slatter is even now at work on the index. At Harvard University Press, Lindsay Waters has been a source of great encouragement over several years, and Kate Schmit edited the manuscript with great care and sensitivity. My thanks to all of them.

I saved my two greatest personal debts till last. I met Ed Levy within days of my arrival at U.B.C.; he it was who first stimulated my interest in the philosophical foundations of quantum mechanics, who later supervised my dissertation in that area, and who has continued to help me to clarify my thoughts on the subject. Bas van Fraassen and I met at the University of Toronto; since then we have discussed the problems quantum theory raises (along with the architecture of the Renaissance and the plays of Friedrich Dürrenmatt) on two continents and in half a dozen countries. Both have helped me more, perhaps, than they know.

I would also like to express my gratitude to the following firms and institutions:

To Addison-Wesley Publishing Company, Reading, Massachusetts, for permission to reprint a diagram from *The Feynman Lectures on Physics* (1965), by R. P. Feynman, R. B. Leighton, and M. Sands.

To Kluwer Academic Publishers, Dordrecht, Holland, for permission to reprint a diagram from J. Earman's *A Primer on Determinism* (1986).

To Cambridge University Press, Cambridge, U.K., for permission to reprint in Appendix A "An Elementary Proof of Gleason's Theorem," by R. Cooke, M. Keane, and W. Moran, from *Mathematical Proceedings of the Cambridge Philosophical Society* (1985).

To the Frederick W. Hilles Publication Fund of Yale University, with whose assistance the manuscript was prepared.

I seik about this warld unstabille
To find ane sentence convenabille,
Bot I can nocht in all my wit
Sa trew ane sentence fynd off it
As say, it is dessaveabille.

—WILLIAM DUNBAR

INTRODUCTION

The Stern-Gerlach Experiment

Quantum mechanics is at once one of the most successful and one of the most mysterious of scientific theories. Its success lies in its capacity to classify and predict the behavior of the physical world; the mystery resides in the problem of what the physical world must be like to behave as it does. The theory deals with the fundamental entities of physics — particles like protons, electrons, and neutrons, from which matter is built; photons, which carry electromagnetic radiation; and the host of "elementary particles" which mediate the other interactions of physics. We call these "particles" despite the fact that some of their properties are totally unlike the properties of the particles of our ordinary, macroscopic world, the world of billiard balls and grains of sand. Indeed, it is not clear in what sense these "particles" can be said to have properties at all.

Physicists have been using quantum mechanics for more than half a century; yet there is still wide disagreement about how the theory is best understood. On one interpretation, the so-called state functions of quantum mechanics apply only to ensembles of physical systems, on another, they describe individual systems themselves; on one view we can say something useful about a particle only when it interacts with a piece of measuring equipment, on another such a particle can be perfectly well described at all times, but to do so we need a language in which the ordinary laws of logic do not hold.

Are we, perhaps, foolish to seek an interpretation of this theory? Maybe we should take the advice Richard Feynman (1965, p. 129) offers in one of his lectures on *The Character of Physical Law:*

> I am going to tell you what nature behaves like . . . Do not keep saying to yourself, if you can possibly avoid it, "But how can it be like that?" because you will get "down the drain," into a blind alley from which nobody has yet escaped. Nobody knows how it can be like that.

Feynman illustrates this pessimistic conclusion with a well-known thought-experiment, the two-slit experiment to show interference effects with electrons (see also Feynman, Leighton, and Sands, 1965, vol. 3, lecture 1). To the problems raised by this experiment I will return in Chapter 8; in the meantime, another example will allow us to taste the peculiar flavor of quantum theory.

In late 1921 Otto Stern and Walther Gerlach performed the first of a series of experiments on the magnetic properties of various atoms (see Jammer, 1966, pp. 134–136). They vaporized silver in an enameling oven and allowed some of the atoms to escape, collimating them into a narrow beam by means of diaphragms. The beam then passed between the poles of a specially shaped magnet and, some distance further on, it struck a glass plate. The trace the atoms left on the plate showed that they had been deflected as they traversed the magnetic field, and that the beam had been split into two, one half of it being deflected downward and the other upward (Figure I.1). How was this simple result to be explained?

Clearly an interaction between the atoms and the magnetic field was responsible for their behavior. It seemed that each atom acted as a tiny magnet (or, more formally, each had a magnetic moment), and that the splitting was due to the nonuniformity of the field. The DuBois magnets used in the experiment were designed to give a very intense field near the V-shaped pole piece and a less intense field near the other. In a uniform field a small magnet (a compass needle, say) feels no overall force in any one direction: if, like a compass needle, it is constrained by a pivot, it will tend to rotate until it aligns itself with the field; if not so constrained it will precess

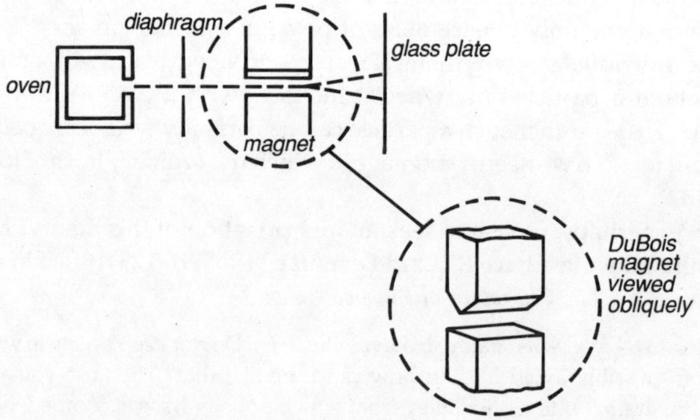

Figure I.1 The Stern-Gerlach apparatus (Experiment V).

round the direction of the field, like a spinning top precessing round the vertical. In a nonuniform field, on the other hand, the magnet will feel a net force in one direction or the other, depending on which pole is in the stronger part of the field.

But to picture a silver atom as a tiny compass needle would be wrong. For if the atoms behaved in that way we would expect to find their magnetic axes oriented randomly as they entered the field; that being so, those deflected most in one direction would be those with their axes aligned parallel with the field gradient, and those deflected most in the other would be those with their axes antiparallel with the field. In addition, however, there would be large numbers of atoms that were not aligned exactly upward or downward and that would suffer deflections intermediate between these two extremes. In other words, instead of two spots of silver on the glass plate, Stern and Gerlach would have seen a smeared line.

Of course, we could take the two spots they observed to show that the magnetic axes of the atoms were oriented either upward or downward but nowhere in between. When the magnets were rotated 90°, however, the beam was again split into two, but now one part was deflected to the left and the other to the right; by parallel reasoning, this would show that the magnetic axes of all the atoms were oriented horizontally. Clearly, the simple compass-needle model of a silver atom will not do.

More formally, we can contrast the behavior of these atoms with that of a compass needle as follows. A classical magnet has a magnetic axis; its magnetic moment is directed along this axis, but this moment has a component in any direction we choose, whose value ranges continuously from a maximum in the direction of the axis through zero along a line perpendicular to it, to a maximum negative value in the opposite direction (see Figure I.2). However, it seems that the components in any direction in space of the magnetic moment of a silver atom can have only one of two values; these are numerically the same as each other, but one is positive with respect to that direction and the other is negative.

At first the experiment was explained in terms of the "magnetic core" hypothesis of Sommerfeld and Landé, a hypothesis long since discarded, which attributed the deflection of the beam to the magnetic properties of the nucleus and inner electrons of an atom. In 1925 an alternative explanation was to hand, proposed by Goudsmit and Uhlenbeck, and it is this explanation which was incorporated into quantum theory as we now know it.

The explanation is roughly this. An electron possesses an intrinsic angular momentum, known as "spin," which gives rise to a magnetic moment. A component of the spin in *any* direction has one of two values, $+\frac{1}{2}\hbar$ or $-\frac{1}{2}\hbar$; hence we list electrons among the "spin-$\frac{1}{2}$ particles." (The constant $\hbar$ is the

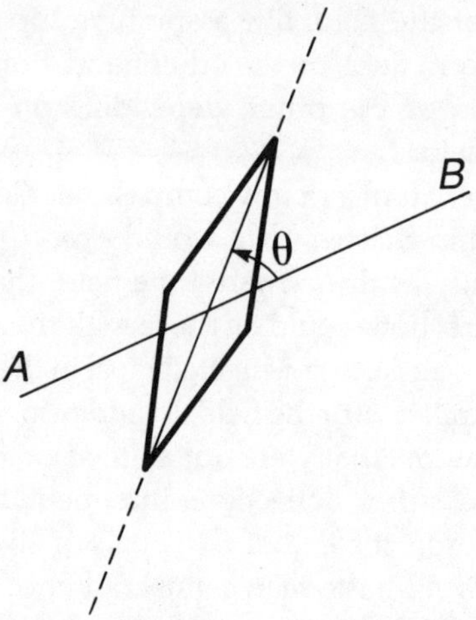

Figure I.2 If the magnetic moment μ of the compass needle is directed along the dotted line, then the component of μ along AB will equal $\mu\cos\theta$.

so-called natural unit of action, the omnipresent constant of quantum theory; it is now usually referred to as Planck's constant, though it would be historically more accurate to reserve that term for h, equal to $2\pi\hbar$.) Like the direction given to a magnetic field, the positive and negative signs are attached conventionally. A silver atom contains 47 electrons; 46 of these are arranged in pairs, with the result that the effects of their spin cancel out and the observed effect is due to the electron left over. In the experiment shown in Figure I.1, which I will call "Experiment V" (for vertical), it is the magnetic moment due to the vertical component of spin of this unpaired electron which the Stern-Gerlach apparatus measures: a positive value for this component means that the silver atom will enter one beam (the "spin-up" beam) while a negative value means that it will enter the other ("spin-down") beam. Incidentally, the protons within the nucleus of the atom are also charged spin-$\frac{1}{2}$ particles, but because of their comparatively large mass, their magnetic moment is much smaller than that of the electrons. The nucleus does contribute to the total magnetic moment of the atom, but to a negligible extent. In this discussion no problem arises when we talk of an atom as a whole, rather than the unpaired electron within it, as having a particular component of spin.

The account just given is, in its broad outlines, correct. But in at least one respect it is seriously misleading. From it we might infer that, when the atoms entered the magnetic field of the apparatus, some were aligned spin-up and some spin-down and that the device just sorted them into two separate beams accordingly. This conclusion would be confirmed were we to block off one of the beams as it left the apparatus, the spin-down beam, let us say. The emerging atoms would now all be spin-up, as we can verify by placing a second magnet in tandem with the first (Figure I.3). No further splitting of the beam would take place, though the beam as a whole would be deflected further upward. Let us call this "Experiment VV."

Now consider a different experiment (Experiment VH) in which the second apparatus is rotated 90° (Figure I.4). The incoming beam—that is, the spin-up beam from the first apparatus—will be split into two horizontally separated beams, spin-left and spin-right. (So far our account and quantum theory are entirely in harmony.) However, now let us block off the spin-right beam. What are we to say of the atoms which now emerge? Our account suggests that they have been through two filters: they have passed the first by virtue of having a spin-up vertical component of spin, and the second by virtue of a spin-left horizontal component of spin. In other words, it suggests that we can specify both the horizontal and the vertical components of spin these atoms possess: were a third apparatus set up to receive this beam, whether the magnetic field gradient were vertical or horizontal, no further splitting would occur.

Unfortunately, this is not the case (Feynman, Leighton, and Sands, 1965, vol. 3, lecture 5). With the axis of the third apparatus set in any direction but horizontal, the emergent beam *will* be split into two. With it vertical (Experiment VHV, Figure I.5) the two parts of the beam will be equal in intensity. This, at least, is what quantum theory predicts for idealized experiments of this kind, and all the evidence from actual experiments, some of which are very close in principle to those described, confirms its predictions. It seems that, somewhere along the line, there is a divergence between the quantum-theoretic analysis of what happens and our account of it: at some point an

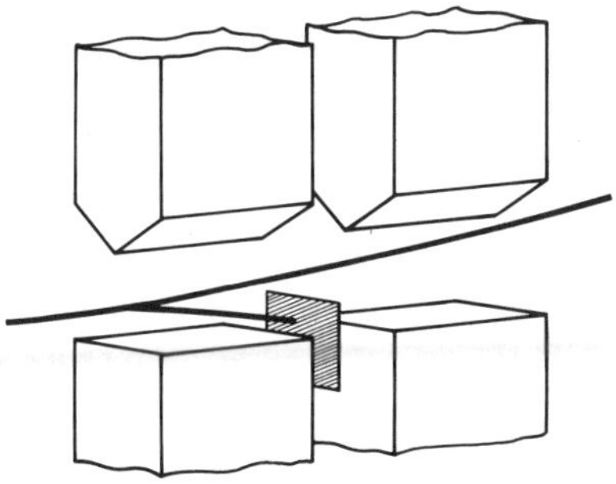

Figure I.3 Experiment VV.

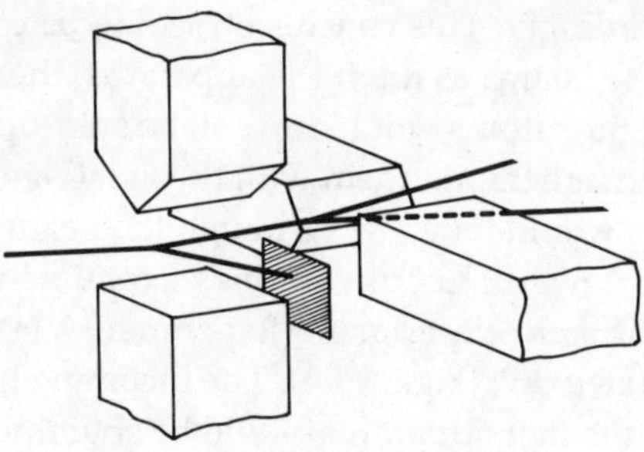

Figure I.4 Experiment VH.

unwarranted assumption or two has found its way into the latter. Within it we find at least four separate assumptions at work:

(1) That when we assign a numerical value to a physical quantity for a system (as when we say that the vertical component of spin of an electron is $+\frac{1}{2}\hbar$), we can think of this quantity as a property of the system; that is, we can talk meaningfully of the electron *having* such and such a vertical component of spin.

(2) That we can assign a value for each physical quantity to a system at any given instant—for example, that we can talk of a silver atom as being both spin-up and spin-left.

(3) That the apparatus sorts out the atoms according to the values of one particular quantity (such as the values of the vertical component of spin), in other words, according to the properties they possess.

(4) That as it does so the system's other properties remain unchanged.

The evidence of Experiments VV and VH is consistent with all of these assumptions; that of Experiment VHV with (1), (2), and (3), but not (4). It looks as though the spin-left, spin-right measurement effected by the second apparatus disturbs the values of the vertical components of spin. But, oddly enough, it disturbs only half of them. According to our interpretation of Experiment VV, all the atoms entering the second apparatus of VH have spin-up vertical components of spin, but as they emerge half of them are spin-up and half spin-down. Or so Experiment VHV informs us, as interpreted on the basis of assumptions (1), (2), and (3).

On this analysis, quantum theory owes us an explanation for the selectivity displayed by the second apparatus. Why is it, we may ask, that half the atoms entering this apparatus are tipped upside down, while the other half journey on undisturbed? Quantum theory declines to tell us. Rather, it suggests that we not only abandon (4) but also look severely at the other principles involved. Assumption (2) may be the first casualty: there may be distinct properties which are incompatible. These properties would not just be mutually exclusive values of one quantity, like spin-up and spin-down, but also properties associated with two different quantities, vertical and horizontal components of spin, for example, or the possibly more familiar pair, position and momentum. The possession of a well-defined value for one such quantity would rule out its possession for the other: to say that an atom was spin-up would rule out our saying that it was also spin-left. But if this is the case, then measurement will not be the simple process suggested by (3); if the vertical and horizontal components of spin are incompatible, and a system has a well-defined vertical component, then a measurement of the horizontal component will not merely reveal what value of the latter the system possesses. The measurement process may have to be seen as in some sense bringing this value about. To say that properties are not revealed by measurement, however, serves to point out an oddity, not only in the quantum concept of measurement but also in the notion of a property at work here. If we accept assumption (1)—that is, the identification of a property with a particular value of a physical quantity—then we may find ourselves dealing with properties of a very peculiar kind. All four assumptions, not just the last of them, need careful scrutiny.

The Stern-Gerlach experiment was highly significant: it supplied the first nonspectroscopic evidence for the quantization of physical quantities. Only discrete values of the components of magnetic moment of a system were permissible, compared with the continuum of values possible on the classical view. The importance of the work was immediately recognized, Sommerfeld stating that, "With their bold experimental method Stern and Gerlach demonstrated not only the existence of space quantization, they also

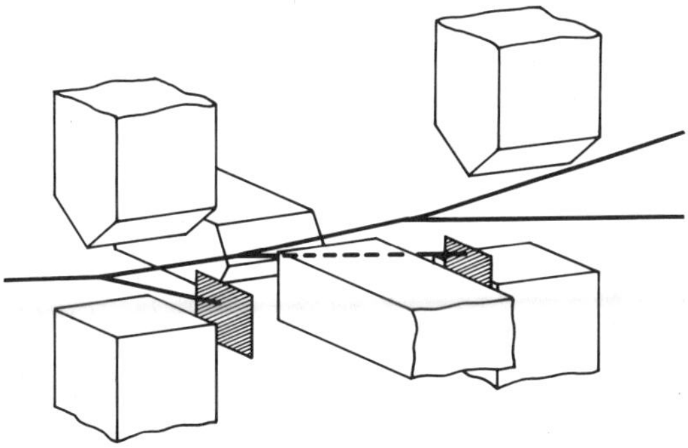

Figure I.5 Experiment VHV.

proved the atomistic nature of the magnetic moment, its quantum-theoretic origin and its relation to the atomic structure of electricity" (Jammer, 1966, p. 134).

Yet, notwithstanding its success, the Stern-Gerlach experiment immediately presents us with some of the problems to which Feynman alluded.* These problems arise when we try to reconcile quantum theory, and the experimental results with which it deals, with intuitively appealing principles of interpretation. To see these problems more clearly, we need to become better acquainted with the theory itself. As for the principles with which the theory conflicts, they may be just the legacy of an outmoded physics, old bottles into which, with the usual result, we are pouring new wine. It may be that our way of describing the world is inadequate, and the metaphysical notions implicit in it inappropriate, for dealing with a realm so far removed in scale from our everyday experience. This, I take it, is what Feynman suggests, albeit with a more graphic turn of phrase.

* For a contemporary view of the problems it raises, see Einstein and Ehrenfest (1922), reprinted in Ehrenfest (1959), pp. 452–455.

I

The Structure of Quantum Theory

1

Vector Spaces

No real insight into quantum theory is possible without an acquaintance with the mathematics it employs. Luckily it isn't hard to get some feeling for this mathematics; in fact, apart from some supplementary material in Chapter 5, the present chapter contains virtually all the background material drawn on in the rest of this book.

The mathematics in question is the theory of vector spaces (sometimes called "Hilbert spaces"). In this chapter I give a three-part sketch of the vector-space theory developed, with quantum mechanics in mind, by P. A. M. Dirac and John von Neumann in the early 1930s (Dirac, 1930; von Neumann, 1932; see Bub, 1974, pp. 3–8, on differences between the two). Sections 1.1–1.4 deal with a simple geometrical example of a vector space, the plane. This is a two-dimensional real space which we call $\mathbb{R}^2$; that is to say, each point on it can be specified by two real numbers (x and y coordinates in a standard Cartesian system). Sections 1.5–1.7 generalize this material to the case of a two-dimensional complex space, $\mathbb{C}^2$, in which each point is represented by two complex numbers. The remaining sections (1.8–1.16) carry the generalization a stage further and present an abstract characterization of a vector space. These spaces can be of any, even infinite, dimensionality; however, it so happens that a great many of the problematic features of quantum theory can be presented in terms of electron spin, and the quantum theory of the spin-$\frac{1}{2}$ particle involves just the two-dimensional space $\mathbb{C}^2$. For this reason—and of course for the delectation of the reader—Section 1.7 comprises a set of problems dealing with $\mathbb{C}^2$. Apart from one exercise in Section 1.14, these are the only problems set in the chapter, but many of the results quoted without proof in other sections can be obtained by a few minutes work with paper and pencil. I have indicated the approximate level of difficulty of each proof by stars (☆): the harder the proof, the greater the number of stars.

1.1 Vectors

Consider the two-dimensional real space of the plane of the paper, $\mathbb{R}^2$. We pick a particular point in $\mathbb{R}^2$ and call it the *zero vector,* $\mathbf{0}$. The other vectors in $\mathbb{R}^2$ are arrows of finite length which lie within the plane with their tails at zero; any arrow of this kind is a nonzero vector of $\mathbb{R}^2$. (See Figure 1.1.)

We can define *vector addition,* the operation by which we add two vectors to form a third, as follows. Given two vectors $\mathbf{u}$ and $\mathbf{v}$, we construct a parallelogram with $\mathbf{u}$ and $\mathbf{v}$ as adjacent sides (see Figure 1.2). The diagonal of this parallelogram, which passes through $\mathbf{0}$, will also be a vector: call it $\mathbf{w}$. This vector is the vector sum of $\mathbf{u}$ and $\mathbf{v}$. We write,

$$\mathbf{w} = \mathbf{u} + \mathbf{v}$$

We also define *scalar multiplication,* that is, the operation of multiplying a vector by a number. The vector $2\mathbf{v}$, for instance, is the arrow like $\mathbf{v}$ but twice as long. Multiplying $\mathbf{v}$ by a negative number, -1.5 say, yields an arrow in the opposite direction to $\mathbf{v}$ and half as long again as $\mathbf{v}$ (see Figure 1.3). It follows that, for any $\mathbf{v}$,

$$\mathbf{v} + (-1)\mathbf{v} = \mathbf{0}$$

Note that $\mathbf{0}$ here denotes the zero vector, not the number zero.

So far we have proceeded entirely geometrically, using a geometrical construction to obtain $\mathbf{u} + \mathbf{v}$ and giving a geometrical meaning to $a\mathbf{v}$ (where a is a real number). However, an alternative, arithmetical approach is open to us. We may impose a coordinate system on our space and then refer to each vector by the coordinates of its tip. Each vector will be designated by a pair of numbers, which we write as a column, thus:

$$\begin{pmatrix} x \\ y \end{pmatrix}$$

The numbers x and y by which we denote a particular vector $\mathbf{v}$ will of course

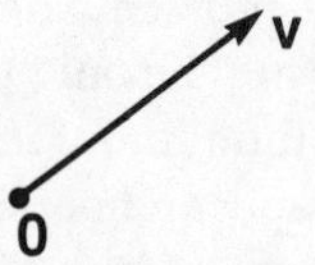

Figure 1.1

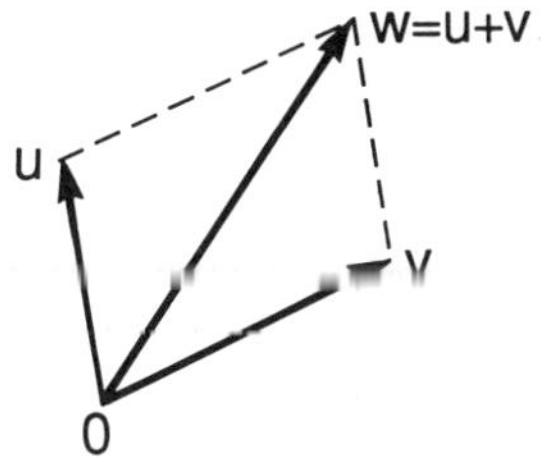

Figure 1.2

vary according to the coordinate system we have chosen (see Figure 1.4), or, as we say, according to the *basis* we use. Provided we are consistent and don't switch haphazardly from one to another, in principle it doesn't matter what basis we choose, though one may be more convenient than another. In every basis the zero vector is represented by

$$\begin{pmatrix} 0 \\ 0 \end{pmatrix}$$

Unless otherwise stated, we shall assume from now on that we are using a single (arbitrarily chosen) fixed basis.

Corresponding to the operations of vector addition and scalar multiplication carried out on vectors, we can perform very simple arithmetical operations on representations of vectors. It is easily shown that,

$$\text{if} \quad \mathbf{v} = \begin{pmatrix} x \\ y \end{pmatrix} \quad \text{and} \quad \mathbf{u} = \begin{pmatrix} x' \\ y' \end{pmatrix}, \quad \text{then}$$

$$\mathbf{v} + \mathbf{u} = \begin{pmatrix} x + x' \\ y + y' \end{pmatrix} \quad \text{and} \quad a\mathbf{v} = \begin{pmatrix} ax \\ ay \end{pmatrix} \qquad (\star)$$

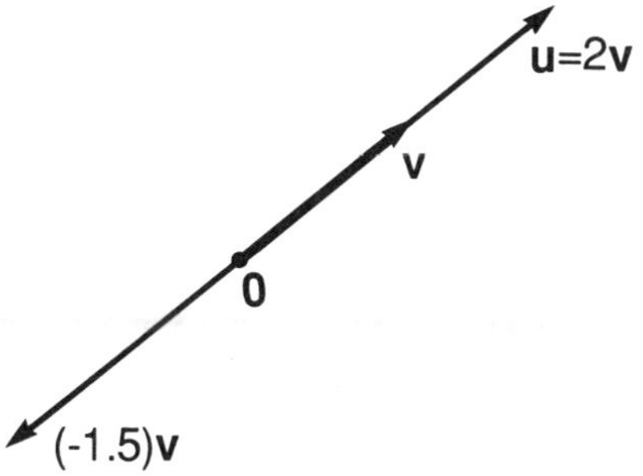

Figure 1.3

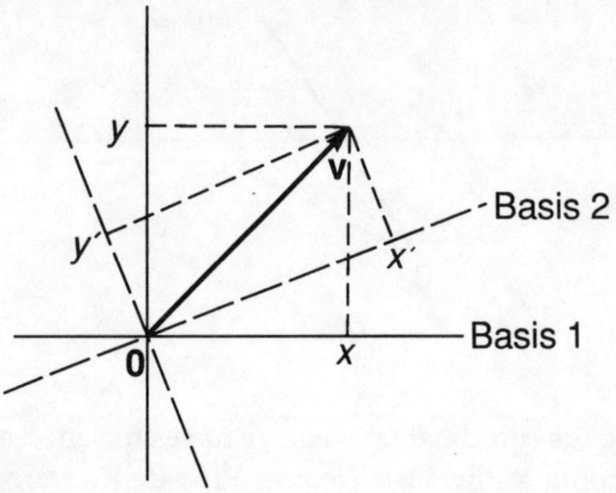

Figure 1.4 $\mathbf{v} = \begin{pmatrix} x \\ y \end{pmatrix}$ in basis 1; $\mathbf{v} = \begin{pmatrix} x' \\ y' \end{pmatrix}$ in basis 2; thus the same vector can be represented in many different ways.

Note that

$$\mathbf{v} + (-1)\mathbf{v} = \begin{pmatrix} x \\ y \end{pmatrix} + \begin{pmatrix} -x \\ -y \end{pmatrix} = \begin{pmatrix} x-x \\ y-y \end{pmatrix} = \begin{pmatrix} 0 \\ 0 \end{pmatrix} = \mathbf{0}$$

as required.

1.2 Operators

We now consider *operators* on our set of vectors. An operator transforms any vector in the space into another vector; one example is a rotation operator, which swings any vector round through a certain angle without altering its length. We will denote operators by boldface capital letters and write $\mathbf{A}\mathbf{v}$ for the vector which results when the operator $\mathbf{A}$ acts on the vector $\mathbf{v}$. In Figure 1.5 $\mathbf{v}'$ is the vector we get by swinging $\mathbf{v}$ round through an angle θ (counterclockwise), and so we write,

$$\mathbf{v}' = \mathbf{R}_\theta \mathbf{v}$$

where $\mathbf{R}_\theta$ is the operator which produces this rotation.

Another kind of operator is a reflection operator, which, as the name indicates, produces the reflection of any vector on the other side of a given line. Figure 1.6 shows the effect of the reflection operator $\mathbf{S}_y$ which reflects vectors about the y-axis. Note that if $\mathbf{u}$ is a vector lying along this axis, then $\mathbf{S}_y\mathbf{u} = \mathbf{u}$. In other words, $\mathbf{u}$ is mapped onto itself by $\mathbf{S}_y$.

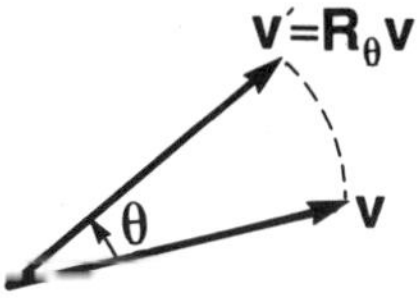

Figure 1.5

Neither reflection nor rotation operators change the lengths of vectors, but some operators do. We can consider, for instance, the operator which just doubles the length of each vector, or the one which reduces its length by half. There is also a *zero operator,* which transforms every vector in the space into the zero vector.

One of the most important classes of operators we deal with is that of *projection operators.* An example of such an operator is shown in Figure 1.7. This is the projection operator $\mathbf{P}_x$, which, as we say, *projects a vector onto* the x-axis. This takes any vector

$$\begin{pmatrix} x \\ y \end{pmatrix}$$

and transforms it into the vector

$$\begin{pmatrix} x \\ 0 \end{pmatrix}$$

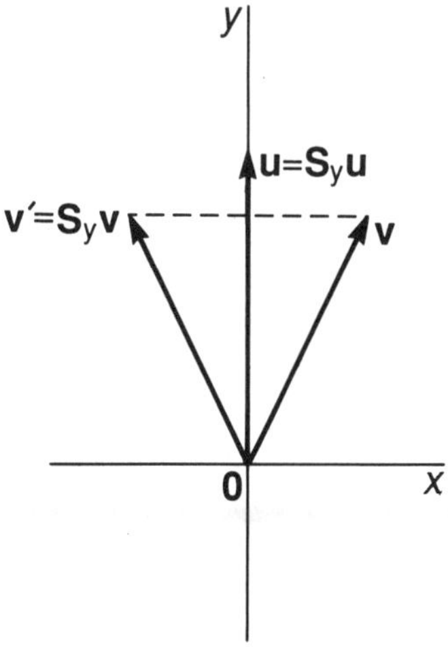

Figure 1.6

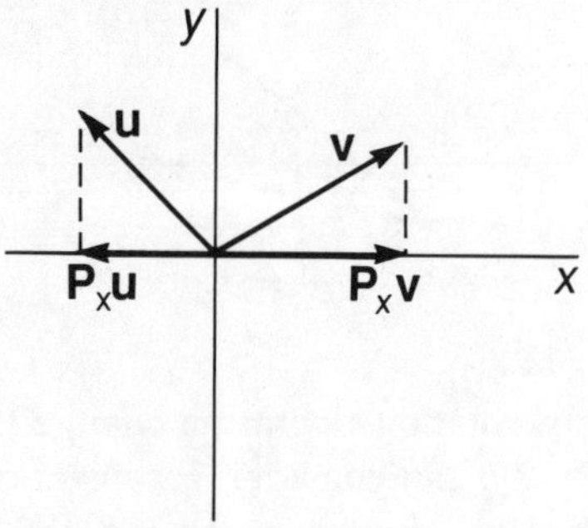

Figure 1.7

lying along the x-axis with its tip immediately below

$$\begin{pmatrix} x \\ y \end{pmatrix}$$

Notice that, while for a given vector **v** there is only one vector $\mathbf{P}_x\mathbf{v}$ (or else $\mathbf{P}_x$ would not be an operator), nevertheless we may well have distinct vectors **u** and **v** such that $\mathbf{P}_x\mathbf{u} = \mathbf{P}_x\mathbf{v}$ (see Figure 1.8). In this way projection operators differ from rotation and reflection operators.

We may, of course, perform a series of operations on a given vector **v**. We may, for instance, rotate it through an angle θ to produce $\mathbf{R}_\theta\mathbf{v}$ and then project the resulting vector onto the x-axis, producing $\mathbf{P}_x(\mathbf{R}_\theta\mathbf{v})$. Now, provided θ is neither $0°$ nor $180°$, this vector is different from the one we get if we perform the operations in the reverse order. In other words, $\mathbf{R}_\theta(\mathbf{P}_x\mathbf{v}) \neq \mathbf{P}_x(\mathbf{R}_\theta\mathbf{v})$ (unless **v** is the zero vector). To see this, consider that any vector $\mathbf{P}_x(\mathbf{R}_\theta\mathbf{v})$ must lie along the x-axis, while any vector $\mathbf{R}_\theta(\mathbf{P}_x\mathbf{v})$ must be along a line at an angle θ to this axis.

We can define the operator **AB** as that operator which, when applied to an arbitrary vector **v**, yields the vector **A(Bv)**. In other words, the operator **AB** is effectively an instruction to apply first the operator **B** and then the operator **A**. We have just shown that, in general, $\mathbf{AB} \neq \mathbf{BA}$, but the equality may hold for particular operators **A** and **B**; for example, if **A** and **B** are both rotation operators, then $\mathbf{AB} = \mathbf{BA}$. We say then that **A** and **B** *commute*. On a point of notation: in the concatenation **AB**, both **A** and **B** are operators, and **AB**, which is also an operator, is called the product of **A** and **B**. In the concatenation **Av**, however, **A** is an operator but **v** is a vector, and one should not think of what is happening as multiplication.

We saw in the previous section that any vector of $\mathbb{R}^2$ can be represented by a pair of numbers. Does a similar arithmetical representation of operators exist? Yes, provided we restrict ourselves to *linear operators.* An operator **A** is *linear* provided that, for all vectors **u** and **v** and for any number c,

(1.1) $$\mathbf{A}(\mathbf{u} + \mathbf{v}) = \mathbf{A}\mathbf{u} + \mathbf{A}\mathbf{v}$$

(1.2) $$\mathbf{A}(c\mathbf{v}) = c(\mathbf{A}\mathbf{v}).$$

All the operators discussed in this book are linear.

Any linear operator on $\mathbb{R}^2$ may be represented by a 2×2 matrix of real numbers

$$\begin{pmatrix} a & b \\ c & d \end{pmatrix}$$

such that if

$$\mathbf{v} = \begin{pmatrix} x \\ y \end{pmatrix}$$

then

(1.3) $$\mathbf{A}\mathbf{v} = \begin{pmatrix} a & b \\ c & d \end{pmatrix}\begin{pmatrix} x \\ y \end{pmatrix} = \begin{pmatrix} ax + by \\ cx + dy \end{pmatrix}$$ (☆☆)

It is trivial to prove the converse, that any such matrix represents a linear operator.

To perform the manipulations in (1.3), think of taking the top line $(a \;\; b)$ of the matrix, rotating it so that it matches up with the vector **v** (multiply a by x and b by y), and then adding ax to by to get the top entry of the vector **Av**.

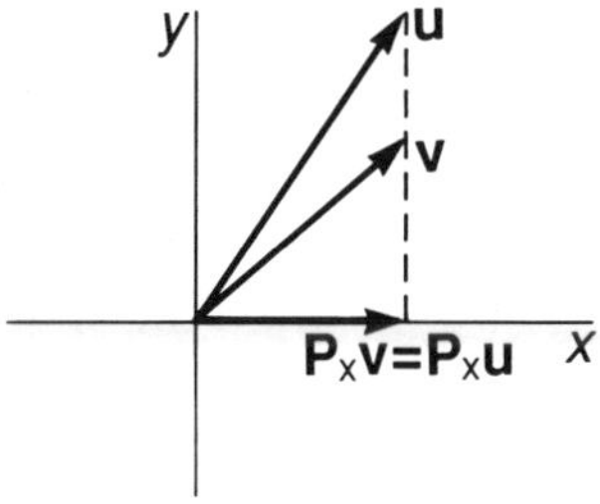

Figure 1.8

The bottom entry is obtained by doing the same with the bottom line of the matrix. (For help with the proof of this theorem, or for a fuller account of elementary vector-space theory, consult any book on linear algebra, such as Lang, 1972.)

The operators we have looked at all have simple matrix representations. For instance,

$$\mathbf{S}_y = \begin{pmatrix} -1 & 0 \\ 0 & 1 \end{pmatrix} \quad \text{and} \quad \mathbf{P}_x = \begin{pmatrix} 1 & 0 \\ 0 & 0 \end{pmatrix} \tag{☆}$$

A little thought should show why these operators have the representations shown, and it is a useful exercise to show that

$$\mathbf{R}_\theta = \begin{pmatrix} \cos\theta & -\sin\theta \\ \sin\theta & \cos\theta \end{pmatrix} \tag{☆☆}$$

We include in our class of operators the identity operator

$$\mathbf{I} = \begin{pmatrix} 1 & 0 \\ 0 & 1 \end{pmatrix}$$

This is the operator that leaves any vector as it found it: $\mathbf{Iv} = \mathbf{v}$, for all $\mathbf{v}$.

If we have two operators **A** and **B**, with representations

$$\begin{pmatrix} a & b \\ c & d \end{pmatrix} \quad \text{and} \quad \begin{pmatrix} e & f \\ g & h \end{pmatrix}$$

what is the representation of their product **AB**? It is the matrix which, when we operate with it on the vector **v** according to the rule (1.3), yields the same results as operating with **B** and **A**, in that order. A little brisk manipulation shows that

$$\mathbf{AB} = \begin{pmatrix} ae + bg & af + bh \\ ce + dg & cf + dh \end{pmatrix} \tag{☆}$$

(We obtain the top left-hand entry by matching the top line of **A** with the left column of **B**, the top right entry by matching the top line of **A** with the right column of **B**, and so on.)

It's worth going into this in more detail. Let

$$\mathbf{v} = \begin{pmatrix} x \\ y \end{pmatrix}$$

Then if

$$(\mathbf{AB})\mathbf{v} = \begin{pmatrix} px + qy \\ rx + sy \end{pmatrix}$$

we will know that the matrix representation of **AB** is

$$\begin{pmatrix} p & q \\ r & s \end{pmatrix}$$

Now

$$\mathbf{Bv} = \begin{pmatrix} e & f \\ g & h \end{pmatrix}\begin{pmatrix} x \\ y \end{pmatrix} = \begin{pmatrix} ex + fy \\ gx + hy \end{pmatrix}$$

and so

$$\mathbf{A}(\mathbf{Bv}) = \begin{pmatrix} a & b \\ c & d \end{pmatrix}\begin{pmatrix} ex + fy \\ gx + hy \end{pmatrix} = \begin{pmatrix} a(ex + fy) + b(gx + hy) \\ c(ex + fy) + d(gx + hy) \end{pmatrix}$$
$$= \begin{pmatrix} (ae + bg)x + (af + bh)y \\ (ce + dg)x + (cf + dh)y \end{pmatrix}$$

Since, by definition, $(\mathbf{AB})\mathbf{v} = \mathbf{A}(\mathbf{Bv})$, it follows that,

$$\mathbf{AB} = \begin{pmatrix} ae + bg & af + bh \\ ce + dg & cf + dh \end{pmatrix}$$

We can now confirm a previous result. Examining the matrix representations of $\mathbf{R}_\theta\mathbf{P}_x$ and $\mathbf{P}_x\mathbf{R}_\theta$ we find that

$$\mathbf{R}_\theta\mathbf{P}_x = \begin{pmatrix} \cos\theta & 0 \\ \sin\theta & 0 \end{pmatrix} \quad \text{and} \quad \mathbf{P}_x\mathbf{R}_\theta = \begin{pmatrix} \cos\theta & -\sin\theta \\ 0 & 0 \end{pmatrix} \tag{☆}$$

Thus, as we showed before, in general $\mathbf{P}_x$ and $\mathbf{R}_\theta$ do not commute. (Note, however, what happens when $\theta = 0°$ or $\theta = 180°$.)

This is a convenient point at which to start what will be a successive generalization of the notion of a projection operator. So far we have just considered projections onto the x and y axes; however, we can project onto any line through 0. That is, given any line L, at an angle θ to the x-axis, say, and an arbitrary vector $\mathbf{v}$, we can think of $\mathbf{v}$ as the sum of two other vectors $\mathbf{v}_L$ and $\mathbf{v}_{L^\perp}$, such that $\mathbf{v}_L$ is in L and $\mathbf{v}_{L^\perp}$ is in the line $L^\perp$ at right angles to L (see

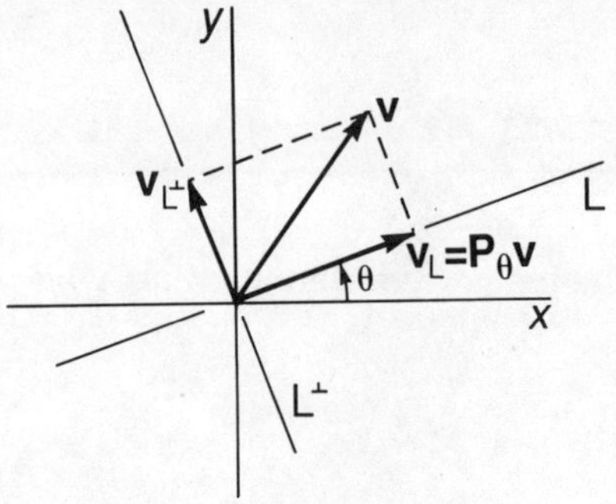

Figure 1.9 $\mathbf{P}_\theta$ projects onto L.

Figure 1.9). That is, the vector $\mathbf{v}$ can be written as the sum: $\mathbf{v} = \mathbf{v}_L + \mathbf{v}_{L^\perp}$. We now define the projection operator $\mathbf{P}_\theta$ onto the line L as the operator $\mathbf{P}_\theta$ such that $\mathbf{P}_\theta\mathbf{v} = \mathbf{v}_L$. As an exercise it's worth showing that

$$\text{(1.4)} \qquad \mathbf{P}_\theta = \begin{pmatrix} \cos^2\theta & \cos\theta \cdot \sin\theta \\ \cos\theta \cdot \sin\theta & \sin^2\theta \end{pmatrix} \qquad (☆☆)$$

The addition of two linear operators is easily defined: we write, for all vectors $\mathbf{v}$,

$$(\mathbf{A} + \mathbf{B})\mathbf{v} = \mathbf{A}\mathbf{v} + \mathbf{B}\mathbf{v}$$

We obtain the matrix representation of $\mathbf{A} + \mathbf{B}$ by simply adding corresponding entries; if, as before,

$$\mathbf{A} = \begin{pmatrix} a & b \\ c & d \end{pmatrix} \quad \text{and} \quad \mathbf{B} = \begin{pmatrix} e & f \\ g & h \end{pmatrix}, \quad \text{then}$$

$$\mathbf{A} + \mathbf{B} = \begin{pmatrix} a+e & b+f \\ c+g & d+h \end{pmatrix} \qquad (☆)$$

We can also define the multiplication of the operator $\mathbf{A}$ by the scalar a: we specify that, for all vectors $\mathbf{v}$, $(a\mathbf{A})\mathbf{v} = a(\mathbf{A}\mathbf{v})$. Each element in the matrix of $a\mathbf{A}$ is then a times the corresponding entry in the matrix for $\mathbf{A}$.

Alternatively, we could regard this multiplication as a special case of the multiplication of operators; to multiply any vector by the scalar a is effectively to operate on it with the matrix

$$\begin{pmatrix} a & 0 \\ 0 & a \end{pmatrix}$$

Hence we have the operator equation:

$$a\mathbf{A} = \begin{pmatrix} a & 0 \\ 0 & a \end{pmatrix} \mathbf{A}$$

Note finally that we write $\mathbf{A} - \mathbf{B}$ for the operator $\mathbf{A} + (-1)\mathbf{B}$.

1.3 *Eigenvectors and Eigenvalues*

Consider the operator **A** with matrix representation

$$\begin{pmatrix} 0 & 2 \\ 2 & 0 \end{pmatrix}$$

acting on the vector

$$\mathbf{v} = \begin{pmatrix} 3 \\ 3 \end{pmatrix}$$

In this case

$$\mathbf{Av} = \begin{pmatrix} 6 \\ 6 \end{pmatrix} = 2\mathbf{v}$$

That is, the vector which results is just a multiple of the vector we started with. This is not always so with this operator; if we evaluate **Au**, where

$$\mathbf{u} = \begin{pmatrix} 3 \\ 0 \end{pmatrix}, \quad \text{we get} \quad \mathbf{Au} = \begin{pmatrix} 0 \\ 6 \end{pmatrix} \neq 2\mathbf{u}$$

Thus **A** does not simply double the length of all vectors. In fact, if we interpret **A** geometrically, we find that it corresponds to the operation of first doubling the length of a vector, then rotating it 90° counterclockwise, and finally reflecting the result about the y-axis. (To see this, check that

$$\begin{pmatrix} 0 & 2 \\ 2 & 0 \end{pmatrix} = \begin{pmatrix} -1 & 0 \\ 0 & 1 \end{pmatrix} \begin{pmatrix} 0 & -1 \\ 1 & 0 \end{pmatrix} \begin{pmatrix} 2 & 0 \\ 0 & 2 \end{pmatrix} \tag{☆}$$

using the method of matrix multiplication given in Section 1.2.)

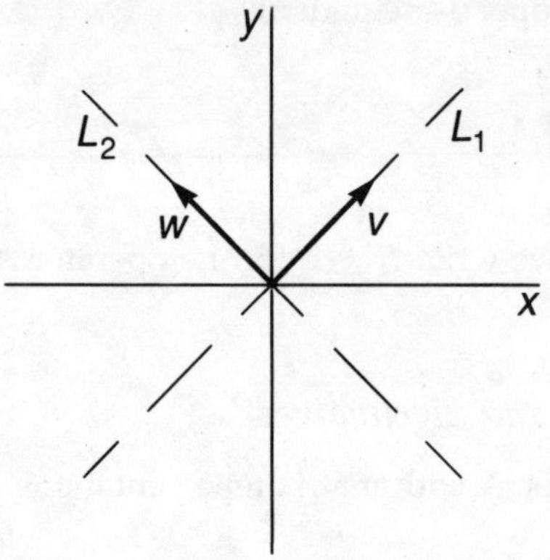

Figure 1.10 **v** and **w** are eigenvectors of **A**, where $\mathbf{A} = \begin{pmatrix} 0 & 2 \\ 2 & 0 \end{pmatrix}$.

However, for any vector $\mathbf{v}'$, lying along the same line as

$$\begin{pmatrix} 3 \\ 3 \end{pmatrix}$$

(that is, any vector lying along the line L_1 at 45° to our axes—Figure 1.10), and hence of the form

$$\begin{pmatrix} x \\ x \end{pmatrix}$$

we find that $\mathbf{A}\mathbf{v}' = 2\mathbf{v}'$ (☆). Also, we can check very quickly that if **w** is a vector of the form

$$\begin{pmatrix} -x \\ x \end{pmatrix}$$

that is, a vector lying along L_2, then

$$\mathbf{A}\mathbf{w} = \begin{pmatrix} 2x \\ -2x \end{pmatrix} = -2\mathbf{w}$$

Vectors of the form $\mathbf{v}'$ and **w** are known as *eigenvectors* of **A**, and the *eigenvalues* corresponding to them are 2 and -2, respectively. More formally,

(1.5) **v** is said to be an *eigenvector* of a linear operator **A**, with corresponding *eigenvalue a*, if $\mathbf{v} \neq \mathbf{0}$ and $\mathbf{A}\mathbf{v} = a\mathbf{v}$.

Note that we do not allow the zero vector to be an eigenvector of any vector.

Not all operators have eigenvectors. For instance, the rotation operator $\mathbf{R}_\theta$ has, in general, no eigenvectors, since, unless $\theta = 0°$ or $\theta = 180°$, the vector $\mathbf{R}_\theta\mathbf{v}$ cannot lie along the same line as the vector **v**. When $\theta = 0°$, $\mathbf{R}_\theta$ is the identity operator **I**; for the two special cases, **I** and $\mathbf{R}_{180}$, every vector is an eigenvector; the corresponding eigenvalues are $+1$ and -1, respectively. Likewise, any purely multiplicative operator has every vector in the space as an eigenvector.

Now consider the reflection operator $\mathbf{S}_y$ and the projection operator $\mathbf{P}_\theta$. Do these admit eigenvectors, and, if so, how many? In general, obviously, the vector $\mathbf{S}_y\mathbf{v}$ does not lie along the same line as **v**. However, it does so in two special cases: first, when **v** lies along the y-axis (so that $\mathbf{S}_y\mathbf{v} = \mathbf{v}$); and, second, when **v** lies along the x-axis (so that $\mathbf{S}_y\mathbf{v} = -\mathbf{v}$). Thus we have two classes of eigenvector and two eigenvalues, $+1$ and -1. The projection operator $\mathbf{P}_\theta$ maps all vectors onto the line L_θ at an angle θ to the x-axis (see Figure 1.11). Thus any vector in this line is an eigenvector of $\mathbf{P}_\theta$, with eigenvalue 1. Now consider a vector **v** along the line $L_{\theta+90°}$ at right angles to L_θ. For this vector we have $\mathbf{P}_\theta\mathbf{v} = \mathbf{0} = 0\mathbf{v}$. As always, the symbol **0** denotes the zero *vector,* while the symbol 0 denotes the *number* zero. In fact we have here a special case of the eigenvector equation $\mathbf{A}\mathbf{v} = a\mathbf{v}$ in which $a = 0$. (Note that, although the zero vector is not an admissible eigen*vector,* the number zero is a perfectly good eigen*value.*) We see that the eigenvectors of

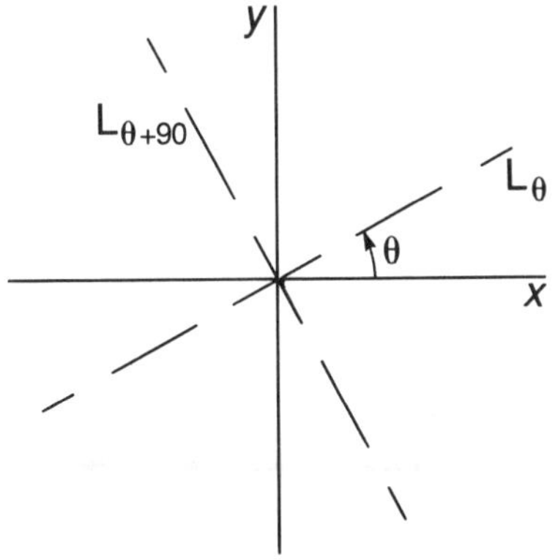

Figure 1.11 Eigenvectors of $\mathbf{S}_y$ lie along y-axis (eigenvalue 1) or along x-axis (eigenvalue -1); eigenvectors of $\mathbf{P}_\theta$ lie along L_θ (eigenvalue 1) or along $L_{\theta+90}$ (eigenvalue 0).

$\mathbf{P}_\theta$ lie along either L_θ or $L_{\theta+90}$, and the corresponding eigenvalues are 1 and 0 in the two cases.

These examples suggest some very general conclusions. The operators we have looked at fall into three classes. One class has no eigenvectors at all: this class includes all the rotation operators except $\mathbf{R}_0$ and $\mathbf{R}_{180}$. In the second class we find the projection and reflection operators and the example **A** used at the beginning of this section. In each of these cases all the eigenvectors lie along one or the other of two lines. With each set of eigenvectors (that is, with all the eigenvectors lying along a particular line) is associated a particular eigenvalue; thus to each operator of this type we can associate a pair of distinct eigenvalues. Now, in the examples we looked at, the two lines containing the eigenvectors are at right angles one to the other. While this is not the case for *all* the operators on $\mathbb{R}^2$ that (as we say) admit two eigenvectors with distinct eigenvalues, nevertheless this result holds for a very significant subclass of such operators, namely those among them which are *symmetric*. The matrix representing a symmetric operator on $\mathbb{R}^2$ may be recognized by the fact that its top right element is equal to its bottom left element.

The third class contains operators like **I** and $\mathbf{R}_{180}$. They admit all the vectors in the space as eigenvectors, all sharing a common eigenvalue. Note that these operators are also symmetric.

We can now use the operator

$$\mathbf{A} = \begin{pmatrix} 0 & 2 \\ 2 & 0 \end{pmatrix}$$

to illustrate an important result. Clearly **A** is symmetric: further, it has two eigenvalues, a_1 and a_2, where $a_1 = 2$ and $a_2 = -2$. The eigenvectors lie along two lines, at 45° and at 135° to the x-axis; to the eigenvalue a_1 corresponds the line L_1 in Figure 1.10, and to the eigenvalue a_2 corresponds L_2. We can find the matrices which represent the projection operators onto these lines. Using (1.4), we obtain:

$$\mathbf{P}_1 = \begin{pmatrix} \frac{1}{2} & \frac{1}{2} \\ \frac{1}{2} & \frac{1}{2} \end{pmatrix} \quad \text{and} \quad \mathbf{P}_2 = \begin{pmatrix} \frac{1}{2} & -\frac{1}{2} \\ -\frac{1}{2} & \frac{1}{2} \end{pmatrix}$$

Now compute the operator $a_1\mathbf{P}_1 + a_2\mathbf{P}_2$.

$$a_1\mathbf{P}_1 + a_2\mathbf{P}_2 = +2\begin{pmatrix} \frac{1}{2} & \frac{1}{2} \\ \frac{1}{2} & \frac{1}{2} \end{pmatrix} + -2\begin{pmatrix} \frac{1}{2} & -\frac{1}{2} \\ -\frac{1}{2} & \frac{1}{2} \end{pmatrix}$$

$$= \begin{pmatrix} 1 & 1 \\ 1 & 1 \end{pmatrix} + \begin{pmatrix} -1 & 1 \\ 1 & -1 \end{pmatrix}$$

$$= \begin{pmatrix} 0 & 2 \\ 2 & 0 \end{pmatrix} = \mathbf{A}$$

This result turns out to be quite general. That is, if we take a symmetric operator **A** which admits two eigenvectors with distinct eigenvalues a_1 and a_2, then the eigenvectors corresponding to a_1 all lie within a line L_1, and those corresponding to a_2 all lie within a line L_2 ($L_1 \perp L_2$). If $\mathbf{P}_1$ projects onto L_1 and $\mathbf{P}_2$ onto L_2, then, as in the case above,

(1.6) $$\mathbf{A} = a_1\mathbf{P}_1 + a_2\mathbf{P}_2$$

It's worth approaching these ideas in a slightly different way. Any linear operator **A** on $\mathbb{R}^2$ may be "decomposed" into the sum of other linear operators, as follows. Let

$$\mathbf{A} = \begin{pmatrix} a & b \\ c & d \end{pmatrix}$$

$$\mathbf{B}_1 = \begin{pmatrix} 1 & 0 \\ 0 & 0 \end{pmatrix} \quad \mathbf{B}_2 = \begin{pmatrix} 0 & 1 \\ 0 & 0 \end{pmatrix} \quad \mathbf{B}_3 = \begin{pmatrix} 0 & 0 \\ 1 & 0 \end{pmatrix} \quad \mathbf{B}_4 = \begin{pmatrix} 0 & 0 \\ 0 & 1 \end{pmatrix}$$

Then

$$\mathbf{A} = a\mathbf{B}_1 + b\mathbf{B}_2 + c\mathbf{B}_3 + d\mathbf{B}_4$$

However, we are interested in a more narrowly defined sense of "decomposition."

(1.7) If **A** is a symmetric operator on $\mathbb{R}^2$, then there exists a pair of projection operators $\mathbf{P}_1$ and $\mathbf{P}_2$, projecting onto mutually perpendicular lines, such that $\mathbf{A} = a_1\mathbf{P}_1 + a_2\mathbf{P}_2$.

This is called the *spectral decomposition theorem* for $\mathbb{R}^2$. There are two cases: (i) $a_1 \neq a_2$, (ii) $a_1 = a_2$.

In both cases (that is, whenever **A** is symmetric), **A** admits eigenvectors. When $a_1 \neq a_2$, the decomposition of **A** into the weighted sum of two projection operators is unique. Furthermore, all eigenvectors of **A** lie either along the line onto which $\mathbf{P}_1$ projects or along the line onto which $\mathbf{P}_2$ projects. Those in the first line have corresponding eigenvalue a_1, while those in the second have corresponding eigenvalue a_2. When $a_1 = a_2$, *all* vectors of $\mathbb{R}^2$ are eigenvectors of **A**, and the decomposition is not unique. For any pair of projection operators, $\mathbf{P}_1$ and $\mathbf{P}_2$, projecting onto mutually perpendicular lines, we have $\mathbf{A} = a_1\mathbf{P}_1 + a_2\mathbf{P}_2$.

1.4 *Inner Products of Vectors in* $\mathbb{R}^2$

The introduction of the notion of the *inner product* of two vectors, also called the *dot product* or the *scalar product,* enables us to give numerical expression to such geometrical ideas as the length of a vector and the orthogonality of vectors. (Vectors at right angles one to the other are said to be *orthogonal.*) Using the notation introduced by Dirac, we denote the inner product of two vectors **u** and **v** by $\langle\mathbf{u}|\mathbf{v}\rangle$. We define it for $\mathbb{R}^2$ as follows:

(1.8) $$\text{If } \mathbf{u} = \begin{pmatrix} x_1 \\ y_1 \end{pmatrix} \text{ and } \mathbf{v} = \begin{pmatrix} x_2 \\ y_2 \end{pmatrix}, \text{ then } \langle\mathbf{u}|\mathbf{v}\rangle = x_1x_2 + y_1y_2.$$

The + here is the plus sign of ordinary arithmetical addition. We see that, although **u** and **v** are vectors, their inner product is just a number. For instance, let $\mathbf{u} = \begin{pmatrix} 2 \\ 1 \end{pmatrix}$ and $\mathbf{v} = \begin{pmatrix} 3 \\ 4 \end{pmatrix}$; then $\langle\mathbf{u}|\mathbf{v}\rangle = (2)(3) + (1)(4) = 10$.

How does this number acquire a geometrical significance? Consider the case when

$$\mathbf{u} = \mathbf{v} = \begin{pmatrix} x \\ y \end{pmatrix}$$

In this case $\langle\mathbf{u}|\mathbf{v}\rangle = \langle\mathbf{u}|\mathbf{u}\rangle = x^2 + y^2$. Here the geometrical significance is clear; by Pythagoras' theorem, $\langle\mathbf{u}|\mathbf{u}\rangle$ is equal to the square of the length of the vector **u**. We denote the length of the vector **v** by $|\mathbf{v}|$ and observe that

(1.9) $$|\mathbf{v}| = \sqrt{\langle\mathbf{v}|\mathbf{v}\rangle}$$

If $|\mathbf{v}| = 1$, then we say that **v** is *normalized.* Given any vector **v**, we can always produce a normalized vector collinear with **v** by dividing **v** by its own length; in other words $\mathbf{v}/|\mathbf{v}|$ is a normalized vector along the same line as **v**.

In general, the inner product of two vectors yields a number proportional to the length of each and to the cosine of the angle between them. Thus, surprisingly, the inner product of two vectors is independent of our choice of x and y axes; I say "surprisingly" because the way we calculate inner products (using x and y coordinates) involves reference to a particular coordinate system. The general result, for two vectors **u** and **v** at an angle ϕ to each other, is:

$$\langle \mathbf{u}|\mathbf{v}\rangle = |\mathbf{u}||\mathbf{v}|\cos\phi \tag{1.10}$$

I will not prove this general result, but will show that it yields the right answer in the case of two normalized vectors, **u** and **v**, such that **u** lies along the x-axis and **v** is at an angle ϕ to it (see Figure 1.12). In this case

$$\mathbf{u} = \begin{pmatrix}1\\0\end{pmatrix} \quad \text{and} \quad \mathbf{v} = \begin{pmatrix}\cos\phi\\ \sin\phi\end{pmatrix}$$

(**v** is normalized, since $\cos^2\phi + \sin^2\phi = 1$, for all ϕ). We obtain $\langle \mathbf{u}|\mathbf{v}\rangle = (1)(\cos\phi) + (0)(\sin\phi) = \cos\phi$, as (1.10) requires.

(To prove the more general result, first see what the effect on $\langle \mathbf{u}|\mathbf{v}\rangle$ would be if **u** and **v** were not normalized but were along the same lines as before, and then compare the inner products $\langle \mathbf{u}|\mathbf{v}\rangle$ and $\langle \mathbf{R}_\theta\mathbf{u}|\mathbf{R}_\theta\mathbf{v}\rangle$ for an arbitrary angle θ.)

Equation (1.10) tells us that when $\cos\phi = 0$, then $\langle \mathbf{u}|\mathbf{v}\rangle = 0$. Thus for two vectors at right angles, the inner product is zero. Such vectors are said to be *orthogonal* to each other.

Now consider a normalized vector **v** and a line L at an angle ϕ to **v**. If **P** is the projection operator onto L, then

$$\langle \mathbf{v}|\mathbf{P}\mathbf{v}\rangle = \cos^2\phi \tag{1.11}$$

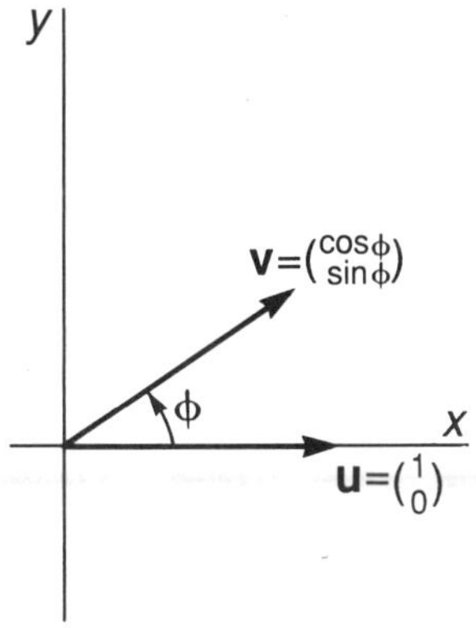

Figure 1.12

Before we obtain a general proof of this, consider the case when $\mathbf{P} = \mathbf{P}_x$. In this case

$$\mathbf{v} = \begin{pmatrix} \cos\phi \\ \sin\phi \end{pmatrix} \quad \text{and so} \quad \mathbf{P}_x\mathbf{v} = \begin{pmatrix} \cos\phi \\ 0 \end{pmatrix}$$

(See Figure 1.13.) It follows that $\langle \mathbf{v}|\mathbf{P}_x\mathbf{v}\rangle = \cos^2\phi + (\sin\phi)(0) = \cos^2\phi$, in accordance with (1.11). In the general case, we see from trigonometry that $|\mathbf{Pv}| = |\mathbf{v}| \cos\phi$. By (1.10),

$$\langle \mathbf{v}|\mathbf{Pv}\rangle = |\mathbf{v}||\mathbf{Pv}| \cos\phi = |\mathbf{v}|^2\cos^2\phi = \cos^2\phi$$

since $\mathbf{v}$ is normalized. It is also clear that $\langle \mathbf{v}|\mathbf{Pv}\rangle = |\mathbf{Pv}|^2 = \langle \mathbf{Pv}|\mathbf{Pv}\rangle$.

Further, if $\mathbf{P}_1$ and $\mathbf{P}_2$ are projection operators onto two perpendicular lines (see Figure 1.14), then $|\mathbf{v}|^2 = |\mathbf{P}_1\mathbf{v}|^2 + |\mathbf{P}_2\mathbf{v}|^2$, for any vector $\mathbf{v}$. Both these considerations show that, if $\mathbf{v}$ is normalized, then $0 \leq |\mathbf{Pv}|^2 \leq 1$, for any projection operator $\mathbf{P}$. The significance of these and analogous results will be evident when we look at quantum theory. Within the theory, the probabilities of events are given by expressions of the form $|\mathbf{Pv}|^2$, hence the importance of showing that when $\mathbf{v}$ is normalized this expression can take values only between zero and one.

1.5 *Complex Numbers*

In the vector space $\mathbb{R}^2$ we have permitted multiplication of vectors by real numbers. We say that $\mathbb{R}^2$ is a vector space *over the field of the reals.* The next step is to consider a vector space over the field of *complex* numbers. The generalization is straightforward, once we have a grasp of what such numbers are.

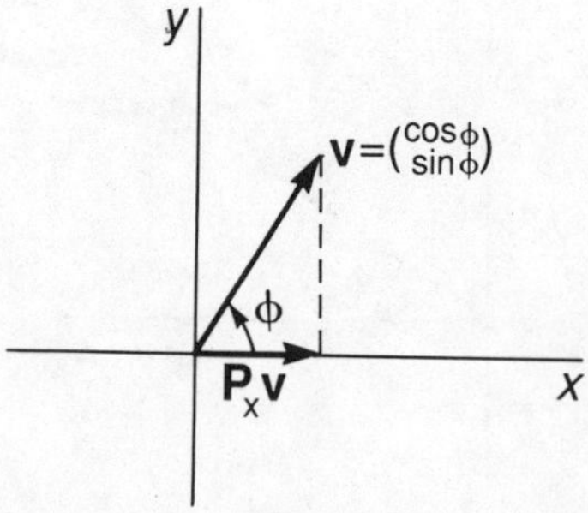

Figure 1.13

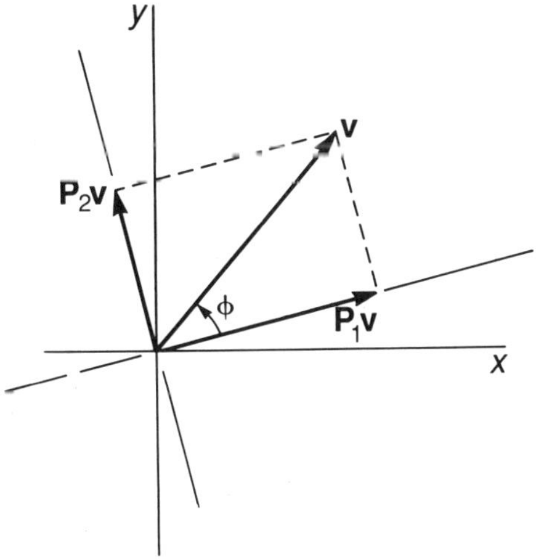

Figure 1.14

As is well known, the number 36 is the square of 6, and also the square of -6; there is no real number x such that $x^2 = -36$. However, we can imagine the sort of properties such a number would have, if it existed. It would be twice the square root of -9, for instance, so that it would conform to the equation $(x/2)^2 = x^2/4$, and it would be a root of the equation $x^2 + 36 = 0$.

In fact, if we included "imaginary" numbers like x in our set of numbers, then every quadratic equation would be capable of solution. Equations like $x^2 - 36 = 0$ would have real solutions, whereas those like $x^2 + 36 = 0$ would have imaginary solutions, the square roots of negative numbers. If the inclusion of imaginary numbers is worrying, it is worth considering the sense in which a negative number, -6 say, is real—or, come to that, the sense in which 6 itself is real. Of course, the sum of your worries may not be decreased by such considerations.

From what has been said, if a is a positive real number, then $-a$ is negative, and $\sqrt{-a}$ will be imaginary. Our imaginary numbers are to conform to the same rules as the real numbers, so

$$\sqrt{-a} = \sqrt{(a)(-1)} = (\sqrt{a})(\sqrt{-1})$$

Because a is positive, $\sqrt{a}$ is a real number. Thus any imaginary number can be written as the product of a real number and the square root of -1. (We can in fact define an imaginary number in this way if we wish.) We denote the square root of -1 by i; thus $\sqrt{-36} = 6i$.

We can add and subtract imaginary numbers:

$$2i + 0.5i = 2.5i = 4i - 1.5i$$

We can multiply them by real numbers:

$$2(3i) = 6i = (3i)2$$

We can also multiply two imaginary numbers together; if we do so the answer is real. For example,

$$(2i)(3i) = 6i^2 = (6)(-1) = -6$$

When we add a real number a to an imaginary number ib we obtain a *complex number,* $a + ib$. This expression for a complex number cannot be further simplified.

Notice that a and b are both real numbers; in this section and the next, I will use $a, b, d, e, \ldots$ to denote real numbers; when I wish to talk of complex numbers I will use $c_1, c_2, \ldots$

We add and subtract complex numbers in a straightforward way:

$$(a + ib) + (d + ie) = (a + d) + i(b + e)$$

The sum of two complex numbers is thus the sum of their real parts plus the sum of their imaginary parts, and is again a complex number.

Similarly, consider the product of two complex numbers:

$$\begin{aligned}(a + ib)(d + ie) &= ad + a(ie) + (ib)d + (ib)(ie)\\ &= ad + iae + ibd - be\\ &= (ad - be) + i(ae + bd)\end{aligned}$$

This is again a complex number.

We may remark that both real and imaginary numbers are special cases of complex numbers. The complex number $a + ib$ is real provided $b = 0$, and it is imaginary whenever $a = 0$.

Now consider the product of $a + ib$ and $a - ib$. The formula for the product yields

$$(a + ib)(a - ib) = a^2 + b^2$$

This is both real and positive. We call $a - ib$ the *complex conjugate* of $a + ib$, and conversely. We denote by c^* the complex conjugate of the complex number c. Thus $(a + ib)^* = a - ib$, and $(a - ib)^* = a + ib$. For all c, $(c^*)^* = c$, but $c^* = c$ if and only if c is real. We have just shown that $(c^*)(c)$ is always real and positive.

Observe that the use of complex numbers enables us to factorize expressions like $a^2 + b^2$, which previously resisted factorization.

The quantity $|c| = \sqrt{(c)(c^*)}$ is known as the *norm* of c. We are often interested in complex numbers of norm 1; from the definition of the norm, it follows that if $c = a + ib$ and $|c| = 1$, then $a^2 + b^2 = 1$. This in turn implies that there is an angle θ such that $a = \cos\theta$ and $b = \sin\theta$. Thus any complex number of norm 1 can be written in the form:

$$c = \cos\theta + i\sin\theta = e^{i\theta}$$

(The number e is the base of so-called *natural* logarithms; it is the sum of the infinite series:

$$e = 1 + 1 + \frac{1}{2!} + \frac{1}{3!} + \cdots$$

For any x,

$$e^x = 1 + x + \frac{x^2}{2!} + \frac{x^3}{3!} + \cdots$$

For our purposes, however, we can think of $e^{i\theta}$ simply as a notational convenience for $\cos\theta + i\sin\theta$.)

Finally, I should add that many mathematicians find this approach to complex numbers, which emphasizes the role of $\sqrt{-1}$, faintly disreputable. They define complex numbers as ordered pairs (a,b) of reals which obey certain algebraic relations, so that, for instance, $(a,b) + (d,e) = (a + d, b + e)$, and $(a,b)^* = (a,-b)$. The reader is invited to reconstruct the material of this section along these lines.

1.6 *The Space* $\mathbb{C}^2$

Let us now return to the study of vectors, and look at the complex space $\mathbb{C}^2$. Whereas in $\mathbb{R}^2$ each vector was represented by a pair of real numbers

$$\begin{pmatrix} a \\ b \end{pmatrix}$$

to each vector of $\mathbb{C}^2$ we associate a pair of complex numbers

$$\begin{pmatrix} c_1 \\ c_2 \end{pmatrix}$$

In contrast with the situation in $\mathbb{R}^2$, however, no direct geometrical representation of a vector in $\mathbb{C}^2$ is possible. For present purposes we say that the pair of numbers *is* the vector.

Vector addition and scalar multiplication go on much as before.

$$\text{If} \quad \mathbf{u} = \begin{pmatrix} c_1 \\ c_2 \end{pmatrix} \quad \text{and} \quad \mathbf{v} = \begin{pmatrix} c_3 \\ c_4 \end{pmatrix}, \quad \text{then} \quad \mathbf{u} + \mathbf{v} = \begin{pmatrix} c_1 + c_3 \\ c_2 + c_4 \end{pmatrix}$$

as in the case when our vectors were pairs of reals. We allow scalar multiplication by any complex number:

$$\text{if} \quad \mathbf{v} = \begin{pmatrix} c_1 \\ c_2 \end{pmatrix}, \quad \text{then} \quad c\mathbf{v} = \begin{pmatrix} cc_1 \\ cc_2 \end{pmatrix}$$

The number 0 is a complex number, and so, as before, the zero vector is given by

$$\mathbf{0} = \begin{pmatrix} 0 \\ 0 \end{pmatrix}$$

An operator on a complex space is like an operator on a real space: it is an instruction to transform a vector into some other vector. As in $\mathbb{R}^2$, to each linear operator on $\mathbb{C}^2$ there corresponds a 2×2 matrix of numbers, but in this case the numbers are complex. For instance, a typical operator on $\mathbb{C}^2$ is represented by the matrix

$$\begin{pmatrix} 2 & 1 - i \\ 1 + i & 3 \end{pmatrix} = \mathbf{A}$$

The algorithm for determining $\mathbf{A}\mathbf{v}$, given $\mathbf{A}$ and $\mathbf{v}$, is the same as before, as is the procedure for finding the matrix $\mathbf{AB}$, the product of $\mathbf{A}$ and $\mathbf{B}$, given those matrices. For example, let $\mathbf{A}$ be as above, and let

$$\mathbf{v} = \begin{pmatrix} 1 \\ 1 + i \end{pmatrix}$$

Then

$$\mathbf{Av} = \begin{pmatrix} 2 & 1-i \\ 1+i & 3 \end{pmatrix} \begin{pmatrix} 1 \\ 1+i \end{pmatrix} = \begin{pmatrix} (2)(1) + (1-i)(1+i) \\ (1+i)(1) + (3)(1+i) \end{pmatrix}$$

$$= \begin{pmatrix} 4 \\ 4(1+i) \end{pmatrix} = 4\mathbf{v}$$

We see that $\mathbf{v}$ is an eigenvector of $\mathbf{A}$, with corresponding eigenvalue 4. It turns out that the vector

$$\mathbf{u} = \begin{pmatrix} 1-i \\ -1 \end{pmatrix}$$

is also an eigenvector of $\mathbf{A}$. In this case the corresponding eigenvalue is 1 (thus $\mathbf{Au} = \mathbf{u}$).

These eigenvalues are real. In this respect the operator $\mathbf{A}$ is not quite typical; it is a member of a particular class of operators known as *Hermitian* operators. These operators are going to play an important role when we look at quantum theory: they will represent physical quantities, and their eigenvalues will be the possible values of those quantities; clearly it befits a measurable quantity that its possible values should be real. I will postpone a formal definition of a Hermitian operator until Section 1.12; it is the analogue in complex space of a symmetric operator on a real space, and it has similar identifying characteristics. Whereas the off-diagonal elements of a symmetric matrix on $\mathbb{R}^2$ were equal, those of a Hermitian operator on $\mathbb{C}^2$ are complex conjugates of each other. (The diagonal elements of a 2×2 matrix are the top left and bottom right elements; the off-diagonals, therefore, are the bottom left and top right elements.) In the example above, the elements in question are $1 - i$ and $1 + i$. We also require that the diagonal elements (2 and 3 in this case) be real. As in this example, the sum of the diagonal elements of a Hermitian operator is always equal to the sum of its eigenvalues.

For operators on complex spaces, as for those on real spaces, the maximum number of distinct eigenvalues is equal to the dimensionality of the space. In the case of a real space we also found that eigenvectors of symmetric operators whose eigenvalues were distinct were always at right angles to each other. The Hermitian operators on $\mathbb{C}^2$ have the same property, but it's not informative to say so until we know what meaning we can give to "at right angles" in the complex case. We approach this via the notion of inner product.

It is in the definition of inner product that the first important amendment to our computational rules appears.

$$\text{Let}\quad \mathbf{u} = \begin{pmatrix} c_1 \\ c_2 \end{pmatrix} \quad \text{and} \quad \mathbf{v} = \begin{pmatrix} c_3 \\ c_4 \end{pmatrix}. \quad \text{Then}$$

(1.12) $\langle \mathbf{u}|\mathbf{v}\rangle = c_1{}^*c_3 + c_2{}^*c_4$

and so, in general, $\langle \mathbf{u}|\mathbf{v}\rangle$ is not equal to $\langle \mathbf{v}|\mathbf{u}\rangle$. In fact we can prove that one is the complex conjugate of the other:

(1.13) $\langle \mathbf{v}|\mathbf{u}\rangle = \langle \mathbf{u}|\mathbf{v}\rangle^*$ (☆)

But now consider the inner product $\langle \mathbf{u}|\mathbf{u}\rangle$. From (1.12), $\langle \mathbf{u}|\mathbf{u}\rangle = c_1{}^*c_1 + c_2{}^*c_2$. We know that, for any complex number c, c^*c is a positive real number; thus, for any vector $\mathbf{u}$ of $\mathbb{C}^2$, $\langle \mathbf{u}|\mathbf{u}\rangle$ is real and positive.

This means that even in complex space we can talk of the length of a vector; we define it by writing

(1.14) $|\mathbf{v}| = \sqrt{\langle \mathbf{v}|\mathbf{v}\rangle}$

without the risk of having a length turn out to be either an imaginary number or the square root of such a number.

As before, we say that $\mathbf{v}$ is *normalized* if $|\mathbf{v}| = 1$, and that $\mathbf{u}$ and $\mathbf{v}$ are *orthogonal* if $\langle \mathbf{u}|\mathbf{v}\rangle = 0 = \langle \mathbf{v}|\mathbf{u}\rangle$. This gives us a definition of orthogonality for use in complex spaces, where the geometrical idea of a right angle is inappropriate. If $\mathbf{u}$ and $\mathbf{v}$ are orthogonal, we write $\mathbf{u} \perp \mathbf{v}$.

Armed with this definition, we can return briefly to the topic of eigenvectors and eigenvalues. We find that, if $\mathbf{v}_1$ and $\mathbf{v}_2$ are both eigenvectors of a Hermitian operator $\mathbf{A}$ on a complex space, such that $\mathbf{A}\mathbf{v}_1 = a_1\mathbf{v}_1$, $\mathbf{A}\mathbf{v}_2 = a_2\mathbf{v}_2$, and $a_1 \neq a_2$, then $\mathbf{v}_1 \perp \mathbf{v}_2$. In the example given,

$$\mathbf{v}_1 = \begin{pmatrix} 1 \\ 1+i \end{pmatrix} \quad \text{and} \quad \mathbf{v}_2 = \begin{pmatrix} 1-i \\ -1 \end{pmatrix}$$

We see that

$$\begin{aligned} \langle \mathbf{v}_1|\mathbf{v}_2\rangle &= (1^*)(1-i) + (1+i)^*(-1) \\ &= (1)(1-i) + (1-i)(-1) \\ &= 0 \end{aligned}$$

as required.

As with the definitions of inner product, length, and orthogonality, wherever possible we find suitable generalizations in $\mathbb{C}^2$ of the concepts familiar from the real space $\mathbb{R}^2$. For instance, the analogues in $\mathbb{C}^2$ of the lines of $\mathbb{R}^2$ are the *one-dimensional subspaces* of $\mathbb{C}^2$. If two vectors of $\mathbb{R}^2$ lie along the same line, then one is a multiple of the other; similarly, if two vectors $\mathbf{v}$ and $\mathbf{v}'$ lie within the same one-dimensional subspace of $\mathbb{C}^2$, then $\mathbf{v}' = c\mathbf{v}$, where c is some (complex) number, and conversely. We usually use the term *ray* instead of the cumbersome *one-dimensional subspace.*

Let us now generalize the notion of a *projection operator.* We do this by following the route taken in Section 1.2; we can usefully use a diagram (Figure 1.15), provided that we remember that what we see in the diagram is only the analogue in $\mathbb{R}^2$ of what we have in $\mathbb{C}^2$.

Let L be any ray of $\mathbb{C}^2$, and $\mathbf{v}$ be any vector of $\mathbb{C}^2$. Then there exist two vectors $\mathbf{v}_L$ and $\mathbf{v}_{L^\perp}$, such that (i) $\mathbf{v}_L + \mathbf{v}_{L^\perp} = \mathbf{v}$, (ii) $\mathbf{v}_L$ lies within L, and (iii) $\mathbf{v}_{L^\perp} \perp \mathbf{v}_L$. Further, for a given vector $\mathbf{v}$ and ray L, $\mathbf{v}_L$ and $\mathbf{v}_{L^\perp}$ are unique. As in the analogous case in $\mathbb{R}^2$ (see Figure 1.15), we can define the projection operator $\mathbf{P}$ onto L by writing, for any vector $\mathbf{v}$, $\mathbf{Pv} = \mathbf{v}_L$, where $\mathbf{v}$, $\mathbf{v}_L$, and $\mathbf{v}_{L^\perp}$ stand in the relations given by (i), (ii), and (iii) above.

As in $\mathbb{R}^2$ we find that, for every vector $\mathbf{v}$ and every projection operator $\mathbf{P}$,

$$\langle \mathbf{v}|\mathbf{Pv}\rangle = |\mathbf{Pv}|^2 = \langle \mathbf{Pv}|\mathbf{Pv}\rangle$$

This is always real and positive; furthermore, whenever $\mathbf{v}$ is normalized,

$$0 \leq \langle \mathbf{v}|\mathbf{Pv}\rangle \leq 1$$

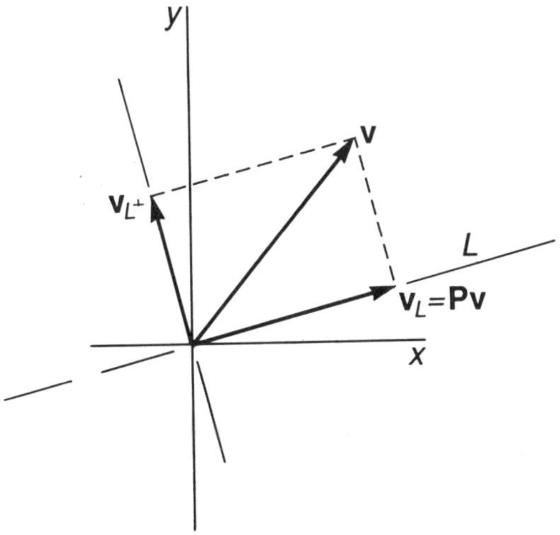

Figure 1.15

A Hermitian operator on $\mathbb{C}^2$, like a symmetric operator on $\mathbb{R}^2$, can be decomposed into a weighted sum of projection operators. Consider the Hermitian operator $\mathbf{A}$ on $\mathbb{C}^2$ with distinct (real) eigenvalues a_1 and a_2. Let $\mathbf{v}_1$ and $\mathbf{v}_2$ be corresponding eigenvectors, and $\mathbf{P}_1$ and $\mathbf{P}_2$ be projection operators onto the rays containing $\mathbf{v}_1$ and $\mathbf{v}_2$, respectively. (We call these rays the subspaces *spanned* by the vectors.) Then, as before, the spectral decomposition theorem gives us:

$$\mathbf{A} = a_1\mathbf{P}_1 + a_2\mathbf{P}_2 \tag{1.15}$$

For example, consider again the operator

$$\mathbf{A} = \begin{pmatrix} 2 & 1-i \\ 1+i & 3 \end{pmatrix}$$

The projection operator $\mathbf{P}_1$ onto the ray containing

$$\begin{pmatrix} 1 \\ 1+i \end{pmatrix} \text{ is } \frac{1}{3}\begin{pmatrix} 1 & 1-i \\ 1+i & 2 \end{pmatrix}$$

and the projection operator $\mathbf{P}_2$ onto the ray containing

$$\begin{pmatrix} 1-i \\ -1 \end{pmatrix} \text{ is } \frac{1}{3}\begin{pmatrix} 2 & -1+i \\ -1-i & 1 \end{pmatrix}$$

The eigenvalues are 4 and 1, respectively, and a brisk calculation shows that (1.15) holds. As an exercise (☆☆), it is worth considering how one could show that $\mathbf{P}_1$ and $\mathbf{P}_2$ are given by these particular matrices.

1.7 *The Pauli Spin Matrices*

To echo Eco (1979), every book defines the role of its ideal reader. Even so, some do it less subtly than others. Here are a few problems on the space $\mathbb{C}^2$.

These problems are not simply mathematical exercises; in later chapters the results will be applied to a particular physical example, namely to the quantum theory of the fermion or spin-$\frac{1}{2}$ particle. As indicated in the previous section, in quantum mechanics physical quantities like momentum and energy are represented by Hermitian operators; Chapter 2 shows how these operators enter into theoretical calculations. The exercises below involve three operators used to represent the components of spin of a fermion

—the quantities we met in the discussion of Stern and Gerlach's results in the Introduction. The matrix representations of these operators are shown below.

$$\mathbf{S}_x = \frac{1}{2}\begin{pmatrix} 0 & 1 \\ 1 & 0 \end{pmatrix} \qquad \mathbf{S}_y = \frac{1}{2}\begin{pmatrix} 0 & -i \\ i & 0 \end{pmatrix} \qquad \mathbf{S}_z = \frac{1}{2}\begin{pmatrix} 1 & 0 \\ 0 & -1 \end{pmatrix}$$

The three matrices involved are known as the *Pauli spin matrices.*

PROBLEMS

1. Show that $\mathbf{S}_x$ and $\mathbf{S}_y$ do not commute, and evaluate $\mathbf{S}_x\mathbf{S}_y - \mathbf{S}_y\mathbf{S}_x$. Express this difference in terms of $\mathbf{S}_z$, and show that this relation holds cyclically among the three operators.
2. Let

$$\mathbf{x}_+ = \frac{1}{2}\begin{pmatrix} \sqrt{2} \\ \sqrt{2} \end{pmatrix}, \qquad \mathbf{x}_- = \frac{1}{2}\begin{pmatrix} \sqrt{2} \\ -\sqrt{2} \end{pmatrix},$$

$$\mathbf{y}_+ = \frac{1}{2}\begin{pmatrix} 1-i \\ 1+i \end{pmatrix} \qquad \mathbf{y}_- = \frac{1}{2}\begin{pmatrix} 1-i \\ -1-i \end{pmatrix}$$

Show that $\mathbf{x}_+$ and $\mathbf{x}_-$ are eigenvectors of $\mathbf{S}_x$, and that $\mathbf{y}_+$ and $\mathbf{y}_-$ are eigenvectors of $\mathbf{S}_y$. In each case, what are the corresponding eigenvalues?
3. Show (i) that $\mathbf{x}_+$ and $\mathbf{y}_+$ are both normalized; and (ii) that $\mathbf{x}_+$ is orthogonal to $\mathbf{x}_-$, and that $\mathbf{y}_+$ is orthogonal to $\mathbf{y}_-$. Why might one expect (ii) to be the case?
4. Determine the eigenvectors and corresponding eigenvalues of $\mathbf{S}_z$.
5. Let $\mathbf{P}_{x+}$ be the projection operator onto the one-dimensional subspace of $\mathbb{C}^2$ containing $\mathbf{x}_+$. We extend the notation in an obvious way to $\mathbf{P}_{x-}$, $\mathbf{P}_{y+}$, and so on. Then

$$\mathbf{P}_{x+} = \frac{1}{2}\begin{pmatrix} 1 & 1 \\ 1 & 1 \end{pmatrix} \qquad \mathbf{P}_{x-} = \frac{1}{2}\begin{pmatrix} 1 & -1 \\ -1 & 1 \end{pmatrix} \qquad \mathbf{P}_{y+} = \frac{1}{2}\begin{pmatrix} 1 & -i \\ i & 1 \end{pmatrix}$$

(i) Show that $\mathbf{P}_{x-}\mathbf{x}_- = \mathbf{x}_-$ and $\mathbf{P}_{y+}\mathbf{y}_+ = \mathbf{y}_+$. (ii) Determine the vector $\mathbf{P}_{y+}\mathbf{y}_-$. (iii) Show that $\mathbf{P}_{y+}$ is indeed the projection operator onto the ray containing $\mathbf{y}_+$. (iv) Evaluate $\mathbf{P}_{x+}\mathbf{P}_{x-}$ and $\mathbf{P}_{y+}\mathbf{P}_{y+}$ ($= \mathbf{P}^2_{y+}$). Why are these results predictable?
6. Evaluate $\langle \mathbf{x}_+ | \mathbf{P}_{y+}\mathbf{x}_+ \rangle$, $\langle \mathbf{x}_- | \mathbf{P}_{y+}\mathbf{x}_- \rangle$, $\langle \mathbf{y}_+ | \mathbf{P}_{y+}\mathbf{y}_+ \rangle$, and $\langle \mathbf{y}_- | \mathbf{P}_{y+}\mathbf{y}_- \rangle$. Confirm that these are equal to $|\mathbf{P}_{y+}\mathbf{x}_+|^2$, $|\mathbf{P}_{y+}\mathbf{x}_-|^2$, $|\mathbf{P}_{y+}\mathbf{y}_+|^2$, and $|\mathbf{P}_{y+}\mathbf{y}_-|^2$, respectively.

7. Given $\mathbf{S}_y$ and $\mathbf{P}_{y+}$, use the decomposition theorem to determine $\mathbf{P}_{y-}$. Confirm that $\mathbf{P}_{y-}\mathbf{y}_- = \mathbf{y}_-$ and $\mathbf{P}_{y-}\mathbf{y}_+ = \mathbf{0}$.
8. Evaluate $\frac{1}{2}\mathbf{P}_{x+} - \frac{1}{2}\mathbf{P}_{x-}$. Why is this result predictable?

1.8 *Mathematical Generalization*

The comparatively simple mathematics of $\mathbb{C}^2$, where no manipulation more difficult than multiplying complex numbers is involved, enables us to answer basic questions about electrons and their components of spin. To deal with quantum systems in full generality requires an extension and generalization of these ideas. As a preliminary to this generalization, this section is devoted to the topic of mathematical structures; we will return to the subject of vector spaces in Section 1.9.

A mathematical structure consists of a collection of objects (usually mathematical "objects"), together with the relations between those objects, and the operations we can perform on them. Consider, for instance, the set of the rotation operators on $\mathbb{R}^2$ whose effect is to rotate vectors through multiples of 90°. Call this set *Rot*,

$$Rot = \{\mathbf{R}_0, \mathbf{R}_{90}, \mathbf{R}_{180}, \mathbf{R}_{270}\}$$

There are just four members of this set, since a rotation of 360° is equivalent to no rotation at all; in fact, we have $\mathbf{R}_{360} = \mathbf{R}_0 = \mathbf{I}$. Now, given any pair of linear operators **A** and **B**, we can form their product **AB**. A distinguishing feature of the set *Rot* is that the product of any pair of these operators (including the product of any one of them with itself) is again a member of the set. We have, for example: $\mathbf{R}_{90}\mathbf{R}_{180} = \mathbf{R}_{270}$, $\mathbf{R}_0\mathbf{R}_{90} = \mathbf{R}_{90}$, $\mathbf{R}_{270}\mathbf{R}_{270} = \mathbf{R}_{180}$, and so on. We say that multiplication is a *binary operation* on the set.

Consider now the set of four numbers, two real and two imaginary, $\{1, i, -1, -i\}$. We can of course multiply any two of them together in the usual way, and if we do so we find that they have the same property that we observed in the set of four rotation operators: the product of any two of them is also a member of the set: $(i)(-1) = -i$, $(1)(i) = (i)$, $(-i)(-i) = -1$, and so on. Observe that these equations involving numbers exactly match up with the earlier equations involving operators.

We find that each operator from the first set, *Rot*, corresponds to a number from the second; furthermore, to the operation of operator multiplication on *Rot* corresponds the operation of arithmetical multiplication on the set of numbers. The two sets are alike, not in the objects they contain, but in their mathematical structure. When, as in this case, the structural similarity is such that a perfect one-to-one correspondence exists between two sets, we say that they are *isomorphic.*

However, we're interested in a weaker kind of similarity. We want to specify, for instance, the way in which *Rot* is similar to the set of rotations through multiples of 60°. In fact, this set and the two we started with, together with the product operations on them, are all examples of a very general kind of mathematical structure known as a *group,* and defined as follows.

(1.16) $\mathcal{G}$ is said to be a *group* if $\mathcal{G}$ comprises a set G of elements and a binary operation $\circ$ on G; one of the elements of G has particular properties and is known as the *identity* element of the group; for all elements, a, b, c, of G,

(1.16a) $(a \circ b) \circ c = a \circ (b \circ c)$

(1.16b) $a \circ I = a = I \circ a$

where I is the identity element. Additionally, for any element a of G, there is a unique element a' of G such that

(1.16c) $a \circ a' = I = a' \circ a$

We may regard ′ as a singulary operation on G, mapping each member of G into another. (For a general introduction to groups, see Eddington, 1935a, rpt. Newman, 1956, vol. 3, pp. 1558–1573; see also MacLane and Birkhoff, 1979, chap. 2.)

In defining a group I have abstracted certain features of these structures while ignoring others; it is not part of the general definition, for instance, that a group just have four elements. It is not even required that the operation $\circ$ be commutative—that, for all a and b in G, $a \circ b = b \circ a$—although this was the case with both of the groups described here. These two groups belong to a special subclass of groups, the *commutative,* or *Abelian,* groups.

I hope I have said enough to indicate what is involved when we say of a set that it is a structure of a certain kind, like a group. In saying this we are not saying what sorts of objects are in the set, nor how many of them there are (though we may specify this to some degree, as we do when talking of *finite* groups). We are merely saying that we have a set of objects and that we can perform operations on these objects, or on pairs or perhaps trios of these objects, to yield others of the same kind; further, that these operations conform to certain rules, like (1.16a)–(1.16c), above. We may also require that there exist objects in the set with particular properties: for example, every group has to contain an identity element. To describe a structure, we make a list: first on the list is the relevant set of objects, then come the operations performed on that set, and finally we list the elements with specific properties. Thus the first structure we looked at in this section is the group $\langle Rot, \circ, ', \mathbf{R}_0 \rangle$, which includes the set *Rot*, the binary operation of multiplication, the singulary operation which gives the inverse of any element of *Rot*, and the identity element of *Rot*.

I should emphasize that our present concern is not the mathematical theory of groups per se. It so happens that a group is a particularly simple form of mathematical structure and that by talking about groups we can see what is meant by an *operation* on a set, by one structure being *isomorphic* to another, and so on. Armed with these ideas, we can move to a more complicated structure, that of a vector space—recalling, as we go, Russell's (1917, p. 59) suggestion that "Mathematics may be defined as the subject in which we never know what we are talking about, nor whether what we are saying is true."

1.9 *Vector Spaces*

What, then, are the defining properties of a *vector space*, considered abstractly in this way? We have already seen examples of such spaces: the set of arrows in a plane radiating from a given point, and the set of pairs of numbers. In fact, if the numbers are real numbers, the two sets are effectively the same, in that we can translate talk of arrows into talk of pairs of real numbers, and conversely. To use the vocabulary of Section 1.8, the set of arrows in the plane and the set of pairs of real numbers are isomorphic.

When the spaces $\mathbb{R}^2$ and $\mathbb{C}^2$ were introduced, in both cases the operations we met first were vector addition and scalar multiplication. The latter involves multiplying a vector by a scalar, that is, by a number; thus prior to any definition of a vector space we need an analysis of the structure of the set of numbers. The relevant operations on this set are the binary operations of addition and multiplication and the operation which takes us from the number a to the number $1/a$. The elements with special properties are 0 and 1. The structure in question is that of a *field*, $\mathcal{F} = \langle F, +, \cdot, ^{-1}, 0, 1 \rangle$, where the operations and designated elements have familiar properties, such as $a + 0 = a$ and $(a)(a^{-1}) = 1$, for all a in F (see MacLane and Birkhoff, 1979, chaps. 3 and 8).

Both the set of real numbers and the set of complex numbers have the structure of a field. Omitting the formal definition of a field, I will move straight on to the definition of a vector space *over* a field.

Let $\mathcal{F} = \langle F, +^\circ, \cdot^\circ, ^{-1}, 0^\circ, 1 \rangle$ be a field. (The binary operations and zero element are tagged with degree signs to distinguish them from the operations on the vector space, which are customarily represented by the same symbols.) The elements of F will be called *scalars.* Then

(1.17) $\mathcal{V}$ is called a *vector space over* $\mathcal{F}$ if $\mathcal{V} = \langle V, +, \cdot, \mathbf{0} \rangle$, where
V is a nonempty set whose elements are called *vectors;*
$+$ is an operation which takes any pair of vectors and yields a vector (that is, $+$ is a binary operation on V);
$\cdot$ is an operation which takes a scalar and a vector and yields a vector;
$\mathbf{0}$ is a member of V (the *zero vector*);
for all $\mathbf{u}$, $\mathbf{v}$, and $\mathbf{w}$ in V, and for all a and b in F, the following identities hold:

(1.17a) $(\mathbf{u} + \mathbf{v}) + \mathbf{w} = \mathbf{u} + (\mathbf{v} + \mathbf{w})$

(1.17b) $\mathbf{u} + \mathbf{v} = \mathbf{v} + \mathbf{u}$

(1.17c) $\mathbf{v} + \mathbf{0} = \mathbf{v}$

(1.17d) $a \cdot (b \cdot \mathbf{v}) = (a \cdot^\circ b) \cdot \mathbf{v}$

(1.17e) $(a +^\circ b) \cdot \mathbf{v} = a \cdot \mathbf{v} + b \cdot \mathbf{v}$

(1.17f) $a \cdot (\mathbf{v} + \mathbf{u}) = a \cdot \mathbf{v} + a \cdot \mathbf{u}$

(1.17g) $0^\circ \cdot \mathbf{v} = \mathbf{0}$

(1.17h) $1 \cdot \mathbf{v} = \mathbf{v}$

Clearly the examples of vector spaces we have looked at satisfy these axioms. However, so do various other sets of mathematical objects. Consider the set of infinite sequences of numbers; let $\mathbf{x}$ and $\mathbf{y}$ be members of this set, so that $\mathbf{x} = (x_1, x_2, \ldots)$ and $\mathbf{y} = (y_1, y_2, \ldots)$, where x_1, y_1, x_2, y_2 are numbers. We can define vector addition and scalar multiplication by

$$\mathbf{x} + \mathbf{y} = (x_1 + y_1, x_2 + y_2, \ldots) \qquad a \cdot \mathbf{x} = (ax_1, ax_2, \ldots)$$

If we do so, then, because all the clauses of (1.17) are satisfied, we have defined a vector space in which the sequences are the vectors.

Alternatively, consider the set of all complex-valued functions of a real number. Examples are the squaring function, which maps a real number onto its square, the function which maps a real number x onto the complex number $x + ix$, the function which yields the cosine of x, and so on. This set can be made into a vector space as follows. The functions themselves are the vectors in the space; given any two functions, ϕ and ψ, we define their sum $\phi + \psi$, so that, for all real numbers x,

$$(\phi + \psi)(x) = \phi(x) +^{\circ} \psi(x)$$

and we define scalar multiplication by the equation

$$(a \cdot \phi)(x) = a \cdot^{\circ} \phi(x)$$

If we do so (1.17) is satisfied and again the result is a vector space. (The symbol $^{\circ}$ used to distinguish operations performed on numbers from those performed on vectors has now served its purpose. It may be omitted without loss of clarity; however, it is still a useful exercise to see which operation is being referred to by a particular symbol on any given occasion.)

Unless otherwise stated, in what follows vector spaces are assumed to be over the field of the complex numbers.

1.10 *Linear Operators*

The definition of a linear operator given earlier may be repeated without change. An operator $\mathbf{A}$ when applied to any vector $\mathbf{v}$ of vector space $\mathcal{V}$ yields another vector $\mathbf{v}'$; we write $\mathbf{Av} = \mathbf{v}'$. We use the general term *mapping* to indicate the application of an operator to a vector; a mapping is a rule that associates every element of a set with an element of another set, or, as in this case, with an element in the same set. An operator is just a special kind of mapping, and so is a function. We denote a mapping as we would an operator or function.

(1.18) A mapping $\mathbf{A}$ of the set V into itself is called a *linear operator* if for all vectors $\mathbf{u}$ and $\mathbf{v}$ and for any scalar a,

(1.18a) $$\mathbf{A}(\mathbf{v} + \mathbf{u}) = \mathbf{Av} + \mathbf{Au}$$

(1.18b) $$\mathbf{A}(a\mathbf{v}) = a(\mathbf{Av})$$

Examples of linear operators on the space of functions of x are easy to come by. For instance, given a function $\phi(x)$, the expression $x \cdot \phi(x)$ also represents a function of x, whose value is obtained by multiplying the value of $\phi(x)$ by x. Thus x is here an operator, and since (1.18a) and (1.18b) hold (writing x for **A**, ϕ and ψ for **v** and **u**), it is a linear operator. Again, the differential operator d/dx is a linear operator on the space of functions of x. However, though the process of squaring any function ϕ of x—so that $\phi^2(x) = [\phi(x)]^2$—could be regarded as the action of an operator, such an operator would not be linear, because both (1.18a) and (1.18b) would be violated.

The definitions of an eigenvector and an eigenvalue of an operator carry through to the general case:

(1.19) A vector **v** is said to be an *eigenvector* of **A**, with corresponding *eigenvalue* a, if $\mathbf{v} \neq \mathbf{0}$ and $\mathbf{A}\mathbf{v} = a\mathbf{v}$.

We observe, for example, that in our space of functions of x, e^{3x} is an eigenvector of d/dx with eigenvalue 3, since

$$\frac{d}{dx}(e^{3x}) = 3e^{3x}$$

Sums and products of linear operators are defined as before.

(1.20) If **A** and **B** are linear operators on $\mathcal{V}$, then $\mathbf{A} + \mathbf{B}$ and **AB** are linear operators such that, for all **v** in V,

(1.20a) $$(\mathbf{A} + \mathbf{B})\mathbf{v} = \mathbf{A}\mathbf{v} + \mathbf{B}\mathbf{v}$$

(1.20b) $$(\mathbf{A}\mathbf{B})\mathbf{v} = \mathbf{A}(\mathbf{B}\mathbf{v})$$

1.11 *Inner Products on $\mathcal{V}$*

Alongside our abstract definition of a vector space we now want a definition of an inner product. Since the vector spaces we now deal with are not necessarily geometrical, we will not usually be able to give a direct interpretation of this quantity, as we could in the case of $\mathbb{R}^2$. Instead, we pick certain features of that inner product, like the fact that the inner product of any two vectors is a number, and use them as the defining properties of an inner product in general.

Let $\mathcal{V} = \langle V, +, \cdot, \mathbf{0} \rangle$ be a vector space over a field $\mathcal{F}$. (It is assumed here that $\mathcal{F}$ is the field of complex numbers; if $\mathcal{F}$ is the field of the reals then the complex conjugation signs below are redundant.) Then to each pair of vectors **u** and **v** in V we assign a scalar, denoted by $\langle \mathbf{u} | \mathbf{v} \rangle$.

(1.21) $\langle \mathbf{u}|\mathbf{v}\rangle$ is said to be an *inner product* on $\mathcal{V}$ if

(1.21a) $$\langle \mathbf{v}|\mathbf{v}\rangle \geq 0, \text{ and } \langle \mathbf{v}|\mathbf{v}\rangle = 0 \text{ if and only if } \mathbf{v} = \mathbf{0}$$

(1.21b) $$\langle \mathbf{u}|\mathbf{v}\rangle = \langle \mathbf{v}|\mathbf{u}\rangle^*$$

(1.21c) $$\langle \mathbf{u}|a\mathbf{v}\rangle = a\langle \mathbf{u}|\mathbf{v}\rangle$$

(1.21d) $$\langle \mathbf{u}|\mathbf{v} + \mathbf{w}\rangle = \langle \mathbf{u}|\mathbf{v}\rangle + \langle \mathbf{u}|\mathbf{w}\rangle$$

It is clear that the inner products we defined on $\mathbb{R}^2$ and $\mathbb{C}^2$ conform to these conditions. We can extend those definitions of inner product to provide a definition of an inner product on the state of infinite sequences of complex numbers, provided we restrict the space to those sequences $(x_1, x_2, \ldots)$ such that $\Sigma_i x_i^* x_i$ is finite. Given this restriction, we can write, for two vectors $\mathbf{x}$ and $\mathbf{y}$ in the space such that $\mathbf{x} = (x_1, x_2, \ldots)$ and $\mathbf{y} = (y_1, y_2, \ldots)$:

$$\langle \mathbf{x}|\mathbf{y}\rangle = x_1^* y_1 + x_2^* y_2 + \cdots = \sum_i x_i^* y_i$$

The restriction on the sequences is needed to ensure that the inner product defined in this way will always be finite, that is, will be a scalar. The space of such sequences is called ℓ^2.

Similar considerations lead us to define an inner product, not on the vector space of all functions of x, but on the vector space of all square-integrable functions of x, that is, functions $\phi(x)$ such that $\int_{-\infty}^{\infty} \phi(x)^* \phi(x) dx$ is finite. This space is known as L^2; we define an inner product on it by writing, for vectors ϕ and ψ,

$$\langle \phi|\psi\rangle = \int_{-\infty}^{\infty} \phi(x)^* \psi(x) dx$$

A remarkable mathematical fact now presents itself, that the spaces ℓ^2 and L^2 are isomorphic. (See Fano, 1971, p. 269.) That is, we can find a correspondence between sequences in ℓ^2 and square-integrable functions in L^2 such that, if to the sequences $\mathbf{x}$ and $\mathbf{y}$ there correspond functions ϕ and ψ, then (i) to the sequence $\mathbf{x} + \mathbf{y}$ corresponds the function $\phi + \psi$, (ii) to the sequence $a\mathbf{x}$ corresponds the function $a\phi$, and (iii) $\langle \mathbf{x}|\mathbf{y}\rangle = \langle \phi|\psi\rangle$ (provided that each of these inner products is evaluated in the way appropriate to the vectors involved). This isomorphism is relevant to the history of the development of quantum mechanics. The early formulations of the theory, by Heisenberg and Schrödinger, were, respectively, in terms of sequences and of functions; subsequently Schrödinger established that, by virtue of this isomorphism, the two formulations were equivalent (von Neumann, 1932, chap. I.4; see also Stein, 1972, p. 427, n. 10).

Armed with a definition of inner product on a given space, we can define the length of a vector, what it is for a vector to be normalized, and what it is for two vectors to be orthogonal, just as we did when discussing $\mathbb{C}^2$:

(1.22) For all $\mathbf{v}$ and $\mathbf{u}$ in V,

(1.22a) $|\mathbf{v}| = \sqrt{\langle \mathbf{v}|\mathbf{v}\rangle}$

(1.22b) $\mathbf{v}$ is said to be *normalized* if $|\mathbf{v}| = 1$

(1.22c) $\mathbf{v}$ is said to be *orthogonal* to $\mathbf{u}$ if $\langle \mathbf{v}|\mathbf{u}\rangle = 0$

1.12 *Subspaces and Projection Operators*

While we were dealing with arrows radiating from a point, the notion of a subspace of the vector space had a readily visualized geometrical interpretation. Given the fact that we confined the arrows to the plane, we had the following subspaces: the plane itself, all the lines through the zero vector, and the zero vector itself, or, more strictly, the set containing just the zero vector—see (1.23), below. If we had investigated the three-dimensional real space $\mathbb{R}^3$, then the whole space $\mathbb{R}^3$ would have been a subspace, as would every plane which included the zero vector and, as before, every line containing the zero vector, and the set containing only the zero vector. In other words, we would have had subspaces of dimension 3, 2, 1, and 0. Notice that if we add any two vectors lying in a plane, then the result is another vector lying in the same plane; again, if we multiply a vector $\mathbf{v}$ by any number a, the result $a\mathbf{v}$ is in the same plane as $\mathbf{v}$. These results hold not only for the planes of $\mathbb{R}^3$, but for any of its subspaces, and so a generalized definition of a subspace, applicable to all vector spaces, presents itself.

Let $\mathcal{V}$ be the vector space $\langle V, +, \cdot, \mathbf{0}\rangle$.

(1.23) L is said to be a *subspace* of $\mathcal{V}$ if L is a subset of V, and

(1.23a) if $\mathbf{u}$ and $\mathbf{v}$ are in L, then so is $\mathbf{u} + \mathbf{v}$

(1.23b) if $\mathbf{v}$ is in L, then so is $a\mathbf{v}$ (where a is any scalar)

How does this apply to vector spaces of functions of x? As an example, consider the vector space (call it $\mathcal{P}$) which contains just those functions which are polynomials in x, that is, functions of the form $a_0 + a_1x + a_2x^2 +$

$\cdots + a_n x^n$. Then a typical subspace of $\mathcal{P}$ contains all the polynomials of order two or less. (A function of the form $a_0 + a_1 x + a_2 x^2$ is a polynomial of order 2.) Clearly, the addition of two such functions yields another of the same kind, as does multiplication by an arbitrary number a, and this is all we require.

Orthogonality between vectors was defined in Section 1.11. We also say that a vector $\mathbf{v}$ is *orthogonal to a subspace* L if $\mathbf{v}$ is orthogonal to every vector in L, and that two subspaces L_1 and L_2 are orthogonal if every vector in L_1 is orthogonal to every vector in L_2. Note that in Figure 1.16 the planes L_1 and L_2 are at right angles to each other but are not orthogonal, since L_1 contains vectors which are not orthogonal to all vectors in L_2. In particular, the vector $\mathbf{v}$ is common to both.

Note that the zero subspace (containing just the vector $\mathbf{0}$) is orthogonal to all subspaces.

The projection operators we encountered on $\mathbb{R}^2$ and $\mathbb{C}^2$ were projection operators onto rays (one-dimensional subspaces) of $\mathbb{R}^2$ and $\mathbb{C}^2$, respectively. We can define projection operators onto subspaces of any dimension; if L is a plane of $\mathbb{R}^3$, then $\mathbf{P}_L$, the projection operator onto L, maps vectors into L, as shown in Figure 1.17.

We define projection operators in the general case just as we did for $\mathbb{C}^2$. That is, given a subspace L, we can decompose any vector $\mathbf{v}$ into two parts, $\mathbf{v}_L$ and $\mathbf{v}_{L^\perp}$, so that $\mathbf{v}_L$ lies in L, $\mathbf{v}_{L^\perp}$ is orthogonal to L (and hence to $\mathbf{v}_L$), and $\mathbf{v} = \mathbf{v}_L + \mathbf{v}_{L^\perp}$. We then write $\mathbf{P}_L \mathbf{v} = \mathbf{v}_L$, thereby defining the action of $\mathbf{P}_L$ on an arbitrary vector $\mathbf{v}$.

However, an alternative, elegant, and equivalent definition is available, as follows.

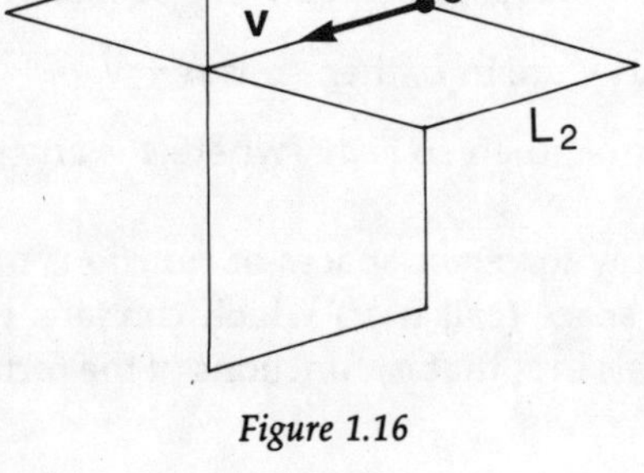

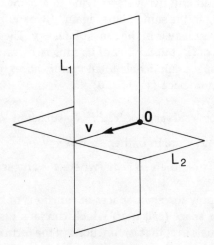

Figure 1.16

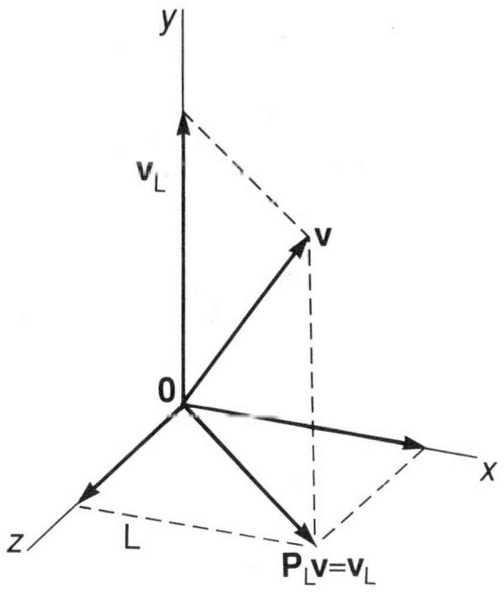

Figure 1.17

We first define a *Hermitian* operator on a complex space equipped with an inner product, and then say what it is for an operator to be *idempotent*.

(1.24) A linear operator **A** on $\mathcal{V}$ is said to be *Hermitian* if, for all vectors **u**, and **v**, $\langle \mathbf{u}|\mathbf{A}\mathbf{v}\rangle = \langle \mathbf{A}\mathbf{u}|\mathbf{v}\rangle$.

(1.25) A linear operator **A** on $\mathcal{V}$ is said to be *idempotent* if $\mathbf{AA} = \mathbf{A}$. (We write $\mathbf{A}^2 = \mathbf{A}$.)

We saw in Section 1.7, for example, that the operator

$$\frac{1}{2}\begin{pmatrix} 1 & -i \\ i & 1 \end{pmatrix}$$

on $\mathbb{C}^2$ is idempotent.

Our new definition of a projection operator is:

(1.26) A linear operator **A** on $\mathcal{V}$ is said to be a *projection operator* if **A** is both Hermitian and idempotent.

It can be shown that such an operator is an operator which has the property of "projecting onto a subspace" in the way described above, and conversely (☆☆). (See Jordan, 1969, pp. 26–27.)

The set of projection operators (or *projectors*) on a vector space is in one-to-one correspondence with the set of subspaces of that space. It includes the zero operator (which projects onto the zero subspace)—the operator $\mathbf{P}_0$ such that, for all $\mathbf{v}$, $\mathbf{P}_0\mathbf{v} = \mathbf{0}$—and also the identity operator $\mathbf{I}$, which projects onto the whole space: for all $\mathbf{v}$, $\mathbf{Iv} = \mathbf{v}$. As we shall see, projectors play an enormously important role in quantum theory; in fact, the discussions of the theory in later chapters are almost entirely in terms of these operators.

I conclude this section with a general proof of a relation we have met a couple of times already. Let $\mathbf{P}$ be any projection operator and $\mathbf{v}$ be any vector, then:

(1.27) $\langle \mathbf{v}|\mathbf{Pv}\rangle = |\mathbf{Pv}|^2$

As proof, consider:

$$\begin{aligned} \langle \mathbf{v}|\mathbf{Pv}\rangle &= \langle \mathbf{v}|\mathbf{P}^2\mathbf{v}\rangle && \text{[idempotence]} \\ &= \langle \mathbf{v}|\mathbf{P}(\mathbf{Pv})\rangle \\ &= \langle \mathbf{Pv}|\mathbf{Pv}\rangle && \text{[Hermiticity]} \\ &= |\mathbf{Pv}|^2 \end{aligned}$$

1.13 *Orthonormal Bases*

A set $\{\mathbf{v}_1,\mathbf{v}_2, \ldots ,\mathbf{v}_n\}$ of vectors *spans* a space $\mathcal{V}$ if any vector $\mathbf{v}$ in $\mathcal{V}$ can be written as a linear combination of $\mathbf{v}_1,\mathbf{v}_2, \ldots ,\mathbf{v}_n$—if, that is, for any $\mathbf{v}$ in $\mathcal{V}$ there exist scalars $a_1,a_2, \ldots ,a_n$ such that $\mathbf{v} = a_1\mathbf{v}_1 + a_2\mathbf{v}_2 + \cdots + a_n\mathbf{v}_n$.

(1.28) The set $\{\mathbf{v}_1,\mathbf{v}_2, \ldots ,\mathbf{v}_n\}$ of vectors is said to be an *orthonormal basis* for $\mathcal{V}$ if

(1.28a) $\{\mathbf{v}_1,\mathbf{v}_2, \ldots ,\mathbf{v}_n\}$ spans $\mathcal{V}$; and for each $\mathbf{v}_i$ and $\mathbf{v}_j$ in $\{\mathbf{v}_1,\mathbf{v}_2, \ldots ,\mathbf{v}_n\}$

(1.28b) $\mathbf{v}_i \perp \mathbf{v}_j$ whenever $i \neq j$, and

(1.28c) $|\mathbf{v}_i| = 1$

The set

$$\left\{\begin{pmatrix}1\\0\end{pmatrix}, \begin{pmatrix}0\\1\end{pmatrix}\right\}$$

forms a convenient orthonormal basis for $\mathbb{R}^2$, and also for $\mathbb{C}^2$. Notice that there is no unique orthonormal basis for any space. For example, we see from Section 1.7 that each of the three sets $\{\mathbf{x}_+,\mathbf{x}_-\}$, $\{\mathbf{y}_+,\mathbf{y}_-\}$, and $\{\mathbf{z}_+,\mathbf{z}_-\}$ is an orthonormal basis for $\mathbb{C}^2$, as are nondenumerably many other pairs of vectors.

An n-dimensional space can be spanned by n mutually orthogonal vectors. If the space is infinitely dimensional, an infinite set $\{\mathbf{v}_i\}$ is required.

If $\{\mathbf{v}_1,\mathbf{v}_2, \ldots ,\mathbf{v}_n\}$ is an orthonormal basis for a vector space $\mathcal{V}$, then any subset of this basis is an orthonormal basis for a subspace of $\mathcal{V}$. The set $\{\mathbf{v}_1,\mathbf{v}_3\}$, for example, is an orthonormal basis for a two-dimensional subspace L; we say that L is *spanned* by $\{\mathbf{v}_1,\mathbf{v}_3\}$, and we also talk of the rays containing $\mathbf{v}_1$ and $\mathbf{v}_3$ *spanning* L. These rays, of course are themselves spanned by $\{\mathbf{v}_1\}$ and $\{\mathbf{v}_3\}$, respectively.

A result that will be important in Section 8.8 is the following. Let $\{\mathbf{v}_1, \ldots ,\mathbf{v}_n\}$ be any orthonormal basis for $\mathcal{V}$. Then any linear operator $\mathbf{A}$ on $\mathcal{V}$ is uniquely determined by the vectors $\mathbf{A}\mathbf{v}_1, \ldots ,\mathbf{A}\mathbf{v}_n$. In other words, to specify $\mathbf{A}$ we need only specify its action on an arbitrary orthonormal basis. This result follows immediately from the definition of linearity in (1.18). For let $\mathbf{v}$ be an arbitrary vector in $\mathcal{V}$; then for some $c_1, \ldots ,c_n$ we have:

$$\mathbf{v} = c_1\mathbf{v}_1 + c_2\mathbf{v}_2 + \cdots + c_n\mathbf{v}_n = \sum_i c_i\mathbf{v}_i$$

And, by linearity,

$$\text{(1.29)} \qquad \mathbf{A}\mathbf{v} = \mathbf{A}\left(\sum_i c_i\mathbf{v}_i\right) = \sum_i (\mathbf{A}c_i\mathbf{v}_i) = \sum_i c_i(\mathbf{A}\mathbf{v}_i)$$

1.14 *Operators with a Discrete Spectrum*

A Hermitian operator which admits eigenvectors is said to have a *discrete spectrum,* and in this case the spectrum consists of the set of eigenvalues of the operator. All Hermitian operators on a finitely dimensional vector space have a discrete spectrum; in the infinitely dimensional case this isn't always so, and I'll discuss the exceptions, and give a general definition of a *spectrum,* in the next section.

It is easily shown, by use of (1.21) and (1.24), that eigenvectors and eigenvalues of Hermitian operators have striking properties.

(1.30) If $\mathbf{A}$ is a Hermitian operator, then its eigenvalues are real. (☆)

(1.31) If $\mathbf{A}$ is a Hermitian operator, such that $\mathbf{A}\mathbf{v}_1 = a_1\mathbf{v}_1$, $\mathbf{A}\mathbf{v}_2 = a_2\mathbf{v}_2$, and $a_1 \neq a_2$, then $\mathbf{v}_1 \perp \mathbf{v}_2$. (☆)

In words, eigenvectors corresponding to distinct eigenvalues are mutually orthogonal. Thus the maximum number of distinct eigenvalues of a Hermitian operator **A** on $\mathcal{V}$ is equal to the dimensionality of $\mathcal{V}$. This result we have already seen for $\mathbb{R}^2$ and $\mathbb{C}^2$; we now consider a vector space $\mathcal{V}$ with dimensionality n.

Let **A** be a Hermitian operator on $\mathcal{V}$. There are two possible cases: (i) **A** has exactly n distinct eigenvalues; (ii) **A** has m distinct eigenvalues, $0 < m < n$.

In case (i), all the eigenvectors corresponding to a particular eigenvalue, a_i say, lie within one ray L_i of $\mathcal{V}$, and every vector in L_i is an eigenvector of **A** with eigenvalue a_i. These rays span $\mathcal{V}$ and are mutually orthogonal. If from each ray L_i we select one normalized vector $\mathbf{v}_i$, then the set $\{\mathbf{v}_i\}$ forms an orthonormal basis for $\mathcal{V}$.

In case (ii), to each eigenvalue a_i there again corresponds a subspace L_i of $\mathcal{V}$ such that $\mathbf{Av} = a_i\mathbf{v}$ if and only if $\mathbf{v}$ is in L_i, and again these subspaces are mutually orthogonal; in this case, however, they are not all one-dimensional. Instead, the following general result holds. Denote by d_i the dimensionality of the subspace corresponding to eigenvalue a_i. Then

$$d_1 + d_2 + \cdots + d_m = n$$

[Case (i) corresponds to the case where $m = n$ and, for all i, $d_i = 1$.] By a curious usage, when $d_i > 1$, we say that a_i is *degenerate.* As in case (i), we can still choose an orthonormal basis for $\mathcal{V}$ consisting only of eigenvectors of **A**: we first choose an orthonormal basis for each L_i (each of which will consist, obviously, only of eigenvectors of **A**) and then form the union of these sets of vectors.

With this as background, here is the general form of the spectral decomposition theorem for a finitely dimensional vector space $\mathcal{V}$.

(1.32) Let **A** be a Hermitian operator on a finitely dimensional vector space $\mathcal{V}$. Then there are real numbers $a_1, \ldots, a_m$ and projectors $\mathbf{P}_1, \ldots, \mathbf{P}_m$ projecting onto mutually orthogonal subspaces of $\mathcal{V}$ ($m \leq n$), such that

$$\mathbf{A} = \sum_{i=1}^{m} a_i \mathbf{P}_i$$

If we add the condition that

(1.32a) $$a_i \neq a_j \quad \text{unless} \quad i = j$$

then this decomposition of **A** is unique.

Note that in the expression for **A** above we are adding operators: we have

$$\mathbf{A} = a_1\mathbf{P}_1 + a_2\mathbf{P}_2 + \cdots + a_m\mathbf{P}_m = \sum_{i=1}^{m} a_i\mathbf{P}_i$$

This sum can now be unpacked in terms of familiar quantities. Each number a_i is an eigenvalue of **A**. The corresponding $\mathbf{P}_i$ is the projection operator onto L_i, the subspace of eigenvectors with eigenvalue a_i. If **A** has n distinct eigenvalues, as in case (i), above, then each projector projects onto a one-dimensional subspace, and uniqueness of decomposition is guaranteed. If, as in case (ii), degeneracy occurs, then condition (1.32a) ensures that each projector $\mathbf{P}_i$ projects onto a subspace L_i containing *all* the eigenvectors with eigenvalue a_i. Now L_i may be more than one-dimensional, and in such a case a further decomposition violating condition (1.32a) is possible. Consider the case when L_i is two-dimensional, and let L_{i_1} and L_{i_2} be any two orthogonal rays spanning L_i, with projectors $\mathbf{P}_{i_1}$, $\mathbf{P}_{i_2}$, respectively. We can show that $\mathbf{P}_i = \mathbf{P}_{i_1} + \mathbf{P}_{i_2}$ (☆☆), and so the term $a_i\mathbf{P}_i$ in the decomposition of **A** may be replaced by $a_i\mathbf{P}_{i_1} + a_i\mathbf{P}_{i_2}$. Notice particularly that *any* pair of mutually orthogonal rays in L_i could be used for this construction, and so this further decomposition is itself not uniquely specifiable by, for example, the requirement that all the $\mathbf{P}_i$ project onto rays.

I have offered a discussion and not a proof of the theorem. (See Jordan, 1969, sec. 14; Fano, 1971, chap. 2.3.) On the basis of this discussion, however, and given one important assumption (which happens to be true), the reader should be able to supply one.

Exercise. Given that every Hermitian operator on a finitely dimensional vector space admits eigenvectors, prove (1.32) (☆☆). *Hint:* Compare the transformation of an arbitrary vector **v** effected by **A** with that effected by $\Sigma_i a_i\mathbf{P}_i$, using the fact that an orthonormal basis for $\mathcal{V}$ exists consisting only of eigenvectors of **A**.

1.15 *Operators with a Continuous Spectrum*

When $\mathcal{V}$ is infinitely dimensional, not all Hermitian operators admit eigenvectors. Some do, and for them an infinitary version of (1.32) holds. Among those that do not, however, are some operators of great importance in quantum theory, like those which represent position and momentum.

Before seeing what form the spectral decomposition theorem takes for them, I will present some of the material of the previous section in a slightly different way. I first define a straightforward ordering relation between projectors in terms of the inclusion relation between subspaces, and then introduce the idea of the *spectral measure* associated with an operator on $\mathcal{V}$.

(1.33) Let $\mathbf{P}_1$ and $\mathbf{P}_2$ project onto subspaces L_1 and L_2 of a vector space $\mathcal{V}$; we define the relation $\leq$ ("less than or equal to") by: $\mathbf{P}_1 \leq \mathbf{P}_2$ if and only if $L_1 \subseteq L_2$ if and only if every vector in L_1 is in L_2.

A spectral measure is a family of projection operators on $\mathcal{V}$ parameterized by the real numbers. In other words, for any real number x there is in the family a projector $\mathbf{P}(x)$ corresponding to it. We don't require that different real numbers always be paired with different projectors. However, as we move along the real line from $-\infty$ to $+\infty$, we require that, if $a < b$, then $\mathbf{P}(a) \leq \mathbf{P}(b)$. Consistent with this is a second requirement: that, as x goes toward $-\infty$, then $\mathbf{P}(x)$ goes toward $\mathbf{P}_0$ (the zero operator) and that, as x goes toward $+\infty$, $\mathbf{P}(x)$ goes toward $\mathbf{I}$. A third requirement ("continuity from the right") I will explain below.

A spectral measure can be associated with any Hermitian operator. Let us look first at the case discussed in Section 1.14, that of a Hermitian operator $\mathbf{A}$ on an n-dimensional vector space $\mathcal{V}$, such that $\mathbf{A}$ has m distinct eigenvalues. We can arrange these eigenvalues in ascending order, so that $a_1 < a_2 \cdots < a_m$. Associated with each eigenvalue a_i there is a subspace (not necessarily one-dimensional) containing all the corresponding eigenvectors. Let $\mathbf{P}_i$ be the projector onto this subspace. The spectral measure $\mathbf{P}(x)$ for $\mathbf{A}$ is now specified as follows.

$$\begin{array}{ll}
\text{For } x < a_1, & \mathbf{P}(x) = \mathbf{P}_0 \\
\text{for } a_1 \leq x < a_2, & \mathbf{P}(x) = \mathbf{P}_1 \\
\text{for } a_2 \leq x < a_3, & \mathbf{P}(x) = \mathbf{P}_1 + \mathbf{P}_2 \\
\vdots & \\
\text{for } a_{m-1} \leq x < a_m, & \mathbf{P}(x) = \mathbf{P}_1 + \mathbf{P}_2 + \cdots + \mathbf{P}_{m-1} \\
\text{for } a_m \leq x, & \mathbf{P}(x) = \mathbf{P}_1 + \mathbf{P}_2 + \cdots + \mathbf{P}_m = \mathbf{I}
\end{array}$$

We can prove that these sums of projection operators, $\mathbf{P}_1 + \mathbf{P}_2$, $\mathbf{P}_1 + \mathbf{P}_2 + \mathbf{P}_3$, and so on, are themselves projection operators, because the subspaces L_1, L_2, and so on that $\mathbf{P}_1$ and $\mathbf{P}_2$ project onto are all mutually orthogonal (☆☆). In fact, the projection operator $\mathbf{P}_1 + \mathbf{P}_2$ is the projection operator onto the subspace spanned by L_1 and L_2, that is, the subspace spanned by the set of eigenvectors with eigenvalue a_1 or a_2. Clearly, since the set of all eigenvectors spans $\mathcal{V}$, $\mathbf{P}_1 + \mathbf{P}_2 + \cdots + \mathbf{P}_m = \mathbf{I}$.

The picture is this. As we move along the real line from $-\infty$ to ∞, $\mathbf{P}(x)$ increases, in the sense given by (1.33), by m "steps." The subspace onto which $\mathbf{P}(x)$ projects just after a step includes the subspace projected onto just before the step, and each step is itself a projection operator $\mathbf{P}_i$. These steps occur at the eigenvalues; the requirement of continuity from the right simply means that, for example, $\mathbf{P}(x) = \mathbf{P}_1$ when $a_1 \le x < a_2$, rather than when $a_1 < x \le a_2$.

The *spectrum* of **A** is the set of points where $\mathbf{P}(x)$ changes value, in this case the set of eigenvalues of **A**.

Now, when **A** is a Hermitian operator on an infinitely dimensional space it is still possible to associate a spectral measure $\mathbf{P}(x)$ with **A**, but it can happen that, where $\mathbf{P}(x)$ increases, it increases continuously rather than by steps. The sets of points over which $\mathbf{P}(x)$ increases are in this case intervals on the real line. Again, the set of all such points is called the *spectrum* of **A**, but now we say that **A** has a *continuous* rather than a *discrete* spectrum.

What does it mean to say, in the continuous case, that $\mathbf{P}(x)$ is *associated with* **A**? We can explain this by analogy with the discrete case. In the discrete case we have, by (1.32),

$$\mathbf{A} = \sum_i a_i \mathbf{P}_i$$

Whence, for any vector **v**,

$$(1.34) \qquad \begin{aligned} \langle \mathbf{v}|\mathbf{A}\mathbf{v}\rangle &= \left\langle \mathbf{v} \middle| \sum_i a_i \mathbf{P}_i \mathbf{v} \right\rangle \\ &= \sum_i a_i \langle \mathbf{v}|\mathbf{P}_i\mathbf{v}\rangle \qquad \text{[by (1.20) and (1.21)]} \end{aligned}$$

Let us look at the inner products $\langle \mathbf{v}|\mathbf{P}_i\mathbf{v}\rangle$. We know from (1.27) that any expression of this form yields a real number. Now, in terms of the spectral measure of **A**, the projector $\mathbf{P}_i$ is the "step" by which $\mathbf{P}(x)$ changes at a_i. Writing $\mathbf{P}(<a_i)$ for the greatest value of $\mathbf{P}(x)$ when $x < a_i$, we have $\mathbf{P}(a_i) = \mathbf{P}(<a_i) + \mathbf{P}_i$, and so

$$\langle \mathbf{v}|\mathbf{P}(a_i)\mathbf{v}\rangle = \langle \mathbf{v}|\mathbf{P}(<a_i)\mathbf{v}\rangle + \langle \mathbf{v}|\mathbf{P}_i\mathbf{v}\rangle$$

whence

$$\langle \mathbf{v}|\mathbf{P}_i\mathbf{v}\rangle = \langle \mathbf{v}|\mathbf{P}(a_i)\mathbf{v}\rangle - \langle \mathbf{v}|\mathbf{P}(<a_i)\mathbf{v}\rangle$$

We see that (i) $\langle \mathbf{v}|\mathbf{P}(x)\mathbf{v}\rangle$ increases monotonically as x moves up the real number line, and that (ii) $\langle \mathbf{v}|\mathbf{P}_i\mathbf{v}\rangle$ is the change in value of $\langle \mathbf{v}|\mathbf{P}(x)\mathbf{v}\rangle$ at $x = a_i$. Thus each term in the sum in (1.34) is the product of a real number a_i and the change of value of $\langle \mathbf{v}|\mathbf{P}(x)\mathbf{v}\rangle$ which occurs there.

Turning to the continuous case, and forsaking mathematical rigor, we can think of $d\langle \mathbf{v}|\mathbf{P}(a)\mathbf{v}\rangle$ as the infinitesimal change in $\langle \mathbf{v}|\mathbf{P}(x)\mathbf{v}\rangle$ which occurs at $x = a$. An analogue to (1.34), using an integral, now gives a generalized version of the *spectral decomposition theorem* (see Fano, 1971, chap. 5.8).

(1.35) For any Hermitian operator $\mathbf{A}$ there is a spectral measure $\{\mathbf{P}(x)\}$ such that, for any vector $\mathbf{v}$,

$$\langle \mathbf{v}|\mathbf{A}\mathbf{v}\rangle = \int_{-\infty}^{\infty} x \, d\langle \mathbf{v}|\mathbf{P}(x)\mathbf{v}\rangle$$

As an example of the spectral measure associated with an operator with a continuous spectrum, consider the operator x (the "position operator") on the space L^2 of square-integrable complex-valued functions of x (see Section 1.11). The spectral measure of x (which we parameterize by the real number y to avoid confusion) is the family $\{\mathbf{E}(y)\}$ of operators on L^2 such that, for any function ϕ in L^2,

$$\mathbf{E}(y)\phi(x) = \begin{matrix} \phi(x) & \text{for } x \leq y \\ 0 & \text{for } x > y \end{matrix}$$

Notice that $\mathbf{E}(y)$ is indeed an operator on L^2, mapping functions onto functions as required. It is easily shown to be linear, idempotent, and Hermitian, and is thus a projection operator. (To show Hermiticity, we need the definition of an inner product on L^2 given in Section 1.11.) Equation (1.35) can be shown to hold in four steps (Jordan, 1969, p. 43), as the reader may care to verify (☆☆).

To revert to the general case, the spectral measure $\mathbf{P}(x)$ associated with an operator $\mathbf{A}$ is a mapping of real numbers to projectors. We can extend this to provide a mapping of measurable subsets of the real line to projectors by writing, for every semi-closed interval $\Delta = \{x: a < x \leq b\}$,

$$\mathbf{P}_\Delta = \mathbf{P}(b) - \mathbf{P}(a)$$

and extending this to other measurable sets of reals in a straightforward way (see Fano, 1971, chap. 4).

We see that, to each Hermitian operator $\mathbf{A}$ and measurable subset Δ of the reals, there corresponds a projection operator $\mathbf{P}^{\mathbf{A}}_{\Delta}$ defined in terms of the spectral measure $\mathbf{P}(x)$ associated with $\mathbf{A}$. The existence of $\mathbf{P}(x)$, and hence of $\mathbf{P}^{\mathbf{A}}_{\Delta}$ for any measurable set Δ, is guaranteed by the spectral decomposition theorem.

To summarize: Let $\mathcal{B}(\mathbb{R})$ be the set of all Borel subsets (measurable subsets) of the reals. Then, given a Hermitian operator $\mathbf{A}$ on a vector space $\mathcal{V}$, the spectral decomposition theorem specifies, for each Δ in $\mathcal{B}(\mathbb{R})$, a unique projection operator $\mathbf{P}^{\mathbf{A}}_{\Delta}$. Stretching our previous usage, we call the family $\{\mathbf{P}^{\mathbf{A}}_{\Delta}: \Delta \in \mathcal{B}(\mathbb{R})\}$ the *spectral decomposition* of $\mathbf{A}$. It has the following properties.

(1.36) In the family $\{\mathbf{P}^{\mathbf{A}}_{\Delta}: \Delta \in \mathcal{B}(\mathbb{R})\}$

(1.36a) $$\mathbf{P}^{\mathbf{A}}_{\mathbb{R}} = \mathbf{I}; \qquad \mathbf{P}^{\mathbf{A}}_{\phi} = \mathbf{P}_0$$

and, for all $\Delta, \Gamma \in \mathcal{B}(\mathbb{R})$

(1.36b) if $\Delta \subseteq \Gamma$, then $\mathbf{P}^{\mathbf{A}}_{\Delta} \leq \mathbf{P}^{\mathbf{A}}_{\Gamma}$

(1.36c) if Δ and Γ are disjoint ($\Delta \cap \Gamma = \phi$), then $\mathbf{P}^{\mathbf{A}}_{\Delta}$ and $\mathbf{P}^{\mathbf{A}}_{\Gamma}$ project onto orthogonal subspaces of $\mathcal{V}$.

We will meet these operators all the time in our discussion of quantum theory.

1.16 *Hilbert Spaces*

The vector spaces we shall use are known as "Hilbert spaces," a term coined by von Neumann (see Stein, 1972, p. 427, n. 10). A Hilbert space is just a vector space on which an inner product has been defined, and which is also complete: a vector space is said to be *complete* if any converging sequence of vectors in the space converges to a vector in the space. All finitely dimensional vector spaces are complete. To show what's involved in the infinite case, let us look at a space which does not meet this condition.

Consider the space S of all *finite* sequences of real numbers. S includes

$$\mathbf{s}_0 = (1)$$

$$\mathbf{s}_1 = (1, \tfrac{1}{2})$$

$$\mathbf{s}_2 = (1, \tfrac{1}{2}, \tfrac{1}{4})$$

$$\vdots$$

$$\mathbf{s}_n = \left(1, \tfrac{1}{2}, \tfrac{1}{4}, \ldots, \frac{1}{2^n}\right)$$

$$\vdots$$

Now $\mathbf{s}_0, \mathbf{s}_1, \ldots$ forms a converging sequence on S, but its limit, that is, the sequence to which it converges, is infinite, and so does not lie in S. Thus S is not complete and so is not a Hilbert space.

On a related topic: in the infinitely dimensional case one should distinguish between subspaces and closed subspaces. Any subspace contains all linear combinations of any finite set of vectors within it [see (1.23)]; a subspace is *closed* if, additionally, it contains the limit vector of any converging sequence of vectors within it. Thus a closed subspace of a Hilbert space is itself a Hilbert space. Quantum mechanics deals with closed subspaces; however, since the examples presented in this book are almost all finitely dimensional, the distinction will largely be ignored in what follows.

This concludes our hasty introductory survey of vector-space theory. In Chapter 5 I return to a few selected topics, prompted by some questions which arise in the discussion of quantum theory in Chapters 2–4.

2

States and Observables in Quantum Mechanics

To understand the conceptual structure of quantum mechanics we need to see how such notions as the *state of a system* and an *observable quantity* are represented within the theory, and how they are used in making predictions. The mathematics used is the mathematical theory of vector spaces, and in Chapter 3 I will discuss why this is a suitable candidate for the job in hand. Prior to any discussion of quantum theory, however, I will look at the way states and observables appear in classical mechanics. This approach offers a useful introduction to these topics on two counts. In the first place, classical mechanics is more familiar to many of us than is quantum theory; second, it's instructive to compare the roles these concepts play in the two theories, since quantum mechanics appears anomalous to us precisely where it departs from our classical expectations.

2.1 *Classical Mechanics: Systems and Their States*

The formulation of classical mechanics I shall use is essentially that given by Hamilton and Jacobi in the nineteenth century (see also Gillespie, 1970). A classical system consists of a single particle or of a set of particles. Some of the particles' properties, like their masses, remain constant with time; others, like their positions, vary. Thus, for a complete description of the system and its behavior we need to know, first, the set Π_c of its constant, unchanging properties and, second, how it is at a particular time, that is, the set Π_v of the instantaneous values of those quantities which vary with time. We also need to know the set Λ of laws which govern both the interactions between the particles and also their interactions with their environment. For instance, if the particles are electrically charged, they will attract or repel each other, and they will also experience forces if the system is placed in an electric field. It is these laws which determine how the system will evolve as time goes on.

The position and momentum of each particle are particularly significant members of Π_v. (The momentum of a particle is the product of its mass and its velocity.) We express this by saying that specification of the position and the momentum of each particle at time *t* gives us the *state* of the system at time *t*. Once the state at time *t* is specified, then specification of Π_c and Λ determines the values of *all* the properties in Π_v at that time.

As an example, consider a system of charged particles. The electrostatic potential energy of that system at time *t* is determined by (a) the relative positions of the particles at that time (given by the state), (b) the charge on each particle (given in Π_c) and (c) the Coulomb law of electrostatic force (given in Λ).

Classical mechanics is usually taken to be deterministic; a complete specification of Π_c and the state at a given time would determine the values of Π_v at all other times, provided the system remains isolated. I return to this point in Section 2.4.

As I mentioned, the state of a system is given by the positions and the momenta of the particles which compose it. Since physical space is three-dimensional, to specify the position of each particle we need three numbers (or *position coordinates*) q_x, q_y, and q_z to locate it relative to an appropriate coordinate system. Similarly, in order to specify the momentum fully, so that we know not only how fast the particle is going but also in what direction, we need three more numbers p_x, p_y, and p_z, the *momentum coordinates,* often called the *components of momentum,* parallel to the three axes of our coordinate system. For each particle these six numbers are independent of one another. Thus, given a system of *n* particles, the state is specified by a total of $6n$ numbers.

In the same way that we can think of a pair of numbers as specifying a point in a two-dimensional space like the plane of the paper, and of a trio of numbers as representing a point in three-dimensional space, we can say that the state of a system is represented by a point in $6n$-dimensional real space. All that we mean by this is that $6n$ independent real numbers are needed to specify the state. This abstract $6n$-dimensional space just consists of all possible sequences of $6n$ real numbers; it is called the *phase space* for the system. We denote the phase space by Ω and the state of the system by ω. Clearly, $\omega \in \Omega$.

For illustration I will often consider the simple case of a single particle constrained to move in one dimension. For this particle the phase space can be represented by a plane (that is, it can be drawn on the paper); specification of the *x* and *y* coordinates of any point in the plane picks out a possible state of the particle by telling us its (single coordinate of) position, q, and its momentum, p; we have $\omega = (q,p)$.

2.2 Observables and Experimental Questions

Let us look in more detail at the way, from Π_c, Λ, and the present state of a system, its other properties are deduced. The total kinetic energy, for example, is determined by the kinetic energy of each particle, T, and this in turn is determined by its mass and its momentum. For each particle we have,

$$T = \frac{1}{2m}(p_x^2 + p_y^2 + p_z^2)$$

where m is the mass of the particle in question. I mentioned electrostatic potential energy in the last section. In contrast, kinetic energy is just the energy due to motion; the position coordinates of the particles are irrelevant. The kinetic energy of the whole system is just the sum of the kinetic energies of the individual particles.

We call physical quantities like kinetic energy *observables*. Like most commentators, I find this usage unfortunate; like them, I will continue to employ it. The simplest examples of observables are position and momentum: their components can be read off from the state by looking at the appropriate coordinates. More generally, with each observable quantity A we associate a function f_A which, for every point in the phase space (in other words, for every state of the system), gives us a real number, the *value* of A. In mathematical terms, to each observable A there corresponds a function $f_A : \Omega \to \mathbb{R}$. Thus, in the case of the single particle moving in one dimension we have,

$$T = f_T(q,p) = \frac{p^2}{2m}$$

Most theoretically significant quantities in classical mechanics have a continuum of possible values, but experimentally, of course, we content ourselves with the rationals, and it is possible to construct artificial "observable quantities" which take on only certain discrete values; an example is "the observable whose value is 1 when the momentum is positive, and 0 otherwise." To call such quantities "artificial" is not to dismiss them: any method of testing a system which just gives a yes/no (or pass/fail) answer measures an observable of this kind, and we can develop an alternative account of the notion of "state" in terms of such tests. I will return to our simple example to show what is involved.

Any measurement made on a system yields answers to questions we can ask about it. If we obtain a measurement of kinetic energy, for example, we answer a whole set of questions of the form, "Is the kinetic energy greater than 1?" "Is the kinetic energy between 1 and 2?" and so on. If we know the state of the system we can give a definite yes or no answer to each such question. We can now ask, "What does the state have to be in order that the kinetic energy shall lie between 1 and 2?" In this case the answer is that q can take any value but that $|p|$ must lie between $\sqrt{2m}$ and $2\sqrt{m}$, values which we obtain from the formula for kinetic energy given above. For a particle of unit mass (that is, for which $m = 1$) the region of the phase space for which either $\sqrt{2m} < p < 2\sqrt{m}$ or $-\sqrt{2m} > p > -2\sqrt{m}$ is shown in Figure 2.1. If, and only if, the state of the system lies within this shaded area can we say that its kinetic energy lies between 1 and 2.

Similarly, for any question we care to ask, there is a region of the phase space that corresponds to it. Consider the vertical line on the diagram: this corresponds to the question, "Is the position of the particle 3 units to the right of the origin?" As the state of the system alters, the point representing it moves around the diagram, and at any time the answer to any experimental question will be yes or no, depending on whether at that time the point lies within the corresponding region or not. Formally, we may regard any given state as acting as a two-valued function on the set of experimental questions, that is, as assigning to each question in the set either the number 1

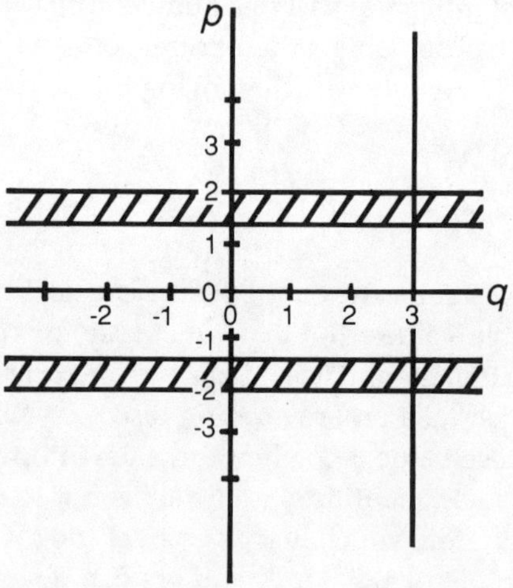

Figure 2.1

(for yes) or 0 (for no). In this vein let us denote the question, "Does observable A have a value within Δ?" (where Δ is some subset of the reals) by (A,Δ), and the value assigned to it by the state by $\omega(A,\Delta)$, thus making it clear that ω is a function. We then obtain

$$\omega(A,\Delta) = 1 \quad \text{if and only if} \quad f_A(\omega) \in \Delta$$

To see that this equivalence holds, consider the conditions under which each side is true. The left-hand side, $\omega(A,\Delta) = 1$, is true when the state of the system is such that the experimental question "(A,Δ)"—that is, the question "Does the observable A have a value within Δ?"—receives the answer yes. But, on the right-hand side, $f_A(\omega)$ gives us the value of the observable A when the system is in state ω; it follows that $f_A(\omega) \in \Delta$ just when $\omega(A,\Delta) = 1$.

The experimental questions we deal with are all of the form (A,Δ), and to each of them corresponds a region, technically a *subset* of the phase space. Later on we shall be concerned with the algebraic structure of the set of experimental questions in classical mechanics; unsurprisingly, it has the structure of the set of subsets of a space.

In the analysis above, the state appeared as a function mapping experimental questions into 1 (yes) or 0 (no). If this account of it seems willfully obscure, the following implausible narrative may be helpful. Two experimenters, one in Moose Jaw and one in Medicine Hat, regularly receive consignments of identical physical systems. Both of them proceed in the same way: each new system is treated in some way or other ("prepared") and then tested. Figure 2.2, which should be thought of as a pair of flow

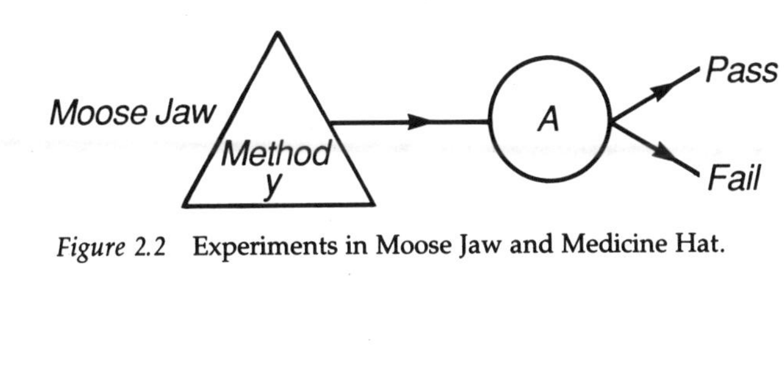

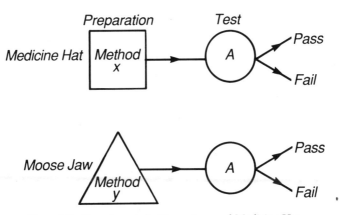

Figure 2.2 Experiments in Moose Jaw and Medicine Hat.

charts rather than as sketches of experimental arrangements, shows the principle. Now imagine that each of the experimenters has a variety of methods of preparation at his or her disposal and that the methods they use are quite different. All methods of testing, on the other hand, are common to both, and all their tests are of the pass/fail sort. Clearly, they can soon find out whether, despite the differences in the modes of preparation, systems prepared using Method *X* by Medicine Hat Man are in effectively the same state as those prepared using Method *Y* by Moose Jaw Woman. They just list the tests run on these systems and compare the results. They will also find it convenient to refer to a prepared state not by specifying its method of preparation (since these are not common to both experimenters), but in terms of the test performances which identify it. Thus the state specification might read, "Test *A*, pass; Test *B*, pass; Test *C*, fail; . . ." and so on. But this is just to regard a state as assigning a value to each experimental question, in other words, to treat it as a function. To a set theoretician, in fact, a function *is* precisely a set of ordered pairs like those we have here.

The two experimenters cannot know whether their specification of a state is complete, that is, whether there is no further test which, with additional equipment, would sort out some apparently homogeneous state still further. If their systems are classical, this knowledge would of course be available to them if they could establish the components of position and momentum for all the particles of their prepared systems. As we have seen, classical mechanics tells us that all significant tests are tests of the values of various functions of these variables.

From this discussion it seems that in classical mechanics we have two ways of thinking of the state of a system. We defined it as a sequence of $6n$ coordinates (where n is the number of particles in the system), each of which tells us a component of position or momentum of a particle. This can be regarded as a description of the system: the specification of the state is effectively a list of some of the system's properties. On the other hand, when we regard it as a two-valued function of the set of experimental questions, then we are drawing attention to the system's dispositions to behave in certain ways. The distinction between properties and dispositions may be challenged; *all* properties, it may be argued, are just dispositions to certain kinds of behavior. I will put this question to one side; for the present I will assume that such a distinction can be made (but see Section 10.2). This granted, then the specification of the state in classical mechanics can be said to have two distinct aspects. As we shall see, in quantum mechanics this is less clearly so: while the specification of the state still serves to summarize a system's dispositions, its descriptive role is moot.

2.3 States and Observables in Quantum Theory

The states I deal with in this section are the so-called *pure states* of quantum mechanics; in Chapter 5 I extend the discussion to *mixed states.* In quantum theory a pure state of a system is given by a vector in a Hilbert space. For certain purposes we need not specify all the components of this vector: for instance, if we are only interested in the *spin* of an electron we need only look at two components, whereas if we are interested in observables which depend only on position and momentum we can disregard those components which refer to the spin. This is why for certain examples (those to do with spin) I shall use pairs of complex numbers to represent the state of an electron, while for others I shall represent its state by a function (which, as we saw in Chapter 1, is an element of a vector space of infinite dimensionality). Effectively, an electron has both a spin-state and a position-state. When these states are pure, each of them can be represented by a vector; the spin-state vector lies in a two-dimensional Hilbert space and the position vector lies in an infinitely dimensional space. Both vectors are normalized, that is, of unit length. Because the spin-state and the position-state are independent, and much of what I say applies equally well to either, I will usually use the term "state" to refer to just one of them. I will call the Hilbert space in which any state is represented the *state space* for the system.

Thus, as in classical mechanics, states are represented by points in a space. However, a classical phase space is finitely dimensional (unless electromagnetic field theory, which requires infinite dimensionality, is being considered), whereas the Hilbert spaces used in quantum theory may be infinitely dimensional. Further, two different vectors $\mathbf{u}$ and $\mathbf{v}$ may both refer to the same state, if they both lie within the same ray (if, that is, there is a complex number c such that $\mathbf{u} = c\mathbf{v}$). Indeed, it is somewhat more precise to regard a ray as representing a pure state (and I will adopt this approach in Chapter 5), but at present the manipulations we perform will involve a representative vector from that ray, and so we take the vector itself to specify the state. And, as I have mentioned, it is assumed that the vector is normalized.

The radical differences between classical mechanics and quantum mechanics appear with the representation of observables. Instead of the real-valued functions of classical theory, quantum mechanics uses Hermitian operators in the Hilbert space to represent observables. Typical examples are the 2×2 matrices which represent the components of spin of a fermion, and the operators x and $-id/dx$ (on the set of square-integrable functions of x) which represent position and momentum, or, more strictly, their components in the x-direction.

Many but not all of these operators admit eigenvectors; as noted in Section 1.15, a notable exception is the position operator x. Such exceptions we will return to later; for the moment we will confine discussion to the operators which admit eigenvectors, that is, to the case when, for the operator **A**, there are vectors $\mathbf{v}_1, \mathbf{v}_2, \ldots$ such that, for each i, $\mathbf{A}\mathbf{v}_i = a_i\mathbf{v}_i$ (and, since **A** is Hermitian, each a_i is a real number).

In these cases, the eigenvalues $a_1, a_2, \ldots$ of the operator are the possible values of the observable quantity which the operator represents. We can see immediately that this aspect of the theory gives us very different results from classical theory: instead of a continuum of possible values, the observables we are now dealing with can have only certain specific values. A measurement of the observable A represented by **A** will yield a given value a_i with certainty, provided that a_i is an eigenvalue of **A** and that the state of the system on which the measurement is carried out is represented by the corresponding eigenvector. In general, however, the state, **v**, of the system will not be an eigenvector of **A**; in such a case we cannot say with certainty what the result of such a measurement would be. Instead we assign to each eigenvalue (or possible value) of **A** a probability calculated as follows.

Let $\mathbf{v}_i$ be the eigenvector with a_i as corresponding eigenvalue, and denote by $\mathbf{P}_i^A$ the projection operator onto the ray containing $\mathbf{v}_i$ (see Figure 2.3). Then, according to quantum theory, the probability $p_{\mathbf{v}}(A,a_i)$ that a measurement of A conducted on a system in state **v** will yield a result a_i is given by

$$p_{\mathbf{v}}(A,a_i) = \langle \mathbf{v} | \mathbf{P}_i^A \mathbf{v} \rangle = |\mathbf{P}_i^A \mathbf{v}|^2 \quad (2.1)$$

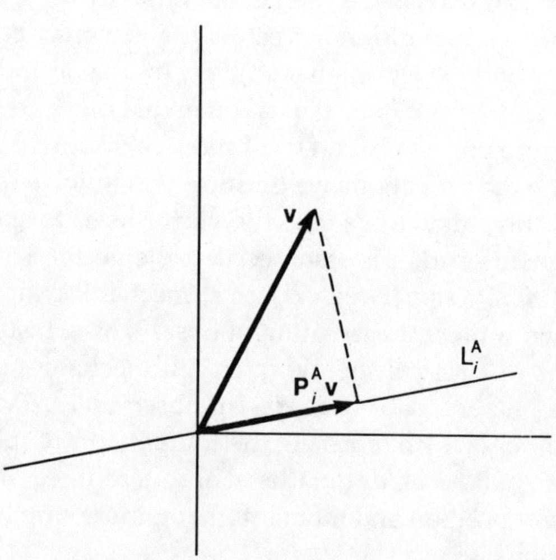

Figure 2.3

Since **v** is normalized, we know from a previous discussion (Section 1.6) that the inner product $\langle \mathbf{v}|\mathbf{P}_i^A\mathbf{v} \rangle$ can only take values from 0 to 1. In other words its values are appropriate to probability measurements.

As examples, consider the operators $\mathbf{S}_x$, $\mathbf{S}_y$, and $\mathbf{S}_z$ used to represent three components of spin of a fermion. They have familiar matrix representations:

$$\mathbf{S}_x = \frac{1}{2}\begin{pmatrix} 0 & 1 \\ 1 & 0 \end{pmatrix} \quad \mathbf{S}_y = \frac{1}{2}\begin{pmatrix} 0 & -i \\ i & 0 \end{pmatrix} \quad \mathbf{S}_z = \frac{1}{2}\begin{pmatrix} 1 & 0 \\ 0 & -1 \end{pmatrix}$$

These are just the spin matrices encountered in Section 1.7. Each operator has eigenvalues $+\frac{1}{2}$ and $-\frac{1}{2}$, and these eigenvalues are the only possible values of each component of spin of a fermion. (Note that we are working in natural units of spin, measuring spin in multiples of Planck's constant $\hbar$.)

The eigenvectors of $\mathbf{S}_x$ are the vectors $\mathbf{x}_+$ and $\mathbf{x}_-$, where, as in Section 1.7,

$$\mathbf{x}_+ = \frac{1}{2}\begin{pmatrix} \sqrt{2} \\ \sqrt{2} \end{pmatrix} \quad \mathbf{x}_- = \frac{1}{2}\begin{pmatrix} \sqrt{2} \\ -\sqrt{2} \end{pmatrix}$$

Similarly, for $\mathbf{S}_y$ and $\mathbf{S}_z$ we have, respectively,

$$\mathbf{y}_+ = \frac{1}{2}\begin{pmatrix} 1-i \\ 1+i \end{pmatrix} \quad \mathbf{y}_- = \frac{1}{2}\begin{pmatrix} 1-i \\ -1-i \end{pmatrix}$$

$$\mathbf{z}_+ = \begin{pmatrix} 1 \\ 0 \end{pmatrix} \quad \mathbf{z}_- = \begin{pmatrix} 0 \\ 1 \end{pmatrix}$$

Recall also that the projection operator $\mathbf{P}_{y+}$ onto the (one-dimensional) subspace spanned by $\mathbf{y}_+$ is given by

$$\mathbf{P}_{y+} = \frac{1}{2}\begin{pmatrix} 1 & -i \\ i & 1 \end{pmatrix}$$

In Section 1.7 we found that (1) $\langle \mathbf{y}_+|\mathbf{P}_{y+}\mathbf{y}_+\rangle = 1$; (2) $\langle \mathbf{y}_-|\mathbf{P}_{y+}\mathbf{y}_-\rangle = 0$; and (3) $\langle \mathbf{x}_+|\mathbf{P}_{y+}\mathbf{x}_+\rangle = \frac{1}{2}$. We can now interpret each of these results as the probability that, when a measurement of a particular observable is carried out on a system in a certain state, one particular value will appear. In each of the three cases we are evaluating the probability that an S_y measurement will yield the result $+\frac{1}{2}$. The eigenvector of $\mathbf{S}_y$ with corresponding eigenvalue $+\frac{1}{2}$ is $\mathbf{y}_+$, and so $\mathbf{P}_{y+}$ is the appropriate projection operator to use in Equation (2.1). The three results correspond to three different states of the particle, the states $\mathbf{y}_+$, $\mathbf{y}_-$, and $\mathbf{x}_+$, respectively. In the first case a measurement of S_y

will yield $+\frac{1}{2}$ with certainty (we say that $\mathbf{y}_+$ is an *eigenstate* of S_y); in the second the probability of such a result is zero, and in the third the chances of such a result are fifty-fifty. Of course, the state of the particle need not be an eigenstate of any of these particular components of spin. For instance, it might be represented by the (normalized) vector

$$\frac{1}{5}\begin{pmatrix} 3i \\ 4 \end{pmatrix}$$

Call this state **u**. Then we can quickly show that, if a measurement of S_y is performed

$$p_{\mathrm{u}}(S_y, +\tfrac{1}{2}) = \frac{1}{50} \quad \text{and} \quad p_{\mathrm{u}}(S_y, -\tfrac{1}{2}) = \frac{49}{50} \qquad (\star)$$

If a measurement of S_x or S_z is performed

$$p_{\mathrm{u}}(S_x, +\tfrac{1}{2}) = \frac{1}{2} \quad \text{and} \quad p_{\mathrm{u}}(S_x, -\tfrac{1}{2}) = \frac{1}{2} \qquad (\star)$$

$$p_{\mathrm{u}}(S_z, +\tfrac{1}{2}) = \frac{9}{25} \quad \text{and} \quad p_{\mathrm{u}}(S_z, -\tfrac{1}{2}) = \frac{16}{25}$$

In each case, there are only two possible outcomes, and so the probabilities of these outcomes add to unity.

Before dealing with operators which do not admit eigenvectors, I will amplify a remark made earlier.

We denote by L_i^A the one-dimensional subspace containing the eigenvector $\mathbf{v}_i$ of the operator **A**, to which corresponds the eigenvalue a_i. Briefly, L_i^A is the subspace onto which $\mathbf{P}_i^A$ projects. Then a measurement of A yields a_i with certainty if, and only if, the vector **v** representing the system's state lies within L_i^A. In that case $\mathbf{P}_i^A\mathbf{v} = \mathbf{v}$, and

$$\begin{aligned} p_{\mathrm{v}}(A,a_i) &= \langle \mathbf{v} | \mathbf{P}_i^A \mathbf{v} \rangle \\ &= \langle \mathbf{v} | \mathbf{v} \rangle \\ &= 1 \end{aligned}$$

With this result in mind, we can now extend the discussion to include those operators which, like the position operator x on the Hilbert space of square-integrable functions of x, admit no eigenvectors. The possible values of position lie anywhere along a continuum, and the operator has a *continu-*

ous spectrum (see Section 1.15). But, whatever species of observable we are dealing with, the following holds true.

Let **A** be an operator representing an observable A. Then to each interval Δ on the real line there corresponds a subspace $L^{\mathbf{A}}_{\Delta}$ of the Hilbert space, such that a measurement of A yields a value within Δ with certainty if and only if the state **v** of the system lies within $L^{\mathbf{A}}_{\Delta}$. Let $\mathbf{P}^{\mathbf{A}}_{\Delta}$ be the projector onto $L^{\mathbf{A}}_{\Delta}$. The expression (2.1) for the probability of a particular experimental outcome now has a straightforward generalization. We write $p_{\mathbf{v}}(A,\Delta)$ for the probability that a measurement of the observable A conducted on a system in state **v** will yield a result in the interval Δ, and obtain

(2.2) $$p_{\mathbf{v}}(A,\Delta) = \langle \mathbf{v} | \mathbf{P}^{\mathbf{A}}_{\Delta} \mathbf{v} \rangle$$

This is the fundamental equation, sometimes called the *statistical algorithm,* of quantum mechanics, relating experimental outcomes to the probabilities of their occurrence. What are the projectors $\mathbf{P}^{\mathbf{A}}_{\Delta}$? They are the operators we met at the end of Section 1.15, belonging to the *spectral decomposition* of **A**.

At the risk of tedious repetition, let me review what has been said, once more using the Pauli spin matrices to illustrate the general result. In quantum mechanics all observable quantities are represented by Hermitian operators on a state space $\mathcal{H}$. Associated with each such operator **A** is a family $\{\mathbf{P}^{\mathbf{A}}_{\Delta}: \Delta \in \mathcal{B}(\mathbb{R})\}$ of projectors on $\mathcal{H}$. If two subsets Δ and Γ of the reals are disjoint (have nothing in common), then two projection operators $\mathbf{P}^{\mathbf{A}}_{\Delta}$ and $\mathbf{P}^{\mathbf{A}}_{\Gamma}$ project onto orthogonal subspaces. (The converse, however, is not true.) In the case of the spin matrix $\mathbf{S}_y$, there are just four projectors in the family, corresponding to these four cases:

(1) If $-\frac{1}{2} \notin \Delta$ and $+\frac{1}{2} \notin \Delta$, then $\mathbf{P}^{\mathbf{S}_y}_{\Delta} = \mathbf{P}_0$;

(2) if $-\frac{1}{2} \in \Delta$ and $+\frac{1}{2} \notin \Delta$, then $\mathbf{P}^{\mathbf{S}_y}_{\Delta} = \mathbf{P}_{y-}$;

(3) if $-\frac{1}{2} \notin \Delta$ and $+\frac{1}{2} \in \Delta$, then $\mathbf{P}^{\mathbf{S}_y}_{\Delta} = \mathbf{P}_{y+}$;

(4) if $-\frac{1}{2} \in \Delta$ and $+\frac{1}{2} \in \Delta$, then $\mathbf{P}^{\mathbf{S}_y}_{\Delta} = \mathbf{I}$.

When Δ contains both $+\frac{1}{2}$ and $-\frac{1}{2}$, as in case (4), the projection operator $\mathbf{P}^{\mathbf{S}_y}_{\Delta}$ is the identity operator, which maps every vector in $\mathcal{H}$ onto itself; it is the projector onto the whole space. In case (4), for any pure state **v**, $p_{\mathbf{v}}(S_y,\Delta) = \langle \mathbf{v} | \mathbf{I}\mathbf{v} \rangle = \langle \mathbf{v} | \mathbf{v} \rangle = 1$. Experiments are certain to yield a result within Δ, since each outcome is either $+\frac{1}{2}$ or $-\frac{1}{2}$. When Δ contains neither of these numbers, as in case (1), the projection operator is the zero operator, which maps all vectors onto the zero vector. In this case we have, $p_{\mathbf{v}}(S_y,\Delta) = \langle \mathbf{v} | \mathbf{P}_0 \mathbf{v} \rangle =$

$\langle \mathbf{v}|\mathbf{0}\rangle = 0$. The interpretation of this result is obvious. In cases (2) and (3), Δ contains just one eigenvalue of $\mathbf{S}_y$; in these cases the projectors $\mathbf{P}^{S_y}_{\Delta}$ are the projection operators onto the rays containing the corresponding eigenvectors, and so (2.2) reduces to (2.1):

$$p_{\mathrm{v}}(S_y,\Delta) = \langle \mathbf{v}|\mathbf{P}^{S_y}_{\Delta}\mathbf{v}\rangle \begin{array}{ll} = \langle \mathbf{v}|\mathbf{P}_{y-}\mathbf{v}\rangle & \text{[case (2)]} \\ = \langle \mathbf{v}|\mathbf{P}_{y+}\mathbf{v}\rangle & \text{[case (3)]} \end{array}$$

The generalization of this example, to the case of an arbitrary Hermitian operator which admits eigenvectors, is straightforward. Consider, for instance, an operator $\mathbf{A}$ admitting eigenvectors $\mathbf{v}_1, \mathbf{v}_2, \ldots,$ with corresponding eigenvalues $a_1, a_2, \ldots$ Then for any interval Δ on the real line which contains just one of these eigenvalues, a_i say, we have $\mathbf{P}^{A}_{\Delta} = \mathbf{P}^{A}_{i}$, where $\mathbf{P}^{A}_{i}$ projects onto the one-dimensional subspace containing $\mathbf{v}_i$. If Δ contains just a_i and a_j, then $\mathbf{P}^{A}_{\Delta}$ projects onto the two-dimensional subspace spanned by $\mathbf{v}_i$ and $\mathbf{v}_j$, and so on.

With complete generality, whether we are dealing with an observable with a discrete or with a continuous spectrum, we can say that to each question of the form, "Will a measurement of A on the system yield a result in the interval Δ?" there corresponds a projection operator $\mathbf{P}^{A}_{\Delta}$ onto a subspace L^{A}_{Δ} of the appropriate phase space. The subspace L^{A}_{Δ} (or, equivalently, the projector $\mathbf{P}^{A}_{\Delta}$) can be said to represent the experimental question (A,Δ). Now, when the idea of an *experimental question* was introduced in the discussion of classical mechanics, each such question corresponded to a sub*set* rather than to a sub*space* of the state space (indeed, the notion of a subspace applies only to vector spaces). In the classical case, a knowledge of the state enables us to answer yes or no to each experimental question (depending on whether or not the point representing the state lies within the relevant subset of state space). We said that the state acted as a two-valued measure on the set of experimental questions. In contrast, knowledge of the quantum-theoretical state only enables us to give a definite yes or no in a few special cases. In general, the state gives us the *probability* of a certain result: the state is effectively a probability function on the set of experimental questions, giving to each question a value in the (closed) interval from 0 to 1.

Let us express this formally. To the question "Will a measurement of A yield a result in the interval Δ?" there corresponds a subspace L^{A}_{Δ} of the Hilbert space. Let $\mathbf{P}^{A}_{\Delta}$ be the projection operator onto L^{A}_{Δ}. Then each state $\mathbf{v}$ of a system defines a function μ_{v} such that $0 \leq \mu_{\mathrm{v}}(L^{A}_{\Delta}) \leq 1$, namely, the function such that $\mu_{\mathrm{v}}(L^{A}_{\Delta}) = \langle \mathbf{v}|\mathbf{P}^{A}_{\Delta}\mathbf{v}\rangle = p_{\mathrm{v}}(A,\Delta)$.

In quantum mechanics there are strong reasons for denying that specifying the state does more than assign probabilities to experimental questions. On this view, the function μ_v is conceptually prior to the vector **v**; this vector then appears as a convenient mathematical way to represent the function in question, and, whereas in classical mechanics the state could be said to have both a descriptive and a dispositional aspect, in quantum theory the descriptive aspect disappears and we are left with the dispositional aspect alone.

This is a view which, ultimately, I will reject (see Section 10.2), but it is

Table 2.1 States and observables in classical and quantum mechanics

	Classical mechanics	Quantum mechanics
State space	$6n$-dimensional real space, Ω (the phase space)	Hilbert space (complex vector space) often infinitely dimensional
Pure state	Point in phase space: $\omega \in \Omega$	(Normalized) vector in state space: $\mathbf{v} \in \mathcal{H}$, $\lvert\mathbf{v}\rvert = 1$
Observable A	Real-valued function on phase space $f_A : \Omega \rightarrow \mathbb{R}$	Hermitian operator on state space $\mathbf{A}: \mathcal{H} \rightarrow \mathcal{H}$
Possible values of observables	Range (f_A), usually a continuum	Two cases: (1) **A** has a discrete spectrum (admits eigenvectors); possible values are eigenvalues of **A** (2) **A** has a continuous spectrum (no eigenvectors); continuum of possible values
Experimental question, "Will measurement of A yield result in Δ?"	Subset of phase space $f_A^{-1}(\Delta) \subseteq \Omega$	Subspace of state space $L_\Delta^A \subseteq \mathcal{H}$
Answer to question	Yes/no answer: yes if and only if $f_A(\omega) \in \Delta$	Probability answer: $p_v(A,\Delta) = \langle \mathbf{v} \vert \mathbf{P}_\Delta^A \mathbf{v} \rangle$
Alternative way to regard state	Two-valued function on set of experimental questions	Function mapping experimental questions into [0,1]

true that there is no obvious analogue in quantum theory for the equation $\omega = (p,q)$ of classical mechanics, which specifies the state in terms of the properties of the system. On this, more later; this is a good point at which to pause and summarize what has been said. To this end, Table 2.1 sets out the main differences between the mathematical representation of quantum theory and that of classical mechanics.

2.4 *Probabilities and Expectation Values*

Two short mathematical notes appear as addenda to the previous section. Both show how we can use the fundamental Equation (2.1) to get further results.

The first applies whenever we have a Hermitian operator, **A**, with a discrete spectrum. Then a set of normalized eigenvectors, $\mathbf{v}_1, \mathbf{v}_2, \ldots$, spans the whole space; for simplicity I will assume that the corresponding eigenvalues, $a_1, a_2, \ldots$, are all distinct (that there is no *degeneracy*). It is trivial to show that in that case the eigenvectors are all mutually orthogonal, as noted in (1.31). Since they span the whole space, we have, for any vector $\mathbf{v}$, $\mathbf{v} = c_1\mathbf{v}_1 + c_2\mathbf{v}_2 + \ldots$, and their orthogonality guarantees that the values of the complex numbers, $c_1, c_2, \ldots$, are uniquely determined for a given $\mathbf{v}$, and also that $\Sigma_i|c_i|^2 = 1$, provided $\mathbf{v}$ is normalized.

We now obtain a very simple expression for $p_{\mathbf{v}}(A,a_i)$, the probability that a measurement of A upon a system in state $\mathbf{v}$ will yield result a_i: in this case,

$$(2.3) \qquad p_{\mathbf{v}}(A,a_i) = |c_i|^2$$

The proof is simple. Let $\mathbf{P}_i$ be the projection operator onto the one-dimensional subspace spanned by the eigenvector $\mathbf{v}_i$. Since the eigenvectors are mutually orthogonal, we have $\mathbf{P}_i\mathbf{v} = c_i\mathbf{v}_i$. It follows that

$$\begin{aligned} p_{\mathbf{v}}(A,a_i) &= \langle \mathbf{v}|\mathbf{P}_i\mathbf{v}\rangle && \text{[by (2.1)]} \\ &= \langle \mathbf{v}|\mathbf{P}_i\mathbf{P}_i\mathbf{v}\rangle && \text{[idempotence, by (1.26)]} \\ &= \langle \mathbf{P}_i\mathbf{v}|\mathbf{P}_i\mathbf{v}\rangle && \text{[Hermiticity, by (1.26)]} \\ &= \langle c_i\mathbf{v}_i|c_i\mathbf{v}_i\rangle \\ &= c_i^*\langle \mathbf{v}_i|c_i\mathbf{v}_i\rangle \\ &= c_i^*c_i\langle \mathbf{v}_i|\mathbf{v}_i\rangle \\ &= c_i^*c_i && \text{[normalization]} \\ &= |c_i|^2 \end{aligned}$$

The second result is an expression for the *expectation value* of an observable, that is, the average value we would expect to obtain if we measured the value of A in a large number of trials on systems all of which were in the same state.

We denote the expectation value of A by $\langle A \rangle$. It is obtained by weighting each possible outcome, a_i, of the measurement by its probability $p_{\mathbf{v}}(A,a_i)$. As before, we confine ourselves to those observables with a discrete spectrum; *en route* to our conclusion we use a result argued for at the end of Section 1.14, that, for an operator $\mathbf{A}$ admitting eigenvectors, $\mathbf{A} = \sum_i a_i \mathbf{P}_i$ (where $\mathbf{P}_i$ projects onto the space spanned by the eigenvector $\mathbf{v}_i$, as before).

We have, then,

$$\begin{aligned} \langle A \rangle &= \sum_i p_{\mathbf{v}}(A,a_i)a_i \\ &= \sum_i \langle \mathbf{v}|\mathbf{P}_i\mathbf{v}\rangle a_i \\ &= \langle \mathbf{v}|\sum_i a_i\mathbf{P}_i\mathbf{v}\rangle \end{aligned}$$

(by the properties of the inner product), and so

$$\langle A \rangle = \langle \mathbf{v}|\mathbf{A}\mathbf{v}\rangle \tag{2.4}$$

Clearly, although it does not appear in the conventional notation, $\langle A \rangle$ is a function of $\mathbf{v}$.

Those with a taste for such things may note that the summation sign appears in three distinct usages in this brief derivation; I leave to them the task of justifying these procedures.

More important, note that although (2.4) was derived only for an operator with a discrete spectrum, it also holds quite generally. The general case, of course, would involve deriving (2.4) from (2.2) rather than from (2.1).

Note also that, in our presentation of quantum theory, we could have postulated (2.4) rather than (2.1); in fact, when $\mathbf{A}$ is the projection operator $\mathbf{P}_i$, (2.1) appears as a special case of (2.4). A projection operator (and the subspace it projects onto) acts as an experimental question, which, as we saw in Section 2.2, is a special kind of observable. To $(P_i,1)$ corresponds the question, "Will a measurement of A yield the result a_i?" P_i is thus the observable whose value is 1 when the measurement of A yields a_i and 0 when the measurement yields any other result. (Recall that the eigenvalues of any projection operator are 1 and 0.) Its expectation value is the weighted average of yes and no answers it elicits, the probability, in other words, that a measurement of A will yield a_i. Thus $\langle P_i \rangle = p_{\mathbf{v}}(A,a_i)$, and since, from (2.4), $\langle P_i \rangle = \langle \mathbf{v}|\mathbf{P}_i\mathbf{v}\rangle$, we obtain Equation (2.1): $p_{\mathbf{v}}(A,a_i) = \langle \mathbf{v}|\mathbf{P}_i\mathbf{v}\rangle$.

2.5 *The Evolution of States in Classical Mechanics*

Both classical mechanics and quantum mechanics specify how the state of a system evolves with time. Obviously, at any instant that a classical system has a nonzero momentum, its position is changing with time, and under the action of a force it will change its momentum. The forces dealt with by classical mechanics are those, like gravity, which depend on the relative positions of pairs of particles or the position of each particle in a *field* of forces. In the Hamilton-Jacobi treatment of the evolution of states, talk of such forces is replaced by talk of energy, and anything that can be said in terms of the former can also be said in terms of the latter; for instance, if we have a particle on the end of a spring, we can specify the behavior of the spring—and hence the motion of the particle—either in terms of the force needed to stretch or compress it by a given amount, or in terms of the mechanical energy stored in it when we do so.

Like any other property of the system, its total energy is determined by its state. It is a function of the position and momentum coordinates of the particles comprising the system. Write q for the sequence of the numbers giving all the (components of) position coordinates for the particles, and p for the sequence giving all the momentum coordinates; then (q,p) specifies the point in phase space which represents the system's state. Thus we have

$$\text{Total energy} = H(q,p)$$

where H is a function known as the *Hamiltonian function* for the system.

It is this function which dictates how the state of a classical system evolves through time. Since the state is specified by $6n$ coordinates, to establish how it changes with time we need to know how each coordinate changes. It turns out that their rates of change can be elegantly expressed by Hamilton's equations, simple formulae involving the Hamiltonian function H. The rate of change of any position coordinate q_i (for example, the y-coordinate of position of the mth particle) is expressed in terms of the dependence of H on the corresponding momentum coordinate (in the example, the y-coordinate of momentum of the mth particle), and conversely. For the whole system we have $3n$ pairs of equations:

$$\frac{dq_i}{dt} = \frac{\partial H}{\partial p_i} \qquad \frac{dp_i}{dt} = -\frac{\partial H}{\partial q_i} \tag{2.5}$$

Note that H is assumed to be differentiable, a point I will return to in the next section. Provided that this assumption holds, the coordinates which specify the state of the system at any time t appear as solutions to this set of differential equations.

Just to see the theory in action, let us take a particularly simple example. Consider a system consisting of a single particle moving in one dimension, along a line. Assume further that this particle is in a force field such that the forces it experiences are just those it would experience were it on the end of a spring; in fact, we will talk as though that were the case. For simplicity, we set the origin of our coordinate system to be the point occupied by the particle when the "spring" is unextended, that is, when the force on it is zero. (See Figure 2.4.)

Since we have a single particle moving in one dimension, two numbers, q and p, suffice to specify the state. The phase space for the particle is a two-dimensional space representable in the plane of the paper. As the particle oscillates to and fro under the influence of the "spring," the energy of the system at any instant is the sum of the kinetic energy of the particle, $p^2/2m$, and the energy stored in the "spring," $kq^2/2$, where p is momentum, m is mass, k is the force on the particle per unit displacement from the origin (numerically, the force needed to stretch the "spring" a unit distance), and q is the position coordinate. We have, then,

$$\text{Total energy} = H(q,p) = \frac{p^2}{2m} + \frac{kq^2}{2}$$

It follows that

$$\frac{dq}{dt} = \frac{\partial H}{\partial p} = \frac{p}{m} \qquad \frac{dp}{dt} = -\frac{\partial H}{\partial q} = -kq$$

A propos of these equations, note that dq/dt is the rate of change of position with time—in other words, the velocity v of the particle—and also that $p = mv$; thus the left-hand equation informs us that $v = v$, which is reassuring, if not very enlightening. Note, however, that the right-hand equation yields Newton's second law of motion, since kq is the force pushing

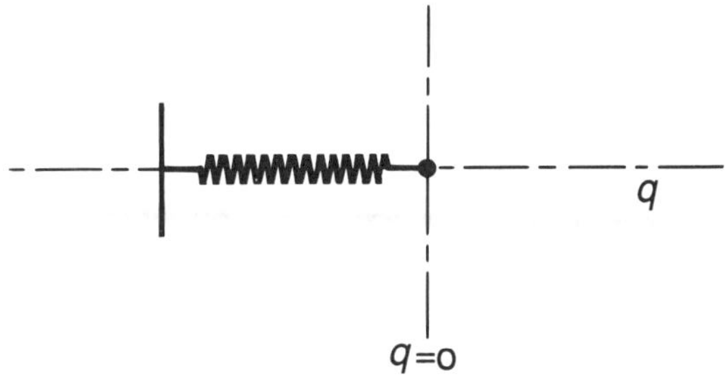

Figure 2.4

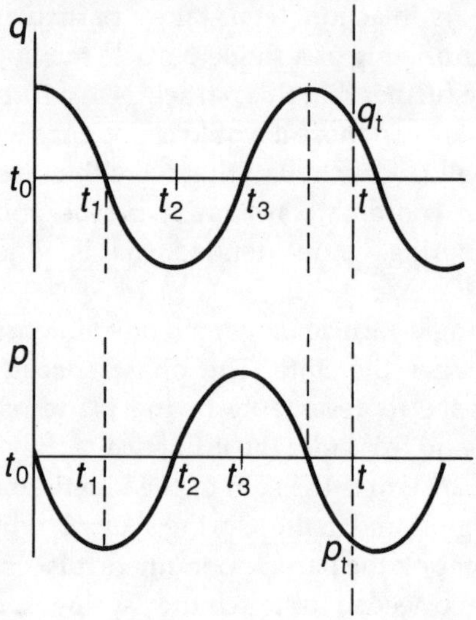

Figure 2.5 Variation of position and momentum with time.

the particle back toward the origin. More relevant to our present concerns is that these equations govern the evolution of the system's state. Assume for argument's sake that the particle is displaced by a distance d and instantaneously at rest at the time $t = 0$, so that its initial state is $(d,0)$. Then the equations tell us that the particle's position and momentum as time goes on are given by the graphs shown in Figure 2.5. To put this another way, as time goes by the state of the particle will follow the trajectory in phase space shown by Figure 2.6; in the absence of retarding forces like friction, this will be an ellipse.

2.6 *Determinism*

In the last decade of the eighteenth century, the Marquis de Laplace wrote:

> We ought then to regard the present state of the universe as the effect of its anterior state and as the cause of the one which is to follow. Given for one instant an intelligence which could comprehend all the forces by which nature is animated and the respective situations of the beings who compose it—an intelligence sufficiently vast to submit these data to analysis—it would embrace in the same formula the movements of the greatest bodies of the universe and those of the lightest atom; for it, nothing would be uncertain, and the future, as well as the past, would be present to its eyes. (1951 [1814], pp. 3–4)

In this way he formulated the doctrine of determinism, the doctrine that, given the present state of the world, all future events are inexorably determined by the laws of nature. Laplace put this metaphysical thesis in epistemic terms by talking of the knowledge available to a "supermind"; this supermind could work out the answer to any question about the future or the past if it had a complete description of how things are now—the "situation of the beings" who comprise the world and the forces which determine how the world changes with time.

The epistemic thesis is stronger than the metaphysical one. The metaphysical thesis is that (1) there is exactly one state ω_1 of the world at time t_1 which is physically compatible with its state ω_0 at t_0 ($t_1 > t_0$); further, (2) these states, ω_0 and ω_1, determine the values of all physical quantities in the world at the times in question. The metaphysical thesis might be true, and the epistemic one false: ω_1 might not be calculable from ω_0, even by a supermind. (For a discussion, see Earman, 1986, chap. 2.) Both theses have been associated with the classical world picture. Indeed, the stronger, epistemic, thesis finds precise expression in the Hamilton-Jacobi version of classical mechanics. Or so it would appear.

Consider a system of particles. We may think of the specification of its state as a precise formulation of what Laplace meant by the "situation of the beings" which comprise it. In order to know all there is to know about the present, a Laplacean supermind would have to know the state of the entire universe. To deduce from this a description of the universe at any time in the past or future, this supermind would need in addition to "comprehend all the forces by which nature is animated," or, equivalently, to know the Hamiltonian function for the entire cosmos.

Our minds, alas, fall short of the Laplacean ideal. Given a system of any complexity, the Hamiltonian may be impossible for us to ascertain, or too cumbersome for us to employ. Nonetheless, Laplace's vision can, and indeed did, function as a regulative ideal for classical physics. That is to say, a metaphysical presupposition, that the universe is deterministic, can govern

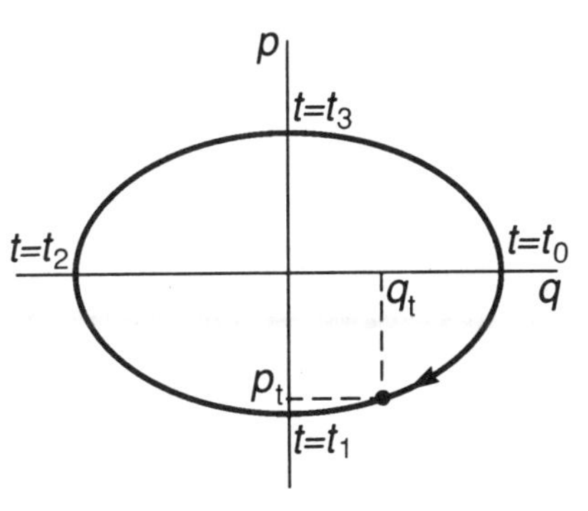

Figure 2.6 Trajectory of state of particle through phase space.

the search for scientific laws. And even our finite intelligences can work out what happens to a particle on the end of an (ideal) spring, as the example in the previous section shows. We obtained the graphs in Figure 2.5 by solving Hamilton's equations. Because Hamilton's equations are first-order differential equations, they can only be solved within a constant term; to obtain unique solutions we plug in the particular values of p and q at one specified time (in this case, when $t = 0$). But from the resulting graphs we can now read off the state of the particle (q_t, p_t) at any time t in the future, and from this state we can deduce all its (mechanical) properties at that time. All this knowledge is available to us through our knowledge of "the forces by which nature is animated" (or, equivalently, the Hamiltonian for the system we are looking at), and the "situation of the beings who compose it," in this case the initial state of the single particle involved.

We can see why Laplace took the universe to be both classically governed and deterministic, but the link between the two is not as clear-cut as he assumed; the laws of classical physics do not entail the thesis of determinism. As Earman (1986, chap. 3) has pointed out, classical physics can be made deterministic only by the adoption of seemingly ad hoc assumptions. Such assumptions are needed, for example, to ensure that the universe is a closed system; within a framework of Newtonian space-time, they turn out to be deeply problematic. Thus, far from entailing the deterministic thesis, classical physics may not even be compatible with it.

Here I will set these fundamental problems on one side and merely indicate how less problematic, but certainly nontrivial, assumptions must be made if the Hamilton-Jacobi formulation of classical mechanics is to be a deterministic theory.

If the state of a classical system of n particles is to evolve deterministically, then all $6n$ differential equations describing this evolution must have unique solutions for any time t. To guarantee this, H must be continuously differentiable (more precisely, it must be differentiable in principle) with respect to q and p for all physically possible states of the system. The curves showing the variation of H with each position and momentum coordinate must be smooth, and exhibit no singularities. This is not an empty requirement. It rules out, for instance, the view that atoms are incompressible spheres of a certain definite radius which exert forces on each other only when they touch. If they were, then the graph representing the force exerted by one atom on another would leap incontinently to infinity as they made contact, and the requirement would be violated (see Figure 2.7). On the assumption that classical mechanics is true, this would mean not merely that no solutions to the set of equations governing the evolution of the universe were calculable, either by our finite minds or by a supermind, but that no unique solutions to these equations *existed.* Both versions of the thesis of determi-

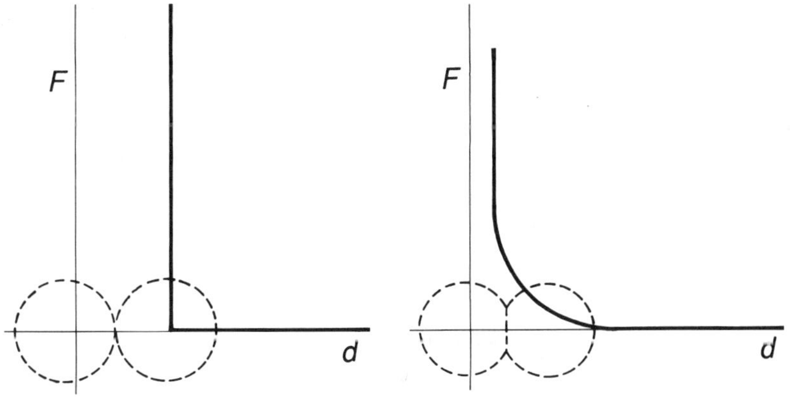

Figure 2.7 Force-distance graphs for *(left)* incompressible and *(right)* compressible spheres.

nism, the epistemic and the metaphysical, would fail to hold; there could be (at least) two distinct states of the world at time t_1, both of which were compatible with a given state at t_0.

2.7 *The Evolution of States in Quantum Mechanics*

Like classical mechanics, quantum theory tells us how the state of a system evolves with time. The key role in the equation governing this evolution is played by an operator rather than by the Hamiltonian function, in line with the general principle that, in quantum mechanics, operators represent physical quantities. As in the classical case, the quantity in question is the total energy of the system; it is represented in quantum theory by a Hermitian operator **H** which we call the *Hamiltonian operator* for the system. The rate of change of the state **v** of a system is given by

$$(2.6)\qquad i\hbar\,\frac{\partial \mathbf{v}}{\partial t} = \mathbf{H}\mathbf{v}$$

and this equation is known as *Schrödinger's time-dependent equation,* or sometimes simply as *Schrödinger's equation.*

There is an equivalent way to describe what happens as time goes on. It is possible to use **H** to construct an operator $\mathbf{U}_t$ which, as the notation implies, is a function of the time. We use this operator to obtain a simple expression for the state $\mathbf{v}_t$ of a system at some time t in terms of its present state $\mathbf{v}_0$:

$$(2.7)\qquad \mathbf{v}_t = \mathbf{U}_t\mathbf{v}_0$$

$\mathbf{U}_t$ is the sum of an infinite series of operators:

$$\text{(2.8a)} \qquad \mathbf{U}_t = \mathbf{I} - \frac{it\mathbf{H}}{\hbar} + \frac{(-it\mathbf{H})^2}{2!\hbar^2} + \frac{(-it\mathbf{H})^3}{3!\hbar^3} + \frac{(-it\mathbf{H})^4}{4!\hbar^4}$$

Each term in this series is well defined in the algebra of operators, and the series converges. Its sum is more easily expressed (see Section 1.5) as

$$\text{(2.8b)} \qquad \mathbf{U}_t = e^{-it\mathbf{H}/\hbar}$$

$\mathbf{U}_t$ is not Hermitian; it is a *unitary operator.*

(2.9) We say that $\mathbf{U}$ is a *unitary operator* on $\mathcal{V}$ if $\mathbf{U}$ is a linear operator on $\mathcal{V}$ which has an inverse, $\mathbf{U}^{-1}$, such that $\mathbf{U}\mathbf{U}^{-1} = \mathbf{I} = \mathbf{U}^{-1}\mathbf{U}$, and, for all $\mathbf{v}$ in $\mathcal{V}$, $|\mathbf{U}\mathbf{v}| = |\mathbf{v}|$.

Unitary operators are the analogues in complex spaces of rotation operators on $\mathbb{R}^2$ and $\mathbb{R}^3$. They leave the lengths of vectors unchanged; thus if $\mathbf{v}_0$ is normalized, so is $\mathbf{U}_t\mathbf{v}_0 = \mathbf{v}_t$; a pure state evolves into a pure state.

The details of the calculation in Equations (2.8 a–b) need not concern us. The important point brought out by Equations (2.8) and (2.9) is that, since $\mathbf{U}_t$ is determined by the operator $\mathbf{H}$ and the time t, the future state is uniquely specified by these two quantities and the present state.

Thus, as far as the evolution of states is concerned, quantum mechanics seems thoroughly Laplacean. How is it, then, that the theory is usually taken to model an indeterministic world? The answer lies in the relation between the quantum state and the values assigned to physical quantities. Recall from Section 2.6 that a deterministic theory is one that (1) not only specifies uniquely the evolution of a system's state, but (2) also assigns, via the state, values to all the physical quantities associated with a system. Quantum theory fulfills the first requirement, but not the second. As I remarked in Section 2.3, a crucial difference between quantum theory and classical mechanics is perhaps this: whereas classical states are essentially descriptive, quantum states are essentially predictive; they encapsulate predictions concerning the values that measurements of physical quantities will yield, and these predictions are in terms of probabilities.

But a bit more needs to be said. It's also true of classical mechanics that the state descriptions it supplies yield predictions about the values that observables will be found to have. Ideally, however, the probability assigned to any experimental question by a pure state of classical theory will be either 1 or 0; classically, probabilities can take values between 0 and 1 either because measurement processes are less than ideal or because information about the state is less than complete. In the quantum case, even given ideal measurements and a precise specification of the state, we obtain nonextremal values of probability.

Thus, in the state-space models we supply for determinist (classical) processes on the one hand and inherently probabilistic (quantum) processes on the other, the distinction between them appears neither as a radical divergence between accounts of the evolution of states, nor simply as a distinction between descriptive and dispositional accounts of states. It appears as a difference between the kinds of predictions a state makes available. Only in the determinist case are these predictions, as we say, *dispersion-free.*

But at this point we can scent a problem. Assume we have a quantum system Q and a measurement apparatus M. If the measurement process is to conform to quantum theory, we would expect the state of the coupled system Q + M to evolve according to Schrödinger's equation, that is, deterministically; nothing so far suggests that a complex system offers an exception to that equation. But if we associate different experimental results with different states of M (its "pointer readings"), and if the evolution of Q + M is deterministic, how is it that results have probabilities other than 1 or 0? I postpone discussion of this question to Chapter 9; for the present, a faint whiff of the problem of measurement can be left to hang in the air.

2.8 Theories and Models

Table 2.1 shows how states and observables are represented in quantum theory; in Section 2.7 we saw how the time-evolution of states is expressed in terms of the action of a family of unitary operators on the vector representing the state. Quantum mechanics, we may say, uses the *models* supplied by Hilbert spaces.

Implicit in this way of presenting quantum mechanics is a general account of scientific theories. A theory T displays a set of models within which the behavior of ideal "possible systems" (or "T-systems") can be represented. For a realist, at least, to accept T is to say that there exist actual systems which are T-systems. (For an antirealist but still model-theoretic view, see van Fraassen, 1980.) The actual solar system, for example, is (approximately) a *Newtonian system,* that is, a system representable within the mathematical models supplied by the theory of classical mechanics. A system S is a *quantum system* if the behavior of S is representable within a Hilbert-space model in the way I have outlined.

This model-theoretic account of a scientific theory is by no means original—it can even be called "the new orthodoxy" in the philosophy of science. (See Suppes, 1967; Giere, 1979; Suppe, 1977, pp. 221–230.) It stands in contrast to "the received view" (the phrase is Putnam's: Putnam, 1962), which takes an axiomatic approach to theories and emphasizes the role of theoretical laws (see Suppe, 1977, pp. 3–61). While I don't quite share Schopenhauer's view of the Euclidean method (it is, he said, as if a man were to cut off both legs in order to be able to walk on crutches; Blanché, 1962), I would reject any claim that an axiom system is the ideal, canonical form for the expression of a scientific theory. The point is this. For any axiom system there exists a class of models; Peano's axioms for arithmetic, for example, have as a model the set of natural numbers. And within science we are not interested in axioms for their own sake, but in the class of models they define. It does not matter how this class is specified, provided that the specification is precise. When we investigate a theory, demands typical of the axiomatic approach—like the requirement that the specification be expressed in a first-order language, or that the predicates of this language be divided into two classes, observational and theoretical—give undue prominence to linguistic matters and are extraneous to our concerns. Thus van Fraassen (1980, p. 44):

> The syntactic picture of a theory identifies it with a body of theorems, stated in one particular language chosen for the expression of that theory. This should be contrasted with the alternative of presenting a theory in the first instance by identifying a class of structures as its models. In this second, semantic, approach the language used to express the theory is neither basic nor unique; the same class of structures could well be described in radically different ways, each with its own limitations. The models occupy center stage.

But when we say that quantum theory uses the models supplied by Hilbert spaces, what sort of models are these? They are models in two apparently dissimilar senses. In the first place, they are models as that term is used in contemporary mathematics; in other words, they are mathematical structures of the kind described in Section 1.8, containing sets of elements on which certain operations and relations are defined. More surprisingly, they are also models in the way that a Tinkertoy construction can be a model of the Eiffel Tower. Just as a point on the model can represent a point on the tower, so, for example, an operator on a Hilbert space can represent a physical quantity.

The two senses are linked in the following way. When we recognize that the Tinkertoy model is a model of the Eiffel Tower, we not only see that points on the model represent points on the tower, but also that certain important relations are preserved in this representation; for example, we would expect the ratio of the overall height to the length of one side of the base to be the same for both the tower and the model. That is to say, we expect the tower and the model to be isomorphic. But isomorphic structures are just the subject matter of model theory in the first, mathematical, sense.

The outline of quantum theory given in this chapter uses the mathematical structure of Hilbert space (a model in the first sense) to provide a representation (a model in the second sense) of the behavior of systems. This behavior has itself been described in very abstract terms; there is a wide gap between the way a working physicist uses quantum theory and the account of the theory I have offered. Of such accounts, Cartwright (1983, pp. 135–136) says,

> One may know all of this and not know any quantum mechanics. In a good undergraduate text these . . . principles are covered in one short chapter. It is true that the Schrödinger equation tells how a quantum system evolves subject to the Hamiltonian; but to do quantum mechanics, one has to know how to pick the Hamiltonian. The principles that tell us how to do so are the real bridge principles of quantum mechanics.

Cartwright gives an instructive account of how an inventive physicist bridges the gap by using models of particular processes "to hook up phenomena with intellectual constructions" (p. 144). "To have a theory of the ruby laser, or of bonding in a benzene molecule," she says, "one must have models for those phenomena which tie them to descriptions in the mathematical theory" (p. 159). These models, however, have a very different function from the mathematical model in which we represent states and observables. They are essentially models in the second, Tinkertoy, sense, which represent actual entities, like a ruby laser, in terms of fictional elements ("two-level atoms" in this instance) whose behavior is amenable to theoretical treatment. These are just useful representations, *simulacra* of what they represent, and are contrasted with the underlying mathematical theory: "a model—a specially prepared, usually fictional description of the system under study—is employed whenever a mathematical theory is applied to reality . . . Without [models] there is just abstract mathematical structure, formulae with holes in them, bearing no relation to reality" (pp. 158–159). This view of the mathematical theory is at odds with my suggestion that the mathematical models supplied by Hilbert spaces are also representational. Such models are not simulacra, nor are they to be contrasted with the theory; in fact, to present the theory is just to exhibit this class of models. In what sense, then, are they more than "abstract mathematical structures"? What, we may ask, do they represent?

Well, to ask this question is precisely to seek an interpretation of quantum theory. When we construct models of the Eiffel Tower or of the ruby laser, we start from these objects and proceed to the task of model building. In the case of quantum theory, we have certain notions like "state" and "observable" which find a representation in the model. Antecedent to the theory, however, these are very insubstantial concepts. We rely on the theory's models to tell us how they are to be understood. The process of interpreting quantum theory is thus the reverse of that of building a model of a preexisting object. We judge our models of the Eiffel Tower and the ruby laser by how well they represent the objects modeled. When we try to interpret quantum theory we assume that the representation the theory offers is a good one and ask Feynman's forbidden question: what sort of world could it represent? In the most abstract, perhaps metaphysical sense, what must the world be like, if it is representable by the mathematical models that quantum theory employs?

3

Physical Theory and Hilbert Spaces

The previous chapter outlined, in rather summary fashion, the way Hilbert spaces supply mathematical models for quantum theory. In fact, Hilbert-space theory was developed for just this purpose. If someone were to ask, "Why Hilbert spaces?" we might think the question a little peculiar; the obvious answer would be, "Because that's the way the world is." But we can refine the question, and ask what it is about the mathematical theory of Hilbert spaces which makes it clearly suitable for the representation of the physical world. More specifically, given the task of representing the quantum world within a mathematical framework, why might we turn to Hilbert-space theory?

The example of classical mechanics shows us that there are possible representations of physical theories which do not involve Hilbert spaces. Of course, this doesn't mean that classical mechanics could not be reformulated in this way. In fact, our strategy for providing a partial answer to the question, "Why Hilbert spaces?" will be to show that the theory of vectors has very general application. We will take as an example a particular physical situation and model it mathematically. The situation will be paradigmatically of the kind with which physical theory deals, but our description will be general enough to leave open the question of what sorts of processes, deterministic or indeterministic, are involved. Similarly its representation, in terms of a vector space, will be general enough to be employed for a variety of physical theories; the particular features of quantum mechanics on the one hand, or classical mechanics on the other, will then appear as additional constraints on these mathematical structures.

The key to the representation is the fact that Pythagoras' theorem, or its analogue, holds in any vector space equipped with an inner product. Consider the space $\mathbb{R}^3$. For any vector $\mathbf{v}$ in $\mathbb{R}^3$,

$$\mathbf{v} = \mathbf{v}_x + \mathbf{v}_y + \mathbf{v}_z$$

Here $\mathbf{v}_x$, $\mathbf{v}_y$, and $\mathbf{v}_z$ are the projections of $\mathbf{v}$ onto an orthogonal triple of rays spanning $\mathbb{R}^3$—or, as we can call them, the *axes* of our coordinate system (see Figure 3.1).

Pythagoras' theorem tells us that

$$|\mathbf{v}_x|^2 + |\mathbf{v}_y|^2 + |\mathbf{v}_z|^2 = |\mathbf{v}|^2$$

and so, if $\mathbf{v}$ is normalized,

$$|\mathbf{v}_x|^2 + |\mathbf{v}_y|^2 + |\mathbf{v}_z|^2 = 1 \tag{3.1}$$

Let us now assume that we wish to represent three mutually exclusive events that together exhaust all possibilities, and that each event has a certain probability. For instance, if we were rolling a die, the events might be: $x =$ die shows even number; $y =$ die shows 1; $z =$ die shows 3 or 5. If we use the axes of $\mathbb{R}^3$ to represent the events x, y, and z, we can construct a normalized vector $\mathbf{v}$ to represent any probability assignment to these events.

We simply take vectors $\mathbf{v}_x$, $\mathbf{v}_y$, and $\mathbf{v}_z$ along these axes such that $|\mathbf{v}_x|^2 = p(x)$, $|\mathbf{v}_y|^2 = p(y)$ and $|\mathbf{v}_z|^2 = p(z)$, and then add them (vectorially) to yield $\mathbf{v}$.

Since the events x, y, and z are mutually exclusive and jointly exhaustive, we know that $p(x) + p(y) + p(z) = 1$ and it follows from (3.1) that $\mathbf{v}$ is normalized.

This almost trivial construction lies at the heart of the use of vector spaces in physical theory.

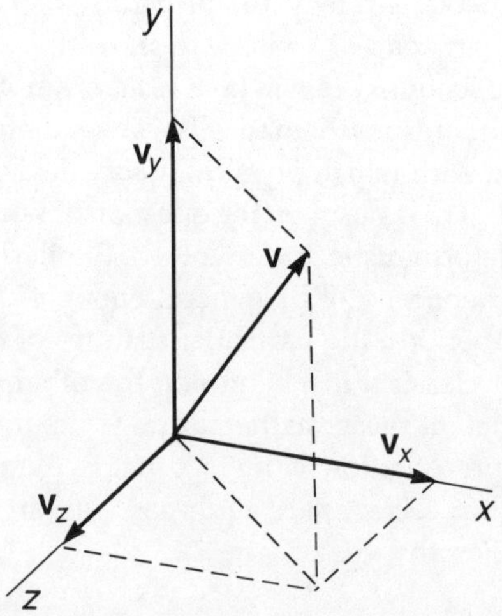

Figure 3.1

3.1 *Minimal Assumptions for Physical Theory*

In developing our general representation of a physical theory we start from one assumption, that the world is such that in certain specifiable circumstances various events can be assigned definite probabilities. I take this assumption to be minimal if we are to have any physical theory at all: we assume that there are links, albeit only probabilistic ones, between one set of occurrences (the initial circumstances) and another (the resulting events).

If the world were fully determined then the assumption would still hold, although ultimately all the probabilities involved would take either one or zero as values.

To place our theory in a specific context, let us imagine modified versions of the schematic experiments described in Section 2.2. In each of those experiments, a preparation of a system was followed by a test, and the result of this test was assumed to depend on the mode of preparation. The tests were all of the pass/fail kind, and it was tacitly assumed that a given method of preparation would always yield the same test results. We may relax both these conditions. We will consider a test for which there are a number of possible outcomes: for present purposes we will assume their number to be at most denumerably infinite, so that they may be labeled x_1, x_2, x_3, and so on. This allows us to consider any test which involves assigning a rational number to some physical quantity (indeed, it goes beyond the bounds of physical plausibility). Further, we will assume that there is a statistical correlation between a given mode of preparation and a particular outcome; in other words, that once a system has been prepared, each outcome x_i acquires a certain probability $p(x_i)$ whose value depends on the method of preparation used.

The question arises whether, by talking in terms of these schematic experiments, we introduce additional assumptions, thereby losing the generality of approach we are after. In particular, are such assumptions brought into play by our talk of a *system,* which is first to be prepared and then tested? As long as we talk only of one particular preparation-measurement procedure, they are not. Effectively, all we are assuming is that there is a physical interaction between one piece of equipment, the preparation apparatus, and another, the measurement apparatus; we express this by saying that a system prepared by one is tested by the other, but this could be thought of purely as a figure of speech.

Perhaps the situation becomes more problematic when we discuss how experimental outcomes using one apparatus are related to outcomes from another. Certainly the term *system* then refers (or, to the scrupulous, appears to refer) to whatever is in common between two, possibly very different, preparation-measurement procedures. But this just shows that the minimal assumption we started with, that in certain circumstances various events can be assigned definite probabilities, does not, on its own, ground the activity of theorizing. If indeed talk of "systems" betrays a second assumption, that there can be something in common between two different processes, this is scarcely *problematic.* How else does theorizing proceed? No doubt "something" is vague, and we may be inclined to mistake the nature of the beast in question—after all, experiment clearly showed phlogiston to have a negative weight—but that is just to say that our theory may be wrong. It's not the aim of this chapter to show that only correct theories can use a vector-space representation.

3.2 *The Representation of Outcomes and Events*

As we shall see in Section 3.7, a crucial distinguishing feature of quantum mechanics is the way in which observable quantities are related one to the other. Nonetheless, for the next five sections I will consider a single observable, measured, moreover, by one specific type of experiment.

We assume that this measurement allows a set $\{x_i\}$ of outcomes. (The labels x_1, x_2, and so on need not refer to numerical values: they are merely our way of distinguishing one outcome from another and so could abbreviate such phrases as "Light D went on," "An explosion occurred," and so forth.) This list of outcomes is to be exhaustive, and they are to be mutually exclusive: each repetition of the measurement must yield exactly one outcome from the set. Our first task is to represent this set mathematically. We could, for instance, represent each outcome by a sequence of zeroes and ones, x_1 by $\langle 1,0,0,0, \ldots \rangle$, x_2 by $\langle 0,1,0,0, \ldots \rangle$, x_3 by $\langle 0,0,1,0, \ldots \rangle$, and so on. (Of course, if we have a finite set of outcomes then each sequence can also be finite.) Or, more obscurely, we could raise the index so that it becomes an exponent and think of each outcome as an integral power of x, of x_3 as x^3, for example. As it happens, in both cases, our representation of an outcome is as a basis vector of a vector space (see Section 1.13); in the first instance the space is the space of sequences of real numbers, and in the second it is the space of the polynomials of x with no constant term. This suggests a more general approach. We represent each outcome, not by a vector, but by a *subspace* of a vector space $\mathcal{V}$; to emphasize that the outcomes are mutually exclusive we make these subspaces mutually orthogonal, and to show that they exhaust the alternatives we specify the vector space to be the span of the set of subspaces. (If L is the span of two subspaces M and N, expressed $L = M \oplus N$, then L is the set of vectors $a\mathbf{u} + b\mathbf{v}$ where $\mathbf{u} \in M$, $\mathbf{v} \in N$, and a and b are scalars: the span of a plane in $\mathbb{R}^3$ and a line perpendicular to it is the whole of $\mathbb{R}^3$.)

Need the subspaces be one-dimensional? No: by leaving the dimension unspecified we allow for the fact that our tests may be coarse-grained. Another test which we regard as a refinement of our original procedure might persuade us that what we had previously regarded as one outcome, x_2, say, should properly be regarded as two: x_{2a} and x_{2b}. In that case we would come to regard the subspace corresponding to x_2 as the span of two others. Of course, if we have reason to believe that no further discrimination is possible, that the outcomes are in a sense atomic, then we are at liberty to make the subspaces representing them one-dimensional.

Let us take our original set of outcomes and enlarge it so that it is closed under various operations. We do this by considering subsets of the set $\{x_i\}$ of outcomes: each such subset we call an event, e_i. The operations of union ($e_1 \cup e_2$), intersection ($e_1 \cap e_2$), and complementation ($\bar{e}_1$) can now be brought into play.

To each outcome there corresponds an event: to x_2 (for instance) corresponds the event $e_2 = \{x_2\}$. If $e_1 = \{x_1\}$ and $e_2 = \{x_2\}$, then $e_1 \cup e_2 = \{x_1, x_2\}$; we may say that $e_1 \cup e_2$ occurs provided either that x_1 occurs or that x_2 occurs. A parallel infinitary operation, $\cup_j$, yields, for instance, the event $\cup_i\{x_i\}$, which is certain to occur, since we took the original set $\{x_1, x_2, \ldots\}$ to be exhaustive. We see that, although to every outcome corresponds an event, not every event corresponds to a single outcome.

In like manner, if e_a is the event $e_1 \cup e_3$ and e_b is the event $e_2 \cup e_3$, then the intersection $e_a \cap e_b$ will be the event e_3; and if we have an infinite set of events $\{e_j\}$, then $\cap_j\{e_j\}$ will be the set of those outcomes which all the members of that infinite set have in common. Notice that if $\cup$ and $\cap$ are everywhere defined, then our set of events has to contain the null event, which never happens; this is the event E_0 (which, of course, is not an outcome).

The set of events, together with the operations on it, finds a ready representation in our vector space $\mathcal{V}$. The subspace L_i corresponding to the outcome x_i also represents the event $\{x_i\}$. To the operations $\cup$ and $\cap$ correspond, respectively, the operations of span ($\oplus$) and intersection ($\cap$) on the set of subspaces of $\mathcal{V}$, and infinitary versions of these correspond to $\cup_j$ and $\cap_j$. Not every subspace of $\mathcal{V}$ represents an event, just those subspaces which are (possibly infinitary) spans of the mutually orthogonal subspaces representing the outcomes, together with the zero subspace to represent the null event. As we would hope, the resulting set of subspaces is closed under the operations.

All this is very nice, but one might wonder what it achieves; after all, the set of events already has a structure, that of a field of sets. What is the point, one may well ask, of introducing all the extra structure built into a vector space—a vector space, moreover, on which an inner product must be defined, since we talk of "orthogonality." The answer comes with the introduction of probabilities.

3.3 The Representation of States

As a result of any given method of preparation, each outcome x_i acquires a certain probability $p(x_i)$ of occurrence. If we regard the outcome x_i as the event $\{x_i\}$, then the function p can be extended over the whole set $\mathscr{E}$ of events in such a way that the Kolmogorov probability axioms hold; in other words so that

(3.2a) $p(E_0) = 0$

(3.2b) $p(E_1) = 1$, where $E_1 = \cup_i\{x_i\}$

(3.2c) for events e_i and e_j, $p(e_i \cup e_j) = p(e_i) + p(e_j)$, provided $e_i \cap e_j = E_0$.

Two methods of preparation are identified if and only if to each outcome one gives the same probability as the other. Then, by definition, each distinct method of preparation results in a different assignment of probabilities, that is, a different function p.

Now let us turn to the vector space $\mathcal{V}$. Let L_i be the subspace corresponding to the event e_i, and $\mathbf{P}_i$ the projection operator onto L_i. Since subspaces and projection operators are in one-to-one correspondence we may regard $\mathbf{P}_i$ as representing e_i. Note that the zero operator, $\mathbf{P}_0$, corresponds to E_0 and the identity operator, $\mathbf{I}$, to E_1. We define the *length* of a vector $\mathbf{v} \in V$, as usual, in terms of the inner product with which we have equipped $\mathcal{V}$ and denote it by $|\mathbf{v}|$. The projection $\mathbf{P}_i\mathbf{v}$ of the vector $\mathbf{v}$ onto the subspace L_i will be of length $|\mathbf{P}_i\mathbf{v}|$.

Now let $\mathbf{v}$ be a normalized vector of $\mathcal{V}$. We have $\mathbf{P}_0\mathbf{v} = \mathbf{0}$ and $\mathbf{I}\mathbf{v} = \mathbf{v}$, whence

(3.3a) $|\mathbf{P}_0\mathbf{v}|^2 = 0$

and

(3.3b) $|\mathbf{I}\mathbf{v}|^2 = |\mathbf{v}|^2 = 1$

Further, if $\mathbf{P}_i$ and $\mathbf{P}_j$ project onto orthogonal subspaces L_i and L_j, then $\mathbf{P}_i\mathbf{v}$ is orthogonal to $\mathbf{P}_j\mathbf{v}$; writing $L_i \oplus L_j = L_k$, we obtain

(3.3c) $|\mathbf{P}_i\mathbf{v}|^2 + |\mathbf{P}_j\mathbf{v}|^2 = |\mathbf{P}_k\mathbf{v}|^2$

by Pythagoras' theorem.

Within the limited set of subspaces we are considering, two subspaces are orthogonal if and only if they have just the zero subspace in common. Thus the condition on (3.3c) is that $L_i \cap L_j = 0$ (the zero subspace), and the match between (3.3a–c) and the probability axioms (3.2a–c) is evident.

We can make the match more explicit as follows. Let any (normalized) vector $\mathbf{v} \in V$ define a function $\mu_{\mathbf{v}}$ on the set of subspaces of $\mathcal{V}$ with values in the interval [0,1], such that

$$\mu_{\mathbf{v}}(L_i) = |\mathbf{P}_i\mathbf{v}|^2$$

For the present we restrict this function to the set of subspaces in correspondence with the set of events. We then obtain

(3.4*a*) $\mu_{\mathbf{v}}(0) = 0$

(3.4*b*) $\mu_{\mathbf{v}}(V) = 1$

(3.4*c*) for subspaces L_i and L_j, $\mu_{\mathbf{v}}(L_i \oplus L_j) = \mu_{\mathbf{v}}(L_i) + \mu_{\mathbf{v}}(L_j)$ provided $L_i \cap L_j = 0$.

It appears that our representation of the set of outcomes within the vector space $\mathcal{V}$ has enabled us to represent not only each possible event in $\mathcal{E}$, but also the probability measures on that set. The probabilities of the various events are physically determined by the method of preparation, or, as we may say, by the state of the system being tested. Thus, already, from our generalized "theory" we can begin to see the rationale behind the use of vectors to represent quantum-mechanical states; further, if we look back at Equation (2.1) we find that, both here and in quantum mechanics, probabilities are computed in the same way from the state vector: for any vector $\mathbf{v}$ and projection operator $\mathbf{P}_i$ we have

(3.5) $p(x_i) = \langle \mathbf{v}|\mathbf{P}_i\mathbf{v}\rangle = |\mathbf{P}_i\mathbf{v}|^2$ [see (1.27)]

Equation (3.5) shows that to every normalized vector $\mathbf{v} \in V$ there corresponds a probability measure on $\mathcal{E}$, namely the probability function p such that, for any outcome x_i,

$$p(x_i) = \mu_{\mathbf{v}}(L_i) = |\mathbf{P}_i\mathbf{v}|^2$$

(where the subspace L_i and the projection operator $\mathbf{P}_i$ represent the outcome in question). We can also show the converse, that any probability function p on the particular set of events we are dealing with can be represented by a vector. Let each outcome x_i be represented by the subspace L_i. Now we choose within each subspace L_i a normalized vector $\mathbf{v}_i$, and construct the vector $\mathbf{v}$ as a weighted vector sum of all the vectors $\mathbf{v}_i$: we write

$$\mathbf{v} = \sum_i c_i \mathbf{v}_i$$

and specify that, for each i,

$$|c_i|^2 = p(x_i)$$

Notice that all the vectors $\mathbf{v}_i$ are mutually orthogonal; whence, by Pythagoras' theorem, we know that

$$|\mathbf{v}|^2 = \sum_i |c_i \mathbf{v}_i|^2 = \sum_i |c_i|^2$$

(since $|\mathbf{v}_i| = 1$ for each i), and also that

$$\sum_i |c_i|^2 = \sum_i p(x_i) = 1$$

Thus

$$|\mathbf{v}|^2 = 1$$

or in other words, $\mathbf{v}$ is normalized.

Before showing how $\mathbf{v}$ could be constructed, I emphasized that the probability function it represented was a function defined on a specific set of events, namely the set $\mathscr{E}$ of events associated with the particular experiment we are concerned with. This emphasis is necessary because quantum theory assigns probabilities to events associated with whole families of observables, and these may be measured by a variety of experimental arrangements. It turns out that, although all the events in this enlarged set $\mathscr{E}^*$ can be represented by subspaces of the same vector space, only one of the results shown above is generalizable to $\mathscr{E}^*$. It remains true that any vector on the space can represent a probability function on $\mathscr{E}^*$; however, not all probability functions on $\mathscr{E}^*$ are representable by normalized vectors in the space. I discuss the representation of the others in Section 3.5.

Let us return to the limited class of events associated with a single type of measurement procedure and to the construction which yielded a vector $\mathbf{v}$ for each probability measure on $\mathscr{E}$. It is clear from this construction that p does not have a unique representation in $\mathcal{V}$, or, to put it another way, each vector in $\mathcal{V}$ does not define a distinct state. During the construction we chose from each subspace L_i an arbitrary normalized vector $\mathbf{v}_i$: a different choice would have resulted in a different vector $\mathbf{v}$ representing the same probability measure. There are two reasons why a choice of vectors is available to us. The first is that we have not claimed that our test outcomes are atomic: we have given each subspace L_i arbitrary dimensionality. The second is that, even within a one-dimensional subspace, there is more than one normalized vector. If $\mathcal{V}$ is a vector space over the reals, and $\mathbf{v}_i$ is a normalized vector within a one-dimensional subspace L_i, then so is $-\mathbf{v}_i$; if $\mathcal{V}$ is a complex vector space (and nothing we have said so far rules it out), then each one-dimensional subspace L_i contains an infinite number of normalized vectors: if $\mathbf{v}_i \in L_i$ and $|\mathbf{v}_i| = 1$, then $c\mathbf{v}_i$ will also be a normalized vector within L_i provided that $|c| = 1$, that is, provided c is expressible in the form $\cos\theta + i\sin\theta$ (see Section 1.5). In passing, we may recall from Section 2.3 that, in quantum mechanics too, the second of these considerations applies, and that a pure state is properly thought of as represented by a one-dimensional subspace of a Hilbert space.

3.4 *Determinism, Indeterminism, and the Principle of Superposition*

Although the previous sections have dealt with the representation of a single experiment, in another respect they have been entirely general: no constraints have been laid on the kind of processes to be modeled. The models supplied by vector-space theory are, thus far, suitable for representing all sorts of possible physical processes, deterministic and probabilistic alike. In this section and the next I will show how the differences between such processes are modeled in the theory; they will appear as differences between the sets of possible states which the theory permits.

In Section 3.3 I showed that every normalized vector $\mathbf{v} \in V$ defines a probability measure on the set of events associated with a particular experiment, and also that there is a vector corresponding to each probability measure on that set. Further, I have up to now equated these probability measures with the possible states of the system tested. Among all the various theories which we can formulate using vector spaces, however, there are some in which only certain vectors are eligible to represent states, and, as noted in the last section, there are others in which some states are not representable by a vector at all. I turn now to physical theories of the first kind, and defer discussion of the second to Section 3.5.

Consider, for instance, a theory modeling testing procedures which were fully deterministic: in our description of the experiments there is nothing to say that we *must* be dealing with indeterministic processes. In the deterministic case, if we could specify our preparation procedures with sufficient precision, then each mode of preparation would yield one outcome with certainty. Let us call the states corresponding to these modes of preparation the *pure states* of the theory. The only probability measures involved would then be those which yielded $p(x_i) = 1$ for some outcome x_i and $p(x_j) = 0$ for each other outcome x_j; thus the only vectors which would represent pure states in this theory would be normalized vectors lying within the subspaces representing the individual outcomes: only for a (normalized) vector $\mathbf{v}_i$ lying within L_i do we have

$$|\mathbf{P}_i\mathbf{v}_i| = 1 \quad \text{but}$$

$$|\mathbf{P}_j\mathbf{v}_i| = 0 \quad \text{whenever} \quad j \neq i$$

Bearing this in mind, let us look at one of the ways in which the difference between classical mechanics and quantum theory has been characterized. In chapter 1 of his *Principles of Quantum Mechanics,* Dirac (1930, pp. 10–18) locates the major difference between the two theories in the role played by the *principle of superposition* in quantum mechanics. Put in general terms, the principle states that,

> If there are pure states of a system which yield probability measures p_1 and p_2 on a set of outcomes, then, if a and b are a pair of real numbers such that $0 \leq a \leq 1$ and $0 \leq b \leq 1$, and $a + b = 1$, and p_3 is the probability measure $p_3 = ap_1 + bp_2$, then there is a pure state of the system which yields the probability measure p_3.

In terms of the vectors representing the pure states, it reads,

> If $\mathbf{v}_1$ and $\mathbf{v}_2$ represent possible pure states of a system, then any vector $\mathbf{v}_3 = c_1\mathbf{v}_1 + c_2\mathbf{v}_2$ such that $|\mathbf{v}_3| = 1$ also represents a possible pure state of that system.

We can now see the significance of this principle. It is clear that no deterministic theory can include it, for on such a theory the only vectors allowed to represent pure states lie within the subspaces $L_1, L_2, \ldots$ which represent the outcomes $x_1, x_2, \ldots$. Though these vectors span the whole space, that is, any vector $\mathbf{v}$ can be written as a sum $\Sigma_i c_i \mathbf{v}_i$ of such vectors, we are not free to regard every vector constructed in this way as representing a physically possible pure state. In the two-dimensional case, where there are two possible outcomes x_1 and x_2 represented by the one-dimensional subspaces L_1 and L_2, respectively (see Figure 3.2), then, on a deterministic theory, the

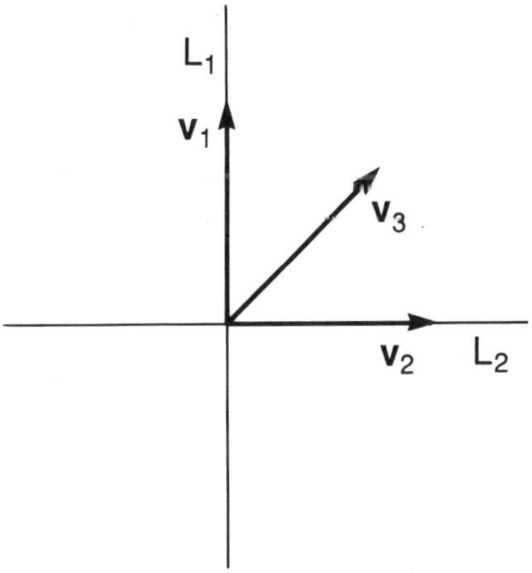

Figure 3.2 The principle of superposition: $\mathbf{v}_3 = (\mathbf{v}_1 + \mathbf{v}_2)/\sqrt{2}$.

(normalized) vectors $\mathbf{v}_1 \in L_1$ and $\mathbf{v}_2 \in L_2$ may represent pure states, but the vector $\mathbf{v}_3 = (1/\sqrt{2})\mathbf{v}_1 + (1/\sqrt{2})\mathbf{v}_2$ may not.

Within quantum mechanics, on the other hand, the principle holds; thus all vectors in the space $\mathcal{V}$ can represent possible physical states, and they may all be written in the form $\Sigma_i c_i \mathbf{v}_i$, that is, as linear sums of vectors within the subspaces which represent outcomes.

3.5 *Mixed States*

Let us now look at a theory in which certain states are not represented by vectors. Consider, for instance, the theory which represents an experimental apparatus of the kind used to demonstrate a binomial distribution. A steel ball is "prepared" by being dropped down a vertical funnel slightly greater in diameter than the ball itself. As it emerges it is "tested" by dropping into an array of horizontal pins, as shown in Figure 3.3. The pins are arranged in horizontal lines, and in any line the distance between adjacent pins is again slightly greater than the diameter of the ball. The pins of each line are staggered with respect to those in the lines immediately above and below, so that, when a ball passes through a gap in one line, it will strike a pin in the line below. Beneath the array there is a series of boxes, each box directly below a gap in the lowest line of pins. Each box corresponds to a different outcome of the test, and each outcome has a certain probability of occurrence.

If the apparatus were symmetrical we would expect it to be equally likely

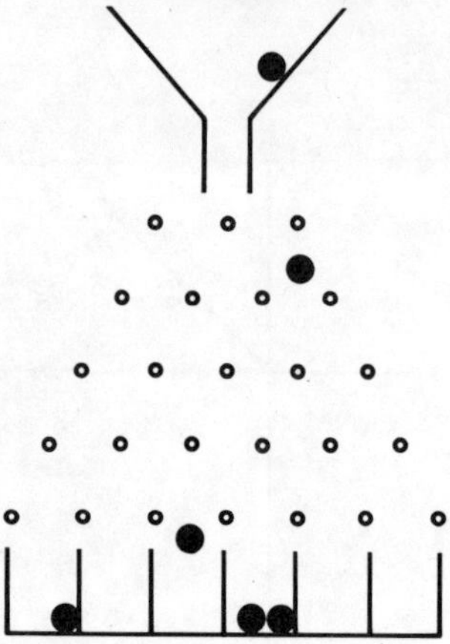

Figure 3.3

that a ball would bounce to the left as to the right after striking a pin. In that case we could assign an expected probability to each outcome as follows. Given n rows of pins there will be $n + 1$ different outcomes, which we can label from the left to right, $x_0, x_1, \ldots, x_n$, and the binomial theorem would lead us to expect that:

$$p(x_k) = \frac{1}{2^n} \frac{n!}{k!(n-k)!}$$

However, we need not confine ourselves to the symmetrical case: we may just assume that some definite probability distribution or other results from the way the apparatus is set up.

Now we may want to accommodate this experiment within a determinist account; we may believe that if we had a truly precise description of the trajectory of the ball as it left the funnel, then we could predict with certainty its path through the array and the outcome that would result. But the probabilities assigned to any outcome by the pure states of a determinist system can only be zero or one, while here we have probabilities lying between these extremes. If we are to deal with these probabilities without abandoning our determinist views, we will have to call on a new notion of state. What we do, in fact, is to describe the ball as it leaves the funnel as being a *mixed state* and to regard each mixed state as a weighted sum of pure states. Let us see first how these mixed states can be represented, and then how they may be interpreted.

In a determinist system each pure state yields probability one to some outcome or other. Given n outcomes there are effectively n distinct pure states, each corresponding to a probability function p_i such that

$$p_i(x_i) = 1 \quad \text{for some } x_i$$

and $p_i(x_j) = 0$ for $i \neq j$. Now, because of the way the apparatus is set up, each of these pure states may have a particular probability of occurring. Let the probability of occurrence of the pure state corresponding to p_i be b_i. Then the probability function p on the set of outcomes can be expressed as a weighted sum of the functions p_i: for each outcome x_j, we have:

$$p(x_j) = \sum_i b_i p_i(x_j) \quad \text{where } \sum_i b_i = 1$$

and we can write,

$$p = \sum_i b_i p_i$$

We see that, provided there are at least two coefficients b_j and b_k greater than zero, p will be the probability function corresponding to a mixed state rather than a pure state.

Within our vector-space representation, each probability function p_i is represented by the function μ_i on the set of subspaces such that

$$\mu_i(L_j) = p_i(x_j)$$

Thus p is represented by the function $\Sigma_i b_i \mu_i$.

Now recall that each function μ_i is such that

$$\mu_i(L_j) = |\mathbf{P}_j \mathbf{v}_i|^2$$

where $\mathbf{v}_i$ is some pure state corresponding to p_i. Note, incidentally: for the reasons given in Section 3.3, more than one vector can represent a given pure state. We may, however, pick a representative $\mathbf{v}_i \in L_i$ and proceed as though there was no such degeneracy. Given, then, a mixed state represented by the weighted sum $\Sigma_i b_i \mu_i$, one may ask why we may not represent it by a vector which is a suitable weighted sum of the vectors $\mathbf{v}_i$. It is certainly not mathematically impossible to do so. In Section 3.3 we saw that, as long as we are confining ourselves to events associated with one particular experiment, we can represent *any* probability measure on the set of these events by a vector. In fact, if we write

$$\mathbf{v} = \sum_i c_i \mathbf{v}_i \quad \text{where} \quad |c_i|^2 = b_i$$

then, for any outcome x_i,

$$\mu_{\mathbf{v}}(L_i) = p(x_i)$$

By doing so, however, we violate the principle that we use vectors to represent only pure states; in a determinist theory the only vectors that do this are the vectors $\mathbf{v}_i$. To put it another way, by doing so we use the principle of superposition.

If we are not to lose an important distinction, we need to find a way of representing the weighted sum of two or more probability functions which is distinct from merely adding the (suitably weighted) vectors which represent them. We do so by finding an alternative representation of pure states. We have already noted that a ray in $\mathcal{V}$ serves to represent a pure state; we use, not the ray, but the projection operator onto it. Mixed states are then represented by weighted sums of projection operators in a very direct way: if each p_i is represented by the projection operator $\mathbf{P}_i$, then $\Sigma_i b_i p_i$ is represented by $\Sigma_i b_i \mathbf{P}_i$. Since $\Sigma_i b_i \mathbf{P}_i$ is not a projector unless there is exactly one coefficient b_i which is nonzero (and hence equal to one), the distinction between pure states and mixed states is made clear.

This treatment of states is developed in Chapter 5. There I will treat the problem of finding an algorithm to relate probabilities to these weighted sums of projectors in the way that the equation

$$p(x_j) = |\mathbf{P}_j \mathbf{v}|^2$$

relates probabilities to the vectors which represent pure states.

Within the situation I have described, mixed states find a ready interpretation: they represent our ignorance of the precise state of affairs as the ball leaves the funnel. For example, if the mixed state were given by

$$\mu = \frac{1}{4}\mu_j + \frac{3}{4}\mu_k$$

and so was representable by $\frac{1}{4}\mathbf{P}_j + \frac{3}{4}\mathbf{P}_k$, this would be taken to mean that the ball was actually in one of the states μ_j or μ_k; the cumulative effect of factors individually too small to allow for means that we do not know which state it is in, but we do know that the ball is three times as likely to be in μ_k as μ_j.

Clearly, any classical theory dealing with systems about which our information is less than complete can use the notion of a mixed state interpreted in this way. Perhaps more surprisingly, mixed states appear in quantum theory as well, but there the "ignorance interpretation," as we may call it, gives rise to a number of problems. I discuss these in Chapter 5.

One question we can pose at this stage is this: what, in quantum mechanics, distinguishes the mixed state represented by $\Sigma_i b_i \mathbf{P}_i$ from the state represented by the vector $\Sigma_i c_i \mathbf{v}_i$, where $|c_i|^2 = b_i$? Each yields the same probability to any given outcome x_i of our experiment (which we may take as measuring some quantum-mechanical magnitude). To put the question more generally: what is the empirical content of the principle of superposition?

A full answer to this is given in Section 3.9, but this much can be said in anticipation. If we are to distinguish operationally between the mixed state S_m represented by $\Sigma_i b_i \mathbf{P}_i$ and the pure state S_p represented by the vector $\Sigma_i c_i \mathbf{v}_i$, then we need a new experiment for which the probability functions given by S_m and S_p will differ. In other words, in order to give content to the principle of superposition we need to consider more than the single experiment which has occupied us so far.

3.6 *Observables and Operators*

I hope the preceding sections have shown how well-suited vectors are to represent the pure states of a quantum-mechanical system. In the same vein we can indicate why it is natural to use an operator to represent a physical magnitude, or observable. The easiest approach is to consider these observables from an operationalist standpoint. (A devout operationalist views the meaning of a physical quantity as being wholly determined by the experimental procedure used to measure it; we can adopt an operationalist approach in this instance, however, without thereby committing ourselves to the whole doctrine.)

To speak guardedly then, at least some physical quantities are the sorts of things which may be measured by the kinds of tests we have described. In such cases the different outcomes of the tests correspond to different values of the quantity in question. Let us take as a simple example an observable A whose value can only be one of the numbers $a_1, a_2, \ldots, a_n$. (Thus, in the language of Chapter 2, A has a finite discrete spectrum.) We assume that our test effectively measures A; this means that the test has as fine a mesh as A requires, so that with each outcome x_i of the test we can associate some single value a_i of the quantity A.

Consider the vector space $\mathcal{V}$ in which we have represented the set of outcomes of the test, each outcome x_i being represented by a subspace L_i.

Since each outcome corresponds to a particular value of the observable A, we could regard it as atomic (in the sense described in Section 3.2), and make each subspace L_i one-dimensional. We need not do this, however, and in the remainder of this section I shall not assume we have done so. As before, we denote by $\mathbf{P}_i$ the projection operator onto L_i. We now construct the operator $\Sigma_i a_i \mathbf{P}_i$ on $\mathcal{V}$, and claim that this operator represents the observable A: in fact, we show this by using the same letter for the operator as for the observable and writing

$$\mathbf{A} = \sum_i a_i \mathbf{P}_i$$

It remains to show just what this claim involves and how it is justified.

As a preliminary, let us distinguish what is happening here from what was going on in the previous section when we constructed the mixed state $\Sigma_i b_i \mathbf{P}_i$. There each $\mathbf{P}_i$ represented a pure state, and (on the ignorance interpretation) each b_i represented the probability of its occurrence. Here every $\mathbf{P}_i$ represents an outcome of an experiment, and each a_i the value of the observable to which the outcome corresponds. Now let us consider the claim itself.

First, we may observe that any operator on $\mathcal{V}$ of the form $\Sigma_i a_i \mathbf{P}_i$ (where all the numbers a_i are real) is Hermitian. Conversely, the spectral decomposition theorem (1.32) tells us (i) that any Hermitian operator on a finitely dimensional vector space is expressible in this way, as a weighted sum of projectors onto mutually orthogonal subspaces, and (ii) that, if all the a_i are distinct, then this decomposition is unique. (One further condition, the compactness of the operator, is required if the space is infinitely dimensional: see Fano, 1971, pp. 81, 291.) This means that we cannot construct the same operator in two distinct ways: if

$$\mathbf{A} = \sum_i a_i \mathbf{P}_i = \sum_j b_j \mathbf{P}'_j$$

(where all the a_i are distinct from one another, as are all the b_j), then $\{a_1, \ldots, a_n\} = \{b_1, \ldots, b_n\}$, $\{\mathbf{P}_i\} = \{\mathbf{P}'_j\}$, and, for any i and j, if $\mathbf{P}_i = \mathbf{P}'_j$ then $a_i = b_j$. Thus, locked up, as it were, in the operator $\mathbf{A}$ is all the information we have about the observable A: that the observable can take the values a_1, a_2, and so on; that we take an outcome x_i of the test to mean that the value of this observable for the system is a_i; and that we represent this outcome x_i within our vector space by the subspace L_i (projection operator $\mathbf{P}_i$).

It is worth noting that the values a_i are the eigenvalues of the operator $\mathbf{A}$ we have constructed, and that each corresponding eigenvector $\mathbf{v}_i$ lies within the subspace L_i. As in quantum theory, eigenvalues of an operator are the permissible values of the corresponding observable.

But this mathematical object, the operator **A**, is not just a memory bank within which we store information about the observable in question. That alone might be enough to justify the claim that **A** *represents* the observable, but more can be said. For we may use this operator, together with the vector representing the (pure) state of the system, to calculate probabilities and expectation values. The algorithms are exactly as they are in quantum theory: from Equation (2.1) we know that, in quantum mechanics, the probability that a measurement of observable A will yield value a_i is given by

$$p_{\mathbf{v}}(A,a_i) = |\mathbf{P}_i^{\mathbf{A}}\mathbf{v}|^2$$

where $\mathbf{P}_i^{\mathbf{A}}$ is the projection operator onto the subspace $L_i^{\mathbf{A}}$ containing the eigenvector $\mathbf{v}_i$ with corresponding eigenvalue a_i. In our experiment, this possible value a_i of the observable is associated with outcome x_i, and that in turn is represented by the subspace L_i, or, equivalently, by the projection operator $\mathbf{P}_i$. This operator $\mathbf{P}_i$, like the operator $\mathbf{P}_i^{\mathbf{A}}$ in quantum theory, is a projection operator from the spectral decomposition of the operator **A**, which represents our observable. Both projection operators enter in the same way into the calculation of probabilities, for in Section 3.3 we defined the state vector **v** as the vector which yielded probabilities to the experimental outcomes according to Equation (3.5)

$$p(x_i) = |\mathbf{P}_i\mathbf{v}|^2$$

From what has been said it is obvious that we should identify $p(x_i)$ in this equation with $p_{\mathbf{v}}(A,a_i)$ from the earlier one.

Given identical procedures for assigning probabilities to the various possible values of a given observable, we could hardly compute expectation values, denoted $\langle A\rangle$, differently in our general representation and in quantum theory: in each case they are calculated by weighting the various possible values by the probability of their occurrence. As in Section 2.4, we obtain

$$\begin{aligned}\langle A\rangle &= \sum_i |\mathbf{P}_i\mathbf{v}|^2 a_i \\ &= \langle \mathbf{v}|\mathbf{A}\mathbf{v}\rangle\end{aligned}$$

3.7 *Relations between Observables: Functional Dependence and Compatibility*

So far we have looked at experiments involving a single type of measurement; though different modes of preparation have been considered, we have not investigated how the results of one kind of test might be related to those of another. We saw in the last section that each test can be thought of as a measurement of a physical quantity, or observable; in this section we will look at some of the ways in which two observables can be related.

As before, we associate an observable with a measurement procedure; the various outcomes from the measurement correspond to values of the observable in question. Again, for simplicity, I will not consider observables with a continuous spectrum; for an observable of that kind, an outcome corresponds to a range of values (a Borel set of the reals), rather than to one value in particular. Most of what we could say about such observables can be inferred from the discussion of observables with a point (or discrete) spectrum.

Let us consider, then, two observables A and B: the values of A are associated with the various outcomes $x_1, x_2, \ldots$ of a suitable experiment, and values of B with outcomes $y_1, y_2, \ldots$ of another. We now ask, what relationships can exist between the probabilities $p(x_i)$ assigned to the outcomes of an A-experiment by a given state and the probabilities $p(y_j)$ which that state assigns to the outcomes of the B-experiment? More formally, let $\mathcal{H}_A$ be the vector space within which we represent the (outcomes associated with) observable A, and $\mathcal{H}_B$ the vector space within which we represent observable B. Then within $\mathcal{H}_A$ there is a set $\{\mathbf{v}_A\}$ of normalized vectors which represent admissible probability measures on the outcomes of measurements of A: we may call these the admissible pure A-states. Similarly, let $\{\mathbf{v}_B\}$ be the set of admissible pure B-states. Then an ordered pair $(\mathbf{v}_A, \mathbf{v}_B)$ will represent a probability measure which simultaneously assigns probabilities to A-outcomes and to B-outcomes. Any relationship that obtains between observables A and B will effect a constraint on the set of ordered pairs which we regard as admissible pure AB-states.

Consider first the relation (or nonrelation) of independence. In this case there are no constraints on the set: if A and B are independent, then the ascription of a set of probabilities to A-outcomes gives us no information about the B-outcomes. We may say that A and B are independent if and only if each ordered pair $(\mathbf{v}_A, \mathbf{v}_B)$ represents an admissible AB-state. Within classical mechanics each component of linear momentum and of position is independent of all the others, and within quantum theory each component of linear momentum is independent of each component of spin. The condition for the independence of A and B requires us to treat $\mathcal{H}_A$ and $\mathcal{H}_B$ as two distinct vector spaces. We may, if we wish, think of the state of a system as a vector in the direct sum of these, $\mathcal{H}_A \oplus \mathcal{H}_B$, and use the ordered pair $(\mathbf{v}_A, \mathbf{v}_B)$ to represent this vector. If we do so, $\mathbf{v}_A$ and $\mathbf{v}_B$ will be the components of $(\mathbf{v}_A, \mathbf{v}_B)$ in the subspaces $\mathcal{H}_A$ and $\mathcal{H}_B$ of $\mathcal{H}_A \oplus \mathcal{H}_B$. This, in effect, is how the independent observables linear momentum and spin are dealt with in quantum theory. Of course, *both* $\mathbf{v}_A$ and $\mathbf{v}_B$ need to be normalized, and so, while we may allow superpositions on $\mathcal{H}_A$, and on $\mathcal{H}_B$, we do not allow superpositions on $\mathcal{H}_A \oplus \mathcal{H}_B$. Such a superposition could yield a component in $\mathcal{H}_B$, say, with norm different from one, and this component would not act as a probability measure on the possible values of B.

Of more interest are the cases in which we can represent A-outcomes and B-outcomes in such a way that both sets of subspaces span the same space, so that $\mathcal{H}_A = \mathcal{H}_B$. Although we can represent independent observables A and B by an operator on a common vector space $\mathcal{H}_A \oplus \mathcal{H}_B$, neither the set of subspaces representing the A-outcomes nor the set of those representing the B-outcomes span the whole of this space. Clearly, however, if $\mathcal{H}_A = \mathcal{H}_B$, consistency demands that $(\mathbf{v}_A, \mathbf{v}_B)$ represents an admissible AB-state only if $\mathbf{v}_A = \mathbf{v}_B$, and so the constraints on $(\mathbf{v}_A, \mathbf{v}_B)$ take a particularly simple form. All the relations we will consider from now on will be of this kind.

To deal first with the most trivial case, it could be that A and B both measure exactly the same physical quantity; although they may use different experimental arrangements, a one-to-one correspondence exists between the outcomes $\{x_i\}$ of the A-experiment and the outcomes $\{y_j\}$ of the B-experiment such that, for any state and any corresponding pair of outcomes (x_i, y_j), we have $p(x_i) = p(y_j)$. In this case it is somewhat less than remarkable that we can find a representation in which $\mathcal{H}_A = \mathcal{H}_B$. Here, where the relation is that of identity, we use the same subspace to represent each of a corresponding pair of outcomes (x_i, y_j). In general, when observables A and B are related to each other, these relations will appear within the Hilbert-space representation as relations between the subspaces representing the A- and the B-outcomes.

Let us take a slightly more complex relationship, that of functional dependence.

(3.6) A is functionally dependent on B provided that each value (outcome) a_i of A corresponds to a set of values (outcomes) $\{b_{i_1}, \ldots, b_{i_j}, \ldots\}$ of B in the following sense: the probability $p(a_i)$ assigned to a_i by any state is the sum $p(b_{i_1}) + \cdots + p(b_{i_j}) + \cdots$ of the probabilities the state assigns to $b_{i_1}, \ldots, b_{i_j}, \ldots$

It follows that each state which assigns probability 1 to any of the outcomes $b_{i_1}, \ldots, b_{i_j}, \ldots$ of B also assigns probability 1 to the outcome a_i of A. Hence the sets $\{b_{i_j}\}$ corresponding to different a_i's are mutually exclusive. In terms of the vector-space representation, we represent an outcome a_i of A by the span L_i^A of the subspaces $L_{i_j}^B$ corresponding to different outcomes

$b_{i_1}, \ldots, b_{i_j}, \ldots$ of B. Thus, by construction, $\mathcal{H}_A = \mathcal{H}_B$. It also follows that the projector $\mathbf{P}_i^A = \Sigma_j \mathbf{P}_{i_j}^B$.

If b_k is any one of the possible values of B which correspond to the value a_i, then we write $f(b_k) = a_i$, and so define a function f that maps the set of possible values of B onto the set of possible values of A. It follows immediately that, if we represent B in our vector space by

$$\mathbf{B} = \sum_j b_j \mathbf{P}_j^B$$

we obtain

$$\mathbf{A} = \sum_i a_i \mathbf{P}_i^A = \sum_i a_i \sum_j \mathbf{P}_{i_j}^B = \sum_k f(b_k)\mathbf{P}_k^B \underset{\text{df}}{=} f(\mathbf{B}) \tag{3.7}$$

As the notation suggests, the last equality is a definition of $f(\mathbf{B})$.

Classical mechanics offers many examples of functional dependencies, albeit between observables with continuous spectra. Consider, for instance, the observables momentum p and kinetic energy T for a single particle moving in one dimension. Since $T = p^2/2m$, to each value of T there correspond two values of p, one positive and one negative, and so T is functionally dependent on p. In fact, as the formula shows, it is a continuous function of p. Similar dependencies exist within quantum theory.

In passing, note that in the three-dimensional (classical) case, $T = (p_x^2 + p_y^2 + p_z^2)/2m$, and so T is functionally dependent on three independent observables, p_x, p_y, and p_z. I won't discuss these more complicated functional dependencies here, though they could be accommodated within the framework we are using.

Instead, let us turn to the case when two observables, A and B, are both functionally dependent on an observable C. In this case A and B are *compatible*. We obtain a representation in which $\mathcal{H}_A = \mathcal{H}_C = \mathcal{H}_B$ by starting with the mutually orthogonal subspaces L_i^C corresponding to C-outcomes. Then, since A is functionally dependent on C, each A-outcome can be represented by the span of some of the spaces L_i^C. So can each B-outcome, and so within $\mathcal{H}_C$ we obtain subspaces corresponding to A- and B-outcomes. The A-subspaces, as we may call them, and the B-subspaces are mutually orthogonal where they do not overlap.

It is convenient to extend the use of the word *compatible* to this relation between subspaces. As an illustration of what the condition involves, we can ask which subspaces within $\mathbb{R}^3$ are compatible with the plane L shown in Figure 3.4. The zero subspace is orthogonal to every subspace, and so is compatible with L. Of the lines through 0, all those within L are compatible

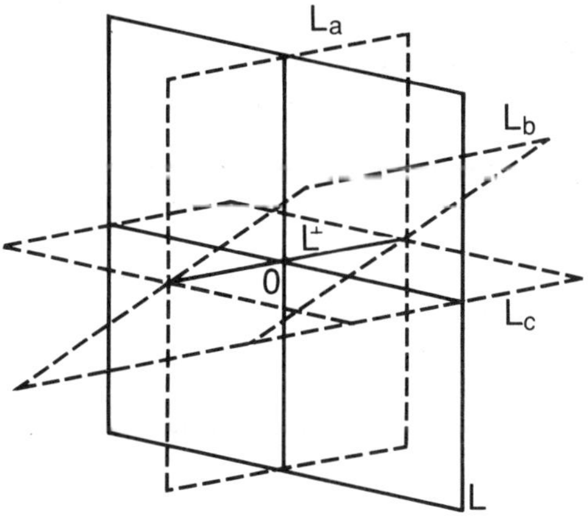

Figure 3.4 Subspaces compatible with L are (a) the zero subspace $\{0\}$; (b) any line in L, and the line $L^{\perp}$ perpendicular to L; (c) the plane L, and any plane obtained by rotating L_a about the line $L^{\perp}$ (for example, L_a, L_b, L_c); (d) the whole space $\mathbb{R}^3$.

with L, as is the line through 0 at right angles to L. Of the planes in $\mathbb{R}^3$ only these are compatible with L: L itself and the planes (shown by dotted lines in the diagram) at right angles to it. Finally, the whole space $\mathbb{R}^3$ is compatible with L. Formally,

(3.8) In any vector space $\mathcal{V}$, subspaces L_a and L_b are said to be *compatible* if there exist mutually orthogonal subspaces L_{a_0}, L_{b_0} and L_c in $\mathcal{V}$ (any or all of which may be the zero subspace) such that

$$L_a = L_{a_0} \oplus L_c \qquad L_b = L_{b_0} \oplus L_c$$

In the theory of vector spaces it is not hard to show that two projection operators $\mathbf{P}_n$ and $\mathbf{P}_m$ commute (that is, $\mathbf{P}_n\mathbf{P}_m = \mathbf{P}_m\mathbf{P}_n$) if and only if they project onto compatible subspaces. This theorem gives us an alternative, and highly convenient, definition of the relation of compatibility between subspaces.

To summarize, if two observables A and B are compatible, then (1) their representations can span a common vector space, and (2) in this representation any pair of subspaces corresponding to their outcomes are compatible. Consider now the operators $\mathbf{A}$ and $\mathbf{B}$ on this space, corresponding to these observables. In our usual notation,

$$\mathbf{A} = \sum_i a_i \mathbf{P}_i^{\mathbf{A}} \qquad \mathbf{B} = \sum_j b_j \mathbf{P}_j^{\mathbf{B}}$$

From (2), all the projection operators $\mathbf{P}_i^A$ and $\mathbf{P}_j^B$ commute with each other; this in turn guarantees that the operators **A** and **B** commute. Thus we obtain the elegant result that compatible observables may be represented by commuting operators.

3.8 *Incompatible Observables*

This chapter began with the question: what is it about the mathematical theory of Hilbert spaces that makes it suitable for providing models for a physical theory? The introduction of incompatible observables prompts a different question: what is it about quantum mechanics that makes its representation in Hilbert spaces so natural? For in quantum mechanics we find observables which are not compatible but yet have a minimal representation on the same Hilbert space. By a "minimal representation" I mean a representation on which each value of the observable is represented by a one-dimensional subspace of the space. (Thus, for the moment, I am continuing to talk only of observables with a discrete spectrum.)

To see what's involved, consider a pair of observables, each of which has two possible values: observable A has values a_1 and a_2, and observable B has values b_1 and b_2. We look first at a single mode of preparation (or state), which assigns probabilities $p(a_1)$, $p(a_2)$, $p(b_1)$, and $p(b_2)$ to the values of these observables, such that $p(a_1) + p(a_2) = 1 = p(b_1) + p(b_2)$.

We can represent the A-state as a vector $\mathbf{v}_A$ in a two-dimensional space whose axes correspond to (A,a_1) and (A,a_2); likewise the B-state can be represented by $\mathbf{v}_B$ in another two-dimensional space. (See Figures 3.5 and 3.6.) Now, as long as we deal with just one state, we can always superimpose the two diagrams, so that the same vector yields both pairs of probabilities. As Figure 3.7 shows, it is just a matter of picking up the B-diagram and rotating it until the vector $\mathbf{v}_B$ in it coincides with $\mathbf{v}_A$ in the A-diagram.

In general, however, we wouldn't expect that this particular superimposed picture would be useful in representing a different preparation procedure. A new state would assign new probabilities to the A-outcomes and to the B-outcomes, representable by two new vectors, $\mathbf{v}'_A$ and $\mathbf{v}'_B$; we would not expect that exactly the same rotation of the B-diagram as before would suffice to make $\mathbf{v}'_A$ and $\mathbf{v}'_B$ coincide (see Figure 3.8). But the remarkable feature of quantum mechanics (or of the systems quantum mechanics describes) is precisely this: that certain observables are related in a way that makes the superimposed picture work for *all* states.

Consider the components of spin of a fermion, S_x, S_y, and S_z. Each of these components has two possible values, $+\frac{1}{2}$ and $-\frac{1}{2}$. (These values are in "natural units," such that $\hbar = 1$.) Accordingly, we can represent the outcomes x^+ and x^- of an S_x-experiment within a two-dimensional Hilbert space

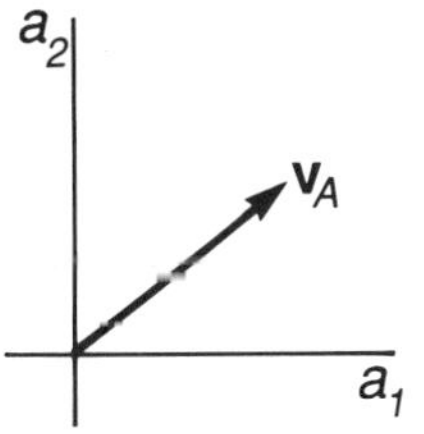

Figure 3.5

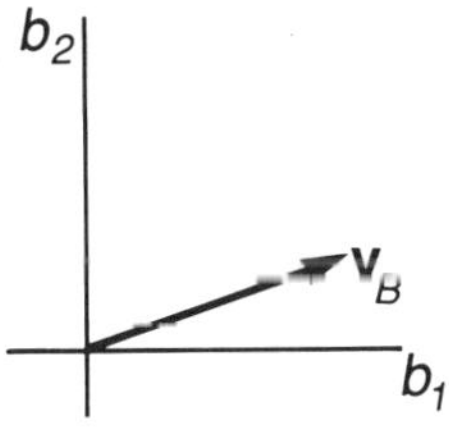

Figure 3.6

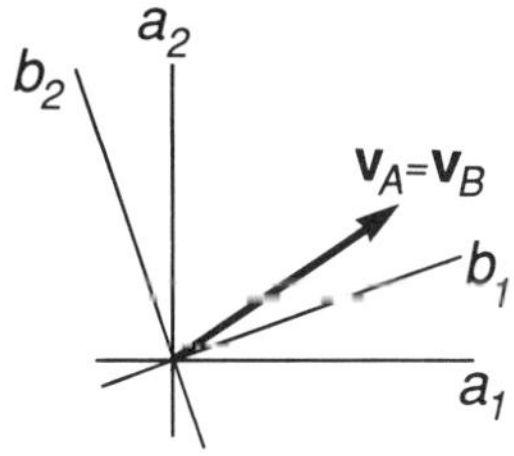

Figure 3.7

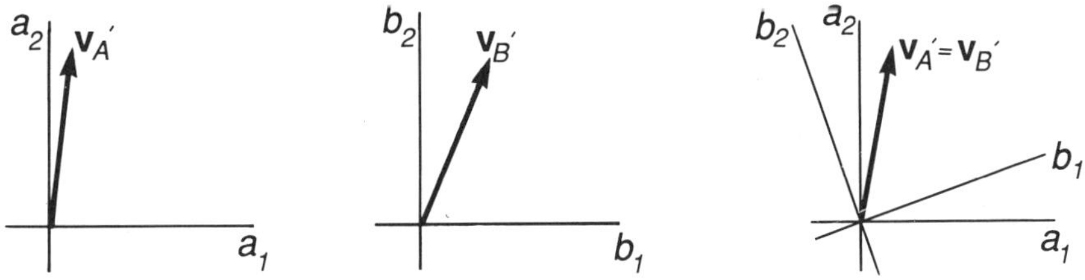

Figure 3.8

$\mathcal{H}_x$, those of an S_y-experiment within a two-dimensional Hilbert space $\mathcal{H}_y$, and those of an S_z-experiment within a two-dimensional Hilbert space $\mathcal{H}_z$. Thus, vis-à-vis this trio of observables, any state can be represented by a triple $(\mathbf{v}_x,\mathbf{v}_y,\mathbf{v}_z)$ of vectors, where $\mathbf{v}_x \in \mathcal{H}_x$, $\mathbf{v}_y \in \mathcal{H}_y$, and $\mathbf{v}_z \in \mathcal{H}_z$. But it turns out that these vectors are not independent; we can use the same two-dimensional Hilbert space to represent all three observables, so that, for *any* pure state, $\mathbf{v}_x = \mathbf{v}_y = \mathbf{v}_z$, and this vector will assign probabilities to all three pairs of outcomes. To do so we first need to make $\mathcal{H}_x$, $\mathcal{H}_y$, and $\mathcal{H}_z$ complex—that is, to use the space $\mathbb{C}^2$ for all three of them—and then to rotate $\mathcal{H}_x$ and $\mathcal{H}_y$, as it were, to fit them on top of $\mathcal{H}_z$.

To speak geometrically—that is, analogically, since $\mathbb{C}^2$ is complex rather than real—within $\mathbb{C}^2$ the rays we use to represent, say, x^+ and z^+ can be obliquely inclined to each other in a way that captures the relation between $p(x^+)$ and $p(z^+)$ for all states of the system. For any pair of spin observables, some, though not all, states are representable in $\mathbb{R}^2$; within the partial representation of S_x and S_z which $\mathbb{R}^2$ affords, the x^+ ray must be at 45° to the z^+ ray, as shown in Figure 3.9. Any normalized vector in $\mathbb{R}^2$ represents a possible assignment of probabilities both to x^+ and x^- and also to z^+ and z^-.

Both in $\mathbb{C}^2$ and in the partial representation in $\mathbb{R}^2$, the rays corresponding to x^+ and to z^+ are oblique one to the other, and hence are, in the technical sense, incompatible. The observables S_x and S_z are likewise incompatible:

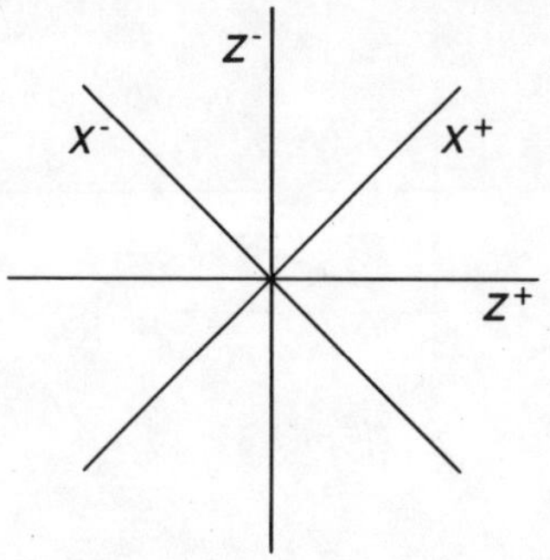

Figure 3.9 Partial representation of S_z and S_x.

the operators representing them do not commute (see problem 1 in Section 1.7).

The term *incompatible* here is a bit misleading. When, for example, we say of two spin components that they are incompatible, we do not merely mean to deny that they are compatible; we also mean to say that a very strong relationship holds between them, of being representable in the same Hilbert space. We are particularly interested in incompatible observables which are, to speak loosely, of the same sort. S_x, S_y, and S_z are all "of the same sort," whereas S_x and S_y^2 are not, despite the fact that they are representable on the same Hilbert space.* We can begin to make this intuitive notion more precise as follows. Consider first a Hilbert space on which S_z is represented. A pair of orthogonal rays in this space represents outcomes z^+ and z^- associated with positive and negative values of S_z. Now observe what happens when we rotate these axes (or perform the complex-space analogue): the axes will come to represent the same values, but of a different component of spin. In the partial representation supplied by $\mathbb{R}^2$, when we have rotated them through 45° they will represent the outcomes x^+ and x^- of S_x.

It turns out that a very simple relation between the operators $\mathbf{S}_x$ and $\mathbf{S}_z$ corresponds to the fact that we can "rotate" axes to transform a representation of S_z-outcomes into a representation of S_x-outcomes, and we can use this relation to specify what exactly being "of the same sort" involves. Recall from Section 2.7 that a unitary operator **U** is the complex-space analogue of a rotation operator.

(3.9) We say that two observables are *mutually transformable* if (a) they are representable in a Hilbert space $\mathcal{H}$ by operators **A** and **B**, and (b) there exists a unitary operator **U** on $\mathcal{H}$ such that $\mathbf{A} = \mathbf{U}\mathbf{B}\mathbf{U}^{-1}$.

* S_y^2 is the observable quantity that is representable by the operator $\mathbf{S}_y^2$.

This relation, which it is tempting to call the *Jarry-relation,* is reflexive, symmetric, and transitive. Note in particular that, if $\mathbf{A} = \mathbf{UBU}^{-1}$, then $\mathbf{B} = \mathbf{U}^{-1}\mathbf{AU}$.

As an example, let $\mathbf{A} = \mathbf{S}_x$ and $\mathbf{B} = \mathbf{S}_z$; the matrix representations of $\mathbf{S}_x$ and $\mathbf{S}_z$ appear in Section 1.7. We now choose $\mathbf{U}$, and hence $\mathbf{U}^{-1}$, so that,

$$\mathbf{U} = \frac{\sqrt{2}}{2}\begin{pmatrix} 1 & -1 \\ 1 & 1 \end{pmatrix} \qquad \mathbf{U}^{-1} = \frac{\sqrt{2}}{2}\begin{pmatrix} 1 & 1 \\ -1 & 1 \end{pmatrix}$$

It is simple to show that $\mathbf{S}_x$ and $\mathbf{S}_z$ are mutually transformable.

Where there are no incompatible observables, the relationship of mutual transformability becomes trivial, as the "transformations" involved reduce to a relabeling of the outcomes of a single experiment. However, mutual transformability is an important characteristic of sets of observables in quantum mechanics, and I discuss one such set in detail in Chapter 4.

Unlike Definition (3.9), the definitions of functional dependence and compatibility given in Section 3.7 made no direct reference to the representation of observables within a Hilbert space. Both definitions, however, can be reformulated in these terms; the definition of functional dependency is a bit cumbersome, and I omit it, but a definition of compatibility of striking simplicity presents itself:

(3.10) Two observables are said to be *compatible* if they are representable on a Hilbert space $\mathcal{H}$ by commuting operators, $\mathbf{A}$ and $\mathbf{B}$.

One advantage of Definitions (3.9) and (3.10) is that neither is restricted to observables with a discrete spectrum. Note in particular that the position and momentum observables, represented by operators $\mathbf{Q}$ and $\mathbf{P}$ on L^2 (where $\mathbf{Q} = x$ and $\mathbf{P} = -id/dx$), are mutually transformable. There is a unitary operator $\mathbf{U}$ on L^2 such that $\mathbf{UPU}^{-1} = \mathbf{Q}$ (see Busch and Lahti, 1985, pp. 65–66). It is known as the *Fourier-Plancherel operator* on L^2, and $\mathbf{P}$ and $\mathbf{Q}$ are said to be *Fourier-connected;* this is just a special case of mutual transformability.

3.9 *The Representational Capacity of Hilbert Spaces*

No physical theory is in fact developed merely by setting up experiments and observing the frequency of occurrence of each of the possible outcomes. The reason is obvious: no experiment takes place in a conceptual vacuum. Only within the context of a theory do we know what experiments are worth performing, or even what procedure is to count as an experiment. Nonetheless, let us imagine this approach being taken. Then the existence of incompatible observables A and B could be shown as follows: for a range of states—that is, modes of preparation of the system dealt with—the probabilities of the various A-outcomes and B-outcomes could be compared and the incompatibility of A and B inferred from the relations among these probabilities. In contrast, on an orthodox approach to quantum theory, we deduce these probability relations from the fact that the operators corresponding to incompatible observables do not commute.

On both approaches, "operational" or orthodox, probability relations associated with incompatible observables give rise to the *uncertainty principle.* I discuss this principle in detail in Chapter 9; roughly, it tells us that certainty about the anticipated result of a given experiment can only be bought at the expense of uncertainty about the anticipated results of others. For the present (and without gross distortion) we can take it to say that there are incompatible observables.

While Dirac took the principle of superposition to be the crucial innovative principle of quantum mechanics, others have cast the uncertainty principle in this role; witness Hanson's remark (1967, p. 45) that "John von Neumann generated all of quantum mechanics from an operationally suitable statement of the uncertainty relations alone." The principle of superposition tells us something about the set of admissible states, the uncertainty principle something about the set of observables encountered in the theory. Any theory which includes either of these principles is, we may say, *inherently probabilistic;* that is, each principle entails that there are pure states which assign to the outcomes of certain experiments probabilities other than one or zero. When the principle of superposition holds we can construct such states from any pair of states which assign a probability of one to different outcomes of a given experiment. For instance, given states p_i and p_j such that, for two distinct outcomes x_i and x_j, $p_i(x_i) = 1$ and $p_j(x_j) = 1$, we can construct a third pure state, p_k, such that, for any outcome x_n of the experiment in question, $p_k(x_n) = c_i p_i(x_n) + c_j p_j(x_n)$, where $0 < c_i \leq c_j < 1$ and $c_i + c_j = 1$. Then $0 < p_k(x_i) = c_i < 1$. Likewise, when observables A and B are incompatible, there are noncompatible subspaces corresponding to outcomes x_i and y_j of A- and B-experiments, respectively. (In geometrical terms these subspaces are oblique one to the other.) In this case, if for some state $p(x_i) = 1$, then $0 \neq p(y_j) \neq 1$; as an example, consider the observables S_x and S_z, with their outcomes x^+ and z^+. Only if all (nonindependent) observables are compatible can we have a determinist theory, if by that we understand that the pure states of the theory assign to experimental questions no values other than one and zero.

Note that, even if we accept (as empirically adequate) an inherently probabilistic theory T, we do not therefore have to deny the thesis of determinism. The theory could be true but incomplete: by proper supplementation it might be made into a determinist theory T* (see Bohm, 1957). Of course this would mean that the "pure states" of T had, so to speak, been misidentified; presumably they would appear as mixed states in T*. Supplementary "hidden-variable" theories of this kind have in fact been proposed for quantum mechanics, and I discuss them in Section 7.8.

Although both the principles under discussion entail that the theory is inherently probabilistic, they are conceptually independent. The existence of incompatible observables does not entail that we can add any (suitably weighted) pair of pure states to obtain another; conversely, we can envisage a theory in which all pairs of observables are either compatible or independent but in which the principle of superposition holds. In the latter case, however, when all pairs of nonindependent observables are compatible, the principle of superposition may have no empirical content. In the absence of incompatible observables there may be no way to distinguish a superposition of two pure states from a mixture of them.

To see what's involved here, let us return to the familiar incompatible observables S_x and S_z and the (pure) states p_{z+} and p_{z-} which assign probability 1 to outcomes z^+ and z^-, respectively, of an S_z-experiment. Note that we have

$$\frac{1}{2} = p_{z+}(x^+) = p_{z+}(x^-) = p_{z-}(x^+) = p_{z-}(x^-)$$

In the space $\mathbb{C}^2$ the states p_{z+} and p_{z-} (the eigenstates of the observable S_z) are represented by the vectors

$$\begin{pmatrix}1\\0\end{pmatrix} \quad \text{and} \quad \begin{pmatrix}0\\1\end{pmatrix}$$

(the eigenvectors of the $\mathbf{S}_z$ matrix: see Section 1.7). Now consider the state represented by the vector

$$\frac{\sqrt{2}}{2}\begin{pmatrix}1\\0\end{pmatrix} + \frac{\sqrt{2}}{2}\begin{pmatrix}0\\1\end{pmatrix} = \frac{\sqrt{2}}{2}\begin{pmatrix}1\\1\end{pmatrix}$$

(see Figure 3.2). This is a superposition of the two eigenvectors of $\mathbf{S}_z$; it is an eigenvector of the $\mathbf{S}_x$ matrix, and represents an eigenstate of the observable S_x. If p_{x+} is the probability function defined by this eigenvector, then

$$p_{x+}(x^+) = 1 \qquad p_{x+}(x^-) = 0$$

$$p_{x+}(z^+) = \frac{1}{2} = p_{x+}(z^-)$$

This function p_{x+} is thus a pure state such that, for each S_z-outcome z_i,

$$p_{x+}(z_i) = \frac{1}{2}p_{z+}(z_i) + \frac{1}{2}p_{z-}(z_i) = \frac{1}{2}$$

On the other hand, if we construct a mixed state p from the equally weighted sum of p_{z+} and p_{z-}, then, while as before, for each S_z-outcome z_i,

$$p(z_i) = \frac{1}{2}p_{z+}(z_i) + \frac{1}{2}p_{z-}(z_i) = \frac{1}{2}$$

we now obtain

$$p(x^+) = \frac{1}{2}p_{z+}(x^+) + \frac{1}{2}p_{z-}(x^+) = \frac{1}{2}$$

or, in other words,

$$p(x^+) = \frac{1}{2} = p(x^-)$$

The (pure) superposition p_{x+} is distinguished from the mixture p not by the probabilities it assigns to the S_z-outcomes, but by those assigned to the S_x-outcomes. It is the existence of an observable S_x incompatible with S_z which enables us to distinguish the mixed state p from the pure state p_{x+}. The fact that different probabilities are assigned to the S_x-outcomes by p and p_{x+} is associated with the fact that the subspaces in $\mathbb{C}^2$ representing these outcomes are (geometrically speaking) obliquely inclined to those representing the S_z-outcomes: as we noted, in the partial representation of S_x and S_z available in $\mathbb{R}^2$ (see Figure 3.9), the x^+ line is at 45° to both the z^+ line and the z^- line.

If all the outcomes in question could be represented by mutually orthogonal subspaces, or by subspaces all of which were generated from one set of mutually orthogonal rays—if, in other words, the observables were compatible—then such differences would not occur. Assume, for instance, that each outcome a of observable A, and each outcome b of observable B (which is not independent of A), can be represented by subspaces M_a and M_b such that

$$M_a = \oplus_i \{L_{a_i}\} \qquad M_b = \oplus_j \{L_{b_j}\}$$

where each of the subspaces L_{a_i} and L_{b_j} is a member of a set $\{L_i\}$ of mutually orthogonal rays of a space $\mathcal{H}$. Assume further that the set $\{M_a\}$ of subspaces corresponding to A-outcomes spans $\mathcal{H}$, as does the set $\{M_b\}$ of those corresponding to B-outcomes. Clearly, A and B are compatible.

We see that any function μ on the set $\{L_i\}$, such that (a) $0 \leq \mu(L_i) \leq 1$ for each L_i in $\{L_i\}$ and (b) $\Sigma_i \mu(L_i) = 1$, determines a probability function p on the sets of A-outcomes and of B-outcomes such that

$$p(a) = \sum_i \mu(L_{a_i}) \qquad p(b) = \sum_j \mu(L_{b_j})$$

Also, to any probability function p there corresponds a function μ, though the latter is not necessarily unique.

Using these ideas, one can easily show that, if p_1, p_2, and p_3 are probability functions on these sets of outcomes, then we can only choose numbers d_1 and d_2 such that

$$p_3(a) = d_1 p_1(a) + d_2 p_2(a) \quad \text{for each } A\text{-outcome } a$$

provided that

$$p_3(b) = d_1 p_1(b) + d_2 p_2(b) \quad \text{for each } B\text{-outcome } b \qquad (☆)$$

Thus, where all observables are compatible, if one probability function is the weighted sum of two others with respect to one set of outcomes, then it must be so with respect to all sets of outcomes.

The conclusion that emerges from this analysis is that, in the absence of incompatible observables, the evidence of experiments like those we are considering would provide no way to distinguish *pure states* which yielded probabilities other than zero and one from *mixtures* which gave the same probabilities. We may say that the principles of uncertainty and superposition are conceptually but not epistemically independent. Where no incompatibility obtains, it is consistent with any evidence of the kind we are considering to regard the appearance of all probabilities in the theory (save zero and one) as the result of our ignorance about an essentially determined state of affairs. On this view the only possible pure states would be those represented by functions μ_j such that

$$\begin{aligned} \mu_j(L_i) = \delta_{ij} &= 1 \quad \text{if } i = j \\ &= 0 \quad \text{if } i \neq j \end{aligned}$$

All other states would be mixtures.

Some final remarks about the significance of incompatible observables need to be made. We have seen that a Hilbert-space representation is possible for a wide class of theories; we would, however, regard it as peculiarly fitted for a theory which had these features: in the space in which we represent the states and observables of the theory, (1) each ray (or normalized vector within that ray) represents a pure state, (2) every subspace of $\mathcal{H}$ represents an experimental question, and (3) every Hermitian operator represents an observable. To echo a point made just now, these features are not entirely distinct. If all observables were compatible, not only would the Hilbert space have, as it were, some surplus capacity for the representation of observables, but a number of rays would represent the same pure state; in the simple two-dimensional case shown in Figure 3.10, if any outcome of any experiment could be represented using just one pair of mutually orthogonal subspaces, L_1 and L_2, then no distinction could be made between the pure states represented by $\mathbf{v}_1$ and $\mathbf{v}_2$: whichever we projected onto L_1 and L_2, we would obtain the same probabilities.

Be that as it may, a theory with all these features would employ all the representational capacity, so to speak, of the Hilbert space. The question is, does quantum mechanics do so? Well, the principle of superposition, whenever it obtains, guarantees the first feature. There are systems which do not exhibit strictly quantum behavior, however, and for which the principle fails. These include, obviously, classical systems which can be, at different times, in distinct states S_1 and S_2 but can never be in a superposition of the two. There are also other, nonclassical examples: for example, it is useful to consider a proton and a neutron as two different states of a nucleon, but no superposition of proton-state and neutron-state exists (Beltrametti and Cassinelli, 1981, chap. 5). However, there are many systems for which feature (1) does hold, and for which, therefore, any vector in the Hilbert space can represent a pure state.

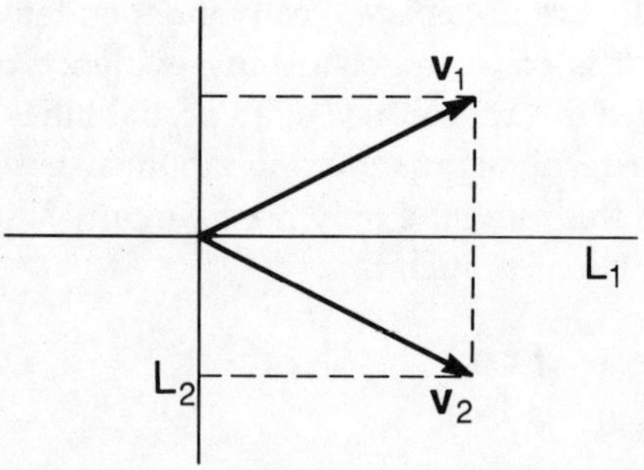

Figure 3.10

Now the existence of incompatible observables is not enough to guarantee either (2) or (3). For example, in the Hilbert space of square-integrable functions of x there are incompatible observables P and Q (momentum and position) but, it seems, no genuine observables corresponding to the Hermitian operators $\mathbf{P} + \mathbf{Q}$ or $\mathbf{PQ} + \mathbf{QP}$, to name but two (see Wigner, 1973, p. 369). For the Hilbert spaces representing spin systems, however, (1), (2) and (3) all hold; this was established by Swift and Wright (1980). To demonstrate (3) Swift and Wright showed that under certain idealizing assumptions—in particular, the assumption that we can create in the laboratory any electromagnetic field consistent with Maxwell's equations—an arbitrary Hermitian operator on a spin system can be measured using a suitable generalization of the Stern-Gerlach experiment. (They also ignore masking effects due to charge; see Section 10.1.)

Thus, at least in the case of spin systems, quantum theory makes use of the full representational capacity of a Hilbert space.

3.10 *The Schrödinger Equation*

In quantum theory, the state of a system at any time t_1 specifies the probabilities attaching to outcomes of any experiment performed at that time. If the experiment is carried out at a later time t_2 ($t_1 < t_2$), the probabilities will not, in general, be the same as at t_1; we say that between t_1 and t_2 the state of the system has *evolved.* Whereas at t_1 it was representable by a vector $\mathbf{v}_1$ in the appropriate Hilbert space $\mathcal{H}$, at t_2 it is representable by $\mathbf{v}_2$. (I assume here that the initial state is a pure state.) It is the latter state $\mathbf{v}_2$ which assigns probabilities to outcomes of experiments conducted at time t_2.

The Schrödinger equation of quantum theory describes how the state evolves through time. That is to say, it enables us to use the present state of the system to assign probabilities to future experiments. As we saw in Section 2.7, if $t_2 - t_1 = t$, then the dynamical evolution of a system's state is described by the equation

$$\mathbf{v}_2 = \mathbf{U}_t \mathbf{v}_1$$

where $\mathbf{U}_t$ is a unitary operator on $\mathcal{H}$. Furthermore, this operator is a complex function of the Hamiltonian operator $\mathbf{H}$, which represents the total energy of the system; we have Equation (2.8b):

$$\mathbf{U}_t = e^{-i\mathbf{H}t}$$

(I have here suppressed the constant $\hbar$.)

As this equation shows, **H** defines not just a single unitary operator **U**, but a family $\{\mathbf{U}_t\}$ of such operators indexed by the time t. The question we now address is: why should the dynamical evolution of states be given by operators of this kind? Is there, so to speak, an *a priori* derivation of Schrödinger's equation?

Note first that the family $\{\mathbf{U}_t\}$ has a structure: it forms a one-parameter group parameterized by the real numbers. This statement needs some amplification.

Consider two sets of numbers, the set $\mathbb{R} = \{t: t \text{ is a real number}\}$ and the set $P = \{e^t: t \text{ is a real number}\}$. $\mathbb{R}$ forms a group under the operation of addition, and the identity element of this group is the number zero (see Section 1.8). Since (i) for all $t_1, t_2 \in \mathbb{R}$, $e^{t_1+t_2} = e^{t_1} \cdot e^{t_2}$ and (ii) $e^0 = 1$, it follows that $\langle \mathbb{R},+,0\rangle$ is isomorphic to $\langle P,\cdot,1\rangle$. In other words, P also forms a group (under multiplication) whose identity element is 1.

The set we are interested in, $\{\mathbf{U}_t\}$, is a set not of numbers but of operators, each expressible in the form $e^{-i\mathbf{H}t}$. However, the rules for operator multiplication echo those for arithmetical multiplication:

$$e^{-i\mathbf{H}t_1} \cdot e^{-i\mathbf{H}t_2} = e^{-i\mathbf{H}(t_1+t_2)}$$

Hence the set $\{\mathbf{U}_t\}$ also forms a group isomorphic to $\langle \mathbb{R},+,0\rangle$; the group operation is operator multiplication, and the identity element is the identity operator **I**. It should be clear what is meant when we say that this group is *parameterized* by the real numbers.

We can show that,

(3.11) If **A** is any Hermitian operator on $\mathcal{H}$, then

(i) $e^{-i\mathbf{A}t}$ is a unitary operator on $\mathcal{H}$;
(ii) $\{e^{-i\mathbf{A}t}\}$ forms a group parameterized by the real numbers.

Of more interest to us is the converse theorem, due to Stone. (Fano, 1971, shows this for the finitely dimensional case; see also Jordan, 1969, pp. 51–52.)

(3.12) If $\{\mathbf{U}_t\}$ forms a (weakly) continuous group of unitary operators on $\mathcal{H}$ parameterized by the real numbers, then there is a unique Hermitian operator **A** on $\mathcal{H}$ such that, for all t,

$$\mathbf{U}_t = e^{-i\mathbf{A}t}$$

The significance of this theorem is this: if we can show why the dynamical evolution of states should be given by a weakly continuous one-parameter group of unitary operators, then it will follow from the theorem that there is a single Hermitian operator governing this evolution. (See Jordan, 1969, p. 52; weak continuity is defined below, but see also Fano, 1971, p. 331.) What such an investigation will not show is why this operator should be the Hamiltonian (the energy operator) for the system.

Let us ignore, for the moment, the fact that a Hilbert-space representation of the states of systems exists, and consider a state just as a probability function on a set of experimental questions, a set $\{(A, a_i)$: A an observable, a_i an outcome of an A-experiment$\}$. We assume that the state p_2 at time t_2 is specifiable in terms of the state p_1 at t_1 $(t_1 \leq t_2)$, whatever the latter may be. Thus we can write,

$$p_2 = V_{t_2}^{t_1}(p_1)$$

where $V_{t_2}^{t_1}$ is some function on the set S of states; formally $V_{t_2}^{t_1}: S \rightarrow S$ is a mapping of the set of states into itself.

If the state p_1 is in turn specifiable in terms of the state p_0 at t_0 $(t_0 \leq t_1)$—that is, if

$$p_1 = V_{t_1}^{t_0}(p_0)$$

—then

$$p_2 = V_{t_2}^{t_1}[V_{t_1}^{t_0}(p_0)]$$

and, using the standard notation for the composition of functions, we may write

$$p_2 = (V_{t_2}^{t_1} \cdot V_{t_1}^{t_0})(p_0)$$

We have, of course, $V_{t_0}^{t_0} = V_{t_1}^{t_1} = I$, where I is the identity function. In general, if time is homogeneous—if, that is, no point in time is to be distinguished from any other—$V_{t_2}^{t_1}$ will depend only on the interval $t_2 - t_1$, so that

$$V_{t_2}^{t_1} = V_{t_2 - t_1}^{t_0}$$

This simplifies our notation considerably. We define V_{t_1} by

$$V_{t_1} \underset{\text{df}}{=} V_{t_1}^{t_0}$$

and obtain

$$V_{t_2}^{t_1} = V_t \quad \text{where } t = t_2 - t_1$$

The definition of the product of these functions now gives us, for all t_1, t_2, and t_3,

(3.13a) $$V_{t_1} \cdot V_{t_2} = V_{t_1+t_2} = V_{t_2} \cdot V_{t_1}$$

(3.13b) $$V_{t_1} \cdot (V_{t_2} \cdot V_{t_3}) = (V_{t_1} \cdot V_{t_2}) \cdot V_{t_3}$$

(3.13c) $$V_{t_1} \cdot V_0 = V_{t_1} = V_0 \cdot V_{t_1}$$

(3.13d) $$V_0 = I$$

Thus from just two assumptions, (1) *statistical determinism*, that the state at time t_2 is a function of the state at time t_1 ($t_1 \leq t_2$), and (2) *homogeneity*, that time is homogeneous, it follows that the evolution of states is governed by a family $\{V_t\}$ of functions having the structure of a one-parameter commutative semigroup. By adding the further assumption, (3) *continuity*, that the probabilities given by the state vary continuously with time (so that small changes in time result in small changes in probability), we give $\{V_t\}$ the structure of a *continuous* one-parameter commutative semigroup.

If $\{V_t\}$ is to be a group, then (4) each mapping V_t of S into S must be one-to-one. That is, to each mapping $V_t: S \rightarrow S$ there must correspond an inverse mapping $V_t^{-1}: S \rightarrow S$, so that

(3.13e) $$V_t \cdot V_t^{-1} = V_0 = V_t^{-1} \cdot V_t$$

Mackey (1963, p. 81) called this assumption (4) "*reversibility*," but this name is "not quite appropriate," as Stein (1972, p. 390 and n. 21) has remarked, because the assumption does not imply that, for each possible dynamical evolution of the system, there is another evolution like the first but in the reverse order.

We may associate each inverse mapping V_t^{-1} with a negative number $-t$ by writing

$$V_t^{-1} = V_{-t}$$

and thus obtain what we want, a continuous one-parameter group parameterized by the reals; note, however, that on this account each mapping V_{-t}

(each mapping that, so to say, moves the state backward through time) obtains its physical significance only from V_t, the member of the original semigroup of which it is the inverse.

Two more assumptions are needed to ensure that each operator V_t can be represented by a unitary operator $\mathbf{U}_t$ on a Hilbert space $\mathcal{H}$. The first is (5) *preservation of pure states*, that V_t maps pure states into pure states. Then its representation in $\mathcal{H}$ maps vectors into vectors, and so is an operator $\mathbf{U}_t$ on $\mathcal{H}$. Furthermore, since all vectors representing pure states are normalized, $\mathbf{U}_t$ leaves the lengths of such vectors unchanged.

A second assumption is needed to ensure that $\mathbf{U}_t$ is linear; this may be expressed by either of two requirements. The first is (6a) *preservation of superpositions*, that $\mathbf{U}_t$ preserves superpositions on $\mathcal{H}$: that for all scalars a and b, and for all vectors $\mathbf{u}$ and $\mathbf{v}$,

$$\mathbf{U}_t(a\mathbf{u} + b\mathbf{v}) = a\mathbf{U}_t\mathbf{u} + b\mathbf{U}_t\mathbf{v}$$

The second requirement—equivalent, given (4), to (6a)—is (6b) *preservation of inner product*, that, for all $\mathbf{u}, \mathbf{v} \in \mathcal{H}$,

$$\langle \mathbf{u}|\mathbf{v}\rangle = \langle \mathbf{U}_t\mathbf{u}|\mathbf{U}_t\mathbf{v}\rangle$$

We may get some feel for the physical consequences of (6b) from the following considerations. Let p_0 and q_0 be two pure states, and let us assume that for some experimental question (A,a), $p_0(A,a) = 1$. Now let p_0 and q_0 evolve under the same evolution operator v_t to pure states p_t and q_t, respectively, such that $p_t(B,b) = 1$ for some new experimental question (B,b). Then, provided that (6b) holds for the operator $\mathbf{U}_t$ representing V_t,

$$q_0(A,a) = q_t(B,b)$$

To use a term we have not hitherto come across, (6b) guarantees that *transition probabilities* between states are preserved under dynamical evolution.

Assumptions (5) and (6) between them ensure that each $\mathbf{U}_t$ is a linear operator which leaves the lengths of vectors invariant. Since we have assumed (4) that each $\mathbf{U}_t$ has an inverse, it follows from Definition (2.9) that each $\mathbf{U}_t$ is a unitary operator on $\mathcal{H}$.

Hence, given assumptions (1)–(6), we know that the Hilbert-space representations of the evolution operators satisfy the antecedent of Stone's theorem (3.12). It follows that, if these assumptions are satisfied, then

Schrödinger's equation takes the form

$$i\frac{\partial \mathbf{v}}{\partial t} = \mathbf{A}\mathbf{v}$$

where **A** is a Hermitian operator. As was stated earlier, however, the assumptions do not tell us why this Hermitian operator should be the energy operator for the system.*

* For an argument by analogy with classical mechanics, see Jordan, 1969, pp. 101–102.

4

Spin and Its Representation

In Chapter 3 I showed in general terms why a vector-space representation is appropriate for a theory involving probabilities. I noted that a characteristic feature of quantum theory was that the observables it deals with are, in the technical sense, incompatible, and I focused on observables having a finite number of values. In this chapter I will look at a particular family of such observables, namely the components of spin of the spin-$\frac{1}{2}$ particle, and their representation. The representation of three of these observables (S_x, S_y, and S_z) has been discussed in Sections 1.7 and 2.3.

In part, then, this chapter provides a specific example to illustrate the rather abstract discussion of the last one, but it also addresses a general question, first broached in Section 3.8: from the point of view of physics, does any significance attach to the structure of Hilbert spaces? It might seem that the vector-space formalism is so well adapted to the representation of probabilistic theories that it could be adopted for pretty well any theory of that kind; perhaps its use in quantum theory merely indicates a decision to represent states and observables in a mathematically convenient way. Along these lines Cartwright writes (1983, pp. 135–136), in a passage I have already quoted,

> [Within quantum mechanics] states are to be represented by vectors; observable quantities are represented by operators; and the average value of a given quantity in a given state is represented by a certain product involving the appropriate operator and vector . . .
>
> But notice: one may know all of this and not know any quantum mechanics . . . to do quantum mechanics, one has to know how to pick the Hamiltonian. The principles that tell us how to do this are the real bridge principles of quantum mechanics. These give content to the theory . . .

And Feyerabend (1975, p. 42, n. 9) suggests that

The quantum theory can be adapted to a great many difficulties. It is an open theory, in the sense that apparent inadequacies can be accounted for in an *ad hoc* manner, by adding suitable operators or elements to the Hamiltonian, rather than by recasting the whole structure.

Both sets of remarks are true, but both ignore the fact that the Hilbert-space formalism is, in an important sense, not theory-neutral. This fact has been hinted at in the discussion of minimal representations in Section 3.8 and of representational capacity in Section 3.9. In this chapter it is illustrated by an analysis of one particular problem.

The problem is this. Suppose that we neglect, for the moment, the physical significance of spin, the interaction of spin with a magnetic field, for instance. Are there very general constraints to which the family $\{S_\alpha\}$ of components of spin conform, and which guarantee that the family is representable in $\mathbb{C}^2$ in just the way that quantum theory tells us? According to quantum mechanics, we can represent S_x, S_y, and S_z by the Pauli spin matrices; we can also produce a general form of matrix by which to represent any component of spin. What is it about spin that establishes that this representation must be the right one? Come to that, what is it about spin that establishes that a minimal representation in a Hilbert space exists? We shall find that the possibility of such a representation depends crucially on certain features of the family $\{S_\alpha\}$; we can portray systems, not very dissimilar to quantum systems, whose behavior cannot be modeled in this way. These results will give us good reason to think that Hilbert spaces provide representations of quantum behavior which are not only versatile and adaptable, but physically significant.

4.1 *Symmetry Conditions and Spin States*

We are dealing here with a family $\{S_\alpha\}$ of observables. The index α picks out a direction in space; intuitively, we can set out to measure the component of spin in any direction we choose. We specify α as we would a point on a sphere, by picking out the azimuthal angle ϕ and the longitude θ (see Figure 4.1) and writing

$$\alpha = (\phi, \theta)$$

So that each point on the sphere is represented by just one pair of coordinates we set

$$-\pi < \phi \leq \pi \qquad \frac{-\pi}{2} < \theta \leq \frac{\pi}{2}$$

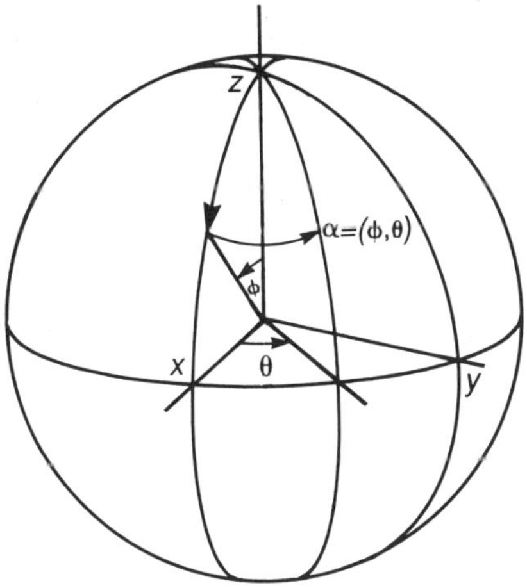

Figure 4.1 Angular coordinates of points on the sphere.

The point α' on the sphere diametrically opposed to α has coordinates $(\phi - \pi, \theta)$ if ϕ is positive and $(\phi + \pi, \theta)$ if θ is negative; α' represents the direction antiparallel to the α-direction.

Each observable S_α is assumed to have just two values, "plus" and "minus." The units we use are not significant, and so we omit the customary $\frac{1}{2}$ or $\frac{1}{2}\hbar$. For the questions $(S_\alpha, +)$ and $(S_\alpha, -)$ we write α^+ and α^-, respectively. If the two values $+$ and $-$ are associated with the directions parallel and antiparallel to α, then we have

$$\alpha^+ = \alpha'^- \qquad \alpha^- = \alpha'^+$$

We assume that a state w of a system assigns a probability to each question α^+. In other words, to each point α on the unit sphere of $\mathbb{R}^3$ a state w assigns a number $p_w(\alpha^+)$, so that, for all α,

$$p_w(\alpha^+) + p_w(\alpha'^+) = 1$$

The *pure states* of the system are those which assign probability 1 to exactly one question α^+ (and hence probability 0 to the complementary question α^-).

Let us now see what the effect is of imposing some very general constraints, like symmetry and continuity, on the way that the probability varies over the sphere. We assume the following to be the case.

(4.1*a*) There exists a family $\{S_\alpha\}$ of observables, indexed by points on the unit sphere S of $\mathbb{R}^3$ (in other words, by directions in physical space).

(4.1*b*) For each point α on S, the observable S_α has two possible values, $+$ and $-$, which we associate with directions parallel and antiparallel to α.

(4.1*c*) The pure states w of the system assign probabilities p_w to all values of the members of $\{S_\alpha\}$.

(4.1*d*) (i) For each pure state w there is one direction in space α_w such that $p_w(\alpha_w^+) = 1$.
(ii) For each direction in space α there is one pure state w such that $p_w(\alpha^+) = 1$.

Alternatively:

(4.1*d*) There is a one-to-one correspondence between states w and directions in space α, such that for w and the corresponding direction in space α_w, $p_w(\alpha_w^+) = 1$. For ease of notation we write p_α for the probability function corresponding to α.

(4.1*e*) For any pure state w, the probability assignments vary continuously over the sphere.

(4.1*f*) For any pure state w, the assignments of probability over the sphere are symmetric about the axis defined by α_w.

(4.1*g*) The set of pure states displays spherical symmetry.

Assumptions (4.1e–g) need some commentary. Let us take the case of a pure state w associated with a particular point χ on the sphere, that is, the pure state w such that $\alpha_w = \chi$. For ease of description I will use a geographical vocabulary and refer to χ as the N-pole of the sphere, to χ' as the S-pole, and so on. To χ the state w assigns probability 1, and to χ' it assigns 0. Assumption (4.1e) tells us that, as we move from χ to χ', we don't get sudden jumps in probability between neighboring points. It rules out, for example, an assignment whereby all points on the northern hemisphere (except χ) are assigned $\frac{3}{4}$, and all points on the equator and the southern hemisphere (except χ') are assigned $\frac{1}{4}$.

Assumption (4.1f) tells us that the assignments of probability are symmetrical with respect to the polar axis $\chi\chi'$. Thus all points on the same line of latitude will be given the same probability, and for every point α on the equator,

$$p_\chi(\alpha^+) = p_\chi(\alpha'^+) = \frac{1}{2}$$

More formally, assumption (4.1f) guarantees that the probability assigned to α^+ is a function of the angular separation of α and χ on the sphere's surface.

Assumption (4.1g) now tells us that this function is independent of the particular point χ we choose in specifying the state. For example, if the state w_χ assigns probability $\frac{3}{4}$ to points on the sphere at an angular separation of 60° from χ, then the state w_ξ (associated with a point ξ on the sphere) will assign $\frac{3}{4}$ to those points on the sphere at an angle of 60° from ξ.

In sum, under the assumptions (4.1a–g),

(4.2) A continuous function t exists, mapping angles into probabilities ($t:[0,\pi] \to [0,1]$), such that, for all pairs of points α and β on the unit sphere of $\mathbb{R}^3$,

$$p_\alpha(\beta^+) = t(\widehat{\alpha\beta}) = p_\beta(\alpha^+),$$

where $\widehat{\alpha\beta}$ is the angular separation of α and β. Further, $t(0) = 1$ and $t(\pi) = 0$.

We have also seen that $t(\pi/2) = \frac{1}{2}$ and, in general, that

(4.3) $$t(\pi - \lambda) = 1 - t(\lambda) \quad \text{for all } \lambda \text{ such that } 0 \le \lambda \le \pi$$

4.2 *A Partial Representation of Spin in $\mathbb{R}^2$*

We now come to the question of whether the family $\{S_\alpha\}$ of observables, together with a set W of states, can be represented in a Hilbert space. There are two possible values for every observable in the family, and so an ideally simple Hilbert-space representation would use a space of two dimensions. In fact quantum theory tells us that there exists a representation of $\{S_\alpha\}$ in $\mathbb{C}^2$. But before we look at this representation, it will be instructive to see why, for a family $\{S_\alpha\}$ of observables and a set W of states conforming to (4.1), a representation in $\mathbb{R}^2$ is ruled out.

It will be useful to use a rectangular coordinate system for $\mathbb{R}^3$ as well as the angular coordinates we have used so far. We label as the z_+, x_+, and y_+ axes of this rectangular coordinate system the directions in space passing through the points (0,0), ($\pi/2$,0), and ($\pi/2$, $\pi/2$) on S, respectively, as in Figure 4.1. The corresponding observables, S_z, S_x, and S_y, have values denoted by z^+, z^-, x^+, x^-, y^+, and y^-.

Let us restrict ourselves, for the moment, to the subset $\{S_\phi\}$ of observables, where $\{S_\phi\} = \{S_\alpha : \alpha = (\phi,0)\}$. In other words, we limit ourselves to the observables associated with the great circle G on the unit sphere through which both the z-axis and the x-axis pass. For this set $\{S_\phi\}$ of observables we consider in turn three sets of pure states, W_1, W_G, and W_S, and the probabilities they assign. From (4.1d), we know that each set corresponds to a set of points on the unit sphere S. W_1 contains just the state corresponding to the point (0,0); using an obvious notation, we denote by p_{z_+} the associated probability function, so that $p_{z_+}(z^+) = 1$ and, from (4.3), $p_{z_+}(x^+) = \frac{1}{2} = p_{z_+}(x^-)$. W_G is the set of all states corresponding to points on G, while W_S is the set of all pure states and corresponds to the whole sphere S.

For each set W the question is: are the states in W and the observables in $\{S_\phi\}$ representable within the two-dimensional space $\mathbb{R}^2$? It turns out that when $W = W_1$ a representation in $\mathbb{R}^2$ is always available; when $W = W_G$ a representation is possible provided that a certain condition holds; however, when $W = W_S$ no representation in $\mathbb{R}^2$ is possible. *A fortiori*, no representation of W_S and $\{S_\alpha\}$ in $\mathbb{R}^2$ is possible.

To avoid ambiguity we must distinguish between the *physical space* containing the directions (ϕ,0) and the *representation space* from which, by the usual algorithm, we can generate probability assignments. The two values of any S_ϕ in $\{S_\phi\}$ must be represented by orthogonal rays in the representation space, and so we are required to map the points (ϕ,0) on the unit circle G in physical space onto rays $L(\phi)$ in the representation space, in such a way that any two diametrically opposed points on G are represented by orthogonal rays in $\mathbb{R}^2$ (see Figure 4.2). Arbitrarily, we show the ray $L(\phi)$ in the first quadrant when $\phi > 0$ and in the fourth quadrant when $\phi < 0$.

The mapping we need is obvious. Recall that in the first instance we are concerned with a single pure state p_{z_+}. This is to be represented by a unit vector $\mathbf{z}_+$ in $L(z_+)$. As usual, the square of the length of the projection of this vector onto a ray $L(\phi)$ is to give the probability of $(\phi,0)^+$. [I write $(\phi,0)^+$ for the question α^+ when $\alpha = (\phi,0)$.] To obtain, for example, $p_{z_+}(x^+) = \frac{1}{2} = p_{z_+}(x^-)$, we orient $L(x_+)$ and $L(x_-)$ at $\pi/4$ (45°) to the ray $L(z_+)$. In general, for any point (ϕ,0) in G, we orient the ray $L(\phi)$ at an angle ψ_ϕ to the ray $L(z_+)$ given by

$$\cos^2(\psi_\phi) = p_{z_+}[(\phi,0)^+]$$

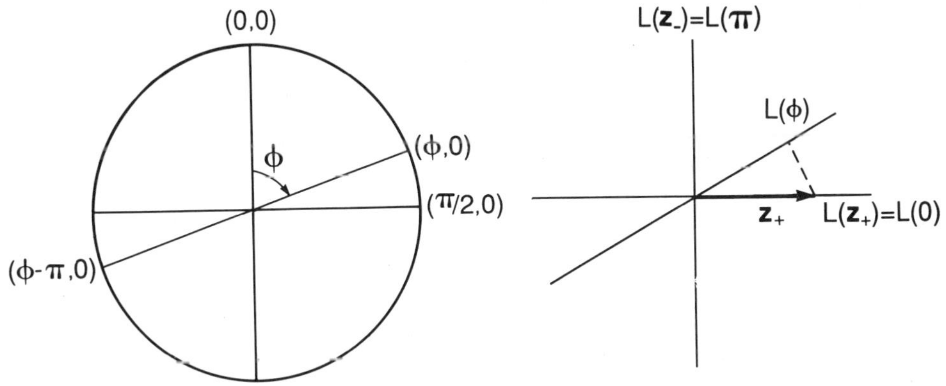

Figure 4.2 Unit circle in physical space *(left)* and representation space $\mathbb{R}^2$ *(right).*

Since, for all α, $p_{z_+}(\alpha) = 1 - p_{z_+}(\alpha')$, $L(\phi)$ is orthogonal to $L(\pi - \phi)$, as required.

In this way we obtain a representation of $\{S_\phi\}$ and W_1 within $\mathbb{R}^2$. Can this construction also give us a representation of $\{S_\phi\}$ and W_G? The question to be answered is this. We have mapped the unit circle G into the set of rays of $\mathbb{R}^2$ in a way that yields the probabilities $p_{z_+}[(\phi,0)^+]$ for each S_ϕ in $\{S_\phi\}$. These are the probabilities assigned by the pure state z_+. But does the construction hold good for pure states associated with other points on G? Are the rays $L(\phi)$ oriented in such a way as to yield the correct probabilities for *all* such states? For instance, consider the state x_+, such that $p_{x_+}(x^+) = 1$. This state must be represented by a unit vector in $L(\pi/2)$. Now this certainly gives the correct probabilities to the possible values of S_z, since we have

$$p_{x_+}(z^+) = p_{x_+}(z^-) = \cos^2\left(\frac{\pi}{4}\right) = \frac{1}{2}$$

and, by our previous construction, $L(x_+)$ is at 45° to $L(z_+)$ and $L(z_-)$ (see Figure 4.3).

However, consider the angle ϕ such that $\psi_\phi = \pi/8$, in other words, the point $(\phi,0)$ on G such that $p_{z_+}[(\phi,0)^+] = \cos^2(\pi/8)$. The subspace $L(\phi)$ is at an angle $\pi/8$ (22.5°) to $L(z_+)$. Clearly, if our representation is to hold good for the state x_+, then the question $(\phi,0)^+$ has to be assigned the same value by x_+ as by z_+. But, on the assumptions (4.1), this means that the point $(\pi/4,0)$, equidistant from (0,0) and $(\pi/2,0)$, must be among the points of G mapped onto $L(\phi)$. (Note that, on the assumptions (4.1), the function t need not be

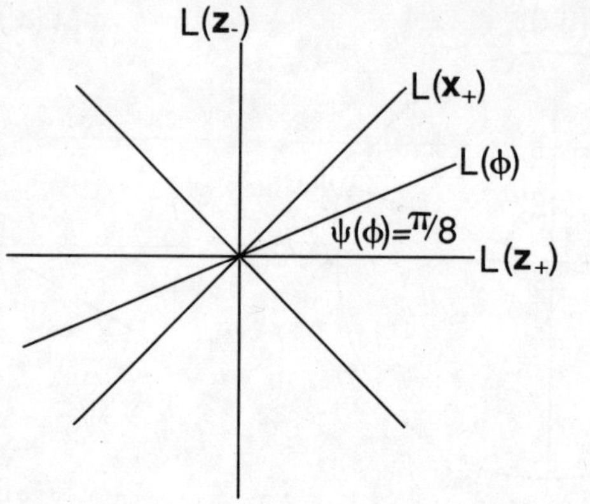

Figure 4.3

one-to-one.) This implies that $t(\pi/4) = \cos^2(\pi/8)$, where, as in (4.2), $t(\widehat{\alpha\beta}) = p_\alpha(\beta^+)$. But now observe, using the results from Section 4.1, that

$$t(\pi) = 0 = \cos^2\left(\frac{\pi}{2}\right)$$

$$t\left(\frac{\pi}{2}\right) = \frac{1}{2} = \cos^2\left(\frac{\pi}{4}\right)$$

$$t\left(\frac{\pi}{4}\right) = \cos^2\left(\frac{\pi}{8}\right)$$

In fact, an extension of the argument given above to pure states associated with the points $(\pi/4,0)$, $(\pi/8,0)$, and so on, shows that, for every nonnegative integer n,

$$t\left(\frac{\pi}{2^n}\right) = \cos^2\left(\frac{\pi}{2^{n+1}}\right)$$

Use of the relation $t(\lambda) = 1 - t(\pi - \lambda)$, together with the continuity assumption, now gives us:

$$t(\lambda) = \cos^2\left(\frac{\lambda}{2}\right) \quad \text{for } 0 \leq \lambda \leq \pi \tag{4.4}$$

Thus the only consistent representation of $\{S_\phi\}$ and W_G in $\mathbb{R}^2$ is remarkably simple: the ray $L(\phi)$ must be at an angle $\phi/2$ to $L(z_+)$, and only if (4.4) holds does our vector-space representation hold good for all the pure states associated with points on the great circle G.

To recapitulate, (4.2) told us that, given certain assumptions about $\{S_\alpha\}$, the probability $p_\alpha(\beta^+)$ is a function of the angular separation of α and β; (4.4) tells us what this function must be if we are to represent the subset $\{S_\phi\}$ of $\{S_\alpha\}$, together with its associated pure states, in $\mathbb{R}^2$; (4.4) is a necessary condition for obtaining a representation of $\{S_\phi\}$ and W_G in $\mathbb{R}^2$.

Equation (4.4) does indeed hold for spin-$\frac{1}{2}$ probabilities, and so the representation we have constructed is perfectly adequate, as far as it goes. But it does not go far enough. The only states that find representation in it are those associated with points on G; for full generality we need to consider, and to represent, the full set W_S of states, or every state corresponding to a point on S. The state y_+, for example, such that, in accordance with (4.2) and (4.3),

$$p_{y_+}(z^+) = \frac{1}{2} = p_{y_+}(x^+)$$

cannot be represented in Figure 4.3. Thus, even as regards all possible probability assignments to members of $\{S_\phi\}$, the representation in $\mathbb{R}^2$ is inadequate.

Moreover, any attempt to represent other members of $\{S_\alpha\}$ on Figure 4.3 is doomed to fail. For what ray is to correspond to $(S_y, +)$? The fact that, for the state z_+, $p_{z_+}(y^+) = \frac{1}{2} = p_{z_+}(x^+)$ suggests that $L(y_+) = L(x_+)$; but, by parallel reasoning in terms of the state x_+, $L(y_+) = L(z_+)$.

Limited though its success is, nevertheless the representation of $\{S_\phi\}$ and W_G in $\mathbb{R}^2$ is not without interest. Effectively, the only consistent representation available is a uniform map of points on the great circle G in physical space to points on a semicircle in the representation space, such that the angular separation of any two points on G is twice the angular separation of their images. This suggests that any consistent representation of the set $\{S_\alpha\}$ of observables and the set W_S of states must respect the symmetries of the set $\{\alpha\}$ of points in physical space. And, in a very precise sense, this is what is achieved by the representation of $\{S_\alpha\}$ and W_S within $\mathbb{C}^2$.

4.3 *The Representation of $\{S_\alpha\}$ in $\mathbb{C}^2$*

By a symmetry of a set of objects we mean a set of mappings of the set onto itself (or automorphisms of the set) which leave invariant some relation or identity characteristic of the set (see Weyl, 1952). If we rotate the unit sphere S of $\mathbb{R}^3$, for example, about an axis through its center, so that the point

(x_1, y_1, z_1) on the sphere becomes the point (x_2, y_2, z_2), then

$$x_1^2 + y_1^2 + z_1^2 = x_2^2 + y_2^2 + z_2^2$$

The identity $x^2 + y^2 + z^2 = 1$ is *invariant under rotations.*

We can readily show that a set of transformations under which an identity is invariant forms a group (see Section 1.8). The symmetry group of S is just the set $SU(3)$ of all rotations of S about its center. Inter alia, this leaves invariant the angular separation of pairs of points on the sphere.

Let us now look at the way symmetry considerations enter into the problem of finding the conditions under which a Hilbert-space representation of $\{S_\alpha\}$ and W_S exists. As we have seen, one task is to find a mapping of points of S onto the rays of some two-dimensional representation space which yields probability assignments consistent with assumptions (4.1). Within the representation space these probabilities are determined by the "angles" between rays. (The term *angle* is metaphorical, if we are in a complex space: in general, probabilities are given by expressions of the form $|<\mathbf{u}|\mathbf{v}>|$, where $\mathbf{u}$ and $\mathbf{v}$ are normalized vectors within the two rays.) The symmetry assumptions (4.1f) and (4.1g) require that, to any automorphism of S under which the angular separation of points of S is invariant (that is, to any rotation of S), there correspond an automorphism of the set of rays of the representation space which leaves invariant the "angles" between them; to such an automorphism, in turn, will correspond a unitary operator on the representation space (see Section 2.7).

We may express this by saying that assumptions (4.1f) and (4.1g) require the group $SU(3)$ of rotations of S to have a representation in the representation space. A group $\mathcal{G}$ is said to *have a representation* within a space $\mathcal{V}$ if there exists a set of unitary operators on $\mathcal{V}$ which, under the operation of operator multiplication, forms a group isomorphic to $\mathcal{G}$. Using this terminology, we can attribute the partial success and ultimate inadequacy of $\mathbb{R}^2$ as the representation space to the fact that, while (obviously) there exists within $\mathbb{R}^2$ a representation of $SU(2)$ (the group of rotations of the unit circle G), there is no representation within it of $SU(3)$.

But, as Felix Klein showed in the late nineteenth century, $SU(3)$ does have a representation within $\mathbb{C}^2$ which is effectively unique (see Goldstein, 1950, chap. 4.5 and bibliography on p. 140). (I say the representation is "effectively" unique because any rotation can be mapped onto two matrices, $\mathbf{M}$ and $-\mathbf{M}$, in $\mathbb{C}^2$.) Further, this representation (which is a mapping of rotation operators on $\mathbb{R}^3$ onto unitary operators on $\mathbb{C}^2$) is consistent with a particular mapping of points of S onto subspaces of $\mathbb{C}^2$, namely the mapping which takes the point $\alpha = (\phi,\theta) \in S$ into the ray $L(\alpha)$, whose projector $\mathbf{P}(\alpha)$ is given by

$$(4.5)\qquad \mathbf{P}(\alpha) = \begin{pmatrix} \cos^2\left(\frac{\phi}{2}\right) & \cos\frac{\phi}{2}\sin\frac{\phi}{2}\,e^{-i\theta} \\ \cos\frac{\phi}{2}\sin\frac{\phi}{2}\,e^{i\theta} & \sin^2\left(\frac{\phi}{2}\right) \end{pmatrix}$$

(Compare this projector with $\mathbf{P}_\theta$, discussed in Section 1.2.)

The argument so far has shown that, if the probabilities associated with $\{S_\alpha\}$ conform to assumptions (4.1a–g), then the only possible representation of $\{S_\alpha\}$ within $\mathbb{C}^2$ will use the mapping given above. But it has not yet been shown that the probability function given by this representation is the function $t(\widehat{\alpha\beta}) = p_\alpha(\beta^+)$, which actually obtains in quantum theory, still less that it is the one which *must* obtain. In the remainder of this section I will deal with the first of these issues; the second I postpone to Section 4.4.

The subspace $L(\alpha)$ projected onto by $\mathbf{P}(\alpha)$ is to represent the experimental question α^+. The pure state w such that $p_w(\alpha^+) = 1$ can be represented by a normalized vector $\boldsymbol{\alpha}_+$ in $L(\alpha)$, where

$$(4.6)\qquad \boldsymbol{\alpha}_+ = \begin{pmatrix} \cos\frac{\phi}{2}\,e^{-i\theta/2} \\ \sin\frac{\phi}{2}\,e^{i\theta/2} \end{pmatrix}$$

It is trivial to show that $\boldsymbol{\alpha}_+$ is indeed in $L(\alpha)$.

If we choose the polar axis to be the z-axis of our coordinate system, as in Figure 4.1, then we obtain, for $\mathbf{x}_+$, $\mathbf{x}_-$, $\mathbf{y}_+$, $\mathbf{y}_-$, $\mathbf{z}_+$, and $\mathbf{z}_-$, vectors familiar from Section 1.7 as the eigenvectors of $\mathbf{S}_x$, $\mathbf{S}_y$, and $\mathbf{S}_z$. These are shown in Table 4.1.

Notice, incidentally, the vectors $\mathbf{z}_+$, $\mathbf{z}_-$, $\mathbf{x}_+$, and $\mathbf{x}_-$, and compare them with Figure 4.3. We see that the $\mathbb{R}^2$-representation obtained in Section 4.2—the representation, that is, of states and observables associated with points in S for which $\theta = 0$—is embeddable in the $\mathbb{C}^2$-representation of $\{S_\alpha\}$.

In order to obtain a general expression for $t(\widehat{\alpha\beta})$, we need only take the most straightforward case, since we know that spherical symmetry obtains. Accordingly, let us assume that the system is in the state z_+. We then expect, from (4.2), that the probability of a result α^+, where $\alpha = (\phi,\theta)$, depends only on the angle ϕ. In fact we get

$$p_{z_+}(\alpha^+) = \langle\, \mathbf{z}_+ | \mathbf{P}(\alpha)\mathbf{z}_+ \,\rangle$$

and, using the expressions for $\mathbf{P}(\alpha)$ and $\mathbf{z}_+$, we obtain

$$\mathbf{P}(\alpha)\mathbf{z}_+ = \begin{pmatrix} \cos^2\frac{\phi}{2} \\ \sin\frac{\phi}{2}\cos\frac{\phi}{2}\,e^{i\theta} \end{pmatrix}$$

whence

$$p_{z_+}(\alpha^+) = \cos^2\frac{\phi}{2} = t(\phi)$$

Given this representation, the function t has a particularly simple form.

It has become apparent that the representation of $SU(3)$ we are forced to by symmetry considerations (provided, that is, some representation is possible) is exactly that used in quantum theory. As a final confirmation of this—and also to display a result of great elegance—let us consider the matrices on $\mathbb{C}^2$ which, on this account, are to represent the observables S_α.

Since we are effectively assuming the possible values of S_α to be $+1$ and -1, we know by the spectral decomposition theorem that, for any $\alpha = (\phi,\theta)$,

$$\mathbf{S}_\alpha = \mathbf{P}(\alpha) - \mathbf{P}(\alpha')$$

Before doing this calculation note that, for each point α on the unit sphere S of $\mathbb{R}^3$, there will be an operator $\mathbf{S}_\alpha$. Although the steps of the calculation are best performed using the angular coordinates of α, in the final stages it is worth moving to Cartesian coordinates, so that $\alpha = (x,y,z)$, where $x^2 + y^2 + z^2 = 1$. We set $\phi = 0$ along the z-axis and $\theta = 0$ along the x-axis, as before.

A wonderfully simple result now presents itself:

(4.7) $$\mathbf{S}_\alpha = \begin{pmatrix} z & x - iy \\ x + iy & -z \end{pmatrix} \qquad (☆☆)$$

The Pauli matrices $\mathbf{S}_x$, $\mathbf{S}_y$, and $\mathbf{S}_z$ appear as special cases of (4.7). In terms of these matrices we obtain

(4.8) $$\mathbf{S}_\alpha = x\mathbf{S}_x + y\mathbf{S}_y + z\mathbf{S}_z \qquad (☆)$$

Table 4.1 Special cases of the formula: $\boldsymbol{\alpha}_+ = \begin{pmatrix} \cos\frac{\phi}{2}\, e^{-i\theta/2} \\ \sin\frac{\phi}{2}\, e^{i\theta/2} \end{pmatrix}$

	Spin states of the spin-$\frac{1}{2}$ particle					
	$\mathbf{z}_+$	$\mathbf{z}'_+ = \mathbf{z}_-$	$\mathbf{x}_+$	$\mathbf{x}'_+ = \mathbf{x}_-$	$\mathbf{y}_+$	$\mathbf{y}'_+ = \mathbf{y}_-$
ϕ	0	π	$\frac{\pi}{2}$	$-\frac{\pi}{2}$	$\frac{\pi}{2}$	$-\frac{\pi}{2}$
θ	0	0	0	0	$\frac{\pi}{2}$	$\frac{\pi}{2}$
$\cos\frac{\phi}{2}$	1	0	$\frac{1}{\sqrt{2}}$	$\frac{1}{\sqrt{2}}$	$\frac{1}{\sqrt{2}}$	$\frac{1}{\sqrt{2}}$
$\sin\frac{\phi}{2}$	0	1	$\frac{1}{\sqrt{2}}$	$-\frac{1}{\sqrt{2}}$	$\frac{1}{\sqrt{2}}$	$-\frac{1}{\sqrt{2}}$
$e^{-i\theta/2}$	1	1	1	1	$\frac{1}{\sqrt{2}}(1-i)$	$\frac{1}{\sqrt{2}}(1-i)$
$e^{i\theta/2}$	1	1	1	1	$\frac{1}{\sqrt{2}}(1+i)$	$\frac{1}{\sqrt{2}}(1+i)$
α_+	$\begin{pmatrix}1\\0\end{pmatrix}$	$\begin{pmatrix}0\\1\end{pmatrix}$	$\frac{1}{\sqrt{2}}\begin{pmatrix}1\\1\end{pmatrix}$	$\frac{1}{\sqrt{2}}\begin{pmatrix}1\\-1\end{pmatrix}$	$\frac{1}{2}\begin{pmatrix}1-i\\1+i\end{pmatrix}$	$\frac{1}{2}\begin{pmatrix}1-i\\-1-i\end{pmatrix}$

4.4 *Conclusion*

The conditions imposed by (4.1) guarantee that, if a representation of $\{S_\alpha\}$ and W_S exists in $\mathbb{C}^2$, then it is the one which employs the Pauli spin matrices. Further, if this representation is faithful, then the function t of (4.2) is given by

$$t(\widehat{\alpha\beta}) = \cos^2 \frac{1}{2}\,(\widehat{\alpha\beta}) \tag{4.9}$$

It follows that, unless we can show why this is the only t-function possible, we have not established that $\{S_\alpha\}$ *must* be representable in $\mathbb{C}^2$. But (4.9) cannot be derived from (4.1a–g). Any monotone function t_ψ of the form

$$t_\psi(\phi) = \cos^2[\psi(\phi)]$$

(where, as the notation implies, $\psi(\phi)$ is a function of ϕ) is consistent with these assumptions, provided that

$$\psi\left(\frac{\pi}{2}-\phi\right)=\frac{\pi}{2}-\psi(\phi)$$

Typical admissible variations of $\psi(\phi)$ with ϕ are shown in Figure 4.4.

As an illustration, consider this whimsical example, proposed by Mielnik (1968, p. 55; see also Beltrametti and Cassinelli, 1981, pp. 204–207). Imagine that we have a spherical container, exactly half full of some liquid. Imagine, further, that the surface of the liquid in the sphere is always a plane through the sphere's center. This container, we assume, can be divided in half by a thin partition along any plane through its center, and whenever this is done we find that all the liquid ends up on one side or other of the partition; thus the liquid exhibits quantum behavior. Furthermore, the side of the partition that the liquid moves to is not determined; rather, there is a certain probability of the liquid's moving to one side of the partition rather than the other, and this probability depends on the orientation of the partition to the original surface of the liquid, as follows. If V_L is the (volume of the) hemisphere originally occupied by the liquid, and V_A is the hemisphere on side A of the partition, then the probability that all the liquid will be found on side A of the partition is given by

$$p(A)=\frac{V_A \cap V_L}{V_L}$$

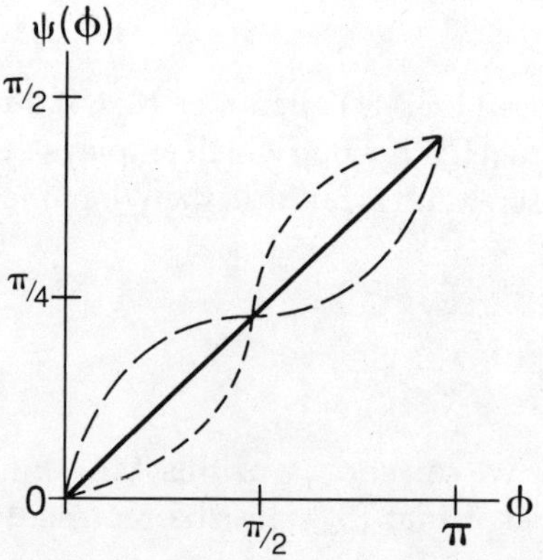

Figure 4.4 Functions $\psi(\phi)$ such that $\psi\left(\frac{\pi}{2}-\phi\right)=\frac{\pi}{2}-\psi(\phi)$.

Thus, for example, if the partition is introduced along the existing surface of the liquid, there is zero probability that the liquid will move to occupy the other half of the sphere.

This imaginary device conforms to (4.1a–g). For any point α on the sphere (see Figure 4.5) there is an observable S_α which we "measure" by the experiment of introducing a partition along the plane equatorial with respect to α. The "value" of this observable is positive if the liquid moves to that side of the partition where α lies, and negative if it moves to the other side. The state w of the system is given by the original orientation of the liquid's surface; the point α_w is the polar point of the hemisphere originally occupied by the liquid.

It's easy to verify that all seven clauses of (4.1) hold but, as Mielnik points out, there is no Hilbert-space representation of such a device. And, in the light of our previous discussion, we can see why: the dependence of the probability $p_\alpha(\beta^+)$ on the angle $\widehat{\alpha\beta}$ is given not by

$$p_\alpha(\beta^+) = \cos^2 \frac{1}{2}\,(\widehat{\alpha\beta})$$

but instead by

$$p_\alpha(\beta^+) = 1 - \frac{\widehat{\alpha\beta}}{\pi}$$

What constraint, then, must we add to (4.1) to guarantee that (4.9) holds? Well, what is nowhere expressed in the assumptions (4.1) is the sense in

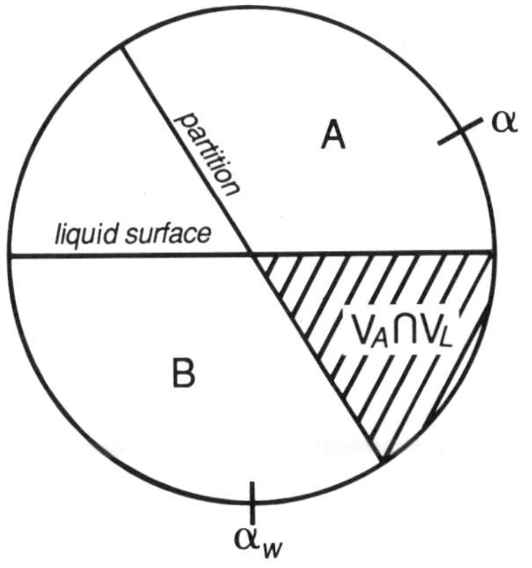

Figure 4.5

which the members of $\{S_\alpha\}$ are components of a physical quantity. From (4.8) we see that, if we *assume* that $\{S_\alpha\}$ is representable as a set of Hermitian operators in $\mathbb{C}^2$, then these are indeed vector operators, which can be resolved into components (Messiah, 1958, vol. 2, p. 509). But it's not obvious how such a relation might be expressible just in terms of the probabilities that states assign to values of S_α. Clearly such *probabilities* cannot add vectorially, on pain of yielding probabilities less than zero.

However, a possible condition on *expectation values* presents itself. We write $\langle S_\alpha \rangle_w$ for the expectation value of S_α, as in Section 2.4; then

$$\langle S_\alpha \rangle_w = p_w(\alpha^+) - p_w(\alpha^-) = 2p_w(\alpha^+) - 1$$

With respect to an arbitrarily chosen Cartesian coordinate system, let α have coordinates α_x, α_y, and α_z (see Figure 4.6). Thus $\alpha = (\phi_\alpha, \theta_\alpha) = (\alpha_x, \alpha_y, \alpha_z)$. We now add to assumptions (4.1) the assumption

$$\langle S_\alpha \rangle_w = \alpha_x \langle S_x \rangle_w + \alpha_y \langle S_y \rangle_w + \alpha_z \langle S_z \rangle_w \tag{4.10}$$

Given (4.10) it follows that

$$t(\widehat{\alpha\beta}) = \cos^2 \frac{1}{2} (\widehat{\alpha\beta})$$

To see this, assume that the system is in a pure state w and that the angular separation of α and α_w is ϕ. We now choose a coordinate system such that

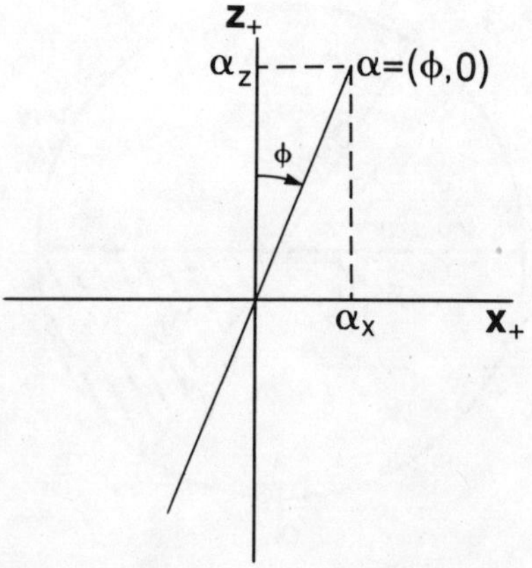

Figure 4.6 Components of $\alpha = (\phi, 0)$.

$\alpha = (\phi,0) = (\sin\phi,0,\cos\phi)$ and $\alpha_w = (0,0) = (0,0,1)$. Then

$$\langle S_x \rangle_w = 0 = \langle S_y \rangle_w \qquad \langle S_z \rangle_w = 1$$

whence, from (4.10),

$$\langle S_\alpha \rangle_w = \cos\phi \langle S_z \rangle_w = \cos\phi$$

$$2p_w(\alpha^+) - 1 = \cos\phi$$

$$p_w(\alpha^+) = \cos^2 \frac{1}{2} (\phi) \qquad \text{[Q.E.D.]}$$

Equivalent to (4.10), given assumptions (4.1), is:

(4.11) For any mutually orthogonal triple of points (α,β,γ) in $\mathbb{R}^3$,

$$\langle S_\alpha \rangle^2 + \langle S_\beta \rangle^2 + \langle S_\gamma \rangle^2 = 1$$

The question posed at the beginning of the chapter now has an answer. Under the assumptions (4.1) and (4.10), a family $\{S_\alpha\}$ of observables and a set W_S of states has a representation in $\mathbb{C}^2$, and this representation, involving the Pauli spin matrices, is just that employed in quantum mechanics for the spin-$\frac{1}{2}$ particle. Further, these assumptions are nontrivial; as Mielnik's example shows, there could be "quantum systems" for which no such minimal representation was possible.

Two more general conclusions can be drawn. The first is that any interpretation of quantum mechanics must recognize that the theory deals with families of observables which are knitted together in a way precisely captured by the Hilbert-space representation. The mutual interdependence of the members of $\{S_\alpha\}$ is not a functional interdependence of the kind found in classical mechanics, but an essentially probabilistic interdependence; the observables are, in the technical sense, mutually transformable, as defined in (3.9). Prima facie, any interpretation which invites us to consider them independently should be mistrusted.

The second is that the way in which the relations between the observables S_α in quantum mechanics are determined by the symmetries of three-dimensional physical space typifies the way in which the relations within any family of mutually transformable observables are determined by underlying symmetries in nature.

5

Density Operators and Tensor-Product Spaces

When the idea of a *mixed state* was introduced in Chapter 3, I suggested that a weighted sum of projectors could represent such a state but postponed the problem of providing a statistical algorithm. The problem is that of finding a natural generalization of Equation (2.1):

$$p_{\mathbf{v}}(A,\Delta) = \langle \mathbf{v} | \mathbf{P}^A_\Delta \mathbf{v} \rangle$$

that is, of the equation whereby to each experimental question (A,Δ) the state assigns a probability.

I will attend to this problem first. In the rest of the chapter I will discuss the vector-space representation of states of complex systems; when two hitherto independent systems interact, they behave as one complex system, and we can represent the states of this complex system, and observables on it, within a new vector space, the *tensor product* of the spaces appropriate to the two component systems.

5.1 *Operators of the Trace Class*

As a first step toward the discussion of mixed states, I introduce the concept of the *trace* of an operator.

Consider a Hermitian operator $\mathbf{A}$ on a Hilbert space $\mathcal{H}$. $\mathbf{A}$ is said to be *positive* if, for all $\mathbf{v}$ in $\mathcal{H}$, $\langle \mathbf{v} | \mathbf{A}\mathbf{v} \rangle \geq 0$. In fact it follows from this condition alone that, if $\mathbf{A}$ is positive, then (i) $\mathbf{A}$ is Hermitian, and (ii) the eigenvalues of $\mathbf{A}$ are positive (☆). Now let $\{\mathbf{v}_i\}$ be an orthonormal basis for $\mathcal{H}$ (see Section 1.13). If $\mathbf{A}$ is positive and $\mathcal{H}$ is finitely dimensional, we can always evaluate $\Sigma_i \langle \mathbf{v}_i | \mathbf{A}\mathbf{v}_i \rangle$, and even in the infinitely dimensional case there are still positive operators $\mathbf{A}$ for which $\Sigma_i \langle \mathbf{v}_i | \mathbf{A}\mathbf{v}_i \rangle$ is finite. We say that an operator $\mathbf{A}$ belongs to the *trace class* provided $\mathbf{A}$ is positive and $\Sigma_i \langle \mathbf{v}_i | \mathbf{A}\mathbf{v}_i \rangle$ is finite. (See Fano, 1971, chap. 5.12.)

This definition is acceptable because, surprisingly, the value of $\Sigma_i\langle \mathbf{v}_i|\mathbf{A}\mathbf{v}_i\rangle$ is independent of the particular orthonormal basis $\{\mathbf{v}_i\}$ which is chosen. [It's a comparatively simple exercise (☆☆) to show this.] Thus its value depends only on **A**, and we call it the *trace* of **A**:

(5.1) $$\mathrm{Tr}(\mathbf{A}) \underset{\mathrm{df}}{=} \sum_i \langle \mathbf{v}_i|\mathbf{A}\mathbf{v}_i\rangle$$

where $\{\mathbf{v}_i\}$ is any orthonormal basis for $\mathcal{H}$.

Since we're at liberty to choose any orthonormal basis whatever to evaluate Tr(**A**), we may as well use the basis which makes life easiest. For instance, let **P** be a projection operator onto a ray of $\mathcal{H}$. In this case we choose an orthonormal basis $\{\mathbf{v}_i\}$ in which one vector, $\mathbf{v}_j$, lies within the ray in question. The other vectors in this basis are all orthogonal to this ray, and so we have

$$\mathbf{P}\mathbf{v}_j = \mathbf{v}_j \quad \text{and} \quad \mathbf{P}\mathbf{v}_i = \mathbf{0} \quad \text{whenever } i \neq j$$

whence

(5.2) $$\mathrm{Tr}(\mathbf{P}) = \sum_i \langle \mathbf{v}_i|\mathbf{P}\mathbf{v}_i\rangle = \langle \mathbf{v}_j|\mathbf{v}_j\rangle = 1$$

It is easy to show that, for any projection operator **P** onto an n-dimensional subspace of $\mathcal{H}$ (where n is finite),

(5.3) $$\mathrm{Tr}(\mathbf{P}) = n$$ (☆)

In addition, we can use the spectral decomposition theorem (1.32) to show that if **A** is in the trace class and there is no degeneracy, then the trace of **A** is the sum of its eigenvalues (☆); since **A** is Hermitian, it follows that Tr(**A**) is always real. When **A** is given a matrix representation, the sum of its diagonal elements gives the trace of **A**.

The trace has the following properties. If a is any real number and **A** and **B** are operators in the trace class, we have

(5.4) $$\mathrm{Tr}(a\mathbf{A}) = a\mathrm{Tr}(\mathbf{A})$$ (☆)

(5.5) $$\mathrm{Tr}(\mathbf{A}+\mathbf{B}) = \mathrm{Tr}(\mathbf{A}) + \mathrm{Tr}(\mathbf{B})$$ (☆)

An important result involves the product of a trace-class operator and a bounded linear operator. **B** is *bounded* if there is a real number b such that, for all $\mathbf{v} \in \mathcal{H}$, $|\mathbf{B}\mathbf{v}| \leq b|\mathbf{v}|$; all continuous operators are bounded (and conversely—see Jordan, 1969, sec. 6), and all linear operators on a finitely dimensional vector space are bounded.

(5.6) If **A** is a trace-class operator and **B** is a bounded linear operator, then **AB** and **BA** are both in the trace class, and $\text{Tr}(\mathbf{AB}) = \text{Tr}(\mathbf{BA})$. (☆☆☆)

(See Jordan, 1969, sec. 22.)

5.2 *Density Operators*

We are particularly interested in a subset of the trace class:

(5.7) **D** is said to be a *density operator* if **D** is a trace-class operator and $\text{Tr}(\mathbf{D}) = 1$.

The terms *statistical operator* and *density matrix* are also used.

From what has been said, any projection operator **P** projecting onto a ray of $\mathcal{H}$ is a density operator. Further, let $\{\mathbf{P}_i\}$ be a family of projection operators projecting onto rays of $\mathcal{H}$. Then, by (5.4) and (5.5),

(5.8) $\mathbf{D} = \Sigma_i a_i \mathbf{P}_i$ is a density operator, provided (a) $0 \leq a_i$, for each a_i, and (b) $\Sigma_i a_i = 1$. (☆)

We see that (5.8) gives us a recipe for constructing density operators from projectors. But does it also give us a prescription for decomposing a density operator? Specifically, (i) can we always express a density operator as a weighted sum of projectors, and (ii) is this decomposition unique?

The answer to (i) is yes. Every density operator **D** admits a set $\{a_i\}$ of eigenvalues. (This is because every density operator is compact: see Fano, 1971, pp. 376, 291.) Assume, for the moment, that there is no degeneracy (see Section 1.14). From the discussion in the previous section, these eigenvalues are all positive and add to one, and the spectral decomposition theorem (1.32) then guarantees that a set $\{\mathbf{P}_i\}$ of projectors exists (each projector $\mathbf{P}_i$ projecting onto a ray containing eigenvectors of **D** with eigenvalue a_i) and that $\mathbf{D} = \Sigma_i a_i \mathbf{P}_i$.

Even if there is degeneracy, we can still apply the spectral decomposition theorem and stipulate that each $\mathbf{P}_i$ project onto a ray of $\mathcal{H}$. We will then find that not all the a_i are distinct, that $a_j = a_k$, for instance. But all this means is that some a_i are going to appear more than once in the summation that yields $\Sigma_i a_i = 1$ in clause (b) of (5.8).

The possibility of degeneracy, however, is one reason we cannot guarantee a unique decomposition for **D** (in other words, why the answer to the second question is no). Assume, for instance, that we have $a_j = a_k$. Then the rays onto which $\mathbf{P}_j$ and $\mathbf{P}_k$ project span a plane L_{jk} in $\mathcal{H}$, and, if $\mathbf{P}'_j$ and $\mathbf{P}'_k$ are projectors onto any two orthogonal rays of L_{jk}, we can replace $\mathbf{P}_j$ and $\mathbf{P}_k$ in $\{\mathbf{P}_i\}$ by $\mathbf{P}'_j$ and $\mathbf{P}'_k$ to form a new family $\{\mathbf{P}'_i\}$ of projectors (such that, for $j \neq i \neq k$, $\mathbf{P}'_i = \mathbf{P}_i$). We then obtain,

$$\mathbf{D} = \sum_i a_i \mathbf{P}_i = \sum_i a_i \mathbf{P}'_i$$

As an example, consider the projection operators associated with the Pauli spin matrices (see Section 1.7). The rays projected onto by $\mathbf{P}_{x+}$ and $\mathbf{P}_{x-}$ span the whole space $\mathbb{C}^2$, as do those projected onto by $\mathbf{P}_{y+}$ and $\mathbf{P}_{y-}$ and those projected onto by $\mathbf{P}_{z+}$ and $\mathbf{P}_{z-}$. Numerical computation confirms that

$$\frac{1}{2}\mathbf{P}_{x+} + \frac{1}{2}\mathbf{P}_{x-} = \frac{1}{2}\mathbf{P}_{y+} + \frac{1}{2}\mathbf{P}_{y-} = \frac{1}{2}\mathbf{P}_{z+} + \frac{1}{2}\mathbf{P}_{z-} \qquad (\star)$$

More fundamentally, the very construction employed in (5.8) ensures that density operators do not, in general, have a unique decomposition. For in that construction there was no requirement that the rays onto which the projectors $\mathbf{P}_i$ projected were to be mutually orthogonal. Yet we know from the spectral decomposition theorem that for each **D** there exists a set $\{\mathbf{P}'_j\}$ of projectors onto mutually orthogonal rays such that $\mathbf{D} = \Sigma_i b_i \mathbf{P}'_i$. Thus, in general, we have

$$\mathbf{D} = \sum_i a_i \mathbf{P}_i = \sum_j b_j \mathbf{P}'_j \quad \text{but} \quad \{\mathbf{P}_i\} \neq \{\mathbf{P}'_j\}$$

and so a density operator has a nonunique decomposition. In fact, any density operator **D** which is not itself a projector is expressible in an infinite number of ways as a weighted sum of projectors onto rays, according to the formula $\mathbf{D} = \Sigma_i a_i \mathbf{P}_i$ (with $a_i \geq 0$ for each a_i and $\Sigma_i a_i = 1$).

5.3 *Density Operators on* $\mathbb{C}^2$

In this section, following Beltrametti and Cassinelli (1981, chap. 4.2), I quote a number of results for the operators on $\mathbb{C}^2$. They are generalized for operators on the space $\mathbb{C}^n$ by U. Fano (1957, sec. 7). The reader is invited to supply the proofs of these statements.

Consider the four operators on $\mathbb{C}^2$:

$$\sigma_1 = \begin{pmatrix} 0 & 1 \\ 1 & 0 \end{pmatrix} \quad \sigma_2 = \begin{pmatrix} 0 & -i \\ i & 0 \end{pmatrix} \quad \sigma_3 = \begin{pmatrix} 1 & 0 \\ 0 & -1 \end{pmatrix} \quad \mathbf{I} = \begin{pmatrix} 1 & 0 \\ 0 & 1 \end{pmatrix}$$

These are, of course, familiar: $\sigma_1 = 2\mathbf{S}_x$, $\sigma_2 = 2\mathbf{S}_y$, and $\sigma_3 = \mathbf{S}_z$ (see Section 1.7).

Let $\mathbf{A}$ be a linear operator on $\mathbb{C}^2$.

(5.9) If $\mathbf{A}$ is Hermitian, then there are real numbers ρ_1, ρ_2, ρ_3, and ρ_4 such that

$$\mathbf{A} = \rho_1\sigma_1 + \rho_2\sigma_2 + \rho_3\sigma_3 + \rho_4\mathbf{I} \qquad \text{[see Section 1.6]} \qquad (\star)$$

(5.10) If $\mathbf{A}$ is a density operator, then $\rho_4 = \frac{1}{2}$. (☆)

(5.11) If $\mathbf{A}$ is a projection operator, then
(i) $\rho_4 = \frac{1}{2}$ and
(ii) $\rho_1^2 + \rho_2^2 + \rho_3^2 = \frac{1}{4}$ (by idempotence). (☆)

Hence, writing $r_1 = 2\rho_1$, and so on,

(5.12) If $\mathbf{A}$ is a projection operator, then $\mathbf{A}$ may be written in the form

$$\mathbf{A} = \frac{1}{2}(r_1\sigma_1 + r_2\sigma_2 + r_3\sigma_3 + \mathbf{I})$$

where $r_1^2 + r_2^2 + r_3^2 = 1$. (☆)

(5.13) Any three real numbers r_1, r_2, and r_3 such that $r_1^2 + r_2^2 + r_3^2 = 1$ specify a projection operator on $\mathbb{C}^2$; the set of all projection operators on $\mathbb{C}^2$ is in one-to-one correspondence with the set of points on the unit sphere of $\mathbb{R}^3$. (☆)

Let p_1 and p_2 be the points on the unit sphere of $\mathbb{R}^3$ corresponding to the projectors $\mathbf{P}_1$ and $\mathbf{P}_2$ on $\mathbb{C}^2$.

(5.14) A density operator on $\mathbb{C}^2$ expressible as the weighted sum of $\mathbf{P}_1$ and $\mathbf{P}_2$ is represented by a point within the unit sphere of $\mathbb{R}^3$ on the line p_1p_2 (see Figure 5.1). (☆)

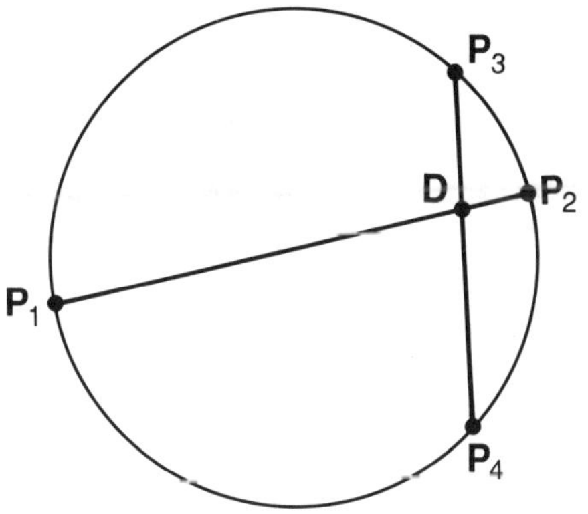

Figure 5.1 The set of density operators on $\mathbb{C}^2$; $\mathbf{D} = a_1\mathbf{P}_1 + a_2\mathbf{P}_2 = b_1\mathbf{P}_3 + b_2\mathbf{P}_4$; $\mathbf{P}_1$ is orthogonal to $\mathbf{P}_2$.

(5.15) If **A** is a density operator on $\mathbb{C}^2$, then **A** may be written in the form

$$\mathbf{A} = \frac{1}{2}(r_1\sigma_1 + r_2\sigma_2 + r_3\sigma_3 + \mathbf{I})$$

where $r_1^2 + r_2^2 + r_3^2 \leq 1$. (☆☆)

The last two results of this section are included solely on account of their elegance; they will not be used in what follows.

(5.16) The set of Hermitian operators on $\mathbb{C}^2$ forms a four-dimensional vector space over the reals, and $\{\sigma_1, \sigma_2, \sigma_3, \mathbf{I}\}$ forms a basis for this space. (☆)

(5.17) $\frac{1}{2}\mathrm{Tr}(\mathbf{AB})$ supplies an inner product for this space; with respect to this inner product, the basis $\{\sigma_1, \sigma_2, \sigma_3, \mathbf{I}\}$ is orthonormal (see Section 1.9). (☆)

5.4 *Pure and Mixed States*

We can now answer the question posed at the beginning of this chapter: what algorithm can generate the quantum-mechanical probabilities for mixed states?

Let $\mathbf{P}_\mathbf{v}$ be the projector onto the ray containing a normalized vector **v**, and let **Q** be any projector on the space $\mathcal{H}$. If $\{\mathbf{v}_i\}$ is any orthonormal basis for $\mathcal{H}$, then, by definition,

$$\begin{aligned}\mathrm{Tr}(\mathbf{QP_v}) &= \sum_i \langle \mathbf{v}_i | \mathbf{QP_v v}_i \rangle \\ &= \mathrm{Tr}(\mathbf{P_v Q}) \qquad \text{[by (5.6)]}\end{aligned}$$

Using the strategy used to derive (5.2), let us take a basis $\{\mathbf{v}_i\}$ containing $\mathbf{v}$ as one of its members. Then $\mathbf{P_v v} = \mathbf{v}$, and $\mathbf{P_v v}_i = \mathbf{0}$ when $\mathbf{v}_i \neq \mathbf{v}$, whence

$$\mathrm{Tr}(\mathbf{P_v Q}) = \sum_i \langle \mathbf{v}_i | \mathbf{QP_v v}_i \rangle = \langle \mathbf{v} | \mathbf{Qv} \rangle$$

But this is exactly the expression occurring in the statistical algorithm of quantum theory; if $\mathbf{Q} = \mathbf{P}^A_\Delta$—that is, $\mathbf{Q}$ is the projector onto the subspace representing the experimental question (A,Δ)—we have, by (2.2),

$$\langle \mathbf{v} | \mathbf{Qv} \rangle = \langle \mathbf{v} | \mathbf{P}^A_\Delta \mathbf{v} \rangle = p_{\mathbf{v}}(A,\Delta)$$

It follows that, if we represent a pure state by the projector $\mathbf{P_v}$ rather than the vector $\mathbf{v}$, then $p_{\mathbf{v}}(A,\Delta)$, the probability that this pure state assigns to (A,Δ) is given by

(5.18) $$p_{\mathbf{v}}(A,\Delta) = \mathrm{Tr}(\mathbf{P_v P}^A_\Delta)$$

Notice that, by taking $\mathbf{P_v}$ to represent a certain pure state, we eliminate the oddity we noticed in Section 3.3, that two distinct vectors can represent the same state. This happens when $\mathbf{u} = c\mathbf{v}$ and $|c| = 1$. Since any two such vectors lie within the same ray, there is only one projector corresponding to the state they represent.

We see that a projector $\mathbf{P_v}$ onto a ray acts as a probability measure μ_p on the set $S(\mathcal{H})$ of subspaces of $\mathcal{H}$, such that, for any $L \in S(\mathcal{H})$,

$$\mu_p(L) = \mathrm{Tr}(\mathbf{P_v P}_L)$$

(where $\mathbf{P}_L$ projects onto L). It is straightforward to show that, if we have a (finite) set of probability measures $\{\mu_i\}$, then any weighted sum $\Sigma_i a_i \mu_i$ of such measures is also a probability measure, provided that (a) $a_i \geq 0$, for each a_i, and (b) $\Sigma_i a_i = 1$. (To see this, confirm that the Kolmogorov axioms (3.2) and their generalizations (8.4) all hold.)

But now consider a density operator $\mathbf{D}$, where $\mathbf{D} = \Sigma_i a_i \mathbf{P}_i$. Each $\mathbf{P}_i$ projects onto a ray of $\mathcal{H}$, and to each corresponds a probability measure μ_i on $S(\mathcal{H})$.

For any subspace L and projector $\mathbf{P}_L$ we have, using (5.4) and (5.5),

$$\begin{aligned}\mathrm{Tr}(\mathbf{D}\mathbf{P}_L) &= \mathrm{Tr}\left(\sum_i a_i \mathbf{P}_i \mathbf{P}_L\right)\\ &= \sum_i a_i \mathrm{Tr}(\mathbf{P}_i \mathbf{P}_L)\\ &= \sum_i a_i \mu_i(L)\end{aligned}$$

Since $\mathbf{D}$ is a density operator, the constraints on the a_i are just those we need; thus to $\mathbf{D}$ there corresponds the probability measure $\mu_{\mathrm{D}} = \Sigma_i a_i \mu_i$ on the set $S(\mathcal{H})$ of subspaces of $\mathcal{H}$. To each subspace L of $\mathcal{H}$ it assigns the weighted sum of the probabilities assigned by the pure states $\mathbf{P}_i$ according to the algorithm

(5.19) $\quad \mu_{\mathrm{D}}(L) = \mathrm{Tr}(\mathbf{D}\mathbf{P}_L)$

Thus, if L represents the experimental question (A,Δ), we can now generalize the statistical algorithm of quantum mechanics as follows:

(5.20) $\quad p_{\mathrm{D}}(A,\Delta) = \mathrm{Tr}(\mathbf{D}\mathbf{P}^A_\Delta)$

Within this equation, the density operator $\mathbf{D}$ represents the state of a system.

The use of density operators allows us to give a vector-space representation to *mixed states.* Mathematically, these are just appropriately weighted sums of pure states, so that, for instance, if $\mathbf{P}_1$ and $\mathbf{P}_2$ represent distinct pure states, then any density operator $\mathbf{D} = a_1\mathbf{P}_1 + a_2\mathbf{P}_2$ (with $a_1 > 0$, $a_2 > 0$, and $a_1 + a_2 = 1$) represents a mixed state. We express this fact by saying that the set of states forms a *convex set,* of which the *extremal points* are the pure states. This geometrical mode of expression seems particularly apt in the case of $\mathbb{C}^2$, where the terms *convex set* and *extremal point* find a literal representation. Recall from Section 5.3 that the set of density operators on $\mathbb{C}^2$—that is, the set of all states—can be put into one-to-one correspondence with the set of points in the unit ball of $\mathbb{R}^3$. Within the set of states, the extremal points, or pure states, represented by projectors onto the rays of $\mathbb{C}^2$, are in one-to-one correspondence with the points on the surface of this ball (in other words, with the points on the unit sphere of $\mathbb{R}^3$). Of course, after the discussion of the spin-$\frac{1}{2}$ particle in Chapter 4, this latter fact should hardly come as a surprise.

Let me once more emphasize the distinction between a superposition and a mixture of two pure states, using, yet again, the example of spin. Consider the pure states $\mathbf{z}_+$ and $\mathbf{z}_-$ (equivalently, $\mathbf{P}_{z+}$ and $\mathbf{P}_{z-}$). We can form a superposition $\frac{1}{2}\mathbf{z}_+ + \frac{1}{2}\mathbf{z}_-$ of these states, which we normalize to yield $\sqrt{2}(\frac{1}{2}\mathbf{z}_+ + \frac{1}{2}\mathbf{z}_-) = \mathbf{x}_+$ (equivalently, $\mathbf{P}_{x+}$). This is a pure state. However, $\frac{1}{2}\mathbf{P}_{z+} + \frac{1}{2}\mathbf{P}_{z-}$ represents a mixed state: as we saw in Section 5.2,

$$\frac{1}{2}\mathbf{P}_{z+} + \frac{1}{2}\mathbf{P}_{z-} = \frac{1}{2}\mathbf{P}_{x+} + \frac{1}{2}\mathbf{P}_{x-} = \frac{1}{2}\mathbf{P}_{y+} + \frac{1}{2}\mathbf{P}_{y-} \neq \mathbf{P}_{x+}$$

This particular mixed state, in which the particle is, as we say, completely *unpolarized*, is one we shall come across again in future chapters.

The customary interpretation of mixed states used to be the *ignorance interpretation*. According to this interpretation, a system in a state $\mathbf{D} = a_1\mathbf{P}_1 + a_2\mathbf{P}_2$ was really in some pure state ($\mathbf{P}_1$ or $\mathbf{P}_2$), and the coefficients a_1 and a_2 represented the likelihoods of its being in one or the other; these were *epistemic* probabilities, representing our best estimates of the chances.

This interpretation of a mixed state is clearly appropriate to a classical theory (see Section 3.5), but it is open to two objections in the quantum-mechanical case. The first stems from the nonuniqueness of decomposition: as we saw in Section 5.2, any density operator **D** which is not itself a projector can be decomposed in an infinite number of ways. Now this may just mean that our ignorance when we represent a state by **D** is (vastly) greater than we had assumed; still, it does seem odd that when we cannot say which are the possible pure states of a system, we can assign to a particular pair of them probabilities which add to one. In the case of the unpolarized spin-$\frac{1}{2}$ particle, for instance, can we say that there is a probability of 0.5 that the particle is in the $\mathbf{x}_+$ state and a probability of 0.5 that it is in the $\mathbf{x}_-$ state, and that the same holds true for the $\mathbf{y}_+$ state and the $\mathbf{y}_-$ state, and for the $\mathbf{z}_+$ state and the $\mathbf{z}_-$ state, not to mention thc nondenumerable infinity of other pairs of states associated with different directions in space? And this is not merely a difficulty associated with the central point of the set of states; *all* mixed states allow an infinite number of decompositions.

It may be that the particular decomposition we should consider is in all cases determined for us by the preparation the system has undergone. If so, this is a fact that the formal specification of the state fails to reveal. And there still remains a second, possibly more telling, objection against the ignorance interpretation, which I will spell out in Section 5.8.

Nonetheless, even though the ignorance interpretation is suspect, the following remains true.

Assume that we prepare an ensemble of systems in a mixed state **D** and that **D** can be decomposed according to the equation $\mathbf{D} = \Sigma_i a_i \mathbf{P}_i$. Then our estimate of the relative frequency of any given experimental result from this ensemble is exactly what we would get if the ensemble consisted of various subensembles, each in a pure state $\mathbf{P}_i$, and each of these subensembles were represented in the whole ensemble with relative frequency a_i. This follows from the fact that, for any projector $\mathbf{P}$,

$$\mathrm{Tr}(\mathbf{DP}) = \sum_i a_i \mathrm{Tr}(\mathbf{P}_i\mathbf{P})$$

5.5 *The Dynamical Evolution of States*

When we use density operators to represent states, Schrödinger's equation takes the form

$$\mathbf{D}_t = \mathbf{U}_t\mathbf{D}_0\mathbf{U}_t^{-1} \tag{5.21}$$

$\mathbf{U}_t$ is the same unitary operator that appears in (2.8b):

$$\mathbf{U}_t = e^{-i\mathbf{H}t}$$

Equation (5.21) extends Schrödinger's equation to mixed states. A notable feature of the dynamical evolution it describes is that it leaves invariant the convex structure of the set of states. Assume, that is, that a mixture $\mathbf{D}$ is a weighted sum of two pure states, $\mathbf{P}_a$ and $\mathbf{P}_b$, so that

$$\mathbf{D} = a\mathbf{P}_a + b\mathbf{P}_b$$

Let $\mathbf{D}$, $\mathbf{P}_a$, and $\mathbf{P}_b$ evolve under (5.21) in time t to $\mathbf{D}'$, $\mathbf{P}'_a$, and $\mathbf{P}'_b$, respectively. Then

$$\mathbf{D}' = a\mathbf{P}'_a + b\mathbf{P}'_b$$

A corollary of this rule is that if we prepare an ensemble in a mixed state $\mathbf{D}$ which is statistically indistinguishable from a collection of subensembles, each in a pure state $\mathbf{P}_i$ (as in the case discussed in the last paragraph of the previous section), then the ensemble and the collection will remain indistinguishable under dynamical evolution.

Of course, if the ignorance interpretation of mixed states is the correct one, this is as it should be; an ensemble in a mixed state is not just statistically indistinguishable from a collection of subensembles, it *is* such a collection and the preservation of the convex structure of the set of states is just what we would expect.

If the ignorance interpretation is rejected, however, the assumption that, statistically, mixed states behave as though it were true is one that leads to striking results. A theorem due to Kadison (1951), effectively the converse of the result quoted above, shows the consequences of assuming (C) *preservation of convexity:* that the convex structure of the set of states is preserved under dynamical evolution.

Let f_t be a mapping of the set S of density operators on a Hilbert space $\mathcal{H}$ onto itself: $f_t: S \to S$. Then

(5.22) If f_t preserves the convex structure of the set S, then there is a unitary operator $\mathbf{U}_t$ on $\mathcal{H}$ (with inverse $\mathbf{U}_t^{-1}$) such that, for every density operator $\mathbf{D}$ in S,

$$f_t(\mathbf{D}) = \mathbf{U}_t\mathbf{D}\mathbf{U}_t^{-1}$$

Recall now the "derivation" of the Schrödinger equation offered in Section 3.10. We see that the assumption (C) does the work of the assumptions (4), (5), and (6) made there. In other words, if we assume (1) statistical determinism, (2) homogeneity of time, (3) continuity, and (C) preservation of convexity, then the dynamical evolution of a system is given by a family $\{\mathbf{U}_t\}$ of unitary operators forming a weakly continuous one-parameter group parameterized by the reals (see Simon, 1976; also Beltrametti and Cassinelli, 1981, pp. 52–55, 252–254). As before, Stone's theorem tells us that there is a Hermitian operator $\mathbf{A}$ such that, for all t,

$$\mathbf{U}_t = e^{-i\mathbf{A}t}$$

5.6 Gleason's Theorem

In Section 5.4 I showed that the probability measures on the set $S(\mathcal{H})$ of subspaces of a Hilbert space include not only those representable by normalized vectors (the pure states), but also those representable by density operators on the space (both pure states and mixed states). The vectors and density operators generate probabilities according to the (by now) familiar algorithms

$$\mu_{\mathbf{v}}(L) = \langle \mathbf{v} | \mathbf{P}_L \mathbf{v} \rangle \quad \text{and} \quad \mu_{\mathbf{D}}(L) = \mathrm{Tr}(\mathbf{D}\mathbf{P}_L)$$

respectively.

The question arises: does this exhaust the set of possible probability measures on $S(\mathcal{H})$? In other words, is every probability measure on $S(\mathcal{H})$ representable by a density operator? To this question, "The affirmative answer was assumed by von Neumann, conjectured by Mackey, and proved by Gleason" (Beltrametti and Cassinelli, 1981, p. 115; see Mackey, 1963; Gleason, 1957).

The formal statement of Gleason's theorem runs as follows.

(5.23) Let μ be any measure on the closed subspaces of a separable (real or complex) Hilbert space $\mathcal{H}$ of dimension at least 3. There exists a positive self-adjoint operator $\mathbf{T}$ of the trace class such that, for all closed subspaces L of $\mathcal{H}$,

$$\mu(L) = \mathrm{Tr}(\mathbf{T}\mathbf{P}_L)$$

The term *self-adjoint* is effectively synonymous with *Hermitian* (but see Fano, 1971, p. 279). If we demand that μ be a probability measure, thus requiring that $\mu(\mathcal{H}) = 1$, then $\mathrm{Tr}(\mathbf{T}) = 1$; in other words, $\mathbf{T}$ is a density operator.

Note that Gleason's theorem only applies to Hilbert spaces of dimensionality higher than two. Thus the space $\mathbb{C}^2$ used for most of our examples is in this regard anomalous. This doesn't mean that we can't represent spin states by density operators on $\mathbb{C}^2$, but rather that we can't know that this exhausts the set of possible states. As will appear in Chapter 6, this fact is linked to the possibility of a "hidden-variable reconstruction" of the spin statistics for the spin-$\frac{1}{2}$ particle.

To use the discreet euphemism preferred by mathematicians, Gleason's original proof of the theorem is nontrivial. However, in 1985 an "elementary" proof was given by Cooke, Keane, and Moran, and this is reproduced in Appendix A.

The heart of the theorem is the proof that, in Gleason's terms, every frame function is regular. A *frame function* of weight W for $\mathcal{H}$ is a real-valued function f defined on the unit sphere of $\mathcal{H}$ (that is, an assignment of real numbers to the normalized vectors of $\mathcal{H}$) such that, for every orthonormal basis $\{\mathbf{v}_i\}$ of $\mathcal{H}$,

$$\sum_i f(\mathbf{v}_i) = W$$

In other words, whatever orthonormal basis we choose, the assignments f makes to its members always add to the same result.

It follows that a frame function for $\mathcal{H}$ is also a frame function for a closed subspace of $\mathcal{H}$, albeit with a (possibly) different weight, and hence that all normalized vectors in a ray are assigned the same value by a given frame function (☆). At the risk of belaboring the obvious, frame functions of weight 1 are significant to us because we regard any set of mutually orthogonal rays which spans $\mathcal{H}$ as representing a set of mutually exclusive and jointly exhaustive outcomes of a possible experiment; the probabilities assigned to these rays should therefore add to 1.

A frame function is said to be *regular* if there exists a self-adjoint (Hermitian) operator $\mathbf{T}$ on $\mathcal{H}$ such that, for all normalized vectors $\mathbf{v}$,

$$f(\mathbf{v}) = \langle \mathbf{v} | \mathbf{T}\mathbf{v} \rangle$$

It is straightforward (☆) to show that (5.23) follows from the fact that all frame functions are regular.

The importance of the theorem can be summarized in this way. A quantum-mechanical state gives a simultaneous assignment of probabilities to all experimental questions involving observables in a given family (for example, to all questions involving components of spin). Quantum theory allows us to represent all members of this family on the same Hilbert space $\mathcal{H}$, and tells us that certain states are representable by vectors in $\mathcal{H}$. With respect to these (pure) states, the structure of the set of all these experimental questions—the structure of the set of quantum-mechanical *events*—is that of the set $S(\mathcal{H})$ of subspaces of $\mathcal{H}$. Gleason's theorem tells us what the set of all *possible* states on this structure is: it contains just those states which are representable by density operators on $\mathcal{H}$; they form a convex set with the pure states as its extremal points.

As we shall see in the next chapter, any straightforward account of the *properties* of a quantum-mechanical system is ruled out by this result.

5.7 *Composite Systems and Tensor-Product Spaces*

When two quantum-mechanical systems interact, they form a composite system. States and observables of this composite system are then represented in a vector space $\mathcal{H}^A \otimes \mathcal{H}^B$ formed from the spaces $\mathcal{H}^A$ and $\mathcal{H}^B$ in which the states of the two component systems, A and B, are represented; $\mathcal{H}^A \otimes \mathcal{H}^B$ is known as the tensor product of $\mathcal{H}^A$ and $\mathcal{H}^B$. (See Jauch, 1968, chap. 11.7, 11.8; Beltrametti and Cassinelli, 1981, chap. 7.)

We construct $\mathcal{H}^A \otimes \mathcal{H}^B$ so that, if $\{\mathbf{v}_i^A\}$ is an orthonormal basis for $\mathcal{H}^A$ and $\{\mathbf{u}_j^B\}$ is an orthonormal basis for $\mathcal{H}^B$, then the set of pairs $(\mathbf{v}_i^A, \mathbf{u}_j^B)$ forms an orthonormal basis for $\mathcal{H}^A \otimes \mathcal{H}^B$. We use the notation $\mathbf{v}_i^A \otimes \mathbf{u}_j^B$ for the pair $(\mathbf{v}_i^A, \mathbf{u}_j^B)$.

The inner product of the tensor-product space is defined in terms of the inner products on $\mathcal{H}^A$ and $\mathcal{H}^B$:

$$\text{(5.24)} \quad \langle \mathbf{v}_i^A \otimes \mathbf{u}_m^B | \mathbf{v}_j^A \otimes \mathbf{u}_n^B \rangle = \langle \mathbf{v}_i^A | \mathbf{v}_j^A \rangle \langle \mathbf{u}_m^B | \mathbf{u}_n^B \rangle$$

Since the set $\{\mathbf{v}_i^A \otimes \mathbf{u}_j^B\}$ spans $\mathcal{H}^A \otimes \mathcal{H}^B$, this equation defines an inner product on the whole tensor-product space. In any vector space, $|\mathbf{v}| = 0$ if and only if $\mathbf{v}$ is the zero vector [see (1.21)]; it follows from (5.24) that, for any $\mathbf{v}^A \in \mathcal{H}^A$ and $\mathbf{u}^B \in \mathcal{H}^B$,

(5.25) $$\mathbf{v}^A \otimes \mathbf{0} = \mathbf{0} = \mathbf{0} \otimes \mathbf{u}^B$$

For our purposes, the details of the construction of $\mathcal{H}^A \otimes \mathcal{H}^B$ are not important (see Jauch, 1968), chap. 11.7; van Fraassen, 1972, pp. 351–362). But a highly significant result of this construction is that the set of vectors expressible in the form $\mathbf{v}^A \otimes \mathbf{u}^B$ is only a proper subset of $\mathcal{H}^A \otimes \mathcal{H}^B$. In other words, although every vector in the space we construct is a linear sum of vectors expressible in the form $\mathbf{v}^A \otimes \mathbf{u}^B$, not every vector in the space is itself expressible in that form. Thus the tensor product of $\mathcal{H}^A$ and $\mathcal{H}^B$ is not simply the Cartesian (or *topological*) product of $\mathcal{H}^A$ and $\mathcal{H}^B$, but includes it as a proper subset.

Since all vectors in a space are linear sums of the basis vectors, we can define linear operators in terms of the transformations they effect on the latter (see Section 1.13). We use this fact to define an operator $\mathbf{A}^A \otimes \mathbf{A}^B$ on $\mathcal{H}^A \otimes \mathcal{H}^B$ in terms of the action of linear operators $\mathbf{A}^A$ and $\mathbf{A}^B$ on $\mathcal{H}^A$ and $\mathcal{H}^B$, respectively, by writing:

(5.26) $$(\mathbf{A}^A \otimes \mathbf{A}^B)(\mathbf{v}_i^A \otimes \mathbf{u}_j^B) = \mathbf{A}^A\mathbf{v}_i^A \otimes \mathbf{A}^B\mathbf{u}_j^B$$

and extending this, by linearity, to the whole of $\mathcal{H}^A \otimes \mathcal{H}^B$.

These operators are Hermitian, provided that $\mathbf{A}^A$ and $\mathbf{A}^B$ are. They represent observables on the composite system, measurable by measuring $\mathbf{A}^A$ for system A and $\mathbf{A}^B$ for system B. If a measurement is performed on only one of the component systems ($\mathbf{A}^B$ on system B, say), then we represent this as a measurement of $\mathbf{I} \otimes \mathbf{A}^B$ on the composite system.

5.8 *The Reduction of States of Composite Systems*

We represent states of a composite system just as we do states of a simple system, by density operators, or (in the special case of pure states) by normalized vectors. But these operators and vectors are now to be defined on a tensor-product space. If the two component systems are in pure states $\mathbf{v}^A$ and $\mathbf{u}^B$, then the composite system is also in a pure state $\mathbf{v}^A \otimes \mathbf{u}^B$. However, because not all vectors in $\mathcal{H}^A \otimes \mathcal{H}^B$ are expressible in the form $\mathbf{v}^A \otimes \mathbf{u}^B$, the converse is not, in general, true. The question then arises, does every state, pure or mixed, of the composite system allow a unique *reduction* into states of the component systems?

Let us make this question more precise. Let **D** be a density operator on $\mathcal{H}^A \otimes \mathcal{H}^B$ representing a state of the composite system. Assume that the spectral decompositions of arbitrary Hermitian operators $\mathbf{A}^A$ and $\mathbf{A}^B$ on $\mathcal{H}^A$ and $\mathcal{H}^B$ are given by $\{\mathbf{P}^A\}$ and $\{\mathbf{P}^B\}$, respectively. The question is now, are there states $\mathbf{D}^A$ and $\mathbf{D}^B$ of the component system which, for all observables $\mathbf{A}^A$ and $\mathbf{A}^B$, and for all Δ and $\Gamma \subseteq \mathbb{R}$, satisfy the equations below?

(5.27a) $\quad \mathrm{Tr}[\mathbf{D}(\mathbf{P}^A_\Delta \otimes \mathbf{I})] = \mathrm{Tr}(\mathbf{D}^A\mathbf{P}^A_\Delta)$

(5.27b) $\quad \mathrm{Tr}[\mathbf{D}(\mathbf{I} \otimes \mathbf{P}^B_\Gamma)] = \mathrm{Tr}(\mathbf{D}^B\mathbf{P}^B_\Gamma)$

In each case, the trace is to be defined on the appropriate space.

These equations just express a consistency requirement: probabilities of outcomes of measurements on either system are to be the same whether or not we consider that system as a component of a larger one.

It turns out that, for any state **D** of the composite system, $\mathbf{D}^A$ and $\mathbf{D}^B$ are uniquely specified by (5.27) (see Jauch, 1968, chap. 11.8). But there are pure states **D** of the composite system which reduce into mixed states $\mathbf{D}^A$ and $\mathbf{D}^B$ of the component systems. (An example of this is discussed in Chapter 8.) This fact is of considerable importance for our interpretation of mixed states, since it shows that, in this case at least, an ignorance interpretation cannot be maintained. (See Section 5.4.) Consider a composite system in the *pure state* **D**, of which the component states are the mixed states $\mathbf{D}^A$ and $\mathbf{D}^B$. For the sake of argument, assume that $\mathbf{D}^A = a_1\mathbf{P}^A_1 + a_2\mathbf{P}^A_2$, while $\mathbf{D}^B = b_1\mathbf{P}^B_1 + b_2\mathbf{P}^B_2$, with $a_1 \neq a_2$ and $b_1 \neq b_2$, so that there are no problems of degeneracy. Then, according to the ignorance interpretation of $\mathbf{D}^A$ and $\mathbf{D}^B$, system A is really in one of the pure states $\mathbf{P}^A_1$ or $\mathbf{P}^A_2$, and system B is really in one of the pure states $\mathbf{P}^B_1$ or $\mathbf{P}^B_2$. These four states may also be represented by vectors $\mathbf{v}^A_1$, $\mathbf{v}^A_2$, $\mathbf{u}^B_1$, and $\mathbf{u}^B_2$, respectively, such that $\mathbf{P}^A_1\mathbf{v}^A_1 = \mathbf{v}^A_1$, and so on. But this would mean that the composite system is really in one of the four states $\mathbf{v}^A_1 \otimes \mathbf{u}^B_1$, $\mathbf{v}^A_1 \otimes \mathbf{u}^B_2$, $\mathbf{v}^A_2 \otimes \mathbf{u}^B_1$, or $\mathbf{v}^A_2 \otimes \mathbf{u}^B_2$, with probabilities a_1b_1, a_1b_2, a_2b_1, a_2b_2, respectively— in other words, that the composite system is in a *mixed state.* Since this contradicts our original assumption, the ignorance interpretation simply will not do. I return to this point in Section 9.6.

Another significant feature of the relation between composite and component states is that, in the event that the component states are mixed states $\mathbf{D}^A$ and $\mathbf{D}^B$, then $\mathbf{D}^A \otimes \mathbf{D}^B$ is not the only composite state satisfying (5.27). In other words, the composite state is not uniquely defined by $\mathbf{D}^A$ and $\mathbf{D}^B$. This suggests that there is, in general, more information available from a specification of a composite state than from a specification of its component states. The importance of this will appear in Chapter 8.

In sum, if the composite and component states satisfy (5.27), then:

(5.28a) If the component states are pure (that is, representable by vectors $\mathbf{v}^A$ and $\mathbf{u}^B$), then the composite state is pure and is represented by $\mathbf{v}^A \otimes \mathbf{u}^B$.

(5.28b) If the component states are mixed, then the composite state is not uniquely defined by them; in particular, it may sometimes be a pure state not expressible in the form $\mathbf{v}^A \otimes \mathbf{u}^B$.

(5.28c) Any composite state $\mathbf{D}$ defines uniquely two component states, $\mathbf{D}^A$ and $\mathbf{D}^B$.

(5.28d) If (and only if) the composite state is expressible in the form $\mathbf{v}^A \otimes \mathbf{u}^B$ are the component states pure.

II

The Interpretation of Quantum Theory

6

The Problem of Properties

This book is really an extended examination of the statistical algorithm of quantum mechanics, that is, of the equation

$$p_{\mathrm{D}}(A,\Delta) = \mathrm{Tr}(\mathbf{D}\mathbf{P}^A_\Delta)$$

which, in the case of pure states, reduces to

$$p_{\mathrm{v}}(A,\Delta) = \langle \mathbf{v}|\mathbf{P}^A_\Delta \mathbf{v}\rangle$$

In Part One, I looked at the right-hand side of these equations; I was concerned to sort out the mathematical theory of Hilbert spaces and to show how naturally and elegantly they lend themselves to the representation of a probabilistic theory. In Part Two I turn to the left-hand side and to the problems which appear when we seek a deeper understanding of what the algorithm tells us. These problems are easier to state than to resolve. First, how are we to understand the quantities (A,Δ) to which the theory assigns probabilities? Second, what concept of probability does the theory invoke? Third, what account can such a theory give of the measurements to which the algorithm implicitly refers? More briefly, in Part Two I ask whether looking for answers to the question, "How can the world be like that?" is as conducive to despair as Feynman suggests.

6.1 *Properties, Experimental Questions, and the Dispersion Principle*

Recall from Chapter 2 that, in classical mechanics, a pair (A,Δ) can be thought of as a *property* of a system. Associated with a system there are physical quantities (*observables* in our terminology); the values of these observables change over time as the system's state changes, but at any time a measurement of any quantity will (ideally) yield a value within any desired range of accuracy. A specification of the state gives us these values; as we saw, the classical state ω acts as a two-valued function on the set of pairs (A,Δ): when $\omega(A,\Delta) = 1$, the system possesses the property in question; when $\omega(A,\Delta) = 0$, it does not.

In this way classical mechanics allows us to preserve certain elements of the ontological structure of the world first enunciated in Aristotle's *Categories.** Where Aristotle had talked of "substance" and "quantity," in classical mechanics we speak of "system" and "property." The question this chapter addresses is whether these categorial elements can be preserved in an interpretation of quantum theory.

In the discussion of quantum theory in Chapter 2, a pair (A,Δ) was described as an "experimental question." But what exactly does such a question ask? In classical mechanics too, the pair can be thought of as a question: it asks of system whether it has the property (A,Δ), to which the state gives the answer yes or no. The functions defined by the states of quantum theory, however, are not two-valued; their values lie anywhere in the interval [0,1]. Nor do classical states—states, that is, which assign to every question either a yes or a no—emerge as special cases. In any theory which uses the full representational capacity of a Hilbert space, there will be questions represented by incompatible subspaces to which no state simultaneously assigns the limiting values 1 or 0. Thus there will be no *dispersion-free* states. This is easily seen geometrically. Consider, for example, $(S_z,+)$ and $(S_x,+)$. As we saw in Section 4.2, we can represent these experimental questions, together with a selection of states (including $\mathbf{z}_+$, $\mathbf{z}_-$, $\mathbf{x}_+$, and $\mathbf{x}_-$), in $\mathbb{R}^2$ (Figure 4.3). Clearly, any vector lying in, or at right angles to, the $(S_z,+)$ ray will be at 45° to the $(S_x,+)$ ray. But these are the only vectors which assign limiting values to $(S_z,+)$, and they all assign a probability of $\frac{1}{2}$ to $(S_x,+)$. In fact, imagine the state vector $\mathbf{v}$ moving round the representation space $\mathbb{R}^2$. Then $p_{\mathbf{v}}(S_z,+) = \cos^2\psi$, but $p_{\mathbf{v}}(S_x,+) = \cos^2(\psi - \pi/4)$, and we see that each probability approaches a limiting value only when the other approaches $\frac{1}{2}$ (Figure 6.1). This holds even if we move to $\mathbb{C}^2$, for none of the additional states representable in $\mathbb{C}^2$ but not in $\mathbb{R}^2$ assigns a limiting value to either question.

For observables with a continuous spectrum, the situation is even more

* In *Categories* 6 Aristotle suggests that the only quantities of substance are position, length, area, and volume, but in *Physics* IV.14 locomotion (speed) also appears as a quantity. These works are included in Aristotle (1984), among many other editions.

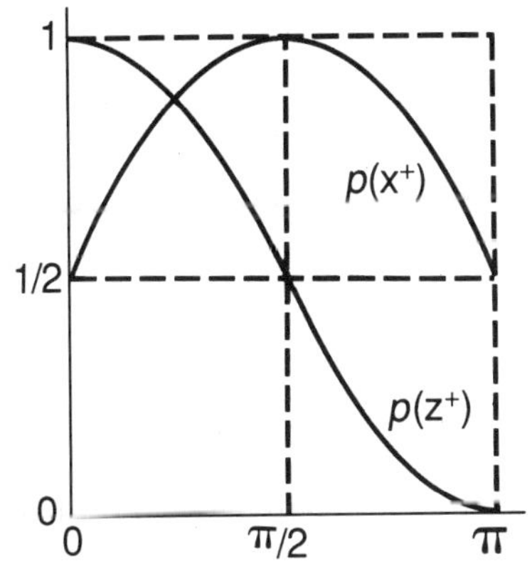

Figure 6.1 Probabilities of $(S_z,+)$ and $(S_x,+)$ for the state α_+, where $\alpha = (\phi,0)$, as ϕ varies from 0 to π.

striking. Consider the noncommuting observables position (Q) and momentum (P). If the system is, as we say, *localized* in a finite interval $[a,b]$, that is, if it is in a state **v** such that

$$p_v(Q,[a,b]) = 1$$

then the only $\Delta \subseteq \mathbb{R}$ such that

$$p_v(P,\Delta) = 1$$

is the set $\mathbb{R}$ itself (Busch and Lahti, 1985; see also Section 9.1).

In quantum theory the *dispersion principle* holds: there are no dispersion-free states (see Section 9.1). But neither the claim that the pairs (A,Δ) represent properties nor the claim that individual systems possess a full range of such properties is necessarily at odds with this principle. Imagine the following hypothetical situation. At all times each observable for a system has a well-defined value. Thus, for any putative property (A,Δ) at any juncture, either the system has that property or it does not. Our present theory, however, can only predict the probability that a given system has the property in question; as a description of reality the theory is incomplete. If, in this situation, we were to rest content with the theory we had, then there would be serious and systematic limitations to our knowledge of the world. On Einstein's view, this is just the situation in which we are placed by quantum mechanics.

6.2 *The EPR Argument*

Einstein's reservations about quantum theory are well known. It was not that he rejected the theory; rather, he declined to regard any theory which just yielded probabilities as a candidate for an ultimate, complete account of the world. His remark chiding Born for believing in "the God who plays dice" is now proverbial (letter of September 7, 1944, reprinted in French, 1979, pp. 275–276; for an interesting analysis of Einstein's views, see Fine, 1984).

But these reservations went beyond expressions of distaste for probabilistic theories. With Podolsky and Rosen, in 1935 Einstein coauthored a remarkable paper, now often referred to simply as "EPR." The title asks, "Can Quantum Mechanical Description of Reality Be Considered Complete?" The answer given is that it cannot; surprisingly, the argument uses results obtained from the theory itself.

Einstein, Podolsky, and Rosen sometimes talk of the completeness of a theory, sometimes of the completeness of the description of physical reality given by a theory. They use the former as an abbreviation for the latter; the assumption of the paper, that a physical theory should provide a representation of physical reality, is explicitly stated: "The physical concepts with which the theory operates . . . are intended to correspond with the objective reality" (EPR, p. 777).

The relation their account suggests between physical reality, on the one hand, and its mathematical representation by a theory, on the other, is this. Theoretical physics employs mathematical models. Of these models only certain elements represent existing features of the physical world. Ptolemaic astronomy, to take a historical example, used a complex array of rotating circles mounted one on another. Yet (for Ptolemy at any rate) not all the points on these circles represented elements of reality, but only those points which represented the Sun, the Moon, Mercury, Venus, and so on. EPR looks at the mathematical model supplied by quantum theory and gives us a sufficient condition for an element of that model to represent an element of reality:

> *If, without in any way disturbing a system, we can predict with certainty (i.e., with probability equal to unity) the value of a physical quantity, then there exists an element of physical reality corresponding to this physical quantity.* (P. 777)

I will call this the *EPR criterion* for physical reality. The quotation above makes it clear that the "elements of physical reality" they are concerned with are values of physical quantities. These are thought of as properties (A,a) of systems, as in classical mechanics, and (on our account) are representable by subspaces L_a^A of a Hilbert space. A necessary condition for the completeness of a theory, EPR says, is that "*every element of the physical reality must have a counterpart in the physical theory*" (p. 777).

What Einstein, Podolsky, and Rosen now claim about position and momentum applies equally well to the two noncommuting observables S_z and S_x for the spin-$\frac{1}{2}$ particle:

If both of them had simultaneous reality—and thus definite values—these values would enter into the complete description, according to the condition of completeness. If then the wave function provided such a complete description of reality, it would contain these values . . . (P. 778)

As we have seen, the spin state vector cannot "contain" the values of S_z and S_x simultaneously. However, the fact that they both can't enter at one time into the kind of description which the state vector provides may just indicate that they cannot have simultaneous reality. We could say, for instance, that in the state $\mathbf{z}_+$ the particle has the property $(S_z,+)$; the value of S_z is predictable with certainty, and so there is an element of reality corresponding to it. However, we could also say that, in this state, the particle has neither the property $(S_x,+)$ nor the property $(S_x,-)$, that neither of these properties constitutes an element of reality.

Einstein, Podolsky, and Rosen saw that the fact that quantum mechanics admits no dispersion-free states does not, on its own, tell us whether the theory is complete or not. As they write,

From [the dispersion principle] it follows that either (1) *the quantum-mechanical description of reality given by the wave function* [in our terminology the *state vector*] *is not complete* or (2) *when operators corresponding to two physical quantities do not commute the two quantities cannot have simultaneous reality.* (P. 778)

Now it may be surprising that, by using the theory itself, one could ever be led to embrace alternative (1) of this disjunction. Although the EPR criterion is only a sufficient condition for the ascription of reality, if this is the only criterion we have, then what we regard as real will be limited by what we can predict with certainty. But these predictions are provided by the theory. How can a theory fail to predict with certainty something which it predicts with certainty?

6.3 *Bohm's Version of the EPR Experiment*

The EPR strategy is to describe an experimental arrangement involving correlated pairs of particles. These particles interact and then separate; thereafter measurements made on one particle can be used, via the correlations, to generate predictions about the other. These predictions have probability one, and so, according to the EPR criterion, properties of the second particle acquire the status of elements of reality. Furthermore, since we may choose what measurement to carry out on the first particle, such predictions can be made about either of two incompatible observables. But it is implausible that the reality of a property of the second particle depends on what measurement is carried out on the first; hence values of *both* of these observables should be considered elements of reality. Since this contradicts alternative (2) of the EPR disjunction, we are therefore led to alternative (1): the quantum-mechanical description of reality is not complete.

In the thought experiment the paper describes, the incompatible observables in question are position and momentum. I will describe an analogous experiment suggested in 1951 by Bohm, in which the observables are different components of spin of the spin-$\frac{1}{2}$ particle.

It is possible to prepare pairs of particles, such as an electron-positron pair, whose total spin in any direction is zero. If the pair then separates, theory suggests that if, for instance, an S_z experiment is carried out on each system, then the results will always be opposite in sign: if the result of measuring S_z on the electron is $+$, then on the positron it will be $-$, and vice versa. The same holds for all directions in space (that is, for S_x, S_y, and so on), provided that both experiments measure the same component of spin.

It's worth sketching the formalism by which quantum mechanics reaches this result; the general result, Equation (6.1), will be important later. We represent the spin state of a single spin-$\frac{1}{2}$ particle on a two-dimensional complex space; call it $\mathcal{H}$. States of the composite system, electron + positron, will be represented in the tensor-product space $\mathcal{H}^e \otimes \mathcal{H}^p$ of two such spaces (see Section 5.7). Now let $\mathbf{v}_+$ and $\mathbf{v}_-$ be the eigenvectors for some component of spin $\mathbf{S}^e_\alpha$ for the electron, and let $\mathbf{u}_+$ and $\mathbf{u}_-$ be the eigenvectors of the *same* component of spin, $\mathbf{S}^p_\alpha$, for the positron. The *singlet spin state* in which the system is prepared is given by

$$\mathbf{\Psi} = \frac{1}{\sqrt{2}}(\mathbf{v}_+ \otimes \mathbf{u}_-) - \frac{1}{\sqrt{2}}(\mathbf{v}_- \otimes \mathbf{u}_+)$$

The intriguing thing about this state is that it is independent of the direction α; that is, we get the same vector in $\mathcal{H}^e \otimes \mathcal{H}^p$ no matter what component of spin we choose to work with, provided only that we choose the same component for both systems. Compare this with the single system, for which

$$\frac{1}{\sqrt{2}}\mathbf{z}_+ - \frac{1}{\sqrt{2}}\mathbf{z}_- = \mathbf{x}_- \neq \frac{1}{\sqrt{2}}\mathbf{x}_+ - \frac{1}{\sqrt{2}}\mathbf{x}_-$$

Ψ gives us a specification of the state of the composite system. To measure an observable on the composite system we can perform an experiment on each of the component systems; for instance, we may measure S^e_α on the electron and S^p_β on the positron. Such a (joint) observable is represented by the operator $\mathbf{S}^e_\alpha \otimes \mathbf{S}^p_\beta$ on $\mathcal{H}^e \otimes \mathcal{H}^p$. The probabilities computed by using the standard quantum-mechanical algorithm on the tensor-product space are joint probabilities, the probability, for instance, that a measurement of S^e_α on the electron will yield + and that a measurement of S^p_β on the positron will also yield +. It turns out that, for the singlet spin state, this joint probability is given by

$$(6.1) \qquad p_\Psi[(S^e_\alpha,+),(S^p_\beta,+)] = \frac{1}{2}\sin^2\frac{1}{2}(\widehat{\alpha\beta}) \qquad (\star\star)$$

where $\widehat{\alpha\beta}$ is the angle between the directions α and β.

Notice that when $\widehat{\alpha\beta} = 0$ (when α and β coincide) there is zero probability that both measurements will yield +; this is exactly in line with what was said earlier, that if the result of measuring S^e_z (say) is +, then the result of measuring S^p_z must be −. In fact we have, for any direction α,

$$(6.2) \qquad p_\Psi[(S^e_\alpha,+),(S^p_\alpha,-)] = \frac{1}{2} = p_\Psi[(S^e_\alpha,-),(S^p_\alpha,+)]$$

Effectively, in these cases $\widehat{\alpha\beta} = 180°$.

The argument now runs as follows. Assume that we perform an S_α measurement on the electron of a given pair. Then, without disturbing the positron, we will be able to predict with certainty what value of S_α a measurement would reveal for it. Thus, according to the EPR criterion, the value of S_α for the positron is an element of reality. But we could as easily have measured S_β for the electron (where β is distinct from α), and thereby been able to predict with certainty the value of S_β for the positron. It follows that the value of S_β for the positron is equally an element of reality. The representation furnished by the state vector for a single particle is therefore incomplete, since it does not contain elements which are counterparts of both these elements of reality.

The crucial moves in the argument are these. After the interaction, the second particle (the positron in our example) is regarded as physically independent of the first. (This condition is sometimes known as the *locality condition.*) Because of the correlations resulting from the interaction we may obtain information about the properties of the positron by means of experiments performed on the electron, but these properties are assumed to exist independently of what happens to the electron once the pair has separated. In particular they are assumed to exist independently of the fact that we perform measurements upon it. Notice that although certainty of prediction is a sufficient condition for ascription of reality, what exists is not to be *identified* with what we can predict. This lifts the paradox we met at the end of Section 6.2: there is no suggestion that we can predict with certainty the values, for example, of both S_x^p and S_z^p at the same time. For any given pair, we can choose to perform either an S_x^e or an S_z^e experiment. Each of these experiments would reveal an element of reality associated with the positron. It is because (if locality obtains) our choice will not disturb the positron in any way that we can claim that both these elements of reality exist simultaneously. In the words of EPR, to make "the reality [of S_z^p and S_x^p] depend on the process of measurement carried out on the first system, which does not disturb the second system in any way" is something that "no reasonable definition of reality could be expected to permit" (EPR, 1935, p. 780).

The summary I have given departs from EPR, not only by reworking the argument in terms of spin components as Bohm suggested, but also by putting it in terms of incompatible *properties* of the second particle, whereas EPR assigns it two distinct *states.* (I discuss EPR in terms of states in Chapter 8; see also Beltrametti and Cassinelli, 1981, pp. 69–72.) I have rewritten it in this way partly to emphasize that the argument, if valid, does not convict quantum theory of internal inconsistency. Nor was that its aim. As will appear, there are other deep problems which the EPR experiment raises, but here I have been concerned to bring out the thesis argued by the original authors, that we can regard quantum mechanics as complete only at the cost of abandoning a particular—and appealing—account of physical reality.*

6.4 *The Statistical Interpretation*

Einstein's realism about the properties of systems went hand in hand with a specific interpretation of quantum theory, now generally called the *statistical interpretation.* At one time the phrase referred to any account of quantum theory which accepted Born's rule for deriving probabilities from the squares of projections of the state vector (or "wave-function," as it was generally called); in fact von Neumann (1932, p. 210) used the phrase in just this sense. Now, however, the Born rule is effectively part of quantum theory, and we understand by the "statistical interpretation" an interpretation of quantum theory which views the state description provided by the

* For a detailed analysis of EPR, see Hooker (1972); for a full account of responses to it, see Jammer (1974, chap. 6).

state vector or density operator as applicable to an ensemble of similarly prepared systems, rather than to an individual system (Ballentine, 1970).

The term *ensemble* is borrowed from statistical thermodynamics; it refers to a conceptual entity: a set of similarly prepared particles. As Ballentine (1970, p. 361) points out, this should not be confused with a beam of particles, whose individual members may well interact with each other.

On this interpretation, the state description provides statistical information about such ensembles; a natural, though not necessary, concomitant of this is the view that quantum mechanics is a classical statistical theory, in that the probabilities yielded by the state vector give the relative frequencies of occurrence of properties among the members of the ensemble. If, for example, an ensemble of spin-$\frac{1}{2}$ particles were in the $\mathbf{z}_+$ state, so that $p(S_x,+\frac{1}{2}) = p(S_x,-\frac{1}{2}) = \frac{1}{2}$, then half of the members of the ensemble would have the property $(S_x,+\frac{1}{2})$ and half the property $(S_x,-\frac{1}{2})$. Which property any particular system had would be revealed upon measurement.

It is clear that, on this interpretation, the description of individual systems offered by quantum mechanics is invariably less than complete.

The view I have sketched here has three components, which can be called the *Precise Value Principle* (PVP), the *Relative Frequency Principle* (RFP), and the *Faithful Measurement Principle* (FMP). (I use the nomenclature of Healey, 1979, here, and the general direction of this chapter is closely aligned with that of his paper. RFP is implicit in his account, though not explicitly stated.) According to PVP, whatever the state of a system (or, more properly, of the ensemble containing the system), each observable has a precise value for the individual system. According to RFP, the quantum-mechanical statistics represent the relative frequency of occurrence of these values within the ensemble. FMP suggests that every successful measurement reveals the (preexisting) value of that observable for the particular system under test. FMP thus tells us that, if the value a of an observable A occurs in an ensemble with relative frequency n, then (ideal) measurements of A will yield that value with the same frequency.* Thus the measured frequencies coincide with the existing frequencies of particular values, provided, that is, that the measured sample can be thought of as a genuine ensemble.

Elements of this view are to be found in the work of Einstein and of Popper. Certainly, both believed that the quantum-mechanical formalism applied to ensembles of systems, and both espoused PVP. (See, for example, Einstein, 1948; Popper, 1982; Ballentine, 1972.) And, as Healey points out, without FMP, PVP has little empirical content. Note, however, that Popper

* In an acidulous footnote Fine (1979, p. 152) disputes this correlation, but his objection to it seems, instead, to be a rejection of FMP.

(1982, pp. 64–74) did not interpret probabilities as relative frequencies, preferring instead a *propensity* interpretation.

Independently of any cachet bestowed by its pedigree, the statistical interpretation is prima facie a very plausible and attractive view of quantum theory. Unfortunately it cannot be maintained—at least, not in the simple form in which I have presented it.

6.5 *Kochen and Specker's Example*

The statistical interpretation, as presented in the previous section, will be threatened by any counterexample to PVP. Such a counterexample is offered by Kochen and Specker (1967); if their result holds, then we cannot regard the properties of systems in the way that the statistical interpretation suggests.

The example they use involves a spin-1 system. Whereas for the spin-$\frac{1}{2}$ particle there are only two possible values, $+\frac{1}{2}$ and $-\frac{1}{2}$, of any component of spin, for a spin-1 system there are three: $+1$, 0, and -1. Thus the square S_α^2 of any component of spin can take as values only $+1$ and 0. Kochen and Specker show, first, that, if we take any triple of these squares, S_α^2, S_β^2, and S_γ^2, corresponding to three mutually perpendicular directions in space, α, β, and γ, then for all states of the system a measurement will show two of them to have value 1 and the third 0. PVP would then require us to assign 1 or 0 to each direction in space, and to do so in such a way that, of any three mutually perpendicular axes, α, β, γ, two receive value 1 and the third 0. By a geometrical argument, Kochen and Specker show that this cannot be done.

This is a very remarkable result—how remarkable can be seen by comparing this situation with that of the components of spin of the spin-$\frac{1}{2}$ particle, whose possible values are just $+\frac{1}{2}$ and $-\frac{1}{2}$. In this case, PVP suggests that each direction in space must receive a value different from that given to the diametrically opposed direction. Clearly, one elementary way to do this is to imagine a sphere split into two; to one hemisphere we assign $+\frac{1}{2}$, and to the other we assign $-\frac{1}{2}$. Whether or not we could ever generate the quantum-mechanical statistics from such an assignment of values is, of course, a very different question. The point is that Kochen and Specker's example shows that, for certain systems, even that trivial kind of assignment is denied us. Recall, in this connection, that Gleason's theorem applies only to a space of dimensionality three or greater. (See Section 5.6.)

Let us look at Kochen and Specker's argument in more detail. Since, for the spin-1 particle, there are three possible values of each component of spin, a three-dimensional vector space is needed to represent the spin states of such a system. We use the space $\mathbb{C}^3$, on which operators are given by 3×3 matrices of complex numbers; the rules for manipulating them are natural extensions of those used for the 2 × 2 matrices of $\mathbb{C}^2$ (see Section 1.6). The analogues of the Pauli spin matrices for the x-, y-, and z-components of spin are

$$\mathbf{S}_x = \begin{pmatrix} 0 & 0 & 0 \\ 0 & 0 & -i \\ 0 & i & 0 \end{pmatrix} \quad \mathbf{S}_y = \begin{pmatrix} 0 & 0 & i \\ 0 & 0 & 0 \\ -i & 0 & 0 \end{pmatrix} \quad \mathbf{S}_z = \begin{pmatrix} 0 & -i & 0 \\ i & 0 & 0 \\ 0 & 0 & 0 \end{pmatrix}$$

We see that

$$\mathbf{S}_x^2 = \begin{pmatrix} 0 & 0 & 0 \\ 0 & 1 & 0 \\ 0 & 0 & 1 \end{pmatrix} \quad \mathbf{S}_y^2 = \begin{pmatrix} 1 & 0 & 0 \\ 0 & 0 & 0 \\ 0 & 0 & 1 \end{pmatrix} \quad \mathbf{S}_z^2 = \begin{pmatrix} 1 & 0 & 0 \\ 0 & 1 & 0 \\ 0 & 0 & 0 \end{pmatrix}$$

The operators $\mathbf{S}_x$, $\mathbf{S}_y$, and $\mathbf{S}_z$ do not commute with each other; like the Pauli matrices, they obey a cyclic commutation relation (see Section 1.7). The operators $\mathbf{S}_x^2$, $\mathbf{S}_y^2$, and $\mathbf{S}_z^2$, on the other hand, commute with each other. Each of them has eigenvalues 0 and 1, and so these are the possible values of the observables they represent. Their sum is given by

$$\mathbf{S}_x^2 + \mathbf{S}_y^2 + \mathbf{S}_z^2 = 2\mathbf{I}$$

Since all vectors in $\mathbb{C}^3$ are eigenvectors of $2\mathbf{I}$, with eigenvalue 2, it follows that measurements of the sum of $\mathbf{S}_x^2$, $\mathbf{S}_y^2$, and $\mathbf{S}_z^2$ (strictly, of the observable represented by their sum) will always yield value 2. Thus, of the trio of observables, S_x^2, S_y^2, S_z^2, two have value 1 and the third 0. By symmetry this is true for any trio $S_\alpha^2, S_\beta^2, S_\gamma^2$, provided that α, β, and γ are mutually perpendicular directions in space.

Two assumptions are being made here (compare Healey, 1979; Stairs, 1983b). The first is that there are (unique) observables which are represented by $\mathbf{S}_x^2$, $\mathbf{S}_y^2$, $\mathbf{S}_z^2$, and $\mathbf{I}$. Second, we assume that when one operator is written as a function of others, as when we write

$$\mathbf{S}_x^2 + \mathbf{S}_y^2 + \mathbf{S}_z^2 = 2\mathbf{I}$$

then the possible values of the corresponding observables are functionally related in just the same way, so that we can add the values of S_x^2, S_y^2, and S_z^2 to obtain a value for $2I$. (I is the "observable" whose value for any system is always 1.)

As for this second assumption, there seems little reason to doubt it, at least when, as here, the observables are compatible, and the functions involved are simple sum and product functions. For, as was shown in Section 3.7, such functional relations among compatible operators are defined on just this basis. Kochen and Specker address the first assumption by proposing an experiment which would yield values to the observable represented by

$$\mathbf{K} = a\mathbf{S}_x^2 + b\mathbf{S}_y^2 + c\mathbf{S}_z^2$$

The system they consider is an atom of orthohelium. Thus they establish not only that $2\mathbf{I}$ represents a genuine observable (when $a = b = c$), but also that S_x^2, S_y^2, and S_z^2 are actually commeasurable as well as being compatible. For the possible values of $\mathbf{K}$ (its eigenvalues) are $a + b$, $b + c$, and $c + a$, which will be distinct provided that a, b, and c are. From our second assumption, these values correspond to the cases when S_z^2, S_x^2, and S_y^2, respectively, have value 0.

There remains the question of the uniqueness of the observables represented by the $\mathbf{S}$ matrices (by $\mathbf{S}_x^2$, for example), but I will defer discussion of this until Section 6.8.

I will give the impossibility proof in an elegant version due to Friedberg (first published in Jammer, 1974, p. 325).

Let us assume (A): We can assign a value of 0 or 1 to each point on a sphere in such a way that, of any orthogonal triple of points, just one receives value 0. Call such an assignment an *A-assignment.* We then show: (I) There is an angle β such that, if any point p on the sphere receives value 0 on an A-assignment, then so does any point q at an angular distance β from p. (II) If one point on the sphere receives value 0 on an A-assignment, then, from (I), so do all the others. But (II) contradicts our original assumption; it follows that no A-assignment exists.

In what follows, our notation shows A-assignments assigning values to vectors rather than to points on the unit sphere; for example, we understand by $v(\mathbf{x} + \mathbf{y})$ the value given by an A-assignment to the point q on the sphere where it is pierced by the vector $\mathbf{x} + \mathbf{y}$ (in its positive direction).

To show (I): Consider an orthonormal triple of vectors, $\{\mathbf{x},\mathbf{y},\mathbf{z}\}$, from the center of the sphere. From this triple we generate two more orthogonal (but not normalized) triples of vectors: $\{\mathbf{x} + \mathbf{y}, \mathbf{x} - \mathbf{y}, \mathbf{z}\}$, $\{\mathbf{x} + \mathbf{z}, \mathbf{y}, \mathbf{x} - \mathbf{z}\}$. We now show that there is no A-assignment v such that,

(6.3) $$v(\mathbf{x} + \mathbf{y}) = 1 = v(\mathbf{x} - \mathbf{y})$$

(6.4) $$v(\mathbf{x} + \mathbf{z}) = 1 = v(\mathbf{x} - \mathbf{z})$$

For such an assignment would yield, from (6.3), $v(\mathbf{z}) = 0$ and, from (6.4), $v(\mathbf{y}) = 0$, thus violating assumption (A).

Now consider the vectors $(\mathbf{y} + \mathbf{z}) - \mathbf{x}$ and $(\mathbf{y} + \mathbf{z}) + \mathbf{x}$. It is easy to show by vector geometry that

$$(\mathbf{x} + \mathbf{y}) \perp [(\mathbf{y} + \mathbf{z}) - \mathbf{x}] \perp (\mathbf{x} + \mathbf{z})$$
$$(\mathbf{x} - \mathbf{y}) \perp [(\mathbf{y} + \mathbf{z}) + \mathbf{x}] \perp (\mathbf{x} - \mathbf{z})$$

Since no two perpendicular vectors can both be assigned 0 by an A-assignment, it follows that there is no A-assignment v such that

$$v[(\mathbf{y} + \mathbf{z}) + \mathbf{x}] = 0 = v[(\mathbf{y} + \mathbf{z}) - \mathbf{x}]$$

since this would yield

$$1 = v(\mathbf{x} + \mathbf{y}) = v(\mathbf{x} + \mathbf{z}) = v(\mathbf{x} - \mathbf{y}) = v(\mathbf{x} - \mathbf{z})$$

and we have already proved that such assignments are forbidden.

In this way we have found two vectors, $(\mathbf{y} + \mathbf{z}) - \mathbf{x}$ and $(\mathbf{y} + \mathbf{z}) + \mathbf{x}$, which cannot both be assigned 0 by an A-assignment. By taking their inner product (see Section 1.4) we see that the angle α between them is $\cos^{-1}(\frac{1}{3}) \simeq 70°$. Since the choice of the basis $\{\mathbf{x},\mathbf{y},\mathbf{z}\}$ was arbitrary, it follows that no two points on the sphere whose angular separation is α can be assigned 0 by an A-assignment.

Now let $\mathbf{w}$ be a normalized vector in the x-y plane, lying between $\mathbf{x}$ and $\mathbf{y}$, and making an angle α with $\mathbf{y}$. Then $\mathbf{w}$ makes an angle β with $\mathbf{x}$, where

$$\beta = \sin^{-1}\left(\frac{1}{3}\right) = 90° - \alpha$$

If v is any A-assignment for which $v(\mathbf{w}) = 0$, then $v(\mathbf{y}) = 1$, and, since $\mathbf{w} \perp \mathbf{z}$, $v(\mathbf{z}) = 1$. It follows that $v(\mathbf{x}) = 0$.

Again, this may be generalized: if the angular separation of two points p and q on the sphere is β, then for any A-assignment v, $v(p) = 0$ implies $v(q) = 0$. This proves (I).

To show (II), let p and q be any two distinct points on the sphere. We show that there is a finite sequence of points $\langle p_1, p_2, \ldots, p_n \rangle$ where $n \geq 2$, such that $p_1 = p$, $p_n = q$, and the angular separation between any pair of successive points, p_i and p_{i+1}, is β. Then, from (I), any A-assignment assigning 0 to p also assigns 0 to q. Starting at p, we mark on the great circle through p and q a sequence of points, so that the angular separation of each from its predecessor is β, and such that the last, p_j say, has an angular separation from q less than or equal to β. Clearly, if the angular separation of p_j and q is equal to

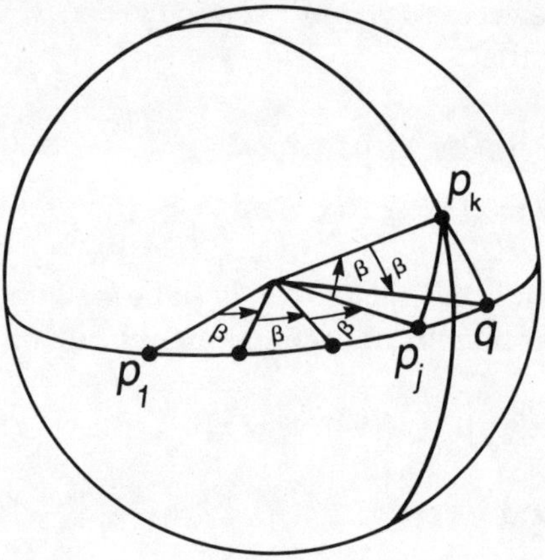

Figure 6.2

β, then the required sequence is $\{p, \ldots, p_j, q\}$. If the angular separation of p_j from q is less than β, then, by continuity, there is a p_k whose angular separation from both p_j and q is equal to β (see Figure 6.2), and the required sequence is $\{p, \ldots, p_j, p_k, q\}$.

This concludes the proof.

6.6 *Generalizing the Problem*

The formalism of quantum mechanics entered the argument of the previous section in one place only: it was used to establish that the sum of the values of S_x^2, S_y^2, and S_z^2 must be equal to 2. However, we can use an extension of the impossibility proof to show that PVP cannot hold in any physical theory that uses the full representational capacity of a Hilbert space of three or more dimensions, that is, in which there is a one-to-one correspondence between experimental questions pertaining to a certain class of observables and the set of subspaces of such a space.

Let us assume that we have, as we may say, a *full set*, $\{A_i\}$, of observables, each with n values ($n \geq 3$), representable on a Hilbert space $\mathcal{H}$. $\mathcal{H}$ will have n dimensions, and to any orthogonal n-tuple of rays will correspond the values $a_1, \ldots, a_n$ of some observable A_i in the set. (I assume that there is no degeneracy.) These rays will represent the properties (A_i, a_1), (A_i, a_2), . . . , (A_i, a_n).

If PVP held we should be able to assign a value to every observable simultaneously. That is, of each orthogonal n-tuple of rays, exactly one would be given the value 1 ["The system has property (A_i, a_k)," say] and the others the value 0 ["The system does not have the properties (A_i, a_1), (A_i, a_2), etc."]. The impossibility proof in the previous section showed that in a three-dimensional real space we cannot assign the values 0, 1, and 1 consistently to each orthogonal triple of rays; trivially, we cannot assign the values 1, 0, and 0, either. The proof extends straightforwardly to complex spaces within which there are orthogonal triples of vectors, that is, to any space of dimension three or greater. The crucial condition on assignments, the condition impossible to fulfill, is that, of any mutually orthogonal set of rays spanning the space, exactly one be assigned the value 1 while the others are all assigned 0. In this extended proof, we replace talk of angular separation of points on the sphere by formulations involving the inner product of two vectors. (Recall that, in $\mathbb{R}^3$, $\langle \mathbf{x}|\mathbf{y}\rangle = |\mathbf{x}| \cdot |\mathbf{y}| \cdot \cos\theta$.)

Alternatively, the (generalized) impossibility proof can be viewed as a corollary of Gleason's theorem (see Section 5.6). For assume a function f exists mapping all rays of a Hilbert space $\mathcal{H}$ onto $\{0,1\}$, which has value 1 for exactly one ray of each set of mutually orthogonal rays which span $\mathcal{H}$. Such a function would, in Gleason's terminology, be a frame function, and from his theorem it follows that, provided $\mathcal{H}$ has dimensionality higher than two, there exists a density operator $\mathbf{D}$ on $\mathcal{H}$ such that

$$f(\alpha) = \mathrm{Tr}(\mathbf{D}\mathbf{P}_\alpha)$$

for each ray α (and associated projection operator $\mathbf{P}_\alpha$).

Now consider the spectral decomposition of $\mathbf{D}$: $\mathbf{D} = \Sigma_j b_j \mathbf{P}_j$. We can find a set of mutually orthogonal rays spanning $\mathcal{H}$, such that each $\mathbf{P}_j$ of this decomposition projects onto one member of the set. (However, if not all the coefficients b_j are distinct, this set will not be uniquely specified by $\mathbf{D}$; see Section 1.14.) The function f represented by $\mathbf{D}$ will take value 1 for exactly one member of this set: call this ray i. Then

$$f(i) = 1 = \mathrm{Tr}(\mathbf{D}\mathbf{P}_i) = \mathrm{Tr}\left(\sum_j b_j \mathbf{P}_j \mathbf{P}_i\right)$$

Since $\mathbf{P}_j\mathbf{P}_i = 0$ except when $i = j$, and $\mathbf{P}_i^2 = \mathbf{P}_i$, it follows that

$$1 = \mathrm{Tr}(b_i \mathbf{P}_i) = b_i \mathrm{Tr}(\mathbf{P}_i) = b_i$$

But $\mathbf{D}$ is a density operator; we have $b_j \geq 0$ for all j, and $\Sigma_j b_j = 1$. Thus $\mathbf{D}$ is the projection operator $\mathbf{P}_i$, and hence, for any ray α in $\mathcal{H}$ distinct from i, $\mathbf{P}_\alpha \neq \mathbf{P}_i$, and so

$$f(\alpha) = \mathrm{Tr}(\mathbf{P}_i\mathbf{P}_\alpha) < 1$$

(Recall from Section 5.4 that $\mathrm{Tr}(\mathbf{P}_i\mathbf{P}_\alpha) = \langle \mathbf{v}_\alpha | \mathbf{P}_i \mathbf{v}_\alpha \rangle$, where $\mathbf{v}_\alpha$ is a normalized vector in α.)

Hence i is the only ray in $\mathcal{H}$ assigned 1 by f, contrary to our assumptions. It follows that no such function exists.

All the proofs given here are open to the following objection. They make the assumption that a full (and hence nondenumerable) set of observables exists for the space $\mathcal{H}$ (as does the version given by Bell; see Bub, 1974, pp. 69–70). Now, as we saw in Section 3.9, while this assumption may be well-founded for the space $\mathbb{C}^2$ of the spin-$\frac{1}{2}$ particle, it may not be true in general in quantum theory. Kochen and Specker's own proof, on the other hand, makes no such assumption. They show that the required mapping fails in three-dimensional space for a set of triples involving only 117 points. As they point out, this avoids the objection that "it is not meaningful to assume that there are a continuum number of quantum mechanical propositions" (Kochen and Specker, 1967, p. 70).

6.7 *The Bell-Wigner Inequality*

In 1964, J. S. Bell dealt another blow to the straightforward statistical interpretation outlined in Section 6.4, by taking the discussion of EPR a step further; he showed that the assumptions made by Einstein, Podolsky, and Rosen did not simply show that the quantum-mechanical formalism was incomplete, but led to results which were actually at odds with quantum-mechanical predictions. Here is his argument in the form in which it was later presented by Wigner (1970).

Let us assume that, for each particle in a (Bohm-style) EPR experiment, the values of three arbitrary components of spin are all elements of reality. Call these components S^1_a, S^1_b, S^1_c, and S^2_a, S^2_b, S^2_c. Then we can write the values of these three components for the pair of particles in the form $(i,j,k;l,m,n)$, where i, j, k represent the values of S^1_a, S^1_b, S^1_c, and l, m, n those of S^2_a, S^2_b, S^2_c, respectively. Each of i, j, k, l, m, n can have two values ($+$ or $-$), and these are anticorrelated, so that if $j = +$ then $m = -$, and so on. Hence $(+,-,+;-,+,-)$ is a possible assignment of values, whereas $(+,-,+;+,-,-)$ is not. There are then only eight possible assignments of values which can have a nonzero probability of occurrence; we can label these assignments 1–8, and write:

$$p(1) = p(+,+,+;-,-,-) \qquad p(5) = p(-,+,+;+,-,-)$$

$$p(2) = p(+,+,-;-,-,+) \qquad p(6) = p(-,+,-;+,-,+)$$

$$p(3) = p(+,-,+;-,+,-) \qquad p(7) = p(-,-,+;+,+,-)$$

$$p(4) = p(+,-,-;-,+,+) \qquad p(8) = p(-,-,-;+,+,+)$$

Now

$$p[(S^1_a,+);(S^2_b,+)] = p(3) + p(4)$$
$$p[(S^1_b,+);(S^2_c,+)] = p(2) + p(6)$$
$$p[(S^1_a,+);(S^2_c,+)] = p(2) + p(4)$$

Since all these probabilities are nonnegative, it follows that,

$$(6.5) \qquad p[(S^1_a,+);(S^2_c,+)] \leq p[(S^1_a,+);(S^2_b,+)] + p[(S^1_b,+);(S^2_c,+)]$$

This relation is known as "the Bell-Wigner inequality."

As we saw in Section 6.3, quantum mechanics gives us a formula for computing these joint probabilities. We have, from Equation (6.1),

$$p_\Psi[(S^1_a,+);(S^2_b,+)] = p_\Psi(S^1_a \otimes S^2_b,+,+) = \frac{1}{2}\sin^2\frac{1}{2}(\widehat{ab})$$

But consider the case when a, b, and c are coplanar, $\widehat{ac} = 120°$, and the direction b bisects the angle between a and c. In this case,

$$\frac{1}{2}\sin^2\frac{1}{2}(\widehat{ac}) = \frac{1}{2}\sin^2 60° = \frac{3}{8}$$
$$\frac{1}{2}\sin^2\frac{1}{2}(\widehat{ab}) = \frac{1}{2}\sin^2\frac{1}{2}(\widehat{bc}) = \frac{1}{2}\sin^2 30° = \frac{1}{8}$$

And, contrary to what the Bell-Wigner inequality requires,

$$\frac{1}{2}\sin^2\frac{1}{2}(\widehat{ac}) > \frac{1}{2}\sin^2\frac{1}{2}(\widehat{ab}) + \frac{1}{2}\sin^2\frac{1}{2}(\widehat{bc})$$

We see that, although the derivation of the Bell-Wigner inequality given here starts from the anticorrelations predicted by quantum theory, its conclusion conflicts with other predictions that the theory makes. How does this happen? If we examine the derivation, we find that a cluster of assumptions, largely unacknowledged, does most of the work within it. This cluster of assumptions, therefore, is responsible for the divergency. The assumptions are (1) that the principles PVP, RFP, and FMP characteristic of the statistical interpretation all hold, and (2) that the properties of one system are unaffected by measurements conducted on the other. All of these would be congenial to Einstein, Podolsky, and Rosen; in fact most are either assumed (explicitly or implicitly) or entailed by their argument. Collectively we can refer to them as the assumption of "local realism."

Bell's result gives a surprising turn to discussions of EPR. It was never suggested by Einstein, Podolsky, and Rosen that quantum theory was *wrong* in its predictions, but rather that it failed to satisfy a particular criterion of completeness. But it now appears that to accept their conclusion is to make certain assumptions which are actually *inconsistent* with quantum theory. Thus, if we test the theory's predictions for coupled systems, we are also, surprisingly, testing a cluster of metaphysical assumptions. For, should the theory's predictions be confirmed, and the Bell-Wigner inequality be violated, this would offer a severe challenge to these assumptions; one might even be tempted to say that they were falsified.

I return to this topic in Chapter 8, but a few preliminary remarks are in order. Since the difference between what quantum theory predicts and what the Bell-Wigner inequality demands was first pointed out, a number of experiments have been performed to see whether the inequality holds (see Clauser and Shimony, 1978; d'Espagnat, 1979). The results, though not unanimous, have largely borne out the predictions of quantum theory; we may take the evidence of those favorable to quantum theory as particularly significant, since the requirement that certain predictions are precisely realized is more stringent than the requirement that a certain inequality obtains. The consensus of opinion is that these results have been a remarkable test of the theory, which it has survived.

6.8 Hidden Variables

The theorems of Bell and of Kochen and Specker make it clear that, if the quantities (A,Δ) appearing in the statistical algorithm are indeed properties of a system, then these properties don't attach to the system in a straightforwardly classical way. However, the two papers in which these theorems were originally presented addressed a different, though related question (Bell, 1966; Kochen and Specker, 1967), the question of whether a *hidden-variable* reconstruction of quantum mechanics is possible.

A "hidden-variable" theory, as the name implies, postulates that alongside (or, more graphically, beneath) the measurable quantities dealt with by the theory (position, momentum, spin, and so on) there are further quantities inaccessible to measurement, whose values determine the values yielded by individual measurements of the observables. The quantum-mechanical statistics are to be obtained by "averaging" over the values of the hidden variables. The inaccessibility of these variables may be a contingent and temporary matter, to be remedied as we develop new experimental procedures, or these quantities may be in principle inaccessible (see Jammer, 1974, p. 267).

The suggestion that there may be such "hidden variables" is as old as the probabilistic interpretation of the state vector. It was made by Born (1926b, p. 825) a few months after he first proposed that interpretation: "Anyone dissatisfied with these ideas may feel free to assume that there are additional parameters not yet introduced into the theory which determine the individual event." But almost as old is the denial that such hidden variables can exist. By considering sequences of experiments like the sequence VH, VHV, and so on described in the Introduction, von Neumann was led to believe that the existence of hidden variables would contradict quantum theory. For, on a natural account of hidden variables, these experiments would act as quantum theory tells us they cannot, that is, as a sequence of filters which would eventually yield a homogeneous beam; the value of the hidden variable would be the same for all its members, and it would be incapable of being split further (see Jammer, 1974, p. 267).

Von Neumann's book, *The Mathematical Foundations of Quantum Theory* (1932, chap. 4), contains the first "no-go" theorem for hidden-variable theories (henceforth "HV theories"). A "no-go" theorem is a theorem to show that no HV theory which satisfies certain constraints can reproduce the quantum mechanical statistics.

The constraints suggested by von Neumann have since been challenged as overly stringent, and the theorems of Kochen and Specker and of Bell are now considered much more decisive. Although a survey of HV theories would take us too far afield, I will indicate the kinds of HV theories which these two theorems disallow. (For a survey see Belinfante, 1973, or Jammer, 1974, chap. 7; Bub, 1974, has a good discussion of certain no-go theorems.)

Kochen and Specker ask whether it is possible to construct a classical phase space Ω, involving hidden variables, which allows a "reconstruction" of the quantum statistics. Recall from Chapter 2 that, in a classical theory, a physical quantity A is represented as a real-valued function $f_A : \Omega \rightarrow \mathbb{R}$ on the phase space. Kochen and Specker require that the algebraic relations obtaining among quantum-mechanical observables are preserved in the algebra of these real-valued functions on Ω.

The relations they consider are just those involving compatible (they write "commeasurable") operators on the quantum-mechanical Hilbert space $\mathcal{H}$; to use a term we shall meet in Chapter 7, they require that the *partial algebra* of Hermitian operators on $\mathcal{H}$ be embeddable in the set $\mathbb{R}^\Omega$ of functions from a classical phase space Ω to the reals. It turns out that a necessary condition for this embedding is that a mapping exists of the rays of $\mathcal{H}$ (equivalently, the projectors onto these rays) onto $\{0,1\}$ such that, of any mutually orthogonal set of rays spanning $\mathcal{H}$, exactly one ray receives value 1. But, as we saw in Sections 6.5 and 6.6, there are no such mappings. Hence no HV theory satisfying their requirements is possible.

To see exactly what kind of HV theory this rules out, we need to examine the assumptions Kochen and Specker make. I drew attention to these assumptions in Section 6.5. One of them in particular might be questioned, namely the assumption that a Hermitian operator on a Hilbert space represents a unique observable. The proof rests on the requirement that, if α, β, and γ are any three directions in physical space, then of the observables S_α^2, S_β^2, and S_γ^2, two must be given value 1 and the third 0. It is then assumed that if we assign to S_z^2, say, the value 0 when we encounter it as a member of the triple S_x^2, S_y^2, S_z^2—for example, when we measure $S_x^2 + S_y^2 + S_z^2$—then it must also be given value 0 when it is viewed as a member of the triple $S_{x'}^2$, $S_{y'}^2$, S_z^2, where x' and y' are directions in space different from x and y. It is assumed, in other words, that the value to be assigned to S_z^2 is not *contextual.*

A *contextualist* HV theory would not require this consistency of assignment to S_z^2. On such a theory, a Hermitian operator which belonged to more than one set of mutually compatible operators would not be taken to represent one single observable. Gudder (1970) has shown that (provided we restrict ourselves to a single system) we can always, as it were, piece together HV theories, each dealing with a mutually compatible set of Hermitian operators, and thus produce a contextual HV theory.

Gudder's theorem shows no more than the mathematical possibility of producing such a theory, nor did he claim more for it. It gives no physical grounding for one, and indeed one may think that the move to a contextual theory has sapped the project of much of its motivation.

This reservation apart, it's important to note the restriction to a single system. For if Kochen and Specker's result limits us to contextualist HV theories, then Bell's theorem limits us to nonlocal ones (as does a result by Stairs, 1983b, which applies an argument like Kochen and Specker's to coupled systems). A *local* theory is one in which the hidden variables describing spatially separated systems are independent of one another. However, as soon as we seek an HV theory to deal with composite systems, we are faced with the correlations typical of EPR-type experiments. By abandoning Einstein's assumption that spatially separated systems are independent of each other, and appealing to interactions between the systems concerned, it *may* be possible to reproduce the quantum-mechanical predictions for these experiments. However, it's not possible to reproduce them by recourse to a classical probability space, and *a fortiori* not by recourse to a classical probability space wherein such frequencies appear as relative frequencies of classical states.

The Bell theorem has implications extending beyond the topic of HV theories, and I discuss these implications in Chapter 8. The conclusion to be drawn from it in this section is that no local HV theory for quantum mechanics is possible.

To sum up, any HV theory that reproduces the quantum-mechanical statistics must be both contextual and nonlocal.

6.9 *Interpreting Quantum Theory: Statistical States and Value States*

It seems that quantum mechanics cannot, via an appeal to hidden variables, be reformulated as a theory whose underlying phase space is classical. Furthermore, a straightforwardly classical interpretation of quantum theory itself is ruled out. Where, then, are we to look for another? Come to that, armed with thimbles and care, what exactly are we seeking? To obtain a more precise idea of what is involved in *interpreting a theory*, let us return to a suggestion made in Section 2.8, that to interpret quantum mechanics is to see what kind of world is representable within the class of models the theory employs.

Recall that, on the semantic view of theories, a scientific theory provides a representation, or model, of a certain domain. Thus geometrical optics provides a geometrical representation of the transmission, reflection, and refraction of light, the Bohr theory of the atom a model of atomic structure. Sometimes these models have a physical representation, sometimes they are wholly abstract mathematical structures, but in both cases they supply representations of the phenomena, or, as in the case of the Bohr model, of the structures postulated as underlying the phenomena. The Hilbert spaces of quantum theory are, obviously, of the second, abstract kind.

We interpret the theory by recognizing, in the models the theory provides, elements of a particular conceptual scheme. For example, in the Hamilton-Jacobi theory of classical mechanics for a single particle, the element ω of the phase space is interpreted as an encapsulated summary of the primary qualities of the particle, and the mathematical expression $-\nabla H(\omega)$ $[=(-\partial H/\partial x) - (\partial H/\partial y) - (\partial H/\partial z)$, where H is the Hamiltonian function for the system$]$ is interpreted as the *force* acting on the particle, such forces being the efficient causes responsible for the processes the theory describes.

Thus the theory is interpreted within a particular *categorial framework*. I borrow the phrase from Körner (1969, pp. 192–210); a categorial framework is a set of fundamental metaphysical assumptions about what sorts of entities and what sorts of processes lie within the theory's domain. The *loci classici* for the articulation of the categorial framework of classical mechanics are Kant's *Metaphysical Foundations of Natural Science* and his *Critique of Pure Reason.* This categorial framework was well established prior to the appearance of the Hamilton-Jacobi theory; correspondingly, the task of interpreting the theory was that of looking for familiar sorts of things. If the fit between the categorial framework and the models that the Hamilton-Jacobi theory provided had been less than perfect—if, for example, there had been nothing in the model to correspond to the concept of a primary quality (or objective property), or if what was identified as an efficient cause had allowed a multiplicity of effects (or of what were identified as effects)—then the Hamilton-Jacobi theory would not have been classical mechanics.*

However, in the case of quantum mechanics, a very different situation obtains. The theory uses the mathematical models provided by Hilbert spaces, but it's not clear what categorial elements we can hope to find represented within them, nor, when we find them, to what extent the quiddities of these representations will impel us to modify the categorial framework within which these elements are organized. To interpret the theory is to articulate the categorial framework whose elements have their images within it; we obtain an interpretation by the dialectical process of bringing to the theory a conceptual scheme, and then seeing how this conceptual scheme needs to be adjusted to fit it. Because there are several solutions to this problem, there can be competing interpretations of the same theory. (Compare Holdsworth and Hooker, 1983, who talk of one "quantum mechanics" but several "quantum theories.")

The concept of a *property* can serve to illustrate this rather abstract discussion. Does quantum mechanics allow us to say that a system "has properties"? Certainly we can find represented in Hilbert space values of physical quantities: the subspace L_a^A (equivalently the projector $\mathbf{P}_a^A$) represents the value a of the observable A. But if these subspaces are to be interpreted as properties, then, in addition to the now familiar state represented by a density operator (and called variously the *statistical state* [Kochen, 1978] or the *dynamical state* [van Fraassen, 1981b]), a *value-state* λ (alternatively, a *micro-state* [Hardegree, 1980]) must be attributed to the system. Regardless of whether the statistical state is thought of as applying to individual systems or to ensembles of systems, the value-state must be thought of as applying to individual systems. The value-state will be purely descriptive; whereas the statistical state assigns a probability to each pair (A,a) (regarded as an experimental question), the value-state will specify at any juncture

* "Classical mechanics" is here identified with a class (T_1,I_1), (T_2,I_2), . . . of theories and interpretations.

which of these pairs can be regarded as the system's properties. A value-state will thus map pairs (A,a) onto 1 or 0, depending on whether the system possesses the property in question or not, and so will resemble a classical state.

Two remarks need to be made about this value-state. In the first place, the attribution of properties it provides is over and above the work done by the theory *simpliciter.* We use it to yield an interpretation of the theory which accommodates the notion of the properties of a system, but another alternative is always open to us, that of finding a categorial framework in which the notion does not appear. Second, even if we hang on to properties, the concomitant value-states cannot be just like their classical counterparts. For Kochen and Specker's theorem tells us that, for most quantum systems, there can be no function λ mapping all pairs (A,a) onto 1 or 0 in accordance with PVP—in other words, so that for each A there is exactly one value a for which $\lambda(A,a) = 1$. Any workable account of a value-state must therefore be modified away from adherence to PVP. Different modifications will yield different interpretations of quantum theory.

A number of these interpretations can best be explicated using the vocabulary of "quantum logic"; partly for that reason the next chapter is devoted to that topic.

7

Quantum Logic

Various enterprises are subsumed under the heading *quantum logic.* Two useful introductions to the topic, Mittelstaedt (1981) and van Fraassen (1981a), appear in the same volume; more extended accounts are given by Beltrametti and Cassinelli (1981) and Holdsworth and Hooker (1983). Common to all quantum-logical enterprises is the aim of giving, or utilizing, an algebraic account of quantum theory.

In Sections 7.2–7.4 I define the algebraic structures that quantum logic makes use of (Boolean algebras, partial Boolean algebras, and orthomodular lattices), and show how these structures can be found embedded within Hilbert spaces. In Section 7.5 I look at the work of a group of writers (Mackey, Maczinski, Finkelstein, Jauch, and Piron) who have sought to recapture the Hilbert-space formalism of quantum theory by looking at the algebraic constraints to which the event structure of any theory must conform. Finally, in Sections 7.6–7.9 I show how quantum logic can be thought of as a logic, in the sense in which that word is used when we speak of "deductive logic," and I discuss whether a "quantum-logical" interpretation of quantum mechanics will allow us to salvage the notion of a property of a system.

To illustrate how all these enterprises hang together, I start by examining a very simple classical system, showing, first, how the algebraic structure of a field of sets can coincide with the structure of the set of properties the system can possess and, second, how this structure can also be viewed as a logical structure.

7.1 *The Algebra of Properties of a Simple Classical System*

Consider a simple classical "system" consisting of a box with a transparent lid; the box contains a penny and a quarter and is large enough for the coins to rattle around inside it. At any juncture, each of the coins can be either heads-up or tails-up. We represent this on a two-dimensional classical phase space. (Hughes, 1981, presents this space in living color.) Using standard Cartesian coordinates, let the set P of points such that $y \geq 0$ represent the experimental question (penny, heads-up), and the set $\overline{P}$ such that $y < 0$ represent (penny, tails-up). Similarly, let the set Q of points such that $x \geq 0$ represent (quarter, heads-up), while the set $\overline{Q}$ such that $x < 0$ represents (quarter, tails-up): see Figure 7.1. Since the system is classical, these experimental questions are also possible properties of the system.

The state of the system is represented by a point ω in the phase space; ω specifies which face of each coin is uppermost. For example, if ω lies in the upper left segment of the phase space, $P \cap \overline{Q}$, then the penny is heads-up and the quarter is tails-up. The phase space is classical, not (obviously) in the sense that it involves position or momentum coordinates, but because experimental questions are represented by subsets of the phase space. Note that not all questions are maximally specific; the question $P \cup Q$, for example, receives the answer yes when the system is in any configuration except (penny, tails-up; quarter, tails-up).

We can represent relations between various subsets of this phase space by drawing a network, in which each node represents a subset. Part of this network is shown in Figure 7.2; below the nodes representing P and Q is the node representing $P \cap Q$, and above them is the node representing $P \cup Q$. We now embed this in a diagram which displays all possible subsets of the space obtainable by union and intersection from P, Q, $\overline{P}$, and $\overline{Q}$ (Figure 7.3).

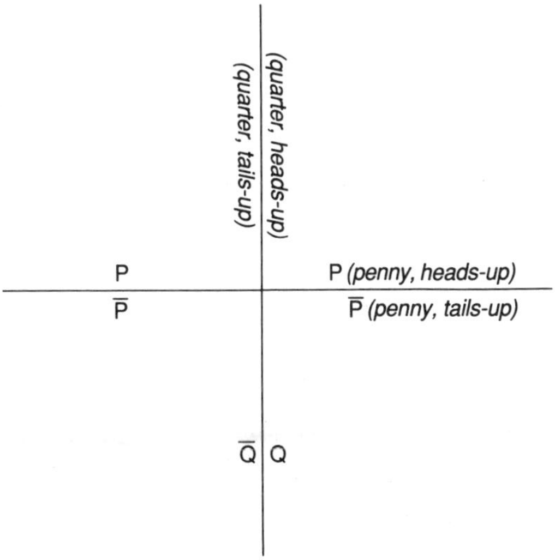

Figure 7.1

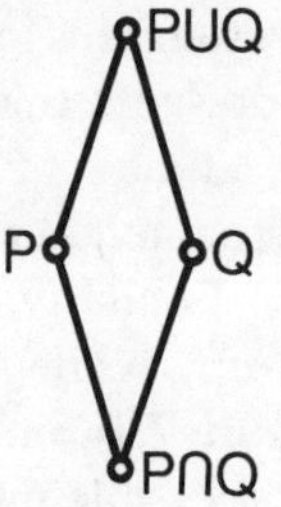

Figure 7.2

At the top of the diagram is the whole space, and at the bottom is the empty set $\varnothing$.

If any point on the diagram can be reached from another by traveling upwards along the lines of the diagram, then the subset represented by the higher node properly contains the subset represented by the lower. Thus a line running upwards between two points (possibly passing through others *en route*) represents the relation of set inclusion.

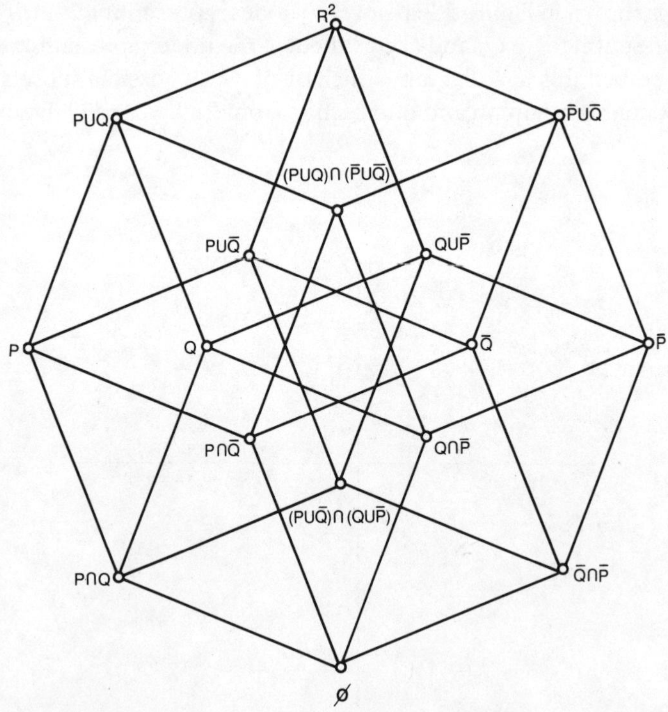

Figure 7.3

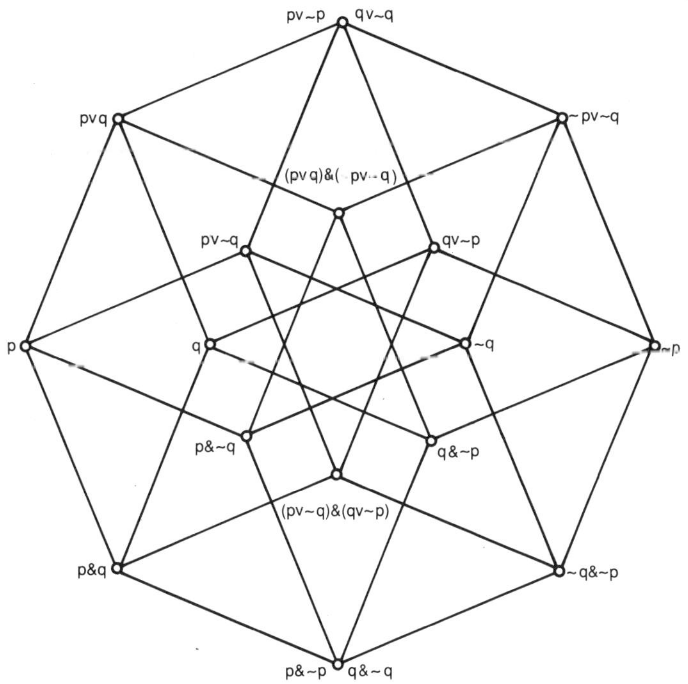

Figure 7.4

Each of these subsets, and hence each node, represents a possible property of the system and so the diagram also displays the relations between these properties. Now, associated with each property is a sentence expressing the fact that the system has the property in question. In fact, the sentence $\omega \in P$ (where ω is the state of the system) expresses the fact that the penny is heads-up.

Let p be synonymous with $\omega \in P$, and q with $\omega \in Q$. Then, using the standard logical connectives & and v for "and" and "or," we can write p & q for $\omega \in P \cap Q$, and $p \vee q$ for $\omega \in P \cup Q$.* Clearly, to each node on the diagram we can attach the corresponding sentence: to the nodes representing P and Q we attach p and q, respectively, and to the nodes representing $\overline{P}$ and $\overline{Q}$ we attach $\sim p$ and $\sim q$, where $\sim$ is to be read as, "It is not the case that . . ." Let Σ_C be the set of sentences which can be formed from p and q by using the connectives &, v, and $\sim$. These three connectives mimic the set-theoretic operations $\cap$, $\cup$, and $\overline{}$, as Figure 7.4 shows.

* Throughout this chapter sentences and sentence schemata of the logical language will not be marked off by quotation marks or quasi-quotation marks. Quelle horreur.

The lowest node on this diagram represents $p \mathbin{\&} {\sim}p$, which is always false, while the highest point represents the sentence $p \vee {\sim}p$, which is always true. The lines on the diagram represent the relation of entailment between sentences. Thus, for example, $p \mathbin{\&} q$ entails p. (We write $p \mathbin{\&} q \models p$.)

Notice that more than one sentence gets attached to a given node. To the lowest node, for example, we attach not only $p \mathbin{\&} {\sim}p$, but also $q \mathbin{\&} {\sim}q$, $(p \mathbin{\&} q) \mathbin{\&} ({\sim}p \mathbin{\&} {\sim}q)$, and so on. Thus, strictly, each node represents a class of sentences, each of which is logically equivalent to all the others in the class. We may say that each node represents a *proposition.*

Thus the same diagram can show (1) the set-theoretic relations among the members of a family of sets, (2) the conceptual relations between the members of a set of properties of a system, and (3) the logical relations holding between the propositions in a certain set. These sets are isomorphic one to another; they all share a common structure. Our next move is to give an abstract characterization of that structure, of the kind discussed in Section 1.8.

7.2 Boolean Algebras

The structure shown in Figure 7.3 is an example of a *Boolean algebra.*

(7.1) We say that $\mathcal{B}$ is a *Boolean algebra* if $\mathcal{B} = \langle B, \vee, \wedge, {}^{\perp}, 0, 1 \rangle$, where B is a set containing at least two elements, 0 and 1 are designated elements of B, $\vee$ and $\wedge$ are binary operations and ${}^{\perp}$ a singulary operation on B, satisfying the identities, for all a, b, c in B,

(7.1a) $a \vee b = b \vee a$ $\qquad$ $a \wedge b = b \wedge a$

(7.1b) $a \vee (b \vee c) = (a \vee b) \vee c$ $\qquad$ $a \wedge (b \wedge c) = (a \wedge b) \wedge c$

(7.1c) $a \vee (a \wedge b) = a$ $\qquad$ $a \wedge (a \vee b) = a$

(7.1d) $a \wedge (b \vee c) = (a \wedge b) \vee (a \wedge c)$ $\qquad$ $a \vee (b \wedge c) = (a \vee b) \wedge (a \vee c)$

(7.1e) $a \vee (b \wedge b^{\perp}) = a$ $\qquad$ $a \wedge (b \vee b^{\perp}) = a$

This axiomatization is due to Sikorsky (1964). At the cost of some redundancy, it displays neatly the symmetry between $\vee$ and $\wedge$; we say that the axioms on the right are the *duals* of those on the left (and vice versa). Clauses (7.1a) and (7.1b) say that both $\vee$ and $\wedge$ are commutative and associative; (7.1c) is known as an "absorption" axiom; (7.1d) tells us that $\wedge$ is distributive over $\vee$ and conversely, and (7.1e) gives us the properties of the complementation operation ${}^{\perp}$. The operations $\vee$ and $\wedge$ are known, respectively, as "join" and "meet."

From these axioms it follows that, for all a and b in B,

(7.2) $$a \vee a = a \qquad a \wedge a = a$$

(7.3) $$a \vee a^{\perp} = b \vee b^{\perp} \qquad a \wedge a^{\perp} = b \wedge b^{\perp}$$

In view of (7.3), there are elements of B, namely $a \vee a^{\perp}$ and $a \wedge a^{\perp}$, which, although they are obtained from a single element a by Boolean operations, do not depend on the choice of a. These are the designated elements 1 and 0 respectively. We have then, by definition,

(7.4) $$1 = a \vee a^{\perp} \qquad 0 = a \wedge a^{\perp}$$

We also find that, for all a and b in B,

(7.5) $$(a^{\perp})^{\perp} = a$$

(7.6) $$(a \wedge b)^{\perp} = a^{\perp} \vee b^{\perp} \qquad (a \vee b)^{\perp} = a^{\perp} \wedge b^{\perp}$$

The identities (7.6) are known as "De Morgan's laws."

An important, though elementary, Boolean algebra Z_2 has just two elements, 0 and 1, as the subscript suggests. In all Boolean algebras, and hence in Z_2,

(7.7)
$$0^{\perp} = 1 \qquad 1^{\perp} = 0$$
$$0 \vee 1 = 1 = 1 \vee 0 \qquad 0 \wedge 1 = 0 = 1 \wedge 0$$
$$0 \vee 0 = 0 = 0 \wedge 0$$
$$1 \vee 1 = 1 = 1 \wedge 1$$

These equations completely characterize the Boolean operations on Z_2.

Any Boolean algebra $\mathcal{B}$ can be homomorphically mapped onto Z_2 (Bell and Slomson, 1969); that is, there are mappings from $\mathcal{B}$ onto Z_2 which, as we say, "preserve the operations" $\vee$, $\wedge$, and $^{\perp}$. Formally:

(7.8) For any Boolean algebra $\mathcal{B} = \langle B, \vee, \wedge, ^{\perp}, 0, 1 \rangle$, there exist functions $h: B \rightarrow \{0,1\}$ such that for all a and b in B,

$$h(a \vee b) = h(a) \vee h(b) \qquad h(a \wedge b) = h(a) \wedge h(b)$$
$$h(a^{\perp}) = [h(a)]^{\perp}$$

The operations $\vee$, $\wedge$, and $^{\perp}$ on the right-hand sides of these equations are operations on Z_2.

The importance of this mapping for classical logic is clear. Consider the Boolean algebra $\mathcal{B}_{16}$ pictured in Figure 7.4; this is the algebra of the set Π_{16} of propositions expressible using just two atomic sentences, p and q, together with the usual connectives. If we think of the two elements, 1 and 0, of Z_2 as *true* and *false*, respectively, then each of the homomorphisms of $\mathcal{B}_{16}$ onto Z_2 offers a systematic way of assigning truth-values to the propositions of Π_{16} (or, more precisely, to the sentences expressing them). On these assignments, as we shall see, the connectives &, v, and ~ are the familiar truth-functional connectives given by truth tables in any introductory logic text (such as Kleene, 1967, p. 9). In the case of $\mathcal{B}_{16}$, there are just four such homomorphisms, each corresponding to a possible assignment of truth-values to p and q.

Each homomorphism is associated with one of the four *atoms* of $\mathcal{B}_{16}$, that is, with one of the points immediately above 0 in the diagram. Each homomorphism maps just one of these atoms onto 1, together with all the points lying above that atom. The set of these elements is said to form an *ultrafilter* on $\mathcal{B}_{16}$. Figure 7.5 shows the elements of $\mathcal{B}_{16}$ which are mapped onto 1 by the homomorphism associated with the atom a. The remainder are mapped onto 0.

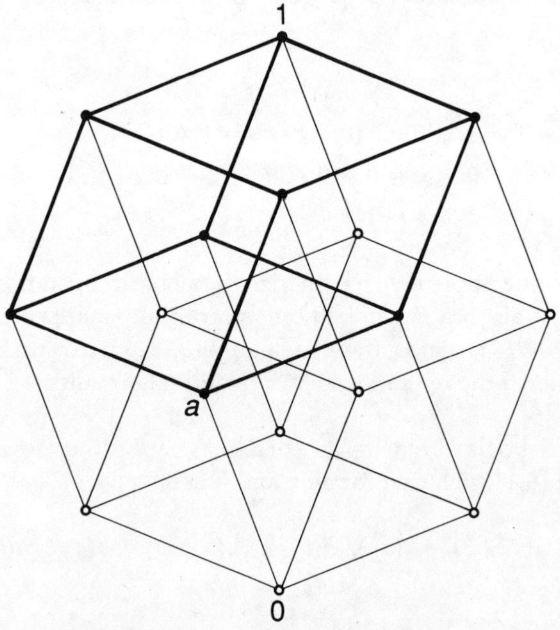

Figure 7.5 A typical ultrafilter on $\mathcal{B}_{16}$.

The generalization of this example to any atomic Boolean algebra is straightforward, but some preliminary work is required.

In the discussion of $\mathcal{B}_{16}$, I have talked of the atoms as points "immediately above" 0. We need an algebraic specification of that relation. Note first that, for all a and b in B,

(7.9) $\quad b = a \vee b$ if and only if $a = a \wedge b$

We use this biconditional to define a relation R on B: we say that

(7.10) $\quad aRb$ if and only if $b = a \vee b$ (if and only if $a = b \wedge a$)

The relation R is reflexive, transitive, and antisymmetric. That is, for all a and b in B,

(7.11a) $\quad aRa$

(7.11b) $\quad aRb$ and bRc together imply aRc

(7.11c) $\quad aRb$ and bRa together imply $a = b$

Such a relation is known as a *partial ordering*. We write $a \leq b$ when aRb; $\leq$ is the relation represented by the lines of the Hasse diagram, as it is called, of $\mathcal{B}_{16}$ in Figure 7.3.

(7.12) $\quad$ We say that a is an *atom* of $\mathcal{B}$ if $a \neq 0$ and, for all b in B, $b \leq a$ implies $b = 0$ or $b = a$.

While all finite Boolean algebras are atomic (that is, they contain atoms), some infinite ones do not. I will restrict present discussion to atomic Boolean algebras, although, in fact, (7.13) and (7.14) below are perfectly general results.

An *ultrafilter* U on an atomic Boolean algebra $\mathcal{B}$ is a set of elements of B containing just one atom a and all points b such that $a \leq b$. We find that, if U is an ultrafilter on a Boolean algebra $\mathcal{B}$, then, for all a and b in B,

(7.13a) $\quad a \vee b \in U$ if and only if either $a \in U$ or $b \in U$ (or both);

(7.13b) $\quad a \wedge b \in U$ if and only if both $a \in U$ and $b \in U$;

(7.13c) $\quad a^{\perp} \in U$ if and only if $a \notin U$.

There is a one-to-one correspondence between the set of ultrafilters on $\mathcal{B}$ and the set of homomorphisms of $\mathcal{B}$ onto Z_2 such that, if U is an ultrafilter on $\mathcal{B}$ and h_U is the corresponding homomorphism, then, for all a in B,

(7.14) $\quad h_U(a) = 1 \quad \text{if and only if} \quad a \in U$

From (7.13) and (7.14) we can see why, if we have a Boolean algebra of propositions, the connectives of the language expressing them behave truth-functionally.

The definition of a Boolean algebra given by (7.1) is purely structural, and so the theorems (7.2)–(7.12) are completely general; no interpretation of $\vee$, $\wedge$, and $^\perp$ is assumed, nor are there restrictions on what B may contain. To emphasize the general nature of a Boolean algebra, and to provide an example which will be useful in the next section, let us look at an interpretation of $\mathcal{B}_{16}$ very different from those we have considered.

Let $\mathcal{A}$ be the algebra $\langle A, \text{LCM}, \text{HCF}, \text{COMP}, 1, 210\rangle$, such that A contains the sixteen numbers 1, 2, 3, 5, 7, 6, 10, 14, 15, 21, 35, 30, 42, 70, 105, 210, while the two binary operations on A yield the lowest common multiple (LCM) and the highest common factor (HCF) of any two numbers in A, and $\text{COMP}(a) = 210/a$, for all a in A. This algebra is isomorphic to $\mathcal{B}_{16}$, that is, we can attach each number to a node on Figure 7.3; the maximum element (1) of this algebra is 210, the minimum element (0) is 1, and the atoms are the primes 2, 3, 5, and 7.

Nonetheless, among all the possible realizations of Boolean algebras, one type of realization has a privileged status: we know from a representation theorem due to M. H. Stone that every Boolean algebra is isomorphic to a field of sets (Bell and Slomson, 1969).

The significance of this theorem for our present purposes is this. The presentation in Section 7.1 may suggest that, because the propositions of a classical theory are represented by subsets of a phase space, their algebraic structure, or logic, is Boolean; however, it is more accurate to say that, because their logic is Boolean, they can be represented by the subsets of a phase space.

7.3 *Posets and Lattices*

Quantum logic deals with a wider class of structures than that of Boolean algebras. Accordingly, in this section we look at the effect of applying successive constraints to a very basic sort of structure, a *partially ordered set*, or *poset*. The effect of these constraints is shown in Figure 7.6, which shows Hasse diagrams of structures which get eliminated at each step.

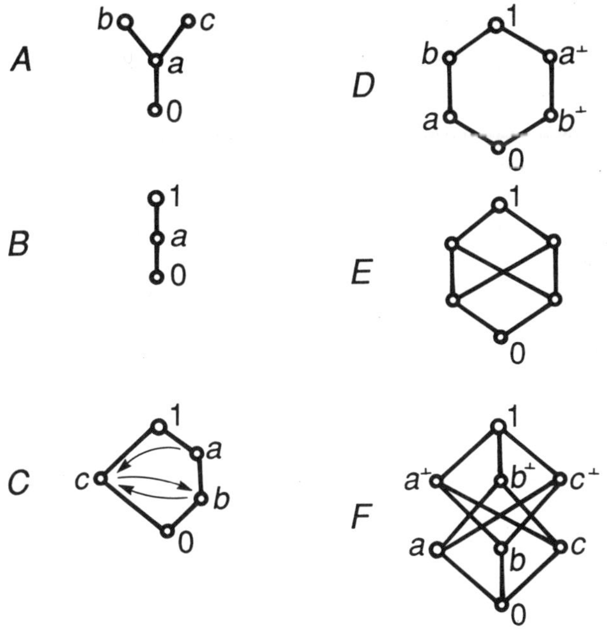

Figure 7.6 Some finite posets and lattices. *A* is a poset with no maximum element: (7.18) fails. (7.18) holds for *B*, but *B* is not complemented: (7.19) fails. (7.19) holds for *C*, but *C* is not orthocomplemented: (7.20) fails. (The arrows show how complementation works.) (7.20) holds for *D*, but *D* is not orthomodular: (7.22) fails. *E* is a poset with maximum and minimum elements, but it is not a lattice. (Nor is *A*.) *F* is an orthocomplemented distributive lattice; it is a Boolean algebra. Compare Figure 7.3 and Figure 7.8.

(7.15) $\mathcal{A} = \langle A, \leq \rangle$ is said to be a *partially ordered set (poset)* if A is a nonempty set and $\leq$ is a reflexive, transitive, and antisymmetric relation on A [see (7.11)].

We do not require that, for all a and b in A, either $a \leq b$ or $b \leq a$. (A set for which this holds is said to be *totally ordered* by $\leq$.) In the rest of this section, $\mathcal{A}$ is taken to be the poset $\langle A, \leq \rangle$.

If a and b are elements of A, then there may exist an element c such that

(7.16a) $a \leq c$ and $b \leq c$;

(7.16b) if $a \leq d$ and $b \leq d$, then $c \leq d$.

Element c is then known as the *supremum* of $\{a,b\}$: $c = \sup\{a,b\} = a \vee b$. Likewise an element e may exist such that

(7.17a) $e \leq a$ and $e \leq b$;

(7.17b) if $f \leq a$ and $f \leq b$, then $f \leq e$.

In this case e is the *infimum* of $\{a,b\}$: $e = \inf\{a,b\} = a \wedge b$.

The supremum of $\{a,b\}$ is also known as the *least upper bound* of $\{a,b\}$, and the infimum of $\{a,b\}$ as the *greatest lower bound* of $\{a,b\}$. As intuitive examples of these bounds, think of LCM and HCF in the Boolean algebra of numbers given in the previous section (in which $a \leq b$ provided that a is a factor of b). Note, however, that though we use the symbols $\wedge$ and $\vee$ for sup and inf, we cannot (yet) identify them with the binary operations on a Boolean algebra.

A poset may have a *maximum* element, 1, or a *minimum* element, 0, or both, such that, for all a in A,

(7.18) $0 \leq a \qquad a \leq 1$

A poset is said to be *complemented* if it has a maximum and a minimum element and if, for all a in A, there exists an element $a^\perp$ in A such that

(7.19) $a \vee a^\perp = 1 \qquad a \wedge a^\perp = 0$

These equations should be read, "Sup$\{a,a^\perp\}$ exists and is equal to 1," and "Inf$\{a,a^\perp\}$ exists and is equal to 0."

$\mathcal{A}$ is said to be *orthocomplemented* if it is complemented and, for all a in A,

(7.20a) $(a^\perp)^\perp = a$;

(7.20b) $a \leq b$ implies $b^\perp \leq a^\perp$.

For an orthocomplemented poset, De Morgan's laws hold for sup and inf wherever they are defined; see (7.6). Notice that, if $\mathcal{A}$ is orthocomplemented, then sup$\{a,b\}$ is defined if and only if inf$\{a,b\}$ is.

We can define a relation of *orthogonality* on an orthocomplemented poset by the following condition:

(7.21) $a \perp b$ if and only if $a \leq b^\perp$

(7.20) guarantees that this relation is symmetric—in other words, that $a \perp b$ implies $b \perp a$.

An important constraint, which will get more attention in the next section, is that of orthomodularity. The following is known as the *orthomodular identity*.

(7.22) $a \leq b$ implies $b = a \vee (b \wedge a^{\perp})$

To define an orthomodular poset in a way applicable to infinite posets we need also the notion of *orthocompleteness*. We first extend the definitions of supremum and infimum in an obvious way to countably infinite sets $\{a_i\}$ of elements of A. Then,

(7.23) $\mathcal{A}$ is said to be *orthocomplete* if it is orthocomplemented and every pairwise orthogonal countable subset of A has a supremum.

(7.24) $\mathcal{A}$ is said to be an *orthomodular* poset if $\mathcal{A}$ is orthocomplete and the orthomodular identity holds.

It may be that sup$\{a,b\}$ and inf$\{a,b\}$ are defined for all pairs, $\{a,b\}$, of elements of A. In that case, $\mathcal{A}$ is said to be a *lattice*. We can now regard $\vee$ and $\wedge$ as binary operations on A and refer to them (unsurprisingly) as "join" and "meet."

Notice that the lattice condition is independent of conditions (7.18)–(7.20) and (7.23)–(7.24). We can apply these constraints to the class of lattices to obtain, successively, lattices with maximum and minimum elements, complemented lattices, orthocomplemented lattices, orthocomplete lattices, and orthomodular lattices.

It is easy to show that, for all lattices, clauses (7.1a–c) of the definition of a Boolean algebra hold (that is, commutativity, associativity, and absorption), as do (7.2) (idempotence) and (7.10), which now appears as a theorem rather than a definition. (7.1e) and (7.4) hold for complemented, and (7.5)–(7.6) for orthocomplemented lattices.

A lattice for which (7.1d) holds is known as a *distributive* lattice. An orthocomplemented distributive lattice is a Boolean algebra.

Now let $\mathcal{A}$ be a complemented distributive lattice. Take $a, b \in A$ such that $a \leq b$. Then

$$\begin{aligned} b &= b \wedge (a \vee a^{\perp}) && [(7.1e)] \\ &= (b \wedge a) \vee (b \wedge a^{\perp}) && [(7.1d)] \\ &= a \vee (b \wedge a^{\perp}) && [(7.10)] \end{aligned}$$

Thus the modular identity is a special case of distributivity. Hence all orthocomplete distributive lattices are orthomodular. However, the converse is not true: in the next section I describe a lattice (Figure 7.8) that is orthomodular but not distributive.

7.4 The Structure of $S(\mathcal{H})$

We now have a vocabulary in which to give an algebraic account of the set of experimental questions in quantum mechanics; in conformity with standard usage, I shall call this set the set of *quantum events*, or just *events*. Since each quantum event is representable by a (closed) subspace of a Hilbert space, quantum logic involves giving an algebraic characterization of the set $S(\mathcal{H})$ of these subspaces.

$S(\mathcal{H})$ forms a lattice $\mathcal{L}(\mathcal{H})$; it is partially ordered by inclusion, and for any pair of subspaces, L and M, there is a greatest subspace which is common to both and a least subspace which contains them both. We may define meet and join on $\mathcal{L}(\mathcal{H})$ by:

(7.25a) $L \wedge M = L \cap M$

(7.25b) $L \vee M = \cap\{N\colon N \in S(\mathcal{H}) \text{ and } L \subseteq N, M \subseteq N\}$

Notice that the latter is not the *union* of two subspaces, but their *span*. The union of two rays, for example, contains just the vectors in the two rays;

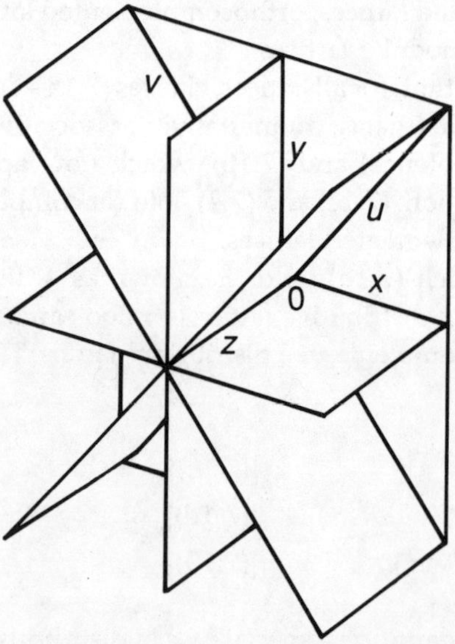

Figure 7.7 Some subspaces of $\mathbb{R}^3$.

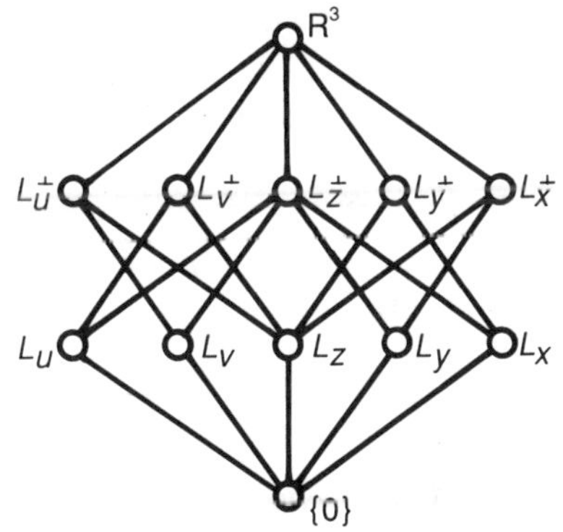

Figure 7.8 The lattice G_{12}.

since it does not contain all linear superpositions of these vectors, it is not a subspace. The span of two rays is the plane containing them both and it is this which, in lattice-theoretic terms, is the *join* of the two rays.

$\mathcal{H}$ is the maximum element and $\{\mathbf{0}\}$ the minimum element of $\mathcal{L}(\mathcal{H})$. The closure (see Section 1.16) of the set of vectors orthogonal to L forms a subspace $L^{\perp}$, which is the orthocomplement of L, obeying (7.19) and (7.20).

Thus the set of subspaces of $\mathcal{H}$ forms an orthocomplemented lattice. It is not distributive, however, as we can see by considering a selection of spaces of $\mathbb{R}^3$. Consider the subspaces shown in Figure 7.7. These are the subspaces generated by two triples of orthogonal vectors, $\{\mathbf{x},\mathbf{y},\mathbf{z}\}$ and $\{\mathbf{u},\mathbf{v},\mathbf{z}\}$. We use an obvious notation: L_x is the ray spanned by $\mathbf{x}$, L_{xy} the plane spanned by $\mathbf{x}$ and $\mathbf{y}$, and so on. Note that four of the vectors, $\mathbf{x}$, $\mathbf{y}$, $\mathbf{u}$, and $\mathbf{v}$, lie in one plane; thus $L_{xy} = L_{uv} = L_{xu} = L_{yv}$, and so on.

The lattice G_{12} of these subspaces (named after Greechie; see Beltrametti and Cassinelli, 1981, p. 102) is shown in Figure 7.8. In this diagram, each one-dimensional subspace is shown immediately below its orthocomplement.

Now consider the subspace $L_x \wedge (L_u \vee L_v)$. Since $L_u \vee L_v = L_{uv} = L_{xy}$, we have $L_x \wedge (L_u \vee L_v) = L_x \wedge L_{xy} = L_x$. On the other hand, since $L_x \wedge L_u = \{\mathbf{0}\}$, and $L_x \wedge L_v = \{\mathbf{0}\}$, we have $(L_x \wedge L_u) \vee (L_x \wedge L_v) = \{\mathbf{0}\} \vee \{\mathbf{0}\} = \{\mathbf{0}\}$. It follows that,

$$L_x \wedge (L_u \vee L_v) \neq (L_x \wedge L_u) \vee (L_x \wedge L_v)$$

and so G_{12} is not distributive, and, *a fortiori*, neither is $\mathcal{L}(\mathbb{R}^3)$. However, the orthomodular identity (7.22) holds of $\mathcal{L}(\mathbb{R}^3)$, and, indeed, of the lattice $\mathcal{L}(\mathcal{H})$ of subspaces of any Hilbert space $\mathcal{H}$. Such lattices are orthomodular.

Our first characterization of $S(\mathcal{H})$, then, is that it has the structure of an *orthomodular lattice.*

I noted in Section 7.3 that all distributive lattices are orthomodular, and it's also true that within any orthomodular lattice we can find sublattices which are distributive. In particular, the set of subspaces which can be generated from any set of mutually orthogonal rays spanning a Hilbert space $\mathcal{H}$ by join, meet, and (ortho)complementation forms a distributive sublattice of $\mathcal{L}(\mathcal{H})$.

G_{12}, for example, contains two distributive sublattices of eight elements, each isomorphic to the lattice shown in Figure 7.6(F); one is generated by L_x, L_y, and L_z, and the other by L_u, L_v, and L_z. These two sublattices are, so to speak, "pasted together" (the term is Bub's) at the points $\{\mathbf{0}\}$, $\mathbb{R}^3$, L_z, and $L_z^\perp$. Each of them is a complemented, distributive lattice—in other words, a Boolean algebra—the elements of which are mutually compatible subspaces of $\mathbb{R}^3$.

This gives an alternative way to characterize algebraically the structure of the set of subspaces of a Hilbert space. Rather than describe it as an orthomodular lattice, we may describe it as a *partial Boolean algebra* (PBA). (The definition given here is equivalent to that in Kochen and Specker, 1965; for a review of work on PBAs, see Hughes, 1985a.)

Consider an indexed family $\mathcal{B} = \{\mathcal{B}_i : i \in I\}$ of Boolean algebras: $\mathcal{B}_i = \langle B_i, \vee_i, \wedge_i, ^{\perp_i}, 0_i, 1_i \rangle$. ($I$ is a set, possibly infinite, of convenient indices.)

$\mathcal{B}$ is said to be a *Boolean manifold* (Hardegree and Frazer, 1981) if

(7.26a) if $i,j \in I$, then there is a $k \in I$ such that $B_i \cap B_j = B_k$;

(7.26b) for all $i,j \in I$, $0_i = 0_j$ and $1_i = 1_j$;

(7.26c) if $a,b \in B_i \cap B_j$, then

$$a \vee_i b = a \vee_j b \qquad a \wedge_i b = a \wedge_j b \qquad a^{\perp_i} = a^{\perp_j}$$

$\mathcal{B}$ is said to be a *partial Boolean algebra* if $\mathcal{B}$ is a Boolean manifold and,

(7.27) for all $a,b,c \in \cup\{B_i\}$, if there are $i,j,k \in I$ such that

$$a,b \in B_i \qquad b,c \in B_j \qquad c,a \in B_k$$

then there is an $m \in I$ such that $a,b,c \in B_m$.

Let $\mathcal{B}$ be a partial Boolean algebra. We define partial operations, $\vee$ and $\wedge$, on $\mathcal{B}$ by:

(7.28) If, for some $i \in I$, $a, b \in B_i$, then

$$a \vee b = a \vee_i b \qquad a \wedge b = a \wedge_i b$$

A complementation operation is defined on $\mathcal{B}$ by:

(7.29) If $a \in B_i$, then $a^{\perp} = a^{\perp_i}$.

A partial Boolean algebra is thus a set of Boolean algebras pasted together in a consistent way, so that, where two or more Boolean algebras overlap, their operations agree with each other. This consistency is assured by (7.26). The condition (7.27) is sometimes called the *coherence condition* (Hardegree and Frazer, 1981, p. 57).

The set $S(\mathcal{H})$ of subsets of a Hilbert space constitutes a partial Boolean algebra $\mathcal{B}(\mathcal{H})$, within which each maximal Boolean algebra $\mathcal{B}_i$ is generated by a set of mutually orthogonal rays spanning $\mathcal{H}$.

We have, it seems, two ways to characterize $S(\mathcal{H})$, as an orthomodular lattice and as a PBA. What exactly is the relation between these two structures? And, further, does either of them fully characterize $S(\mathcal{H})$?

The first question has been answered by two theorems due to Finch and Gudder. It turns out that any orthomodular poset which satisfies a coherence condition is a PBA (Finch, 1969) and, conversely, that any PBA satisfying a transitivity condition is an orthomodular poset (Gudder, 1972). (The coherence condition for posets is given by (7.31) below; a PBA is *transitive* if $a \leq b$ and $b \leq c$ together imply $a \leq c$, for all a, b, and c in the algebra. For an example of an intransitive PBA, see Hughes, 1985b, p. 444, n. 11.) The class of coherent orthomodular posets thus coincides with the class of transitive PBAs. The difference between the lattice and the PBA is this: whereas the lattice operations $\vee$ and $\wedge$ are defined for all pairs of points on the lattice, the operations $\vee$ and $\wedge$ on a PBA are partial operations, defined only for pairs of points, both of which are in the same Boolean subalgebra of the PBA. We call such points *compatible,* noting that in the PBA $\mathcal{B}(\mathcal{H})$ two points are compatible in this sense if and only if the subspaces they correspond to are compatible in the sense of (3.8). But now notice that (3.8), suitably rewritten, gives a purely algebraic definition of compatibility:

(7.30) If a and b are elements of a poset, we say that a is *compatible* with b ($a\$b$), if there are mutually orthogonal elements a_0, b_0, and c in the poset such that $a = a_0 \vee c$ and $b = b_0 \vee c$.

[The orthogonality relation here is, of course, the algebraic relation defined by (7.21).] This definition allows the coherence condition mentioned above to be simply stated:

(7.31) An orthomodular poset $\mathcal{A}$ is said to be *coherent* if, for all a, b, and c in A, $a\$b$, $b\$c$, and $c\$a$ together imply $(a \vee b)\$c$.

This condition on posets does the work of (7.27) (Hardegree and Frazer, 1981).

It turns out that the feature we noted in the case G_{12} is perfectly general: every maximal set of mutually compatible elements of a coherent orthomodular lattice is a Boolean algebra. Thus, to obtain a PBA from a coherent orthomodular lattice $\mathcal{L}$, we just define partial operations on $\mathcal{L}$ which are the restrictions of lattice join and meet to pairs of compatible elements within $\mathcal{L}$. Conversely, there is a natural ordering definable on the transitive PBA $\mathcal{B}(\mathcal{H})$, and there are unique extensions of the partial operations on $\mathcal{B}(\mathcal{H})$ to meet and join with respect to that ordering; the resulting structure is a coherent orthomodular lattice.

The second question remains open. It is not known whether there is a purely algebraic way to specify those partial algebras (or those orthomodular lattices) which are isomorphic to $S(\mathcal{H})$. The sorts of considerations at work in Chapter 4 suggest that the most promising approach would be to consider PBAs on which groups of transformations were definable which reproduced the symmetry groups within Hilbert spaces. These transformations would map one Boolean subalgebra of the PBA onto another; recall that a selection of subspaces $\mathbb{R}^3$ giving rise to G_{12} was obtained by taking one orthogonal triple in $\mathbb{R}^3$ and rotating it about the z-axis to yield another. (See Gudder, 1973, for work along these lines; see also Holdsworth and Hooker, 1983, pp. 135–136, for further references.)

7.5 The Algebra of Events

To the extent that the structure of a Hilbert space can be given algebraically, an algebraic reconstruction of quantum mechanics is possible. The question arises, what is gained by such a reformulation? One attractive possibility is that we can thereby achieve more insight into the way in which the structure of quantum mechanics relates, on the one hand, to that of predecessor theories like classical mechanics, and, on the other, to that of possible successor theories. But, from where we stand now, can anything useful be said about the structure of as yet unformulated theories?

One approach to this project is to consider a linked pair of problems. First, are there *a priori* algebraic constraints which the set of events dealt with by *any* physical theory must satisfy? Second, what further constraints, peculiar to individual theories, lead us to the Boolean algebra of events characteristic of classical mechanics, or to the non-Boolean structure of $S(\mathcal{H})$ we find in quantum theory?

These problems are similar to those broached in Chapter 3. However, that chapter did not set out to deduce the algebraic structure of the set of experimental questions (events) of a theory from an analysis of what constitutes an experimental procedure. Rather, it addressed the question of whether the algebra of events could always be embedded into a Hilbert space, and sought the differences between classical and quantum theory in the extent to which each utilized the machinery that Hilbert-space models made available. In other words, it started with the algebraic models with which the present project, if successful, would conclude. It displayed the structure of Hilbert space and looked at its suitability for representing a physical theory; it did not deduce that structure from pretheoretical considerations.

My aim is to produce a formal specification of the algebra $\mathcal{E}$ of events of a theory; however, I will preface this with some discussion of the operational procedures the algebra is to model and of the problems the approach encounters.

As in Chapter 3, I start with a schematic account of a preparation-measurement procedure. (For a very careful account of a σ-algebra of events along similar lines, see Stein, 1972, pp. 374–378.) Let us divide measurements into two kinds. Those of the first kind yield results on the continuum of real numbers, or within a small range of the reals. Typically we write "$i = 2.21 \pm 0.02\ A$" as a measurement of current. The ranges involved may overlap: $2.21 \pm 0.02\ A$ overlaps with $2.20 \pm 0.02\ A$. Experiments of the second kind yield mutually exclusive outcomes, as when the spin component of a fermion is measured as being either up or down. In each case the set of possible outcomes is exhaustive. We take as the elements of the algebra we are constructing, not outcomes, but *events:* as in Section 3.2, an event is a set (possibly empty) of outcomes associated with one specific measurement device.

The set $\mathcal{E}_A$ of events associated with a specific measurement A then forms a field of sets, that is, a Boolean algebra $\mathcal{B}_A$, whose operations are (as usual) union, intersection, and complementation and whose maximum and minimum elements are, respectively, the null event (the empty set) and the certain event (the set of all possible outcomes of A). If we temper operationalism with idealization, we can say that each event in $\mathcal{E}_A$ will receive the answer yes or no when A is performed. Note that, particularly in the continuous case, we may want to extend $\mathcal{B}_A$ to a Boolean σ-algebra, on which infinitary versions of union and intersection are defined. For simplicity, however, I will confine myself to the finite case from now on.

So far, each measurement procedure has been treated independently. The whole set of events—the set, that is, of events associated with all possible measurement procedures —has been carved up into Boolean algebras, but no relations have been assumed to exist between events associated with different procedures. Note, however, that a complementation operation is everywhere defined, since each event a has a complement $a^\perp$ in the (unique) Boolean algebra which contains it. In addition, we may plausibly identify the null events of all measurement procedures, and also the certain events. The intuition at work here is that two events are identical if no preparation will yield a different result for one than for the other. This rather vague criterion will be made more precise shortly, but for the present it will serve. For since we stipulated that for each measurement procedure the set of outcomes was to be exhaustive, it follows that, whatever preparation procedure is used, the null event, 0, will receive the answer no, and the certain event, 1, the answer yes, no matter what measurement we carry out.

Thus $\mathcal{E}$ is a family of Boolean algebras in one-to-one correspondence with the set of measurement procedures. This family is pasted together at top and bottom; it is an example of a very elementary kind of structure known as an *orthoalgebra.* I defer discussion of such structures until Section 8.1; the present question is, what further constraints can we lay upon $\mathcal{E}$? In particular, in order to relate events associated with different measurement procedures, can we make precise the criterion used just now, when we identified all the null events associated with different measurements, on the grounds that no preparation yielded a different result for one than for another?

Well, every preparation gives a certain probability to the various events of $\mathcal{E}$. We associate with each preparation a *state,* w, which assigns a probability $w(a)$ to each event a of $\mathcal{E}$. This enables us to define a relation $\leq$ on $\mathcal{E}$:

(7.32) We say that $a \leq b$ if, for all states w, $w(a) \leq w(b)$.

If, further, we identify two events a and b whenever, for all states w, $w(a) = w(b)$, then $\leq$ is a partial ordering on $\mathcal{E}$.

It seems that, without significant loss of generality, we have shown that $\mathcal{E}$ must be a poset—a poset, moreover, with maximum and minimum elements and on which a complementation operation has been defined. Alas, dancing in the streets would be premature; without making some significant assumptions we can't expect the complementation operation to mesh properly with the ordering relation. Consider, for instance, the experiment shown diagrammatically in Figure 7.9, which consists of coupling together two Stern-Gerlach apparatuses, one to measure S_z and the other to measure S_y, so that just one of the beams emerging from the S_z apparatus, the z^- beam, say, passes through the S_y apparatus. (This example comes from Beltrametti and Cassinelli, 1981, p. 145; see also Cooke and Hilgevoord, 1981.) If we consider the coupled apparatuses as one experiment, then there will be three possible outcomes, z^+, y^+, and y^-.

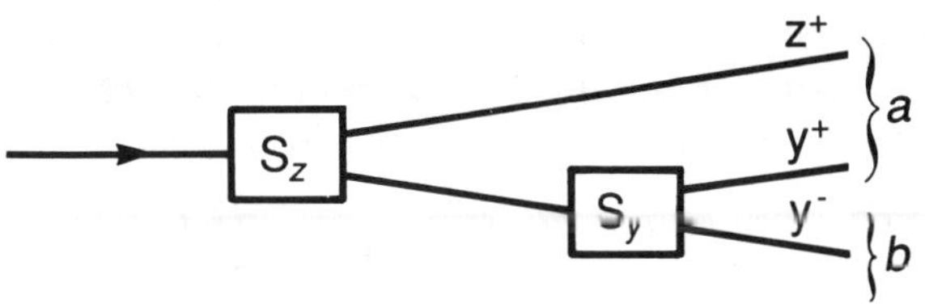

Figure 7.9 Coupled Stern-Gerlach devices.

In this case we will find that, for all states w, $w(y^+) = w(y^-)$. It follows that, if $a = \{z^+, y^+\}$ and $b = \{y^-\}$, then $b \leq a$. Hence $b \vee a = a$. But since a and b are mutually exclusive and jointly exhaustive, $a = b^\perp$. It follows that $b \vee b^\perp = b \vee a = a \neq 1$, contrary to (7.19). Thus the operation $\perp$ is not an orthocomplementation with respect to $\leq$.

How might one outlaw such experimental arrangements? One strategy is to make explicit the assumption that we are dealing with measurement procedures: we may demand that each event have an internal conceptual structure and be recognizable as an experimental question (A,Δ). Then anomalous cases like this one are ruled out, on the grounds that the apparatus does not measure a specific observable. In doing so, however, we lose some of the generality we sought; we confine discussion to possible theories couched in terms of observable quantities and their values. We also assume that we can recognize which experimental devices provide measurements of these quantities and which do not. To the extent that our project is that of prescribing a logical form for the event structure of all successor theories, these constraints seem unduly restrictive. Nonetheless, the approach is still general enough to accommodate theories like quantum theory and classical mechanics.

With these general considerations in mind, let us move to a more formal mode. (The exposition essentially follows Mackey, 1963; see also Maczynski, 1967.) We take as primitive notions those of *observable* and *state;* we also use the resources of number theory, in particular, the notion of a *Borel set of the reals.* (All physically significant sets of reals, and many others, are Borel sets; see Fano, 1971, p. 215.) Let O be the set of observables, S the set of states, $B(\mathbb{R})$ the set of Borel subsets of the reals. A pair (A,Δ), where, as usual, $A \in O$ and $\Delta \in B(\mathbb{R})$, we call an *experimental question.*

Each state w defines a probability function on the set of questions, such that for all $A \in O$ and for all Δ, $\Gamma \in B(\mathbb{R})$, $w(A,\Delta) \in [0,1]$, $w(A,\varnothing) = 0$, $w(A,\mathbb{R}) = 1$, and $w(A,\Delta \cup \Gamma) = w(A,\Delta) + w(A,\Gamma)$ provided $\Delta \cap \Gamma = \varnothing$.

We identify two states ($w_1 = w_2$) if they give the same probability to each question (A,Δ), and we identify two observables A and B if, for all $w \in S$ and for all $\Delta \in B(\mathbb{R})$, $w(A,\Delta) = w(B,\Delta)$. Respectively, these identifications state that the set of questions and the set of states are complete.

We say that two questions are *equivalent*, $(A,\Delta) \sim (B,\Gamma)$, if, for all $w \in S$, $w(A,\Delta) = w(B,\Gamma)$. Each *equivalence class* of questions, $[(A,\Delta)]$, contains all and only questions equivalent to (A,Δ). Modifying our previous usage, we refer to an equivalence class of questions as an *event;* this modification does not affect the substance of what is said. As before, let $\mathcal{E}$ be the set of events.

Clearly, any state w can also be thought of as a function on the set of events such that, for all a in $\mathcal{E}$, if $a = [(A,\Delta)]$, then $w(a) = w(A,\Delta)$. We define a relation of orthogonality on $\mathcal{E}$ as follows.

(7.33) For all $a,b \in \mathcal{E}$, we say that a is *orthogonal* to b ($a \perp b$) if, for all $w \in S$, $w(a) + w(b) \leq 1$.

Now consider the following postulate (Postulate M).

(7.34) If $\{a_i\}$ is a pairwise orthogonal set of events of $\mathcal{E}$, then there is an event b in $\mathcal{E}$ such that, for all states $w \in S$, $w(b) + w(a_1) + w(a_2) + \cdots = 1$.

The Mackey-Maczynski theorem (see Beltrametti and Cassinelli, 1981, chap. 13.6) tells us that

(7.35) If Postulate M holds, then $\mathcal{E}$ is an orthomodular poset with respect to the ordering $\leq$ defined by (7.32).

[The $\leq$ relation, remember, defined in (7.32) is such that $a \leq b$ if, for all $w \in S$, $w(a) \leq w(b)$.] Orthocomplementation on this poset is defined by:

(7.36) $a = b^{\perp}$ if, for all $w \in S$, $w(a) = 1 - w(b)$.

The existence of the orthocomplement of any event is guaranteed by Postulate M; clearly the strength of this postulate is considerable. How might one justify it?

Consider the case when, for some $A \in O$, $a = [(A,\Delta)]$ and $b = [(A,\Gamma)]$, and Δ is disjoint from Γ. In this case, $a \perp b$. It is also plausible to assume that a converse relation holds: that, if $a \perp b$, then there exists a single observable, A, and disjoint Borel sets, Δ and Γ, of real numbers, such that $a = [(A,\Delta)]$ and $b = [(A,\Gamma)]$. This would be true, for instance, if a were the null event, since in that case $a = [(A, \varnothing)]$ for every observable A. Note that if neither event is the null event, then the plausibility of the assumption is increased by the existence of certain states in S. Observe, for example, what happens if there exists a state w_a such that $w_a(a) = w_a(A,\Delta) = 1$. Then for any event $b = [(B,\Gamma)]$ such that $a \perp b$, we have $w_a(b) = 0$, and, to use the language of Sections 3.7 and 3.8, B can be neither independent of A nor (in the quantum-mechanical sense) incompatible with A. But if B is either functionally dependent on A or otherwise compatible with A, then the assumption holds. Of course, in a successor theory, this may not exhaust the list of relations between observables, but it is hard to envision a relation that would produce a counterexample.

Given two orthogonal events, $a = [(A,\Delta)]$ and $b = [(A,\Gamma)]$, associated with a single observable A, we may reasonably postulate the existence of others, specifically of the events $c = [(A,\Delta \cup \Gamma)]$ and $d = [(A,\mathbb{R} - (\Delta \cup \Gamma))]$, such that, for all $w \in S$, $w(c) = w(a) + w(b)$ and $w(c) + w(d) = 1$. Considerations of this kind do not compel assent to Postulate M, but nevertheless they do give it plausibility.

Notice in this regard the effect of defining each event in $\mathscr{E}$ as an equivalence class of questions, and thereby giving it an internal structure. Although the specification of the structure of $\mathscr{E}$ contained in (7.32)–(7.36) is independent of this definition, we look to the internal structure of events, on the one hand, for a criterion for distinguishing well-behaved events from impostors, and, on the other, for arguments to motivate Postulate M.

Let us now look back at the problem we started with, whether *a priori* we can specify any algebraic constraints that the set of events dealt with by a theory must satisfy. We see (1) that, if we think of these events purely experimentally, then the event structure of any theory will be an *orthoalgebra,* and (2) that, given certain assumptions, the event structure of a theory whose expression involves reference to observables and their values will be an *orthomodular poset.*

A stronger claim than (1) has sometimes been made (for example, by Finkelstein, 1969; Jauch 1968, chap. 5; and Piron, 1972) that the set of experimentally specifiable events of any theory must form an orthocomplemented lattice. As these authors point out, classical mechanics and quantum theory both conform to this requirement; the lattice for classical mechanics is characterized by the additional assumption of distributivity, and that of quantum theory by the weaker assumption of modularity. However, there are (to my mind) serious inadequacies in their accounts. In particular, to claim that the set of all events has the structure of a lattice is to claim that, for every pair of events a and b, there exist events $a \wedge b$ and $a \vee b$ which are the infimum and supremum, respectively, of $\{a,b\}$ with respect to a particular ordering of events. For these authors, events are specified in operational terms; thus to make good their claim they need to give a general prescription whereby, from two recipes—one for asking a and the other, possibly using a totally different experimental arrangement, for asking b—there can be generated two more, for $a \wedge b$ and $a \vee b$, with the required properties. It is this problem, of giving experimental definitions of the lattice-theoretic operations, which resists adequate solution.*

The question arises: what further assumptions guarantee that the orthomodular poset $(\mathcal{E},\leq)$ suggested by the Mackey-Maczynski approach will be a lattice? We find (Beltrametti and Cassinelli, 1981, pp. 118, 152, and 297–298) that

(7.37) If (a) $(\mathcal{E},\leq)$ is a separable orthomodular poset,
(b) S is a sufficient (σ—)convex set of states,
(c) for all $a,b \in \mathcal{E}$, if, for some $w \in S$, $w(a) = w(b) = 1$, then there exists $c \in \mathcal{E}$ such that $c \leq a$, $c \leq b$, and $w(c) = 1$,
then $(\mathcal{E},\leq)$ is an orthomodular lattice.

Briefly, $(\mathcal{E},\leq)$ is *separable* if every set of mutually orthogonal events in it is at most countably infinite; S is *sufficient* if, for all $a \in \mathcal{E}$ except the null event, there is a $w \in S$ such that $w(a) = 1$; for an account of convexity, see Section 5.4. Although an assumption like (b) above was at work in our informal justification of Postulate M, the trio (a), (b), and (c) are, to put it politely, nontrivial. Indeed, assumption (c) virtually posits the existence of a lower bound of the pair of events $\{a,b\}$.

Quantum mechanics conforms to the antecedent conditions of (7.37), and so does classical mechanics, though, in the latter case, some work has to be done to show that $(\mathcal{E},\leq)$ is indeed separable. What then distinguishes the two theories, algebraically speaking?

In Section 3.9, the principle of superposition and the uncertainty principle (there glossed as the existence of incompatible observables) were put forward as peculiar to quantum mechanics. Each of these has an algebraic counterpart, as follows. The superposition principle states that

(7.38) If r_1 and r_2 are nonnegative real numbers such that $r_1 + r_2 = 1$, then, if w_1, w_2 are pure states in S, there exists a pure state w_3 in S such that, for all events a in $\mathcal{E}$, $w_3(a) = r_1 w_1(a) + r_2 w_2(a)$.

* For detailed criticisms, see Hughes, 1982; note that the relations on lines 27 and 31 of page 249 of that article should read "$0 < w(q \cdot q^{\perp}) < 1$" and "$T \not\leq (q \cdot q^{\perp})^{\perp}$," respectively. See also Holdsworth and Hooker, 1983, pp. 136–141.

A *pure state* is defined as an extremal point in the convex set S. Incompatibility is defined thus:

(7.39) Let a and b be any two orthogonal elements of $\mathcal{E}$ distinct from the null event; then there exists a non-null event c in $\mathcal{E}$, distinct from both a and b, such that $c < a \vee b$.

No lattice conforming to assumptions (a), (b), and (c), of (7.37) can be distributive if either the superposition principle or the incompatibility principle holds. Neither principle is true of the event structure of classical mechanics.

There is no doubt that algebraic reformulations of these principles add something to our understanding of quantum theory. But no interpretive work is being done by such reformulations. Indeed, no such work can be done by the algebraic approach as long as its aim is seen as that of recapturing algebraically the Hilbert-space formalism of the theory. Furthermore, any algebraic reformulation remains a *partial* reformulation of quantum mechanics, for two reasons. The first is the gap, already remarked on in Section 7.4, between algebraically specifiable structures and the structure of $S(\mathcal{H})$. The second, related, reason is the absence of a dynamical principle from the reformulation. Although, as we saw in Section 3.10, under certain assumptions the set of mappings $f_t : S \rightarrow S$ describing the dynamical evolution of a system forms a group, it is only when these states are representable in a Hilbert space that we can apply Stone's theorem to show that all these mappings are functions of a single observable. To date, quantum logic has provided no equivalent to Schrödinger's equation.

7.6 A Formal Approach to Quantum Logic

"Quantum logic" can refer just to the study of certain algebraic structures and the probability measures definable on them. But traditionally logic has been the science which investigates a family of notions—consistency, validity, entailment, and the like—all of which pertain to (sets of) sentences of a language. Thus a set of sentences can be consistent, one sentence may be entailed by another, and so on. In the remainder of this chapter I look at quantum logic from this viewpoint, and I will use the phrase "quantum logic" in this sense from now on.

We saw in Section 7.1 that the set Σ_C of sentences of a simple language can be mapped onto the set of elements of the Boolean algebra $\mathcal{B}_{16}$, and that the logical relations between the sentences can be "read off" from the algebraic relations between the elements of $\mathcal{B}_{16}$. The connectives of the language are & (conjunction), v (disjunction), and ~ (negation), and the mapping f taking sentences of Σ_C into elements of $\mathcal{B}_{16}$ is such that, for all sentences $A, B \in \Sigma_C$,

(7.40)
$$f(A \,\&\, B) = f(A) \wedge f(B)$$
$$f(A \vee B) = f(A) \vee f(B)$$
$$f(\sim A) = [f(A)]^{\perp}$$

As in Section 7.2, the elements of $\mathcal{B}_{16}$ represent the propositions expressed by the sentences of Σ_C.

A full algebraic treatment of classical logic would consider every mapping f of the (syntactically defined) set Σ_C into an arbitrarily chosen Boolean algebra $\mathcal{B}$ which conformed to (7.40). Here we confine ourselves to a specific algebra and a single mapping, and so talk of consistent sets of *propositions,* and of one *proposition* entailing another, without doing violence to these logical notions. Note, however, that the results (7.41)–(7.43) below hold both in general and *(a fortiori)* for the particular mapping f we choose.

We found that the natural ordering $\leq$ of the elements of the algebra corresponded to a relation $\models$ of entailment among sentences of Σ_C: for sentences $A, B \in \Sigma_C$,

(7.41) $A \models B$ if and only if $f(A) \leq f(B)$

The following purely algebraic theorem also holds. Let $\mathcal{B}$ be a Boolean algebra; then for all $a, b \in \mathcal{B}$,

(7.42) $a \leq b$ if and only if every ultrafilter on $\mathcal{B}$ containing a also contains b.

Whence we obtain,

(7.43) $A \models B$ if and only if every ultrafilter on $\mathcal{B}_{16}$ containing $f(A)$ also contains $f(B)$.

Recall from Section 7.2 that the ultrafilters of $\mathcal{B}_{16}$ play a special role: they represent maximal consistent sets of propositions. Each possible truth-assignment to the sentences of Σ_C is associated with a homomorphism of $\mathcal{B}_{16}$ onto Z_2, that is, with a function that maps all and only the members of some ultrafilter of $\mathcal{B}_{16}$ onto the element 1 of Z_2. Only the propositions lying in the ultrafilter are assigned the value "True" by the associated truth-assignment. Thus (7.43) is the algebraic equivalent of:

(7.44) $A \models B$ if and only if B is true on every truth-assignment to Σ_C on which A is true.

The algebra of propositions of classical logic is Boolean. The question now is this: what are the characteristics of a logic, the algebra of whose propositions has the non-Boolean structure of $S(\mathcal{H})$?

In the present section I will look only at the *formal* characteristics of such a logic; no prior interpretation of the propositions of this logic is assumed. This contrasts with what we did in Section 7.1, where it was always clear what propositions we were dealing with: each node of $\mathcal{B}_{16}$ represented the fact that the penny-quarter system had a certain property—that the penny was tails-up, for example.

With regard to the connectives, the situation is a little different. Since they are *logical* connectives they derive their interpretation from their formal behavior. But again, in contrast to the classical case, no prior interpretation is assumed. Whereas in the example used in Section 7.1 the connectives were assumed to be the truth-functional connectives of classical logic, no such assumption is at work here.

Classically, entailment is usually defined by (7.44), in terms of truth-assignments. Given this definition, (7.41) and (7.43) appear as theorems, capable of proof. In quantum logic, however, comparable statements appear as definitions of logical relations. Any interpretation of the connectives is to be "read off" the algebraic structure; no independent route to it is available.

I will present results quite generally, using the structure G_{12} for illustration. From this one example, we can see straight away that there are two approaches open to us. Like the set of subspaces of a Hilbert space, G_{12} can be considered either as an orthomodular lattice or as a partial Boolean algebra. In this section a lattice-theoretic quantum logic will be described. This may be called orthomodular quantum logic. I will indicate later how this account needs to be qualified on the PBA approach.

Consider a language LQ containing a set Σ_Q of sentences. These sentences are mapped by a function f onto the elements of an orthomodular lattice $\mathcal{L}$. Assume, for example, that Σ_Q contains the atomic sentences p, q, r, s, and t, which are mapped onto the atoms of G_{12}, as shown in Figure 7.10. LQ also contains two binary connectives, $\wedge$ and $\vee$, and a singulary connective, $\neg$. We impose a condition analogous to (7.40), thus establishing a connection

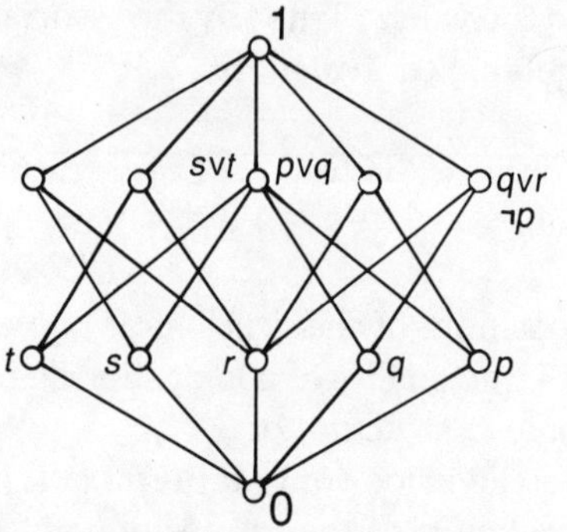

Figure 7.10 Mapping of sentences of Σ_Q onto G_{12}.

between the connectives of *LQ* and the operations on the lattice. For all sentences $A, B \in \Sigma_Q$,

(7.45)
$$f(A \wedge B) = f(A) \wedge f(B)$$
$$f(A \vee B) = f(A) \vee f(B)$$
$$f(\neg A) = [f(A)]^{\perp}$$

We can see from Figure 7.10 that, in our example, $f(\neg p) = f(q \vee r)$, and hence that $\neg p$ is equivalent to $q \vee r$ under the mapping f. As in the classical case, I will confine myself to a single mapping; thus, in what follows, I will omit the phrase "under the mapping f" which, ideally, should accompany all statements about logical relations between the members of Σ_Q. As before, the restriction to a single mapping licenses talk of logical relations between propositions, in this case, quantum propositions.

The orthomodular lattice $\mathcal{L}(\mathcal{H})$ of the set of subspaces of a Hilbert space is *atomic;* that is, there are elements of $\mathcal{L}(\mathcal{H})$, to wit the rays of $\mathcal{H}$, immediately above the zero of $\mathcal{L}(\mathcal{H})$. [(7.12) provides a formal definition.] In what follows I restrict myself to *atomic orthomodular* lattices.

As in the case of an atomic Boolean algebra, an ultrafilter U on such a lattice can be simply defined:

(7.46) U is said to be an ultrafilter on $\mathcal{L}$ if there is an atom a of $\mathcal{L}$ such that $U = \{b\colon a \leq b\}$.

U is then the ultrafilter generated by a. In Figure 7.11 I show a typical ultrafilter on G_{12}.

Now (7.42) holds for $\mathcal{L}$ as for a Boolean algebra; for all a, b, $\in \mathcal{L}$,

(7.47) $a \leq b$ if and only if every ultrafilter on $\mathcal{L}$ containing a also contains b.

We can use each ultrafilter U on $\mathcal{L}$ to define a truth-assignment u (or its analogue) to quantum propositions: for any $a \in \mathcal{L}$,

(7.48) We say that a *holds* under the assignment u if and only if a is in the ultrafilter U.

The function $u: \mathcal{L} \rightarrow \{0,1\}$ is the characteristic function of U; we write $u(a) = 1$ if $a \in U$, and $u(a) = 0$ if $a \notin U$. (7.47) now tells us that the semantic entailment relation on the set of quantum propositions will coincide with the ordering relation on the lattice; for all a, b, $\in \mathcal{L}$,

(7.49) $a \models_Q b$ if and only if a holds whenever b holds if and only if $a \leq b$.

As Putnam (1969, p. 233) pointed out, in many ways the behavior of quantum connectives resembles that of their classical counterparts. The lattice structure of $\mathcal{L}$ guarantees that, for any sentences A, B, and C of Σ_Q,

(7.50a) $A \models_Q A \vee B \qquad B \models_Q A \vee B$

if $A \models_Q C$ and $B \models_Q C$, then $A \vee B \models_Q C$

(7.50b) $A, B \models_Q A \wedge B$

$A \wedge B \models_Q A \qquad A \wedge B \models_Q B$

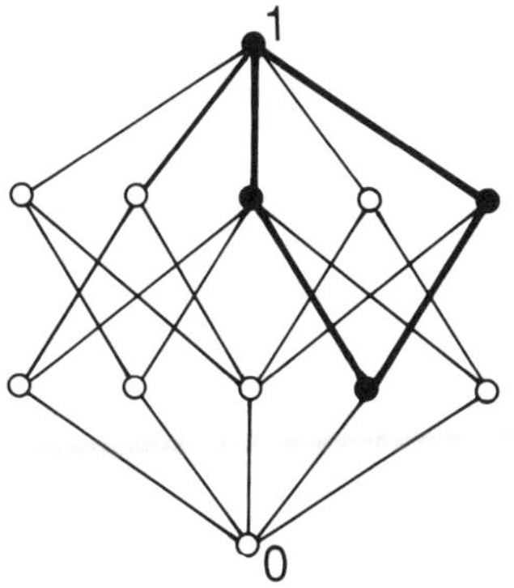

Figure 7.11 Typical ultrafilter on G_{12}.

(7.50c) $A \vDash_Q \neg\neg A$ and $\neg\neg A \vDash_Q A$

$\vDash_Q A \vee \neg A$

$\vDash_Q \neg(A \wedge \neg A)$

[We write $\vDash_Q A$ if A holds on all truth-assignments; note also that the upper line of (7.50b) involves a modest extension of our notation.] There are of course casualties among the theorems of classical logic. Notoriously, $A \wedge (B \vee C) \nvDash_Q (A \wedge B) \vee (A \wedge C)$, since, in general, an orthomodular lattice is not distributive. (Friedman and Glymour, 1972, provide an axiomatization of orthomodular quantum logic which was proved complete by Hughes, 1979; see also Dalla Chiara, 1986, and Gibbins, 1987, chap. 9.)

More fundamentally, we may think, the assignments provided by the ultrafilters on $\mathcal{L}$ do not behave truth-functionally, as classical truth-assignments do. That is to say, the truth-values of compound sentences are not uniquely determined by the truth-values of their components.

Consider, for example, the assignment u determined by the ultrafilter U_q on G_{12} which contains the atom q (see Figure 7.11). On this assignment q holds, but the other atoms do not. The proposition $p \vee q$ lies in the ultrafilter U_q and therefore holds on this assignment. But $p \vee q$ is identical with the proposition $s \vee t$. Hence, on this assignment, we have

(7.51) $u(s) = 0, \quad u(t) = 0, \quad \text{and} \quad u(s \vee t) = 1$

but we also have

(7.52) $u(p) = 0, \quad u(r) = 0, \quad \text{and} \quad u(p \vee r) = 0$

Algebraically, the fact that the truth-assignments of orthomodular quantum logic are not truth-functional appears as the absence of two-valued homomorphisms on nondistributive lattices. Kochen and Specker's theorem tells us that there are none such on $\mathcal{L}(\mathcal{H})$; Jauch and Piron (1963) have shown that the existence of such mappings from an orthomodular lattice $\mathcal{L}$ onto Z_2 implies the distributivity of $\mathcal{L}$.

We can mimic some of the idiosyncracies of orthomodular quantum logic within a classical modal logic. This is done by "translating" the propositions of quantum logic into modal propositions. The "translations" all use the modal operator $\Box$, which can be read as, "It is necessary that . . ." (For an introduction to modal logic, see Hughes and Cresswell, 1968.) We now "translate" a given sentence in Σ_Q by rewriting it, with its quantum connectives replaced by classical, and with the necessity operator added at the front of the sentence; thus $A \wedge \neg B$ is translated as $\Box(\alpha \,\&\, {\sim}\beta)$ (α and β are A and B rewritten, with classical connectives replacing quantum connectives).

G_{12} provides illustrations of the nonclassical features of quantum logic which find analogues in these modal translations. Let u be the quantum-logical truth-assignment determined by the ultrafilter U_q, as before (Figure 7.11), and let v be a truth-assignment to a classical modal logic (S4, say). We have already seen that $u(s) = 0 = u(t)$, but that $u(s \vee t) = 1$. Similarly, we may have $v(\Box\alpha) = 0 = v(\Box\beta)$, but $v[\Box(\alpha \vee \beta)] = 1$, as in the case when α is a contingent proposition and $\beta = {\sim}\alpha$. Again, from Figure 7.11 we see that $u(t) = u(\neg t) = 0$. Likewise, if α is any contingent proposition we have $v(\Box\alpha) = v[\Box({\sim}\alpha)] = 0$.

These remarks bring to mind Gödel's (1933) demonstration that intuitionistic logic can be translated into the classical modal system S4. In fact, Dalla Chiara (1986) has shown that a comparable result holds for quantum logic and a modified Brouwer system. The modal translation she uses is, however, more complex than the one given above, and nothing as precise or as comprehensive as that result is being claimed here; I have merely pointed out some formal affinities between orthomodular quantum logic and the logic of a particular class of modal sentences.

7.7 An Unexceptionable Interpretation of Quantum Logic

In Section 7.6 we saw that, within the lattice of quantum propositions, ultrafilters can be used to define functions which are the analogues of truth-assignments. Let us call these functions "valuations" to avoid making unjustified assumptions. Each valuation u is the characteristic function of some ultrafilter U [see (7.48)] on the lattice.

If $\mathcal{L}$ is atomic, as we assume, then each ultrafilter contains just one atom. Thus, for each valuation u there is exactly one atom a such that $u(a) = 1$, and for all $b \in \mathcal{L}$,

(7.53) $\quad u(b) = 1 \quad \text{if and only if} \quad a \leq b$

Let us now cash this out in terms of quantum systems and their states, and so obtain an interpretation of the propositions of a logic based on the lattice $\mathcal{L}(\mathcal{H})$. We need first to distinguish three kinds of things: quantum events, quantum propositions, and subspaces of a Hilbert space. The subspaces of a Hilbert space act as mathematical representations both of quantum events and of quantum propositions. A quantum proposition is whatever is expressed by a sentence of quantum logic: just what this is we rely on our interpretation to tell us. A quantum event (also called an "experimental question") is a pair (A,Δ). The fact that we are not at this stage giving any further account of these entities does not mean that none is needed; on the contrary, we are still engaged in the project, announced at the beginning of Chapter 6, of gaining more insight into their nature, and, indeed, one reason for seeking an interpretation of quantum logic is that it may help us to do so.

Propositions, events and subspaces are in one-to-one-to-one correspondence; I will use lowercase italic letters $a, b, c, \ldots$ for propositions, $E_a, E_b, E_c, \ldots$ for the corresponding quantum events, and $L_a, L_b, L_c, \ldots$ for the corresponding subspaces of $\mathcal{H}$. Strictly, the three sets form three isomorphic lattices, but I will refer to all three structures indiscriminately as $\mathcal{L}(\mathcal{H})$, relying on context to make clear what the elements of the lattice in question are.

Each atom L_a of $\mathcal{L}(\mathcal{H})$ is a one-dimensional subspace of $\mathcal{H}$ and so represents a pure state of a system. Thus the set of pure states is in one-to-one correspondence with the set of valuations of our quantum logic. Now let $\mathbf{P}_a$ be the projector onto the atom L_a, and for any element L_b of $\mathcal{L}(\mathcal{H})$ (that is, any subspace of $\mathcal{H}$), let $\mathbf{P}_b$ be the projector onto L_b. As we know, each subspace L_b (alternatively, each projector $\mathbf{P}_b$) represents a quantum event E_b, and every such event is assigned a probability by the state; if the state is $\mathbf{P}_a$ this probability is given by,

$$p(E_b) = \mathrm{Tr}(\mathbf{P}_a\mathbf{P}_b) = \langle \mathbf{v}|\mathbf{P}_b\mathbf{v}\rangle$$

where $\mathbf{v}$ is a normalized vector in L_a. We know that

(7.54) $$\mathrm{Tr}(\mathbf{P}_a\mathbf{P}_b) = 1 \quad \text{if and only if} \quad \mathbf{v} \in L_b \quad \text{if and only if} \quad L_a \subseteq L_b$$

An event E_b is assigned probability 1 by a pure state $\mathbf{P}_a$ if and only if the subspace L_b includes L_a. But the latter holds if and only if the proposition b lies in the ultrafilter defined by a. We see that $p(E_b) = 1$ provided that $u(b) = 1$, where u is the valuation corresponding to the (pure) state of the system.

A straightforward and unexceptionable interpretation of quantum logic now presents itself. Let us unpack each quantum event E, so that $E = (A,\Delta)$; the corresponding quantum proposition may be read as, "A measurement of A will yield a result within Δ with probability 1." The truth or falsity of this statement is determined by the state.

Given the possibility of interpreting quantum logic in this way, its resemblance to a logic of modal sentences is not surprising, since the sentential operator, "There is probability 1 that . . . ," is the probabilistic equivalent of the necessity operator $\Box$.

I have called this interpretation of quantum logic "unexceptionable." It is also unambitious. On the proposed reading of quantum propositions, these propositions are just a subset of the predictions quantum mechanics makes about the probabilities of quantum events, and quantum logic offers merely a partial reformulation of quantum theory in the formal mode—that is, a reformulation expressed in terms of sentences and the relations between them. But many devotees of quantum logic were after bigger game. In particular, they took the logico-algebraic approach to quantum theory to offer a way, or various ways, to talk of the properties of systems. The next section looks at one such proposal.

7.8 *Putnam on Quantum Logic*

For an example of a nontrivial logic based on orthomodular lattices, we turn to Hilary Putnam. Though his 1969 paper, "Is Logic Empirical?" only sketched the outlines of such a logic, it presented with splendid vigor some of the most ambitious claims made on quantum logic's behalf. The claims made are these.

(1) Logic is an empirical science; some of the "necessary truths" of classical logic could turn out to be false for empirical reasons (Putnam, 1969, pp. 216, 226).

(2) Just as the general theory of relativity requires us to move to a non-Euclidean geometry, so our best interpretation of quantum mechanics requires the adoption of a nonclassical logic (p. 234).

(3) By adopting a quantum logic we can retain a strong account of the properties of a system (p. 229).

I will discuss (1) in Section 7.9; it turns out to be rather less revolutionary a thesis than one might think. The analogy proposed in (2) is suggestive, and I will myself make use of it in Section 8.9; however, the sense in which I will use the term "quantum logic" is some distance from Putnam's. This section and the next will largely be occupied with claim (3), which I take to be false. Indeed, in a correspondence quoted by Stairs (1983b, p. 588),* Putnam has written that he no longer subscribes to it. In these sections "Putnam" will refer to the Putnam of 1969, continuous with, but epistemically distinct from, his present counterpart.

In formal respects the logic Putnam advocates is that presented in Section 7.6; we are to "read the logic off from the Hilbert space $\mathcal{H}$" (p. 222), and the

* I am much indebted to this paper.

set of subspaces of $\mathcal{H}$ is to be regarded as a lattice. This lattice is nondistributive (see Section 7.3); thus in the corresponding logic the distributive law is not valid, and the inference from $A \wedge (B \vee C)$ to $(A \wedge B) \vee (A \wedge C)$ fails. Putnam boldly asserts that "*all* so-called 'anomalies' in quantum mechanics come down to the *non-standardness of the logic*" (his emphases); once these are given up, he assures us, "every single anomaly vanishes" (pp. 222, 226).

The propositions represented by the subspaces of $\mathcal{H}$ are, for Putnam, property ascriptions, and among the anomalies which will disappear with the adoption of quantum logic are, presumably, those associated with such ascriptions. As examples Putnam uses the values of position and momentum. Observables like these, which have continuous spectra, are independently problematic (see Teller, 1979), and so I will restate his position in terms of two noncommuting observables A and B, each of which has three possible outcomes: respectively, a_1, a_2, a_3, and b_1, b_2, b_3. I will use these lowercase letters to refer to the lattice points corresponding to (A,a_1), et cetera, and also as sentences, "The system has the property (A,a_1)." I assume further that the operators corresponding to A and B share no eigenvectors, so that the lattice we are dealing with is the 14-element lattice shown in Figure 7.12.

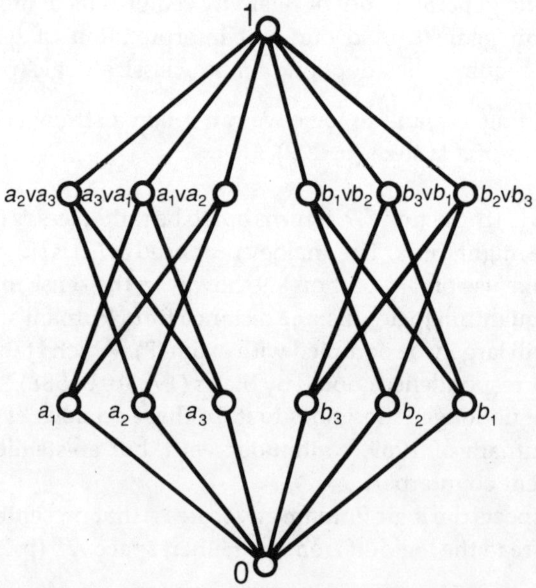

Figure 7.12 Fourteen-element orthomodular lattice.

In this lattice,

$$(a_1 \vee a_2 \vee a_3) = (b_1 \vee b_2 \vee b_3) = 1$$

Since Putnam reads '$a_1 \vee a_2 \vee a_3$' as "The system has an A-value," he regards the conjunction "The system has an A-value and the system has a B-value" as logically true. It is thus a truth of (quantum) logic that every observable for a system has a value (at all times). Note that $a_1 \vee a_2 \vee a_3$ is true even if the system is in a state which makes b_1 (say) true. However, in that state the sentence

(I) $\quad b_1 \wedge (a_1 \vee a_2 \vee a_3)$

is true, but the sentence

(II) $\quad (b_1 \wedge a_1) \vee (b_1 \wedge a_2) \vee (b_1 \wedge a_3)$

is false, since, in the lattice,

$$b_1 \wedge a_1 = b_1 \wedge a_2 = b_1 \wedge a_3 = 0$$

reflecting the fact that no state makes either b_1 and a_1, or b_1 and a_2, or b_1 and a_3 simultaneously true. The fact that we cannot infer (II) from (I) is, of course, one example of the failure of the (classical) distributivity law.

Consider now the objection to Putnam made by Harrison (1983). (He too talks of "position" and "momentum," and in the quotations below I have replaced these words by "B-value" and "A-value," respectively.) Harrison suggests first that, according to quantum theory, if a system has a determinate B-value, it is false that it has any of the A-values specified in the second conjunct of (I). He continues:

> Hence, if quantum theory is true, the truth of the first conjunct in (I) implies the falsity of the second, and (I) itself must be false. Thus the very circumstance, that a particle cannot have a determinate B-value and A-value, which implies the falsity of (II), also implies the falsity of (I), and the difficulty for classical logic is removed. (P. 84)

But his argument from the falsity of a_1, a_2, and a_3 to the falsity of $a_1 \vee a_2 \vee a_3$ relies entirely on his treating $\vee$ as classical truth tables prescribe. Clearly, it is no objection to Putnam's system just to say that truth-table analysis tells us that the truth of a disjunction requires the truth of at least one of the disjuncts. This merely tells Putnam something he already knows: that his system is not classical.

Again, consider Harrison's objection to Putnam's claim that $a_1 \vee a_2 \vee a_3$ is a logical truth:

If the second conjunct in (I) is a logical truth, then quantum theory must be false, for quantum theory just asserts that a particle does not have to have an A-value a_1, or an A-value a_2, etc. for all the A-values there are. (P. 84)

And, of course, if quantum theory were false, then quantum logic would be unnecessary. But once more, and for the same reason, the criticism fails.

Nonetheless, an important question emerges from Harrison's paper. Even if we accept $a_1 \vee a_2 \vee a_3$ as true, why should we read it as "The system has an A-value"? Indeed, what is the content of the claim that the system has an A-value if it can be accompanied by the four statements that (i) this A-value is not a_1, (ii) nor is it a_2, (iii) nor is it a_3, and (iv) these three values of A are all the A-values there are? (See Stairs, 1983b, sec. IV.)

Certainly, Putnam runs into trouble when he makes the further (independent) claim that, not only does the system have an A-value in all states, but that "if I measure I will find it" (Putnam, 1969, p. 230). Assume, for the sake of argument, that the system is prepared in a state which makes b_1 true, and that an A-measurement now yields a_3. If I have simply "found" the A-value of the system, then surely a_3 was true of the system before the measurement, along with b_1. But, as we have noted, on Putnam's quantum logic the conjunction $b_1 \wedge a_3$ is always false.

We may relinquish the claim about measurement, even though it carries away with it Putnam's purported resolution of the measurement problem, and therewith much of the motivation of his project, but then we are left with the odd notion of a "disjunctive property." Apparently the system can have the property (A, $a_1 \vee a_2 \vee a_3$) while having none of the "atomic" properties (A,a_1), (A,a_2), or (A,a_3). Disjunctive properties are not wholly implausible; in fact Teller (1979) has argued that all properties involving continuous quantities are disjunctive, since quantum mechanics never specifies a sharp value for, say, momentum, but at most an interval within which it lies. Nevertheless, in the case of an observable with a discrete spectrum, the acceptance of disjunctive properties seems to dilute to insipidity the claim that, for any system, every observable has a value at all times. The package we have bought seems markedly less attractive than the product which was advertised.

7.9 *Properties and Deviant Logic*

Let us review the situation. Section 7.6 gave a formal account of quantum logic. A set of sentences, closed under the logical connectives $\neg$, $\vee$, and $\wedge$, is supplied with a semantics which maps them systematically onto the elements of a lattice. The purported logical relations between the sentences are then read off from the algebraic relations which hold between these elements. But the logic that results constitutes an alternative to classical logic only when the sentences of this formal language are given a specific interpretation; as Section 7.7 showed, an unexceptionable, if unadventurous interpretation of the lattice elements as modal propositions, $\Box(A,\Delta)$, is available. Under this interpretation quantum logic formalizes a particular account of necessity; it supplements but does not supplant classical logic.

When Putnam says that the rules of quantum logic "conflict with classical logic" and that the lesson to be drawn is that "we must change our logic" (p. 221), he has another interpretation of the formal system in mind. As we saw in Section 7.8 he reads the propositions of quantum logic as indicative propositions ascribing properties to microsystems.

It is this interpretation that has given quantum logic that hint of philosophical perversity—delicious or detestable according to taste—conveyed in the phrase "deviant logic." On the one hand, these are propositions of a kind to which, *prima facie,* we would expect classical logic to apply; on the other, they are just the statements which results like the Kochen and Specker theorem tell us behave in a nonstandard way: given an exhaustive list of the possible values of each observable for a system, at no time can we truly ascribe exactly one of these values to each observable.

Now this problem is going to be faced by anyone who offers an interpretation of quantum mechanics which involves ascribing properties to systems. And no matter what kind of account is given of why the properties behave as they do, this account will always have a counterpart in the formal mode. Assume, for example, that the account posits states of affairs which can or cannot obtain. Then, corresponding to each of these states of affairs there will be a statement which may or may not be truly asserted. Constraints on possible states of affairs will appear in the formal mode as restrictions on what may be truly said about them. It follows that anyone who talks of the properties of systems is committed to some version of "quantum logic."

Witness Harrison, whom we met inveighing "Against Quantum Logic" in Section 7.8. He writes, "I had always supposed that, according to quantum theory, . . . [if] a particle's position is determinate, it is false that it has any of the velocities specified in [an exhaustive list of velocities]" (Harrison, 1983, p. 84). In other words, in quantum mechanics the truth of one atomic proposition—an ascription of position—entails the falsity of another—any specific ascription of velocity. Now any systematic account of such entailments constitutes a logic; further, since no classical conjunction of atomic propositions is a contradiction, this logic will be nonclassical. Thus the arguments Harrison presents do not speak against quantum logic, but in favor of one system rather than another.

In fact, the quantum logic proposed by Reichenbach (1944, secs. 29–33) was concerned with this very question: how should we formalize the relation of mutual exclusivity, or, as he called it, *complementarity* between ascriptions of precise values to incompatible observables. Reichenbach's solution was to move to a three-valued truth-functional logic. Sentences could be true, false, or indeterminate; sentences expressing complementary propositions were such that, if one received the value true (or false), then the other received the value indeterminate. Conjunctions of such sentences were perfectly well formed, but they could never receive the value true.

Reichenbach contrasted his three-valued logic, not with the algebraic analysis of Birkhoff and von Neumann (1936) (the ancestor of all algebraic approaches), but with the Copenhagen interpretation of quantum theory, or, as he termed it, "the Bohr-Heisenberg interpretation" (Reichenbach, 1944, p. 139). The account of property ascriptions offered by this interpretation has a markedly operationalist flavor. According to Bohr, one may ascribe properties to a system, but the concepts involved (position, momentum, and so on) are not applicable to the system at all times. Each becomes applicable only when certain experimental conditions are realized:

> Closer examination reveals that the procedure of measurement has an essential influence on the conditions on which the very definition of the physical quantities rests. (Bohr, 1935b, p. 65)

Note that, as so often, Bohr is here making a point about the conditions of meaningful discourse. These conditions are contextual; if we are dealing with an experimental procedure designed to measure, say, momentum, then we cannot talk meaningfully of the position of a system. Bohr writes of "essentially different experimental arrangements and procedures which are suited either for an unambiguous use of the idea of space location, or for a legitimate application of the conservation theorem of momentum" (Bohr, 1935a, p. 699).

Bohr's account is amenable to formal presentation (though this runs contrary to his own views on semantics; see MacKinnon, 1984). Bub (1979, p. 118) suggests that

> . . . Bohr regards the notion of *truth* as meaningful only in the context of a Boolean possibility structure, i.e., to ascribe a property to a system only makes sense with respect to a structure of possible properties which form a Boolean algebra. In the case of a quantum mechanical system this possibility structure is non-Boolean. The application of the classical notion of truth, or the attribution of physical properties to

such a system, requires reference to a classical measuring system, which fixes a particular Boolean algebra in the non-Boolean possibility structure.

The resulting logic of property ascriptions is strongly reminiscent of one proposed by Kochen in 1978.

On Kochen's account, the set of possible properties of a system is subdivided into Boolean subalgebras, each of which comprises a set of *available* properties, as we may call them. Which properties are available at a given time is determined by the interaction the system has most recently undergone; each interaction will leave the system with a set of available properties, and this set has the structure of an *interaction algebra* (Kochen's term). The spin-$\frac{1}{2}$ particle is a particularly simple case; the interaction algebras are each associated with a direction α in physical space, and have just four elements apiece: $\{\varnothing, (S_\alpha, +\frac{1}{2}), (S_\alpha, -\frac{1}{2}), (S_\alpha, \pm\frac{1}{2})\}$. Hence any such set is a set of available properties.

Among the available properties, only some (at most a half) will be *actual;* typically, a spin-$\frac{1}{2}$ particle may have actual properties $\{(S_x, -\frac{1}{2}), (S_x, \pm\frac{1}{2})\}$. The property $\varnothing$ is never actual; it is available only in a purely technical sense. To use the terminology of Section 6.9, the system has, at any time, a *value-state,* λ. When this is maximally specific—and sometimes it is not, as in the case of the completely unpolarized electron (see Section 8.6)—λ picks out an ultrafilter in the (Boolean) interaction algebra.

The value-state in turn determines the *statistical* state. A new interaction will leave the system with properties in a specific new interaction algebra, but the transitions are not deterministic; each of these (new) available properties is assigned a probability of occurrence by the (old) statistical state. The statistical state assigns a probability to every possible property—in other words, to every property in every interaction algebra. Statistically, the various Boolean algebras all hang together in a familiar way. The family of these algebras forms the partial Boolean algebra characteristic of $S(\mathcal{H})$, each property is representable by a subspace of $\mathcal{H}$, and, as usual, the (pure) statistical states are represented by normalized vectors or by projection operators onto rays of $\mathcal{H}$.

On this interpretation the descriptive and the dispositional aspects of states are distinguished; these two functions of a classical state are performed by two distinct kinds of state. In this division of labor the value-state gives us information about present properties and the statistical state tells us what we may expect from future interactions.

The logic of property ascriptions that emerges is nonclassical; the set of propositions which ascribe properties to systems forms a partial Boolean algebra. Within the language we use to express these propositions, not all sentences can be meaningfully connected; the connectives $\wedge$ and $\vee$ are thus "partial connectives" in the same sense that the operations on a PBA are partial operations. At any time only one maximal Boolean subalgebra of propositions applies to the system. The ultrafilters on that subalgebra act as two-valued truth-assignments to the propositions within it, and to each ultrafilter corresponds a value-state. Among the propositions within this subalgebra the laws of classical logic obtain. The propositions that lie outside it may conveniently be given some third truth-value, neither true nor false, to indicate that neither they nor their negations are true. (Hughes, 1985b, gives a detailed account of the semantics of this logic.)

Algebraically, this is precisely the quantum logic that Bub finds implicit in Bohr's writings. This is not to say that Bohr and Kochen share a common interpretation of quantum theory. Rather, they offer interpretations which differ both in detail and in the metaphysical attitudes they express. In the first place, whereas on Kochen's account the Boolean interaction algebras are selected by any kind of interaction, on Bohr's view the classical nature of measuring instruments gives measurement interactions a special status. Secondly, the ontological commitment urged by Kochen is not shared by Bohr, who indeed took pains to distance himself from others (also associated with the Copenhagen tradition) who held that physical attributes were "created by measurement" (Bohr, 1949).

Nonetheless, formally the logics are exactly the same; on the partial Boolean semantics they employ, sentences conjoining a position ascription and a momentum ascription are not well formed, and hence are meaningless. Thus, although this algebraic logic can be made to collapse to a three-valued semantics, what results is very unlike the logic Reichenbach proposed as an alternative to the Bohr-Heisenberg interpretation. As we have noted, on Reichenbach's logic, conjunctions of complementary propositions are perfectly well formed, though never true; furthermore, unlike the collapsed algebraic logic, Reichenbach's is truth-functional.

These analogies and disanalogies, however, serve only to underscore our previous conclusion: that much of the debate between advocates of quantum logic and their opponents has been misdirected. If Kochen, on the one hand, and Bub, acting on Bohr's behalf, on the other, can start from radically different interpretations of quantum theory and yet produce formally identical quantum logics, then this adds strong support to the view that, whatever interpretation we adopt, the logic of property ascriptions to quantum systems will be nonclassical. The choice we confront is not between adopting, for example, the Copenhagen interpretation and embarking on "the heroic course" of changing our logic (Putnam, 1969, p. 222); it is between adopting a deviant logic and eschewing the notion of a property.

Though it is flattering to believe that talk of properties makes heroes of us all, we may well enquire what work is being done by this notion in any of the proffered interpretations. The answer is, surely, very little. Rather, a metaphysical nostalgia is prompting various responses to the question, how can we make room for the notion of a property within quantum mechanics? If, for example, a particular interpretation-*cum*-logic either yielded something resembling the Precise Value Principle or resolved the measurement problem, then there would be clear-cut reasons, not only for preferring it to the others, but for accepting it. But none do so.

The most we can say is this. If we retain the notion of a property, then either (a) the possession of properties associated with an observable A rules out the simultaneous possession of properties associated with observables incompatible with A; or (b) we have to make sense of the notion of a *disjunctive* property, so that, for example, a particle can have the property $(S_x, \pm\frac{1}{2})$ but neither the property $(S_x, +\frac{1}{2})$ nor the property $(S_x, -\frac{1}{2})$. Kochen, Bohr, and Reichenbach adopt alternative (a), though for different reasons; Putnam, along with other advocates of a lattice-theoretic approach, is forced to alternative (b). Neither alternative, however, is very enticing.

In Section 6.9 I described the task of interpreting quantum theory as that of finding, within the models the theory provides, images of the elements of a categorial framework. The search for properties has yielded only pallid, scarcely recognizable variants of these creatures. Perhaps we should call off the hunt, acknowledge that properties are the unicorns of quantum theory, and confess that none of us is innocent enough to capture one. In doing so we need not condemn all of quantum logic, specifically algebraic quantum logic, as misguided. Even if an emphasis on sentential quantum logics may have proved unhelpful, a more general algebraic program remains. And, just as earlier we distinguished between formal sentential logic and the interpretation of the sentences it manipulated, so now we can distinguish the core of the quantum-logical program from our interpretation of that core (this distinction is due to Stairs, 1983b, p. 578). The core is the idea that the non-Boolean algebraic structures appearing in quantum theory provide the key to our understanding of the quantum world. This core can be retained even when we jettison the interpretation which regards the elements of these structures as properties of systems, the promise of which has proved illusory. On another interpretation, quantum logic provides, in Bub's terms, a non-Boolean possibility structure for quantum *events*. This interpretation is the subject of the next chapter.

8

Probability, Causality, and Explanation

The term *probability* has, up to now, been treated as though it were entirely unproblematic. Surely this is too optimistic by far. There is, for instance, the problem of the *interpretation* of probability: does it represent a degree of belief, or a relative frequency, or a mysterious propensity, or something else again? The view taken in this book is that nearly all the probabilities appearing in theoretical quantum mechanics are *objective* probabilities. That is to say, they inhere in the world and do not simply reflect the degrees of belief of an observer; rather, they determine what this degree of belief should ideally be: if an event E is assigned an objective probability of, say, 0.1, then a fully informed observer should assign a *subjective* probability of 0.1 to E and place her bets accordingly (see Lewis, 1980). I wrote just now that "nearly all" quantum-theoretic probabilities are objective. The possible exceptions occur when a system is in a mixed state. If we adopt the ignorance interpretation of a given mixture, then we assign a subjective probability to each of the pure states represented in it, and each of these in turn assigns objective probabilities to events. Heisenberg, for one, suggested that the interplay between objective and subjective components of probability assignments could be made to do interpretive work, and I discuss his suggestions in Section 9.5. Note, however, that, as we saw in Section 5.8, not all mixtures *can* be given the ignorance interpretation.

Leaving aside the possible exception of mixtures, I will assume that quantum theory deals with objective probabilities. However, I will not discuss how the concept of objective probability is to be interpreted (see, for example, Giere, 1973, 1976; Skyrms, 1980, chap. IA; van Fraassen, 1980, chap. 6), but will instead focus on a problem raised by quantum mechanics for the mathematical theory of probability. Quantum mechanics requires us to modify this theory, or rather to generalize the mathematical account of it given by Kolmogorov (1933). But, surprisingly, this revision yields remarkable benefits; it helps us to provide explanations of the "causal anomalies" which beset quantum theory. Or so I shall suggest.

Running through this chapter, in what I hope will be a euphonious counterpoint, are three main themes: (1) the generalization of probability theory, (2) the "causal anomalies" of quantum mechanics, and (3) the resolution of these anomalies in terms of generalized probability theory. A discussion of scientific explanation appears as a coda.

8.1 *Probability Generalized*

The classical presentation of probability theory was given by Kolmogorov (1933). On this account, probabilities are assigned to sets. In Kolmogorov's original presentation, these sets were said to be subsets of a set E of "elementary events." These "elementary events," however, played no further part in the discussion; following standard practice, I will use the term *event* to refer to any subset of a set E to which a probability is assigned. If a probability is assigned to two events A and B, we also require it to be defined for their union, $A \cup B$, for their intersection, $A \cap B$, and for their complements, $E - A$ and $E - B$. That is to say, a probability function is defined on a field $\mathcal{F}$ of subsets of E.

(8.1) We say that the triple $\langle E,\mathcal{F},p\rangle$ is a *classical probability space* if $\mathcal{F}$ is a field of subsets of E and p is a function $p:\mathcal{F} \rightarrow [0,1]$ satisfying

(8.1a) $p(E) = 1$ and $p(\varnothing) = 0$;

(8.1b) $p(A \cup B) = p(A) + p(B)$, for all $A,B \in \mathcal{F}$ such that $A \cap B = \varnothing$.

In fact it's now usual to define the measure on a σ-field of sets, that is, one which is closed not only under finite union and intersection, but also under (denumerably) infinite union and intersection. In this case (8.1b) becomes:

(8.1b)* If $\{A_i\}$ is any denumerable family of pairwise disjoint members of $\mathcal{F}$ (that is, if $A_i \cap A_j = \varnothing$ whenever $i \neq j$), then $p(\cup_i\{A_i\}) = \Sigma_i p(A_i)$.

Of course, if (8.1b*) is confined to finite families $\{A_i\}$, then it reduces to Kolmogorov's original axiom.

We see that a classical probability measure is a (countably) additive real-valued set function.

Now the "probabilities" defined by quantum-mechanical states are not defined on sets but on quantum events (A,Δ) ("experimental questions"). Thus, in one obvious way, they don't conform to Kolmogorov's definition.

This would be trivial if the algebraic structure of the set of quantum events were isomorphic to a field of sets, that is, if the algebra of quantum events were Boolean. For, as we noted, the fact that Kolmogorov defines events as sets of "elementary events" plays no part in the ensuing mathematical theory. What is important in his account is that the algebraic structure of the set of events is that of a σ-field of sets, that it is a Boolean σ-algebra. In fact, from the point of view of classical probability theory, by defining a probability field in terms of a field of sets rather than a Boolean σ-algebra, Kolmogorov loses no generality (*contra* Popper, 1959, app. *iv; see Bub, 1975), since, by Stone's theorem, any Boolean algebra is isomorphic to some field of sets. (See Section 7.2.)

As we saw in Section 7.4, however, the algebraic structure of the set of quantum events is non-Boolean; the set of subspaces of a Hilbert space can be regarded either as an orthomodular lattice or as a transitive partial Boolean algebra, within which not all pairs of elements are compatible. It seems that the functions assigning probabilities to quantum events are, paradoxically, not probability functions at all, at least, not in Kolmogorov's sense. The importance of this was pointed out by Suppes (1966); clearly, we need to generalize the concept of a probability function so that it is defined on a wider class of algebraic structures than the class of Boolean σ-algebras. Within this wider class, a σ-field of sets, on the one hand, and the set $S(\mathcal{H})$ of subsets of a Hilbert space, on the other, should appear as special cases.

I will confine myself here to a generalization of finitely additive probability functions, defined on *orthoalgebras.*

(8.2) $\langle A,\perp,\oplus,^{\perp},0,1\rangle$ is said to be an *orthoalgebra* if A is a set containing designated elements 0 and 1, $\perp$ is a binary relation on A, $\oplus$ is a partial binary operation on A such that $a \oplus b$ exists if and only if $a \perp b$, $^{\perp}$ is a singulary operation on A, and, for all a,b in A,

(8.2a) if $a \perp b$, then $b \perp a$, and $a \oplus b = b \oplus a$;

(8.2b) $a \perp 0$ and $a \oplus 0 = a$;

(8.2c) $a \perp a^{\perp}$ and $a \oplus a^{\perp} = 1$;

(8.2d) $a \perp a^{\perp} \oplus b$ only if $b = 0$;

(8.2e) $a \perp a \oplus b$ only if $a = 0$;

(8.2f) if $a \perp b$, then $a \perp (a \oplus b)^{\perp}$ and $b^{\perp} \perp a \oplus (a \oplus b)^{\perp}$.

These axioms are due to Hardegree and Frazer (1981). From them we may derive the following theorems:

(8.3a) $0^\perp = 1$; $1^\perp = 0$;

(8.3b) $(a^\perp)^\perp = a$;

(8.3c) $a \oplus b = a \oplus c$ only if $b = c$;

(8.3d) $a \oplus b = 1$ only if $b = a^\perp$.

The symmetric relation $\perp$ is known as the *orthogonality* relation, the operation $\oplus$ is known as the operation of *orthogonal sum*, $^\perp$ is the *complementation* operation. Note that 0 is the only element orthogonal to itself.

We have already met one example of an orthoalgebra in Section 7.5, and it will be useful to review that account here. (As then, the reader is referred to Stein, 1972, pp. 374–378, for a more careful account.) Assume that we can conduct any one of a number of experiments, each of which has a number of mutually exclusive possible outcomes. The set E of *events* is then generated from the set of possible outcomes of all experiments, to form an orthoalgebra, as follows.

An *event* is any set of outcomes associated with a single experiment. Two events are *orthogonal* ($e \perp f$) if they are disjoint sets of outcomes associated with the same experiment. For any pair of orthogonal outcomes, e and f, their orthogonal sum, $e \oplus f$, is defined as the union of the two events. Note that this operation is not defined for two events associated with different experiments; $\oplus$ is thus a partial operation on E. The set of all possible outcomes associated with a particular experiment is the *certain event* for that experiment. The *complement* $e^\perp$ of an event e is the set-theoretic complement of e relative to the certain event for the experiment in question. The empty set, $\varnothing$, is the *null event*, and is common to all experiments; it is orthogonal to all events, and is the zero, 0, of the orthoalgebra. The certain event for any experiment is also identified with the certain event for all others; it is the unit, 1, of the orthoalgebra.

Though the elements of this particular algebra are all sets, the structure $\mathcal{E} = \langle E, \perp, \oplus, ^\perp, 0, 1 \rangle$ is clearly an orthoalgebra and not, in general, a field of sets. But it does have some properties not shared by all orthoalgebras. For instance, within $\mathcal{E}$, the operation $\oplus$ is associative: for all e, f, and g in E,

$$e \oplus (f \oplus g) = (e \oplus f) \oplus g$$

whenever these operations are defined. Successive constraints on orthoalgebras yield a hierarchy of algebraic structures. (See Hardegree and Frazer, 1981; for a summary, see Hughes, 1985a.) A Boolean algebra is an associative orthoalgebra in which all sets of elements are jointly compatible: a set B of elements of an orthoalgebra $\mathcal{A}$ is said to be *jointly compatible* if there exists a set C of pairwise orthogonal members of $\mathcal{A}$ such that each member b of B is the orthogonal sum of some subset of C; in other words, for each $b \in B$, there exist $c_1, c_2, \ldots, c_n \in C$ such that $b = \oplus_i c_i$. When B is the pair $\{a,b\}$, this condition reduces to the familiar definition (7.30).

In the "operational" orthoalgebra $\mathcal{E}$ sketched above, we could regard all events as compatible if all the possible experiments could be performed simultaneously without interfering one with the other. In that case the algebra of events would be embeddable within a Boolean algebra, in fact within a field of sets.

Less stringent constraints than the requirement of universal joint compatibility yield the transitive partial Boolean algebras (equivalently, coherent orthomodular posets) of quantum logic.

We now define a generalized probability function p.

(8.4) A function $p: A \rightarrow [0,1]$ is said to be a *generalized probability function* if the set A forms an orthoalgebra ($\mathcal{A} = \langle A, \perp, \oplus, ^{\perp}, 0, 1 \rangle$), and

(8.4a) $p(0) = 0$, $p(1) = 1$;

(8.4b) for all a and b in A, if $a \perp b$, then $p(a \oplus b) = p(a) + p(b)$.

An infinitary version of this is not problematic (see Gudder, 1976). It requires us to define an operation of infinitary orthogonal sum on an orthoalgebra, defined for countable sets of pairwise orthogonal elements; implicit in this definition is the condition that the orthoalgebra be associative.

Any orthoalgebra $\mathcal{A}$ contains Boolean algebras as substructures. The restriction of a generalized probability function p on $\mathcal{A}$ to a Boolean subalgebra of $\mathcal{A}$ is a Kolmogorov probability function. In fact:

(8.5) If $\mathcal{B}$ is a partial Boolean algebra, any function $p: B \rightarrow [0,1]$ whose restriction to a Boolean subalgebra of $\mathcal{B}$ is a Kolmogorov probability function is a generalized probability function on $\mathcal{B}$.

8.2 *Two Uniqueness Results*

The probability functions we have dealt with throughout this book are functions $p: S(\mathcal{H}) \rightarrow [0,1]$ mapping the set $S(\mathcal{H})$ of closed subspaces of a Hilbert space $\mathcal{H}$ into the interval $[0,1]$. Since $S(\mathcal{H})$ forms a partial Boolean algebra, but not a Boolean algebra, these functions are generalized probability functions rather than Kolmogorov probability functions. Within this PBA, however, there are (maximal) Boolean subalgebras. In fact, any set of subspaces which can be generated from a set of mutually orthogonal rays spanning $\mathcal{H}$ by span, intersection, and orthocomplementation forms a Boolean algebra, and the restriction of any generalized probability function (GPF) to this subalgebra is a Kolmogorov probability function. In the terminology of Section 5.5, any GPF on $S(\mathcal{H})$ is a *frame function*, and we have a representation theorem for all functions of this kind.

Gleason's theorem tells us that the set of GPF's on a Hilbert space $\mathcal{H}$ of dimensionality three or higher is in one-to-one correspondence with the set of density operators on $\mathcal{H}$; to the GPF p there corresponds exactly one density operator $\mathbf{D}$ such that, for every subspace L of $\mathcal{H}$ and associated projection operator $\mathbf{P}$, we have

(8.6) $$p(L) = \mathrm{Tr}(\mathbf{DP})$$

Note that if $\mathcal{H}$ has dimension two, while each density operator on $\mathcal{H}$ yields a GPF, the converse does not hold, witness the probability function on $\mathbb{R}^2$ which assigns 1 to points in the first and third quadrants and 0 to points in the second and fourth.

Gleason's theorem is a very strong result; the measures supplied by the density operators on $\mathcal{H}$ are the only natural extensions of classical probability functions to the non-Boolean structure of the set of quantum-mechanical propositions.

In 1977 Bub (1977) pointed out another highly significant result, that the non-Boolean structure of $S(\mathcal{H})$ also necessitates a revised account of conditional probability. In classical probability theory every Kolmogorov probability function p defines a conditional probability measure $\mathbb{P}$; the probability $\mathbb{P}(A|B)$ of event A conditional on event B is given by

$$\mathbb{P}(A|B) = \frac{p(A \cap B)}{p(B)} \qquad [\text{provided } p(B) \neq 0]$$

For any given nonzero event B, the function $\mathbb{P}(X|B)$ (where X is any event in E) is itself a classical probability measure. In fact, it is the only classical probability measure on the set E of events such that, for all A in E,

$$\text{If} \quad A \subseteq B, \quad \text{then} \quad \mathbb{P}(A|B) = \frac{p(A)}{p(B)}$$

Thus, in the classical case, for events A contained in B, conditionalizing on B just involves a renormalization of p to p', where $p'(B) = 1$.

Now let p be a generalized probability function on $S(\mathcal{H})$, with corresponding density operator $\mathbf{D}$, and let L_B be a subspace such that $p(L_B) \neq 0$.

Then there exists a unique GPF $\mathbb{P}(X|L_B)$ on $S(\mathcal{H})$ such that, whenever $L_A \subseteq L_B$,

$$\mathbb{P}(L_A|L_B) = \frac{p(L_A)}{p(L_B)}$$

The proof of this is given in Appendix B.

By Gleason's theorem, this GPF is representable by a density operator $\mathbf{D}_B$. In Appendix B it is shown that

$$\mathbf{D}_B = \frac{\mathbf{P}_B\mathbf{D}\mathbf{P}_B}{\mathrm{Tr}(\mathbf{P}_B\mathbf{D}\mathbf{P}_B)}$$

where $\mathbf{P}_B$ projects onto L_B.

The denominator is just a normalizing factor, to ensure that $\mathbf{D}_B$ has unit trace. By the properties of the trace [see (5.6)] and idempotence, we obtain

$$\mathbf{D}_B = \frac{\mathbf{P}_B\mathbf{D}\mathbf{P}_B}{\mathrm{Tr}(\mathbf{D}\mathbf{P}_B)}$$

From (8.6) it follows that, if L_A and L_B are subspaces of $\mathcal{H}$ with projection operators $\mathbf{P}_A$ and $\mathbf{P}_B$, then

$$(8.7) \qquad \mathbb{P}(L_A|L_B) = \frac{\mathrm{Tr}(\mathbf{P}_B\mathbf{D}\mathbf{P}_B\mathbf{P}_A)}{\mathrm{Tr}(\mathbf{D}\mathbf{P}_B)} \qquad \text{[Lüders' rule]}$$

Note that in (8.7) there is no restriction on L_A; we do not require that $L_A \subseteq L_B$. However, we see that, as in the classical case, the Lüders rule gives the only probability measure that, for events $L_A \subseteq L_B$, just involves a renormalization of the GPF given by the operator $\mathbf{D}$. This offers strong grounds for regarding it as the appropriate conditionalization rule for GPFs on $S(\mathcal{H})$. Additional grounds for thinking of it as the natural extension of the classical conditionalization rule appear from its behavior in two special cases (see also Bub, 1977, and Section 9.3).

First of all, consider the case when L_A and L_B are compatible. In this case we have

$$\mathbf{P}_A\mathbf{P}_B = \mathbf{P}_B\mathbf{P}_A = \mathbf{P}_C$$

where $\mathbf{P}_C$ projects onto $L_A \cap L_B$. (If $L_A \perp L_B$, then $\mathbf{P}_C$ is the zero operator.)

Using (5.6) we obtain

$$\text{(8.8)} \qquad \mathbb{P}(L_A|L_B) = \frac{\mathrm{Tr}(\mathbf{DP}_C)}{\mathrm{Tr}(\mathbf{DP}_B)} = \frac{p(L_A \cap L_B)}{p(L_B)}$$

By taking compatible subspaces L_A and L_B we remain in one Boolean subalgebra of $S(\mathcal{H})$; in this case, whatever our approach to quantum logic, $L_A \wedge L_B$ is well defined, and is equal to $L_A \cap L_B$. For such subspaces the Lüders rule reduces to classical conditionalization.

Let us look at another kind of situation where we can meaningfully speak of the conjunction of two quantum events. (To reduce the number of symbols floating around, I will use projection operators to represent these events.)

Consider a composite system with two components a and b; the states of the composite system will be represented in the tensor-product space $\mathcal{H}^a \otimes \mathcal{H}^b$. Let $\mathbf{P}^a$ be a projector on $\mathcal{H}^a$ representing a quantum event associated with system a, and $\mathbf{P}^b$ a projector on $\mathcal{H}^b$ representing a quantum event associated with system b.

Assume that the density operator $\mathbf{D}$ on $\mathcal{H}^a \otimes \mathcal{H}^b$ represents the state of the composite system. Then the joint probability of $\mathbf{P}^a$ and $\mathbf{P}^b$ is given, in accordance with (8.6), by

$$p(\mathbf{P}^a,\mathbf{P}^b) = \mathrm{Tr}[\mathbf{D}(\mathbf{P}^a \otimes \mathbf{P}^b)]$$

The probabilities of the individual events are given by

$$p(\mathbf{P}^a) = \mathrm{Tr}[\mathbf{D}(\mathbf{P}^a \otimes \mathbf{I}^b)] \quad \text{and} \quad p(\mathbf{P}^b) = \mathrm{Tr}[\mathbf{D}(\mathbf{I}^a \otimes \mathbf{P}^b)]$$

where $\mathbf{I}^a$ and $\mathbf{I}^b$ are the identity operators on $\mathcal{H}^a$ and $\mathcal{H}^b$, respectively.

Now by Lüders-rule conditionalization,

$$\mathbb{P}(\mathbf{P}^a|\mathbf{P}^b) = \frac{\mathrm{Tr}[(\mathbf{I}^a \otimes \mathbf{P}^b)\mathbf{D}(\mathbf{I}^a \otimes \mathbf{P}^b)(\mathbf{P}^a \otimes \mathbf{I}^b)]}{\mathrm{Tr}\mathbf{D}'}$$

where $\mathbf{D}' = \mathbf{D}(\mathbf{I}^a \otimes \mathbf{P}^b)$.

Using the properties of the trace, operator multiplication on $\mathcal{H}^a \otimes \mathcal{H}^b$, and idempotence, we see that

$$\begin{aligned}\mathbb{P}(\mathbf{P}^a|\mathbf{P}^b) &= \frac{\mathrm{Tr}[\mathbf{D}(\mathbf{I}^a \otimes \mathbf{P}^b)(\mathbf{P}^a \otimes \mathbf{I}^b)(\mathbf{I}^a \otimes \mathbf{P}^b)]}{\mathrm{Tr}\mathbf{D}'} \\ &= \frac{\mathrm{Tr}[\mathbf{D}(\mathbf{P}^a \otimes \mathbf{P}^b)]}{\mathrm{Tr}\mathbf{D}'}\end{aligned}$$

But $\mathrm{Tr}\mathbf{D}' = \mathrm{Tr}[\mathbf{D}(\mathbf{I}^a \otimes \mathbf{P}^b)] = p(\mathbf{P}^b)$, and it follows that

$$\mathbb{P}(\mathbf{P}^a|\mathbf{P}^b) = \frac{p(\mathbf{P}^a,\mathbf{P}^b)}{p(\mathbf{P}^b)} \tag{8.9}$$

exactly as in the classical case.

Before we leave this formal development of generalized probability theory, one thing should be emphasized. The conditional probability given by the Lüders rule is a probability of a quantum event **Q** given another quantum event **P**. Though each event can be regarded as a pair (A,Δ), this internal structure of events is irrelevant to the generalized probability theory given here. In particular, nothing in this discussion of quantum conditionalization bears directly on the question of whether the expression $p(A,\Delta)$ should itself be regarded as a conditional probability and be read as "The probability that a result in the Borel set Δ will occur, given that a measurement of A takes place" ($p(R_\Delta|M_A)$, for short). I postpone this question to Section 10.3.

8.3 *The Two-Slit Experiment: Waves and Particles*

A discussion of quantum theory which made no mention of the two-slit experiment would not quite be Hamlet without the Prince; nonetheless, it might be thought an eccentric departure from tradition. However, I include the experiment here not from a desire to preserve ancestral pieties, but because of its relevance to our present concerns, a relevance which will appear in Section 8.4.

In the experiment—or rather in the idealized version of an experiment* —a source E emits electrons at a steady rate toward a sensitive screen S. Between the source and the screen is a diaphragm, in which there are two slits, A and B. Three experiments are performed. In the first, a, only slit A is open; in the second, b, only slit B is open; in the third, c, both A and B are open. The time of each experiment is long enough for averaging effects to come into play, and in each case the distribution of "hits" on the screen is recorded. The distribution pattern for c (shown at the far right of Figure 8.1) is not just the sum of the patterns for a and b, as it would be if the electrons

* A neutron interference experiment which is the exact analogue of the two-slit experiment has been performed by a group led by Summhammer. It is simply described in Leggett (1986).

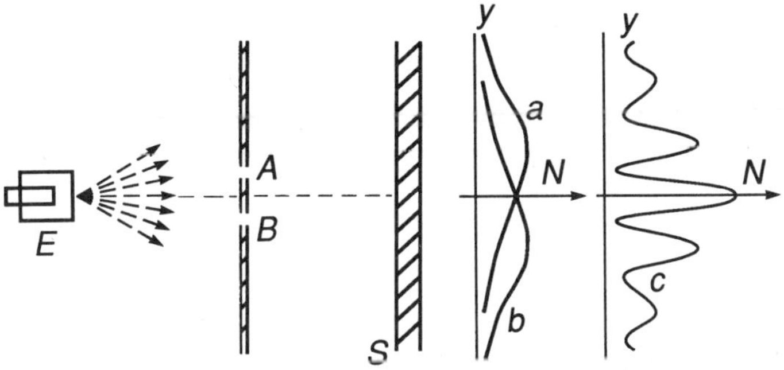

Figure 8.1 The two-slit experiment; curves show distribution of "hits" in experiments *a* and *b* and *(far right)* experiment *c*. (From Feynman, Leighton, and Sands, 1965.)

behaved like classical particles. Instead, it resembles the interference patterns characteristic of waves that have passed through two small apertures (see, for example, PSSC, 1960, pp. 286–294). That is, if we take a small area X of the screen and write

N_A = number of hits on X per unit time in experiment *a*

N_B = number of hits on X per unit time in experiment *b*

N_{AB} = number of hits on X per unit time in experiment *c*

we find that

$$N_{AB} \neq N_A + N_B$$

On a wave interpretation of the interaction between source and screen this is perfectly explicable. If two waves spread out from *A* and *B*, only at a few places on *S* will they arrive in phase; for the most part they will arrive somewhat out of step—in fact when the "crest" of one exactly coincides with the "trough" of the other the two will cancel each other out.

Each of the two classical models of causal processes, the particle model and the wave model, offers a partial description of the source-screen interaction, but neither is fully adequate. Either model, taken on its own, leaves us with a "causal anomaly." (The term is Reichenbach's, 1944, secs. 6, 7.) Anomalous on the wave account is the fact that electrons are individually detectable at the screen; for this "collapse of the wave packet" the account offers no explanation. But the particle account fares no better. Let us assume that, when both apertures are open, a number N'_A of particles reach X per unit time after passing through A, and that a number N'_B reach X per unit time by passing through B. Then, since on a wholehearted particle analysis each particle reaching X must pass through exactly one aperture,

$$N_{AB} = N'_A + N'_B$$

But we know that

$$N_{AB} \neq N_A + N_B$$

and so, either $N_A \neq N'_A$ or $N_B \neq N'_B$.

On this account, the causal anomaly lies in the fact that the opening of B either affects the number of electrons passing through A or else affects the propensity of these electrons to strike the region X on the screen; the particles passing through A mysteriously "know" whether B is open or not.

Each model accounts adequately for some of the phenomena, but neither accommodates them all.

One response to this, and similar anomalies, has been to say that quantum mechanics requires us to forswear a unified description of nature. According to Hanson (1967, p. 43), "The Copenhagen interpretation of quantum mechanics is the view that fundamental nature is indivisibly bipartite—the wave-particle duality." Despite the fact that it has been held by some of the theory's most distinguished practitioners, this view turns out to have slender justification. Let us look at it as it appears in the writings of Niels Bohr. (He discusses the two-slit experiment in Bohr, 1949, pp. 216–218.)

Bohr took the necessity of using two seemingly incompatible descriptions of phenomena as a general epistemological principle and called it the Principle of Complementarity. In the case of the wave-particle duality, the principle takes this form:

(8.10) As a description of microentities and microprocesses, neither a particle description nor a wave description is fully adequate. Between them, however, they form a complete, complementary description.

Underlying this principle is a doctrine which we may summarize as follows.

(1) Conditions for the applicability of scientific concepts are determined by the experimental situation (see, for example, Bohr, 1935a, p. 699).

(2) Experiments can be unambiguously described only in classical terms (see Bohr, 1949, p. 209).

(3) "Any given application of classical concepts precludes the simultaneous use of other classical concepts which in a different connection are equally necessary for the elucidation of the phenomena" (Bohr, 1934, p. 10).

The limitations on classical concepts announced in (3) are due to the indeterminacies associated with the quantum of action: there is always a "finite and uncontrollable interaction between the objects and the measuring instruments in the field of quantum theory" (Bohr, 1935a, p. 700), and this precludes simultaneous ascription of, for example, position and momentum to a particle. I discuss Bohr's interpretation of these indeterminacy relations in Section 9.2. (For a full and sympathetic discussion of Bohr's views, see Hooker, 1972.)

We have met (1) already, in Section 7.9; on Bohr's account, the use of a particular concept (such as momentum or position) presupposes the existence of a particular physical situation; only when that situation obtains is discourse involving that concept meaningful. Similarly with the wave-particle duality. The language associated with a particle model of physical processes acquires meaning in specific experimental contexts. Further, concepts are readily linked to particular models—momentum to the wave model (as the wave number of the wave), and position to the particle model.

Bohr's position is elegantly summarized by Petersen (1963, p. 12):

> In the language of physics there are various sets of concepts such as space and time, and the so-called dynamical concepts like momentum and energy. Corresponding to these different sets of concepts are different types of measuring tools. For example, to determine the position of the object, one must use rulers firmly attached together to form a reference frame. On the other hand, to measure an object's momentum one may let it collide with a freely movable body of known mass, and then measure the resultant velocity of the test body . . .
>
> In quantum physics we use the same concepts [as in classical physics] and thus the same measuring tools, but . . . the dissimilarity between the measuring tools becomes crucially important. Here we cannot use the different types of instruments in combination. We cannot combine the information about the system that we get from one type of instrument with the information we get from another. Therefore a quantum physical phenomenon is characterized by the type of measuring instrument we use. Two phenomena obtained by observing the same system with two different types of instruments are mutually exclusive. Bohr called this logical relation of exclusion complementarity.

The lesson to be drawn is that if we use the same set of concepts in quantum physics as in classical, then we can never obtain a unified description of the behavior of a system. But this prompts the obvious question: why should we accept (2)? Why are the concepts of classical physics to be accorded privileged status? Bohr writes (and italicizes), "*However far the phenomena transcend the scope of classical physical explanation, the account of all evidence must be expressed in classical terms.*" And he argues that only by a "suitable application of the terminology of classical physics" can we describe our experiments to others without ambiguity (1949, p. 209).

This seems wholly implausible. It *may* be that we need to use a classical categorial framework to describe experiments, and hence that such a framework is implicit in the formulation of quantum theory; in fact, I will argue as much in Chapter 10. Nonetheless, this is a far cry from saying (i) that the only vocabulary we can meaningfully employ is that of classical physics, a vocabulary familiar to physicists at the end of the nineteenth century, and (ii) that its operational meaning must forever remain unchanged.

One could challenge this (and with it much of what Bohr says) by denying that there were such things as "operational meanings" (see Hempel, 1954, for a discussion). Similarly, Bohr's views would be instantly rejected by anyone who subscribed to a principle of meaning incommensurability, the view that with a move from one theory to another all terms suffer a radical change in meaning. (This view is discussed by Hacking, 1983, chap. 5.) For example, of the move in question, from classical physics to quantum mechanics, Schrödinger (1935, p. 155) remarked gloomily, "Does not one get the impression that here one deals with fundamental properties of *new* classes of characteristics, that keep only the name in common with classical ones?" But one can take less extreme views and still disagree with Bohr. Without inconsistency, indeed with considerable plausibility, one could maintain (a) that to know what a term means is, among other things, to know the experimental contexts in which its use would be appropriate, (b) that there is some preservation of meaning between theories, and (c) that new theories both bring new concepts into physics and modify the meanings of the concepts that are retained.

According to Rosenfeld, "The classical concepts to which Bohr appeals directly . . . are (in the last resort) not formalizable, but immediately given (as part of common experience)" (pers. com.; see Daneri, Loinger, and Prosperi, 1962, p. 298). Hooker (1972, p. 135) too suggests that classical concepts are "regarded by Bohr as being refined versions of our ordinary, everyday concepts" and that this is the reason Bohr accords them a privileged status. But this position (though not its ascription to Bohr) is untenable. Take, for instance, as ordinary and everyday an instrument as an ammeter. I can, without further elaboration, use the term *ammeter* in describing an experiment to any living physicist. This is because we share a common theoretical vocabulary which includes *electric current.* But the concept of electric current is not a "refined version" of any concept at all that was available to, say, Galileo. Still less can Bohr's claim be made on behalf of magnetic flux density or electrostatic potential, both perfectly good classical concepts.

My point is simply this, that the vocabulary of the experimenter and that of the theoretical physicist (to make a dubious distinction) have always been intertwined; as terms for radically new concepts enter the theoretician's vocabulary, so they will enter the experimenter's. This process did not stop at the stroke of midnight on December 31, 1899.

What holds for the concepts used in the theory holds also for the models in which they appear. One problem which a new theory should not be called upon to answer is why it makes only partial use of the models used by its predecessors. Given the historical matrix from which quantum mechanics emerged, it is not surprising that a great deal of early quantum theory was expressed in terms of wave and particle concepts. For every physicist at the turn of the century, these were ready-to-hand pieces of theoretical equipment. For sound pragmatic reasons physicists were loath to discard them. In 1900, however, with Planck's attribution of particle properties to electromagnetic waves, they began to be used in unorthodox ways; Planck's move was mirrored twenty-five years later by de Broglie's attribution of wave properties to electrons.

What, then, of the so-called wave-particle duality that results? I say more about this duality in Section 10.2; however, we can agree with Bohr that each model, while proving heuristically valuable, offers only a partial analogy to the behavior of light and matter. Further we can agree (how could we not?) that the two models are mutually at odds. We can deny, however, that there is any radical epistemological lesson to be drawn from all this.

These episodes in the prehistory of quantum theory do not teach us to abjure a unified understanding of quantum phenomena in favor of a doctrine of epistemological complementarity, according to which we are compelled to move to and fro between two incompatible ways of picturing the world. They teach us merely that neither of these ways is fully adequate. We can draw a different conclusion than did Bohr, even while agreeing with him that "The two views on the nature of light are rather to be considered as different attempts at an interpretation of experimental evidence, in which the limitations of the classical concepts are expressed in complementary ways" (1934, p. 56).

8.4 The Two-Slit Experiment: Conditional Probabilities

Schrödinger (1953), with whom the concept of the "wave function" originated, maintained to the end of his life that it should be thought of as a mathematical representation of a physical wave, even if this compelled us to a dualist ontology. In contrast, in 1926 Born pointed out that one could interpret wave functions in probabilistic terms. In a discussion of collisions between electrons and atoms he proposed that the function $\Phi(\alpha,\beta,\gamma)$ gave "the probability that the electron will be thrown out in the direction given by the angles α,β,γ," and added in a celebrated footnote, "More careful consideration shows that the probability is proportional to the square of the quantity Φ" (Born, 1926a, p. 865; Wheeler and Zurek, 1983, p. 54).

Effectively, this is the interpretation of the wave function (or state function) used in this book. For Born it was the key to providing a unified particle interpretation of quantum theory: "If one wants to understand [collision processes] in corpuscular terms, only one interpretation [the probabilistic interpretation of Φ] is possible" (Born, 1926a, p. 865). But, initially at least, the use of probabilities still leaves the particle interpretation with the anomaly we met in the last section.

Let A be the event that the electron passes through aperture A, B the event that the electron passes through aperture B, and X the event that the electron strikes the region X of the screen. Then $A \vee B$ is the event that the electron passes through either A or B, A & X is the event that the electron passes through A and strikes region X, and so on. We can write down three conditional probabilities:

$$p(X|A) = \frac{p(X \,\&\, A)}{p(A)} \tag{8.11}$$

$$p(X|B) = \frac{p(X \,\&\, B)}{p(B)} \tag{8.12}$$

$$p(X|A \vee B) = \frac{p[X \,\&\, (A \vee B)]}{p(A \vee B)} \tag{8.13}$$

By expanding (8.13) we obtain

$$p(X|A \vee B) = \frac{p[(X \,\&\, A) \vee (X \,\&\, B)]}{p(A \vee B)} \tag{8.14}$$

and, since

(8.15) X & A and X & B are mutually exclusive events,

it follows that

$$(8.16) \qquad p(X|A \vee B) = \frac{p(X \,\&\, A) + p(X \,\&\, B)}{p(A \vee B)}$$

For simplicity we consider the case when

$$(8.17) \qquad p(A) = p(B)$$

Again, since *A* and *B* are mutually exclusive,

$$(8.18) \qquad p(A \vee B) = p(A) + p(B) = 2p(A)$$

and so

$$(8.19) \qquad p(X|A \vee B) = \frac{p(X \,\&\, A)}{2p(A)} + \frac{p(X \,\&\, B)}{2p(B)} = \frac{1}{2}p(X|A) + \frac{1}{2}p(X|B)$$

If we cash out (8.19) in terms of the relative frequencies with which the event X occurs in experiments *a*, *b*, and *c* (see Section 8.3), we get

$$(8.20) \qquad N_{AB} = N_A + N_B$$

(The factor $\frac{1}{2}$ disappears because we deal with twice as many electrons in experiment *c* as in *a* and *b*.) But, as noted previously, (8.20) is at odds both with quantum theory and with experiment.

One thing that the derivation of (8.19) reveals is that the problem is not just a problem for any particular model of causal processes. For equations (8.11)–(8.19) were established without mention of the particle model; they dealt solely with the probability of an event X conditional on other events *A*, *B*, and *A* v *B*. They give us a purely probabilistic analysis, albeit one that can be supplemented by a causal story involving particles.

Where might the derivation of (8.19) be challenged? First, forsaking the particle model, one might deny (8.15); if *A* and *B* (and hence *A* & X, *B* & X) are not mutually exclusive, then the additivity law appealed to in (8.16) and (8.18) doesn't hold.

Attempts to check (8.15) experimentally have distinctly odd effects. Let us assume, for example, that counters are set up immediately behind the apertures *A* and *B* to register whether both events can take place simultaneously.

Then we find that each electron arriving at the screen has triggered exactly one of the counters, and exclusivity seems to be verified. But the presence of the counters also destroys the pattern at the screen; when they are present (8.20) holds (see Feynman, Leighton, and Sands, 1965, vol. 3, pp. 1.6–1.9). This effect is certainly peculiar, and, as with many quantum effects, it is tempting to see it as symptomatic of a deep-seated epistemological recalcitrance at the quantum level. But I think this temptation should be resisted. The experiment with counters is designed to answer a specific question: are the events *A* and *B* mutually exclusive? The answer it gives is unambiguous: they are.

Of course, our interest in this particular question is a by-product of our search for an account of the interference pattern at the screen, and a remarkable effect of the experiment is that this pattern is replaced by another. Nonetheless, although we would like to know why this effect takes place, that's a separate problem. Even if we couldn't solve it there would be no obvious reason why we shouldn't take the evidence the counters supply at face value; they show that *A* and *B* are indeed mutually exclusive. (A similar point is made by Fine, 1972, p. 25.)

If we accept this result, then we need to locate the problem in the derivation of (8.19) elsewhere. Putnam (1969) suggested that the illicit move in this derivation is that from (8.13) to (8.14) (see Section 7.8). As he pointed out, this move is an application of the distributive law, which doesn't hold within quantum logic. It is certainly true that if we reject the distributive law, then the inference from (8.13) to (8.14), and hence the derivation of (8.19), is blocked. The trouble is, this is a purely negative result. It merely tells us that the additive pattern is not guaranteed at the screen. It gives us no reason why, in general, the interference pattern occurs, nor why the interference pattern becomes the additive pattern when the screen is moved close enough to the diaphragm. (Compare Bub, 1977; see also Gibbins, 1981b, and 1987, pp. 147–151.)

Clearly, the simple rejection of a particular law of logic will not supply much in the way of an explanation of what goes on. And, from Putnam's 1969 paper, one might well think that the only important thing about quantum logic was that it gave up the distributive law. However, as Putnam has recognized (Friedman and Putnam, 1978), the quantum-logical approach can offer a much deeper analysis of the problem than this. This alternative analysis suggests that, rather than sniffing suspiciously at individual moves in the derivation of (8.19), we should reject the whole derivation. For the probabilities we are dealing with are assigned, not by probability functions on a classical probability space, as the derivation assumes, but by generalized probability functions defined on a Hilbert space. In fact Bub has shown that, by replacing classical conditional probabilities by quantum conditional probabilities, and then allowing for one further factor affecting the probability of event X, we obtain the quantum statistics. (See Bub, 1977, and 1979, pp. 100–104; Beltrametti and Cassinelli, 1981, pp. 283–285.) The further factor is the evolution of the system's state between the diaphragm and the screen.

Since the calculations involve an observable with a continuous spectrum (the y-coordinate of position), they look more complicated than those we are used to. However, the principle behind them is very simple. We assume that the electrons arrive at the diaphragm in a pure state Ψ. At the diaphragm a quantum event occurs. In each of the three experiments this event is associated with the y-coordinate of position; events $A = (y,\Delta_A)$, $B = (y,\Delta_B)$, and $A \vee B = (y,\Delta_A \cup \Delta_B)$ occur in experiments a, b, and c, respectively (at least for those electrons which make it to the screen). Conditionalization on any event, using the Lüders rule, yields a new generalized probability function in the Hilbert space, in other words, a new state. Conditionalizing on the event A yields the pure state Ψ_A, while conditionalizing on B yields the pure state Ψ_B. If at this point we appealed to classical probability theory, then conditionalizing on $A \vee B$ would yield a mixture of Ψ_A and Ψ_B, and the resulting probabilities would be half of the sum of those obtained from Ψ_A and Ψ_B, in accordance with (8.19). The surprising and nonclassical feature of Lüders' conditionalization is this, that conditionalizing on $A \vee B$ yields not a mixture of Ψ_A and Ψ_B, but instead a superposition of the two, the pure state $\Psi_{A \vee B}$.

Now, if the screen were very close to the diaphragm, the probability of X would be given by Ψ_A in experiment a, by Ψ_B in experiment b, and by $\Psi_{A \vee B}$ in experiment c. However, since an event at the screen occurs a time t after the corresponding event at the diaphragm, we must use the Schrödinger equation to see how each of the three states Ψ_A, Ψ_B, and $\Psi_{A \vee B}$ evolves in this time and calculate the probabilities of X accordingly. It is this temporal evolution which produces the effects which prompt a wave account of the phenomena, and which we can refer to as the "diffraction" of the state function. Indeed, as we have noted, when the screen and diaphragm are very close together, there are no such effects, and the probabilities given by Ψ_A and Ψ_B add in a thoroughly classical way.

Let us run this formally. The spectral measure associated with the position operator was discussed in Section 1.15. The projection operator corresponding to event A is the operator $\mathbf{P}_A$ such that, for the pure state $\Psi(y)$,

$$\mathbf{P}_A\Psi(y) = \Psi(y) \quad \text{for } y \in \Delta_A$$

$$\mathbf{P}_A\Psi(y) = 0 \qquad \text{for } y \notin \Delta_A$$

Conditionalizing on A (using the Lüders rule) yields a "truncated" wave function $\mathbf{\Psi}_A$, which vanishes outside Δ_A, and within it is just $\mathbf{\Psi}$ renormalized. Similarly, conditionalizing on B and $A \vee B$ yields $\mathbf{\Psi}_B$ and $\mathbf{\Psi}_{A \vee B}$, respectively.

Now if

$$|\mathbf{P}_A \mathbf{\Psi}| = |\mathbf{P}_B \mathbf{\Psi}|$$

then A and B are equiprobable, and

$$\mathbf{\Psi}_{A \vee B} = \frac{1}{\sqrt{2}} \mathbf{\Psi}_A + \frac{1}{\sqrt{2}} \mathbf{\Psi}_B$$

which is a superposition of $\mathbf{\Psi}_A$ and $\mathbf{\Psi}_B$.

In the case when A and B are not equiprobable, we still get a superposition of $\mathbf{\Psi}_A$ and $\mathbf{\Psi}_B$, but one which is unequally weighted.

Now let $\mathbf{U}_t$ be the evolution operator which modifies the state between the diaphragm and the screen, and let Δ_X be the range of y-values covered by the region X. Then, in the experiment c, the state of the system at the screen is $\mathbf{U}_t \mathbf{\Psi}_{A \vee B}$, and, using the usual statistical algorithm (2.1) together with the definition of inner product in L^2 (Section 1.11), we obtain

$$\text{(8.21)} \qquad \begin{aligned} p_c(X) = p_c(y, \Delta_X) &= \langle \mathbf{U}_t \mathbf{\Psi}_{A \vee B} | \mathbf{P}_X \mathbf{U}_t \mathbf{\Psi}_{A \vee B} \rangle \\ &= |\mathbf{P}_X \mathbf{U}_t \mathbf{\Psi}_{A \vee B}|^2 \\ &= \int_{\Delta X} \left| \mathbf{U}_t \frac{1}{\sqrt{2}} (\mathbf{\Psi}_A + \mathbf{\Psi}_B) \right|^2 dy \end{aligned}$$

Within the expansion of (8.21) we find the so-called interference term:

$$\text{Re} \int_{\Delta X} (\mathbf{U}_t \mathbf{\Psi}_A)^* (\mathbf{U}_t \mathbf{\Psi}_B) dy$$

This term gives the difference between $p_c(X)$ and $\frac{1}{2}[(p_a(X) + p_b(X)]$. It only vanishes for all Δ_X when $t = 0$, that is, when the screen is very close to the diaphragm.

Finally, consider the case when there are counters present. Assume, for example, that, with both apertures open, the counter beside the A-aperture registers an electron. Then, after the event $A \vee B$, *another* event A has occurred, to wit, the restriction of the electron to the region round the A-counter. Provided that the counter is sufficiently close to the aperture for no significant evolution of the state to occur between the two, the effect will be a two-stage transition,

$$\Psi \rightarrow \Psi_{A \vee B} \rightarrow \Psi_A$$

With the counters present, the ensemble of electrons will be divided into two subensembles in states Ψ_A and Ψ_B. At the screen this will give the statistics of a mixture of the states $\mathbf{U}_t\Psi_A$ and $\mathbf{U}_t\Psi_B$, and the additive pattern characteristic of classical particles will appear. What was previously an odd and inexplicable effect drops out quite naturally from the analysis.

How does this analysis relate to previous chapters, and where does it leave us? The lesson of Chapters 6 and 7 was that we might be better off if we dispensed with talk of the "properties" of a quantum system. Probably the hardest property to free ourselves from conceptually is that of the system's position in space. For if we stop attributing a position to a system at all times, we will no longer be able to describe the electron in experiment *c* as passing either through aperture *A* or through aperture *B*. Thus we will no longer be able to regard it as mediating a causal process, at least insofar as we require such processes to be characterized by spatio-temporal continuity. We will be left with a story told, not in terms of causal processes, but in terms of quantum events and their probabilities conditional on other quantum events.

Of course, similar stories can be told for classical processes involving probabilities. The difference is that in the classical case, when the probabilities are Kolmogorov probabilities, causal supplements of these stories are available; for an example, consider the way in which the derivation of (8.19) earlier in this section could be supplemented by a causal account in terms of particles. However, when quantum probabilities defined on a Hilbert space are involved, no such causal supplementation is possible. Nevertheless, *contra* Kant, this doesn't make a quantum story unintelligible. And, for all its unfamiliarity, the account of the two-slit experiment outlined above has one great merit: it tallies with the facts.

8.5 *The Bell-Wigner Inequality and Classical Probability*

Like the two-slit experiment, the Bohm version of the EPR experiment raises questions both about causality and about probabilities in quantum mechanics. In Chapter 6, the problem posed by Bell's theorem was presented as a problem for a version of *local realism,* the thesis that (1) quantum propositions (A,Δ) represent properties possessed by individual systems and which measurement reveals, and that (2) the properties of one system cannot be affected by what is done to a second system spatially separated from the first. Although Wigner's formulation of the theorem, in terms of probabilities, was used, these probabilities were interpreted as the statistical interpretation suggests, that is, as relative frequencies of the occurrence of properties within an ensemble.

However, we can now redescribe Wigner's result in terms of probability theory alone. His proof demonstrates that no probability function on a certain kind of classical probability space can yield the probability assignments of quantum theory.

As we saw, Wigner considers assignments of probabilities to sextuples $(i,j,k;l,m,n)$. Each member of a sextuple is either + or −; i, j, and k represent values of certain components of spin, S^1_a, S^1_b, and S^1_c, for particle 1, and l, m, and n values for the same components of spin for particle 2, S^2_a, S^2_b, and S^2_c. These 2^6 sextuples provide a *partition* of a classical probability space, that is, a set of mutually exclusive and jointly exhaustive events. It turns out that no classical probability assignment to this partition can yield the quantum statistics for S^1_a, S^2_a, et cetera.

Bub (1974, chap. 6) has argued that this version of Bell's theorem just provides further evidence that quantum mechanics requires a nonclassical account of probability. Indeed, the problem with the postulated probability space is not far to seek. Effectively, the sextuples defining the members of the partition are assumed to be sixfold classical conjunctions; thus the set $\{(S^1_a,+), (S^1_b,+), (S^1_c,+)\}$, for instance, is assumed jointly compatible. In the event structure of quantum mechanics, however, this is just not so. Nor, crucially, can the quantum Hilbert-space structure be embedded into a classical (Boolean) structure on which this partition might be defined; we know this from Kochen and Specker's (extended) theorem. The postulated classical probability space was therefore doomed to inadequacy, independently of considerations involving coupled systems. Bub concludes that the Bell argument "has nothing whatsoever to do with locality" and emphasizes the point by generating a similar inequality for a single particle, using a classical partition with 2^3 members, each of form (i,j,k) (p. 83).

Accardi and Fedullo (1982) have done likewise. Nonetheless, as Bub now acknowledges, more can be said about the two-particle version of Bell's inequality, in particular about the problems it raises for our concept of causality.

8.6 Bell Inequalities and Einstein-Locality

Let us review and amplify the account of the Bohm version of the EPR experiment given in Section 6.3.

Electron-positron pairs are produced, with the composite system in the so-called singlet spin state $\mathbf{\Psi}$. This is a pure state in the tensor-product space $\mathcal{H}^e \otimes \mathcal{H}^p$:

$$\mathbf{\Psi} = \frac{1}{\sqrt{2}}(\mathbf{v}_+ \otimes \mathbf{u}_-) - \frac{1}{\sqrt{2}}(\mathbf{v}_- \otimes \mathbf{u}_+)$$

where $\mathbf{v}_+$ and $\mathbf{v}_-$ are the eigenvectors of some component of spin, $\mathbf{S}^e_\alpha$, for the electron, and $\mathbf{u}_+$ and $\mathbf{u}_-$ are the eigenvectors of the same component of spin for the positron, $\mathbf{S}^p_\alpha$.

To the vector $\mathbf{\Psi}$ corresponds the density operator $\mathbf{D}_\mathbf{\Psi}$ on $\mathcal{H}^e \otimes \mathcal{H}^p$:

$$\mathbf{D}_\mathbf{\Psi} = \mathbf{P}_\mathbf{\Psi}$$

This yields the two reduced states $\mathbf{D}^e$ and $\mathbf{D}^p$ for the two components of the coupled system; however, these are mixed states rather than pure states (see Section 5.8). In fact, they are mixed states without unique orthogonal decompositions; we have:

$$\mathbf{D}^e = \frac{1}{2}\mathbf{P}^e_{\alpha+} + \frac{1}{2}\mathbf{P}^e_{\alpha-}$$

$$\mathbf{D}^p = \frac{1}{2}\mathbf{P}^p_{\beta+} + \frac{1}{2}\mathbf{P}^p_{\beta-}$$

where α and β are any directions in physical space. If we represent possible states of a spin-$\frac{1}{2}$ particle by points on or within the unit sphere of $\mathbb{R}^3$, as in Section 5.3, then $\mathbf{D}^e$ and $\mathbf{D}^p$ both lie exactly in the center of the sphere. That is to say, the individual particles are completely unpolarized: whatever component of spin is measured on, say, the electron, the probability of the result $+\frac{1}{2}$ is exactly equal to the probability of the result $-\frac{1}{2}$.

However, as we saw in Section 6.3, a strong anticorrelation exists: for any direction α,

(8.22) $$p_\mathbf{\Psi}(S^e_\alpha, +\tfrac{1}{2}; S^p_\alpha, +\tfrac{1}{2}) = \mathrm{Tr}[\mathbf{D}_\mathbf{\Psi}(\mathbf{P}^e_{\alpha+} \otimes \mathbf{P}^p_{\alpha+})] = 0$$

and, in general,

(8.23) $$p_\mathbf{\Psi}(S^e_\alpha, +\tfrac{1}{2}; S^p_\beta, +\tfrac{1}{2}) = \frac{1}{2}\sin^2\frac{1}{2}\widehat{\alpha\beta}$$

The problem is, how are we to explain these correlations? We can sort out putative explanatory accounts into rough groups; *interaction accounts* suggest that the correlations are due to interactions between the component systems after they have separated, while *preparation accounts* trace the correlations back to the original preparation, either of the composite system (type *S*), or of the experimental set-up (type *E*). Each kind of account, it turns out, runs counter to our basic beliefs about causality. (Note that a causal *preparation* account would involve what Salmon, 1984, chap. 6, calls an *interactive fork.* Ah, well.)

As an elementary example of an interaction account, let us hypothesize that the performance of an experiment on one particle (the positron, say) changes the state of the other. Assume, for the sake of argument, that the α-component of spin is measured for the positron and found to have value $+\frac{1}{2}$. Then the probabilities assigned to measurement results on the electron of the same pair will change. Whereas we had, for any direction β, $p(S^e_\beta, +\frac{1}{2}) = 0.5$, the correlation now gives us $p(S^e_\beta, +\frac{1}{2}) = \sin^2\frac{1}{2}\widehat{\alpha\beta}$. But these are just the probabilities assigned to events $(S^e_\beta, +\frac{1}{2})$ when the electron is in the $\boldsymbol{\alpha}_-$ eigenstate of spin (see Chapter 4).

On our hypothesis, the measurement on the positron has effected a change in the state of the electron. Prior to the measurement it was in the mixed state $\mathbf{D}^e$; subsequently it is in the pure state $\mathbf{P}^e_{\alpha-}$. However, the hypothesis seems to raise as many problems as it solves. In particular, how can we account for this interaction without contravening the special theory of relativity (STR)? For it is a fundamental result of that theory, variously called the principle of *Einstein-separability* or *Einstein-locality*, that no causal signals can propagate at a speed faster than light. And, in the first place, most of the experimental tests confirming quantum-mechanical predictions for coupled systems have looked not at spin correlations for an electron-positron pair, but at polarization correlations between photons; these photons travel (of course) at the speed of light, and so only a signal traveling faster than that could pass between them (see Clauser and Shimony, 1978; d'Espagnat, 1979). Second, even if the interaction involved an electron-positron pair (and some have been done using proton-proton pairs), it should be possible to perform an experiment on particle 2 which, although performed later than the experiment on particle 1 in the laboratory frame of reference, is nevertheless space-like separated from it (Taylor and Wheeler, 1963), so that, according to STR, no causal transaction could take place between the two.

STR is one of the most firmly established and best corroborated theories of modern physics. We should be, at least, deeply suspicious of any account of the EPR correlations which violates it. However, as Bell (1964, p. 199) pointed out, it would not be a direct contravention of STR to postulate that the setting of one measurement device affected the results obtained on the other. Such interactions would violate locality in one sense, in that the devices would not function independently of one another, but it would not necessarily violate Einstein-locality; the postulated interactions could propagate at a speed less than that of light and achieve their effects before the actual measurements occurred. The proposed solution is, in effect, a preparation account of type *E*, and traces the correlations to the experimental set-up. It recalls Bohr's dictum: "The problem again emphasizes the necessity of considering the whole experimental arrangement, the specification of which is imperative for any well-defined application of the quantum-mechanical formalism (Bohr, 1949, p. 230). Though Bohr is (again) making a point about the conditions for meaningful discourse, rather than offering a causal account of the correlations, any experiment which puts this particular causal account to the test will also tell us whether Bohr's holistic resolution of the EPR problem is adequate (*contra* Leggett, 1986, p. 44; for Bohr's treatment of EPR see Bohr, 1935a, 1949).

Such an experiment, using correlated polarizations of photons, was suggested by Aspect (1976). His idea was to change "rapidly, repeatedly and independently the orientations of the polarizers." Each change of orientation of a polarizer was to be space-like separated from the corresponding experiment carried out with the other. Aspect continued, "Thus one finds as a consequence of the principle of separability [Einstein-locality] that the response of one polarizer, when analyzing a photon, cannot be influenced by the orientation of the other polarizer at the same time (when analyzing the coupled photon)." The experiment was performed by Aspect, Dalibar, and Roget. They reported that, "The result violates the generalized Bell Inequality . . . and is in good agreement with [the quantum-mechanical prediction]" (Wheeler and Zurek, 1983, p. 442n).

On the one hand, their result both undercuts Bohr's response to the EPR paper and effectively rules out type-*E* preparation accounts of the statistical correlations between the measurements. In order to avoid invoking superluminal signals, these accounts appeal to the prior configuration of the apparatus; however, the statistical relations are the same even when there is, so to speak, no *prior* configuration. On the other hand, the result also confirms our earlier suspicions about interaction accounts. It suggests that all interaction accounts of the EPR correlations, whether they trace these correlations to interactions between the component systems or between the measurement devices, will violate the principle of Einstein-locality.

A statement which is at the same time more general and more precise than this has been proved by Hellman (1982a). He shows that, if any deterministically Einstein-local theory gives anticorrelation results for two distinct observables, so that, for example,

$$p[(S^1_a,+) \text{ and } (S^2_a,+)] = 0$$

and

$$p[(S^1_b,+) \text{ and } (S^2_b,+)] = 0$$

for distinct *a* and *b*, then the theory also yields a version of the Bell inequality known as the CHSH inequality, and is inconsistent with quantum mechanics. (The CHSH inequality was first derived by Clauser et al., 1969; Hellman's proof uses a theorem by Eberhard, 1977.)

Einstein-locality is here precisely defined in terms of models of the physical theory *T*. These are the possible worlds consistent with *T*. We assume that *T* specifies a background of a four-dimensional Minkowski space-time (see Taylor and Wheeler, 1963, chap. 1). Pairs $(\mathbf{x},t)$ in space-time, where $\mathbf{x}$ is a position vector and *t* a time-coordinate, are referred to as *events*; thus "event" is not here to be taken as synonymous with "experimental question." We can talk of two models *agreeing* at an event *e* (that is, at a particular point *e* in space-time) if the same sentences are true at *e* in each model.

Consider any event *e* and any "slice" S_e through the backward light cone from *e*. S_e is part of a plane of simultaneity for some observer; it is a set of events, all with light-like or time-like separation from *e*, and all prior to *e*. (See Figure 8.2.) Then *T* is said to be *deterministically Einstein-local* if, for

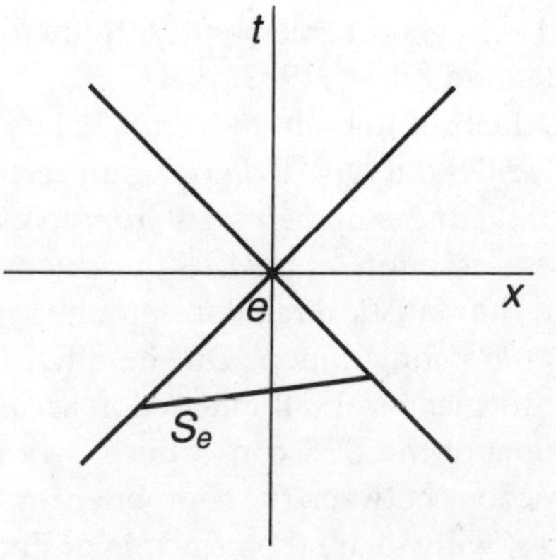

Figure 8.2 Light-cone of event *e*.

every event e and every S_e, any two models agreeing at all events in S_e also agree at e.

The intuition behind this definition is that if the definiens is satisfied, then any differences at e are attributable to differences in events that could, according to STR, be causally related to e.

Notice that Hellman's theorem does not merely sharpen the problem we run into if we try to explain EPR correlations by an interaction hypothesis. It also tells us, first, that quantum mechanics is not a deterministically Einstein-local theory, and, second, that no such theory can generate the quantum-mechanical predictions. In the language of Section 6.8, it rules out the possibility of a contextual, deterministically Einstein-local hidden-variable reconstruction of quantum theory.

As Hellman (1982b) emphasizes, his proof disbars *deterministic* Einstein-local theories, but not *stochastic* Einstein-local theories. A stochastic Einstein-local theory requires the *probability* of a particular measurement outcome on particle 1 to be unaffected by whether or not a measurement is conducted on particle 2. Hellman shows that the requirement of stochastic Einstein-locality is not on its own sufficient to yield Bell-type inequalities. As we shall see in Section 8.8, this is confirmed by the fact that quantum theory is itself stochastically Einstein-local.

To generate Bell-type inequalities we need to supplement this condition by another; Jarrett (1984) suggests that the condition most frequently (and often implicitly) invoked is essentially a *completeness* condition. "Completeness" here is not to be understood in the sense in which Einstein used it (see Section 6.2); like stochastic Einstein-locality, it is a requirement of conditional statistical independence, but whereas stochastic Einstein-locality requires the probability of a particular outcome for particle 1 to be independent of whether or not a measurement is conducted on particle 2, completeness requires it to be independent of the outcome of such a measurement, given that the measurement actually takes place. To bring out this difference, Shimony (1986) refers to the two conditions as "Parameter Independence" and "Outcome Independence," respectively. I will state the completeness condition (Outcome Independence) in terms of measurements of spin, though Jarrett's presentation is more general. To avoid clumsiness, however, a change in notation is called for.*

* "Parameter Independence" is also known as "Surface Locality"; see Section 8.7. The variety of names may seem unfortunate; each was chosen to bring out one feature of the condition in question. The formulation of the completeness condition I use is taken not from Jarrett (1984) but from his 1989 paper, which contains a particularly good—and accessible—discussion of determinism, locality, and completeness.

We write α^e for "an S_α-measurement is performed on the electron," and β^p for "an S_β-measurement is performed on the positron"; we also write $+^e$ for "the outcome of the electron-measurement is $+\frac{1}{2}$," and $+^p$ for "the outcome of the positron-measurement is $+\frac{1}{2}$." Thus, when α^e is the case, $+^e$ is the event $(S^e_{\alpha'}, +\frac{1}{2})$.

Now let λ be the conjunction of all statistically relevant information that the theory supplies *via* the state description of the systems plus their source. Then the theory is *complete* provided that, according to the theory,

$$(8.24a) \quad p(+^e|\lambda,\alpha^e,\beta^p,+^p) = p(+^e|\lambda,\alpha^e,\beta^p)$$

$$(8.24b) \quad p(+^p|\lambda,\alpha^e,\beta^p,+^e) = p(+^p|\lambda,\alpha^e,\beta^p)$$

And, in this notation, the condition of *stochastic Einstein-locality* appears as the pair of equations

$$(8.24c) \quad p(+^e|\lambda,\alpha^e,\beta^p) = p(+^e|\lambda,\alpha^e)$$

$$(8.24d) \quad p(+^p|\lambda,\alpha^e,\beta^p) = p(+^p|\lambda,\beta^p)$$

All these probabilities are classical conditional probabilities. The conditions (8.24a) and (8.24b) tell us that, given a certain preparation of the system plus environment, and given certain settings of the measurement apparatuses (that is, given λ, α^e, and β^p), the occurrence of a particular outcome of the positron-measurement will not affect the probability of occurrence of a particular outcome of the electron-measurement, and vice versa. To quote Jarrett (1984, p. 588):

> The point is, that if the state descriptions are complete in the relevant sense, then conditionalization on the outcome of a measurement on [one] particle entails no further restriction on the physical possibilities that would serve to better define the probabilities for the outcome of possible measurements on [the other].

With justification, he regards this kind of completeness as characteristic of classical theories.

The Bell inequality can be derived from the requirement of stochastic Einstein-locality plus completeness (Jarrett, 1984, p. 582, though the proof is not given). Since quantum mechanics contravenes the Bell inequality, but is stochastically Einstein-local, it is therefore, in Jarrett's sense, incomplete. But, as he says (p. 585),

> Incomplete theories (e.g. quantum mechanics) are not *ipso facto* defective. On the contrary, when the results of Bell-type experiments are taken into account, the truly

remarkable implication of Bell's Theorem is that incompleteness, in some sense, is a genuine feature of the world itself.

To take stock of the various possible accounts of the EPR correlations, we have so far seen that,

(8.25a) deterministic Einstein-local interactive accounts are ruled out by Hellman's result;

(8.25b) type-E preparation accounts are ruled out by the Aspect experiments;

(8.25c) any kind of stochastic Einstein-local preparation account that invokes complete state descriptions is ruled out by Jarrett's result.

In anticipation of Section 8.7 I might also add that the completeness requirement (8.24) strongly resembles part of Reichenbach's and of Salmon's specification of what it is for λ to be the *common cause* of two statistically governed events $+^e$ and $+^p$. As we shall see, it is not only deterministic causality which is threatened by the violation of the Bell inequalities.

8.7 *Bell Inequalities and Causality*

Bell's inequality, or, more accurately, Bell-type inequalities, have been used in a variety of arguments. But, if we leave to one side the versions involving just one particle, these arguments all have a common structure. (This was pointed out by Shimony, 1981; for a comprehensive discussion of Bell's inequality, see Cushing and McMullin, 1989.) The arguments all involve an experimental situation in which pairs of particles are jointly prepared and then separately tested. The inequality is then derived from two distinct sets of premises. The first set, P_{exp}, consists of statements of correlations (or anticorrelations) between experimental results on the two particles, the second, P_{met}, of premises of a more metaphysical kind. From the union of P_{exp} and P_{met} the inequality I is derived:

$$P_{exp} \cup P_{met} \vdash I$$

Quantum mechanics predicts the correlations of P_{exp} but also predicts results at odds with I. Experimental results which bear out the quantum-mechanical predictions thus tell us that I does not hold but that the premises in P_{exp} do. It follows that some or all of the premises in P_{met} must be discarded.

The usual Duhemian reservations of course apply. We might, for instance, consider the allegedly theory-neutral correlation experiments to be so infected with theoretical assumptions that P_{met} could be rescued (see Shimony, 1981). But in the cases to hand there seems little doubt that we are genuinely, and remarkably, putting metaphysical theses to experimental test.

Furthermore, it follows that as many different theses are being tested as there are sets of premises from which Bell-type inequalities can be derived. New derivations of I are thus interesting insofar as they start from different premises and make explicit the set P_{met} of assumptions at work. For example, we have already seen tested (a) the thesis that the quantum statistics may be reconstructed on a classical probability space (Wigner), and (b) the thesis that quantum mechanics (and the world) is deterministically Einstein-local (Hellman).

As with both of these examples, negative results do two related things. They rule out certain kinds of reconstructions or amplifications of quantum theory (hidden-variable theories), and they also rule out the possibility of explaining the EPR correlations in certain kinds of ways. Hellman's result, for instance, tells us that we will look in vain for a deterministically Einstein-local account of them, Jarrett's that we should not accept any stochastically Einstein-local account involving complete state descriptions.

A particularly striking derivation of the inequality, by van Fraassen (1982), is closely related to Jarrett's. It tells us that the correlations are not to be explained by reference to a *common cause*, and threatens any preparation account which invokes that concept. In van Fraassen's derivation, P_{exp} contains, together with the usual anticorrelation statements, premises which he calls statements of "Surface Locality." We have already met them as statements of Parameter Independence (stochastic Einstein-locality): they state that the probability of a particular outcome of an experiment on one particle is not affected by the fact that a measurement is being performed on the other, whatever the latter experiment may be. Van Fraassen makes the point that these premises, like all the others in P_{exp}, are, indeed, obtainable by induction from experiment.

P_{met} contains three different kinds of premises, labeled "Causality," "Hidden Locality," and "Hidden Autonomy." The notion of a *common cause* which these premises are designed to capture is due to Reichenbach (1956, pp. 160–161; see also Salmon, 1984, chap. 6, especially pp. 158–163). He sought an account of a causal mechanism which affected probabilities, and so would be appropriate in a nondeterministic setting. In particular, he wished to supply a causal account of statistical correlations.

He suggested that a correlation between events A and B is attributable to a common cause C provided that C precedes A and B in time, and

(8.26a) $p(A \,\&\, B|C) = p(A|C) \cdot p(B|C)$

(8.26b) $p(A \,\&\, B|\bar{C}) = p(A|\bar{C}) \cdot p(B|\bar{C})$

(8.26c) $p(A|C) > p(A|\bar{C}) \qquad p(B|C) > p(B|\bar{C})$

(Here $\bar{C}$ is the negation of C.)

Condition (8.26a) may be rewritten as

(8.27) $$p(A|C) = \frac{p(A \,\&\, B|C)}{p(B|C)} = p(A|B \,\&\, C)$$

(8.28) $$p(B|C) = \frac{p(A \,\&\, B|C)}{p(A|C)} = p(B|A \,\&\, C)$$

(8.27) tells us that, given C, the probability of *A* is unaffected by the occurrence of *B*, and (8.28) that, given C, the probability of *B* is unaffected by the occurrence of *A*. Similarly for condition (8.26b). Thus, like Jarrett's completeness condition, conditions (8.26a) and (8.26b) are requirements of conditional statistical independence: given C, the two events *A* and *B* are independent; likewise they are independent given $\bar{C}$. These can be intuitively justified as part of the specification of a common cause, either by the arguments used in the last section on behalf of the completeness condition, or in epistemic terms. We may think that two events are independent if knowledge concerning one does not affect our estimate of the probability of the other; condition (8.26a) then says that no extra information would be available, should *A* occur, which would affect the probability of event *B*, other than that contained in the common cause C.

Van Fraassen's postulated common cause is represented by a "hidden variable," λ. The Causality premises are statements of conditional statistical independence, like (8.26a) above, and Hidden Locality and Hidden Autonomy are designed to ensure the temporal priority of the common cause and to locate it in the preparation procedure, rather than in, say, the orientation of the measurement devices, which (as in the Aspect experiments) may be established after the preparation.

From these premises van Fraassen derives the Bell inequality. It follows that another casualty must be recorded in the list begun at the end of Section 8.6:

(8.29) Type-*S* preparation accounts invoking a common cause are ruled out by van Fraassen's result.

However, Reichenbach's analysis is the best, arguably the only, causal account we have of statistical correlations between separated events. No preparation account, it seems, can both save the quantum phenomena and explain them in terms of causal processes. But, from (8.25a), any interaction account which does so will need to invoke superluminal causal signals. Either way, the prospects for a causal explanation of these correlations look bleak.

8.8 Coupled Systems and Conditional Probabilities

As was noted in Section 8.7, van Fraassen derives a Bell-type inequality from five (sets of) premises. Three of these (Causality, Hidden Locality, and Hidden Autonomy) constitute the set P_{met} of "metaphysical" premises capturing the notion of a common cause; the experimental premises of P_{exp} are the assumptions of Perfect Correlation and Surface Locality. Van Fraassen presents the latter assumptions within a very general experimental context, but we can reformulate them without loss in terms of the electron-positron pair that has served as our example of a coupled system. As before, we take the system to be in the singlet spin state. Each of the assumptions is a set of statements about the probability, under certain conditions, of an event $(S^e_\alpha,+)$, where α is an arbitrary direction in space. There are three such probabilities involved: (a) the probability $p(S^e_\alpha,+)$ *simpliciter*; (b) the probability of $(S^e_\alpha,+)$, conditional on an S_β measurement being performed on the system p; (c) the probability of $(S^e_\alpha,+)$, conditional on the event $(S^p_\alpha,+)$. We denote these probabilities by p_a, p_b, and p_c, respectively. Perfect Correlation tells us that $p_c = 0$ (for all directions α in space), and Surface Locality that $p_a = p_b$ for all directions α and β in space [compare (8.24c)].

On van Fraassen's account these statements are to be justified empirically: "These probability statements are directly testable by observed frequencies" (1982, p. 30). The problem is, how are they to be explained?

I will offer a two-part answer to this. In this section I will show that the probability statements are obtainable by straightforward application of the Lüders rule for quantum conditionalization, and then (in Section 8.9) I will justify the claim that this fact alone constitutes an explanation of them.

Throughout this discussion I will talk of a Hilbert space $\mathcal{H}$ as a probability space; strictly, I should talk of the probability space isomorphic to the set $S(\mathcal{H})$ of subsets of $\mathcal{H}$.

As a preliminary, let me deal with a possible objection to applying the Lüders rule in this context. It might seem that in doing so one would be guilty of an equivocation, for the Lüders rule gives conditional probabilities on a non-Boolean set of quantum events whereas, when we regard Perfect

Correlation and Surface Locality as empirical principles, the conditional probabilities appearing in them are thought of as classical conditional probabilities. (Note, in this regard, that van Fraassen's analysis is entirely in terms of a classical probability space.) However, in the cases we are dealing with here, it turns out that the two conditionalizations coincide. It was shown in Section 8.2 that, if A and B are quantum events associated with the two components of a composite system, then the Lüders rule reduces to its classical counterpart (see also Appendix C); we have

$$\mathbb{P}(A|B) = \frac{p(A \,\&\, B)}{p(B)}$$

Let us then return to the electron-positron pair in the singlet spin state $\mathbf{D}_\Psi$ (see Section 8.6). This state of the composite system yields the two reduced states, $\mathbf{D}^e$ and $\mathbf{D}^p$, for the components. The probability p_a is given by

$$p(S^e_\alpha,+) = \mathrm{Tr}(\mathbf{D}^e\mathbf{P}^e_{\alpha+})$$

and for these states, for all α and β,

$$p(S^e_\alpha,+) = \frac{1}{2} = p(S^p_\beta,+)$$

$$p(S^e_\alpha,+;\, S^p_\beta,+) = \frac{1}{2}\sin^2\frac{1}{2}\,\widehat{\alpha\beta}$$

Here, and in what follows, the function p is the union of three generalized probability functions; it takes as arguments events associated with the electron, events associated with the positron, and conjunctions of an electron event and a positron event, giving them the values assigned by the states $\mathbf{D}^e$, $\mathbf{D}^p$, and $\mathbf{D}_\Psi$, respectively.

Perfect Correlation follows trivially from (8.9):

(8.30) $$\mathbb{P}[(S^e_\alpha,+)|(S^p_\beta,+)] = \frac{p(S^e_\alpha,+;S^p_\beta,+)}{p(S^p_\beta,+)} = \sin^2\frac{1}{2}\widehat{\alpha\beta}$$

And when $\alpha = \beta$ we obtain

(8.31) $$p_c = \mathbb{P}[(S^e_\alpha,+)|(S^p_\beta,+)] = 0$$

Note in passing that the probabilities $p(S^e_\alpha,+)$ and $p(S^p_\beta,+)$ are not statistically independent; quantum mechanics, as we expected, violates Jarrett's completeness condition (8.24a–b).

The account of Perfect Correlation given above starts from (8.9), and this in turn is derived by Lüders-rule conditionalization on a tensor-product space. Thus the electron-positron pair is treated as a whole even when the two components are spatially separated. The correlation is not predictable from the states $\mathbf{D}^e$ and $\mathbf{D}^p$ of the two components, but from the state $\mathbf{D}_\Psi$ of the composite system; the system $e + p$ is therefore not reducible to the sum of its parts. Indeed, it is a consequence of the way that quantum mechanics constructs the probability space $\mathcal{H}^e \otimes \mathcal{H}^p$ for $e + p$ from the probability spaces $\mathcal{H}^e$ and $\mathcal{H}^p$ of the components that this is so. In this respect the tensor product of two quantum probability spaces differs radically from the product of two classical probability spaces. Stairs (1984, p. 357; see also 1983a) puts the point admirably:

> Because of the way Boolean algebras (or, more importantly, classical probability spaces) combine, every measure on the product space will either render the systems statistically independent or else will be a statistical mixture of such measures. On the other hand, if the systems are associated with quantum logical fields of propositions, then their product need not exhibit this feature. That is, there may be propositions about the *pair* of systems which are neither equivalent to nor implied by conjunctions such as *a & b*, and there may be measures which are not decomposable into measures which render the subsystems independent.

In general, more information is available when we specify a state $\mathbf{D}$ for a composite quantum system than when we specify the reduced states $\mathbf{D}^a$ and $\mathbf{D}^b$ of its components. For, as noted in Chapter 5, while every state $\mathbf{D}$ yields unique states $\mathbf{D}^a$ and $\mathbf{D}^b$ for the components, the converse holds only when $\mathbf{D}^a$ and $\mathbf{D}^b$ are projectors (pure states). Unless this is the case there is more than one state $\mathbf{D}$ of the composite system which will reduce to $\mathbf{D}^a$ and $\mathbf{D}^b$.

This "quantum holism" is at odds with Einstein's view that, once spatially separated, the two systems could be regarded as independent, but, perhaps surprisingly, it is entirely compatible with Surface Locality—that is, with stochastic Einstein-locality. This principle, like Perfect Correlation, may also be derived by straightforward application of the Lüders rule. It appears as a result of a more general principle which applies both to simple and to composite systems. Assume that, for a given system, a family of mutually exclusive and jointly exhaustive compatible events exists, representable by the set $\{\mathbf{P}_i\}$ of projectors on $\mathcal{H}$. (We have $\Sigma_i \mathbf{P}_i = \mathbf{I}$.) We may think of $\{\mathbf{P}_i\}$ as the spectral decomposition of some observable $\mathbf{A}$. Now let $\mathbf{Q}$ be any event compatible with all the $\mathbf{P}_i$. Then, for any initial state $\mathbf{D}$ of the system,

(8.32) $$p_{\mathbf{D}}(\mathbf{Q}) = \sum_i p_{\mathbf{D}}(\mathbf{P}_i)\mathbb{P}(\mathbf{Q}|\mathbf{P}_i)$$

This equation is provable, either as a corollary of (8.8) or (more directly) as shown below.

$$\sum_i p_{\mathbf{D}}(\mathbf{P}_i)\mathbb{P}(\mathbf{Q}|\mathbf{P}_i) = \sum_i \mathrm{Tr}(\mathbf{DP}_i)\frac{\mathrm{Tr}(\mathbf{P}_i\mathbf{DP}_i\mathbf{Q})}{\mathrm{Tr}(\mathbf{DP}_i)}$$
$$= \sum_i \mathrm{Tr}(\mathbf{P}_i\mathbf{DP}_i\mathbf{Q})$$
$$= \sum_i \mathrm{Tr}(\mathbf{DQP}_i)$$

(by properties of the trace, idempotence of $\mathbf{P}_i$, and compatibility of $\mathbf{Q}$ with $\mathbf{P}_i$).

But

$$\sum_i \mathrm{Tr}(\mathbf{DQP}_i) = \mathrm{Tr}\sum_i(\mathbf{DQP}_i) \qquad \text{[by (5.5)]}$$
$$= \mathrm{Tr}(\mathbf{DQ}\sum_i \mathbf{P}_i)$$
$$= \mathrm{Tr}(\mathbf{DQI})$$
$$= \mathrm{Tr}(\mathbf{DQ})$$
$$= p_{\mathbf{D}}(\mathbf{Q})$$

Equation (8.32) may be interpreted as follows. Consider an observable A represented by an operator $\mathbf{A}$ and a quantum event represented by a projector $\mathbf{Q}$ compatible with $\mathbf{A}$. Provided that we can treat each possible outcome of a measurement of A as a quantum event $\mathbf{P}_i$, the initial probability of $\mathbf{Q}$ when the system is in state $\mathbf{D}$ is equal to its probability conditional on a measurement of A taking place. The latter is calculated as a weighted sum of conditional probabilities $\mathbb{P}(\mathbf{Q}|\mathbf{P}_i)$, and the weight given to each of them is the probability that the A-measurement will yield the $\mathbf{P}_i$ in question.

In the case of a composite system, events associated with one system are always compatible with events associated with the other, since all pairs of operators $\mathbf{A} \otimes \mathbf{I}$ and $\mathbf{I} \otimes \mathbf{B}$ commute. The application of (8.32) to the electron-positron system is thus straightforward. We take the set $\{\mathbf{I}^e \otimes \mathbf{P}^p_{\beta+}, \mathbf{I}^e \otimes \mathbf{P}^p_{\beta-}\}$ to be the family $\{\mathbf{P}_i\}$ of mutually exclusive and jointly exhaustive events. The observable $\mathbf{I}^e \otimes \mathbf{S}^p_\beta$ is then the observable $\mathbf{A}$, and we measure A by measuring S_β for the positron. By taking $\mathbf{P}^e_{\alpha+} \otimes \mathbf{I}^p$ as the event $\mathbf{Q}$, and noting that

$$p(S^e_{\alpha'}+) = \mathrm{Tr}(\mathbf{D}^e\mathbf{P}^e_{\alpha+}) = \mathrm{Tr}[\mathbf{D}_\Psi(\mathbf{P}^e_{\alpha+} \otimes \mathbf{I}^p)]$$

we obtain

(8.33) $$p(S^e_{\alpha'}+) = p(S^p_\beta,+)\mathbb{P}[(S^e_{\alpha'}+)|(S^p_\beta,+)] + p(S^p_\beta,-)\mathbb{P}[(S^e_{\alpha'}+)|(S^p_\beta,-)]$$

Given our interpretation of (8.32), this yields Surface Locality.

Note, however, the proviso expressed in this interpretation, that each possible outcome of a measurement of A be treated as a quantum event $\mathbf{P}_i$. The exact relation between quantum events and measurement outcomes will be discussed in Section 9.4; for the present, we will treat their identification as unproblematic.

The implication of Surface Locality is that no series of experiments performed on the electrons of an ensemble of similarly prepared pairs could give us information about whether any measurements had been performed on the positrons of those pairs. For if we took such an ensemble and performed an S^p_β-measurement on a subensemble of them, then the probability of any event $(S^e_{\alpha'}+)$ would be the same for the subensemble as for the whole ensemble. (Pagels, 1982, pp. 143–152, is very good on this.)

The derivation of Surface Locality just given shows why this is the case. Assume that the pairs are prepared in the singlet spin state $\mathbf{D}_\Psi$. Then, within the subensemble,

$$p(S^p_\beta,+) = \frac{1}{2} = p(S^p_\beta,-)$$

and

$$\mathbb{P}[(S^e_{\alpha'}+)|(S^p_\beta,+)] = \sin^2\frac{1}{2}\widehat{\alpha\beta}$$

$$\mathbb{P}[(S^e_{\alpha'}+)|(S^p_\beta,-)] = \sin^2\frac{1}{2}(\pi - \widehat{\alpha\beta}) = \cos^2\frac{1}{2}\widehat{\alpha\beta}$$

Thus the weighted sum of these conditional probabilities is given by

$$\frac{1}{2}\left(\sin^2\frac{1}{2}\widehat{\alpha\beta} + \cos^2\frac{1}{2}\widehat{\alpha\beta}\right) = \frac{1}{2}$$

which is just the probability of $(S^e_{\alpha'}+)$ within the whole ensemble.

In this illustration I have used the probabilities given by the singlet spin state. Note, however, that Surface Locality (unlike Perfect Correlation) obtains whatever the state of the pairs, as can be seen from the derivation of (8.33).

In some respects the account of the EPR correlations which this analysis gives us resembles an interaction account, in others a preparation account. It is a preparation account in that the source of these correlations is the preparation of pairs of particles in the singlet spin state. It is an interaction account in that an experiment performed on one particle effectively changes the state of the other; conditionalization on an event $(S^p_\alpha,+)$ associated with the positron "projects" the state of the electron into the eigenstate $\alpha-$ of spin. The proof of this last result, to be given shortly, provides a summary of this section. And an examination of this proof will show the crucial respect in which the present account of the EPR correlations differs from those proposed in Section 8.6. There it was tacitly assumed that, whatever type of account was forthcoming, whether interaction or preparation, it would tell a causal story. But, as we saw in Section 8.7, there is good reason to think that no causal explanation can yield the quantum-mechanical statistics. In contrast, the present account has no causal component. To recapitulate, it traces the EPR correlations to three nonclassical features of quantum probability spaces. The first is that, in these spaces, probability measures and density operators are in one-to-one correspondence, the second is that conditionalization on these spaces is given by the Lüders rule, and the third is the way in which the tensor-product spaces associated with composite quantum systems are related to the spaces associated with their components.

As I commented earlier, this third feature tells us that the components of such systems cannot be treated independently, even when they are spatially separated from each other. But we can now see that this particular "nonlocality" need not be thought to conflict with the Special Theory of Relativity.* No superluminal transmission capable of carrying information is involved. If we deal with an ensemble of pairs, this fact is shown by Surface Locality. In the case of a single pair, the occurrence of, say, the event $(S^e_\alpha,+)$ associated with the electron could never on its own tell us that an event $(S^p_\alpha,-)$ had taken place. True, it would tell us that, if an S^p_α-event of any kind had occurred—that is, if S_α had been measured for the positron—then it must have been the event $(S^p_\alpha,-)$. But this fact on its own is not inconsistent with relativity theory. It is easy to imagine unproblematic, everyday examples involving pairs of billiard balls in which similar "superluminal signals" are sent and received, as when, from a prior configuration, the red falls into pocket *a* if and only if the black falls into pocket *b*.

It remains, then, to show how the event $(S^p_\alpha,+)$ "projects" the electron's state from $\mathbf{D}^e$ to $\mathbf{P}^e_{\alpha-}$. Here I will give a purely formal account; the interpretation of this "projection" is discussed in Chapters 9 and 10.

* See Shimony (1980, p. 4); Jarrett (1984, pp. 575–578); Cushing and McMullin (1989). But see also Shimony (1986); and Section 10.2, below.

For any system, complex or composite, in state **D**, the probability of any quantum event B conditional on an event A is that given (via the usual statistical algorithm) by a state **D′**, obtainable from **D** by the Lüders rule. We may say that the event A "projects" the system's state into **D′**. In the case of the composite system $e + p$ we shall find that the event $(S^p_\alpha,+)$ projects the singlet spin state $\mathbf{D}_\Psi$ of the composite system into the state **D′**, where $\mathbf{D}' = \mathbf{P}^e_{\alpha-} \otimes \mathbf{P}^p_{\alpha+}$; hence, whereas $\mathbf{D}_\Psi$ reduced to the mixed states $\mathbf{D}^e$ and $\mathbf{D}^p$ (of e and p, respectively), **D′** reduces to the pure states $\mathbf{P}^e_{\alpha-}$ and $\mathbf{P}^p_{\alpha+}$. The effect of the event $(S^p_\alpha,+)$ is to project the electron's state from $\mathbf{D}^e$ to $\mathbf{P}^e_{\alpha-}$.

To show that, indeed, $\mathbf{D}' = \mathbf{P}^e_{\alpha-} \otimes \mathbf{P}^p_{\alpha+}$, we use α^e_+ and α^e_-, and α^p_+ and α^p_-, for the eigenvectors of the α-component of spin of the electron and the positron, respectively, and define vectors on $\mathcal{H}^e \otimes \mathcal{H}^p$ as follows.

$$\mathbf{v}_{++} = \alpha^e_+ \otimes \alpha^p_+ \qquad \mathbf{v}_{-+} = \alpha^e_- \otimes \alpha^p_+$$

$$\mathbf{v}_{+-} = \alpha^e_+ \otimes \alpha^p_- \qquad \mathbf{v}_{--} = \alpha^e_- \otimes \alpha^p_-$$

The set $\{\mathbf{v}_{++}, \mathbf{v}_{+-}, \mathbf{v}_{-+}, \mathbf{v}_{--}\}$ is an orthonormal basis for $\mathcal{H}^e \otimes \mathcal{H}^p$. (See Section 5.7.)

The singlet spin state $\mathbf{D}_\Psi$ for the composite system is the projector onto the vector $\frac{1}{\sqrt{2}}(\mathbf{v}_{+-} - \mathbf{v}_{-+})$.

According to the Lüders rule, conditionalization on $(S^p_\alpha,+)$ projects $\mathbf{D}_\Psi$ into **D′**, where

$$\mathbf{D}' = \frac{(\mathbf{I}^e \otimes \mathbf{P}^p_{\alpha+})\mathbf{D}_\Psi(\mathbf{I}^e \otimes \mathbf{P}^p_{\alpha+})}{\mathrm{Tr}[(\mathbf{D}_\Psi(\mathbf{I}^e \otimes \mathbf{P}^p_{\alpha+})]}$$

We now evaluate $\mathbf{D}'\mathbf{v}_{ij}$ for $i = \pm$, $j = \pm$. From (5.26), (5.25)—and, for (8.39), from Section 1.12*—we obtain

$$(8.34) \qquad (\mathbf{I}^e \otimes \mathbf{P}^p_{\alpha+})\mathbf{v}_{++} = \mathbf{v}_{++}$$

$$(8.35) \qquad (\mathbf{I}^e \otimes \mathbf{P}^p_{\alpha+})\mathbf{v}_{+-} = \mathbf{0}$$

$$(8.36) \qquad (\mathbf{I}^e \otimes \mathbf{P}^p_{\alpha+})\mathbf{v}_{-+} = \mathbf{v}_{-+}$$

$$(8.37) \qquad (\mathbf{I}^e \otimes \mathbf{P}^p_{\alpha+})\mathbf{v}_{--} = \mathbf{0}$$

$$(8.38) \qquad \mathbf{D}_\Psi \mathbf{v}_{++} = \mathbf{0}$$

$$(8.39) \qquad \mathbf{D}_\Psi \mathbf{v}_{-+} = \frac{1}{2}(\mathbf{v}_{-+} - \mathbf{v}_{+-})$$

* Equation (8.39) is easily obtained using the Dirac notation for projectors, since $\mathbf{D}_\Psi = \frac{1}{2}|\mathbf{v}_{+-} - \mathbf{v}_{-+}\rangle\langle\mathbf{v}_{+-} - \mathbf{v}_{-+}|$; see Dirac (1930, p. 25).

Whence

(8.40) $$(\mathbf{I}^e \otimes \mathbf{P}^p_{\alpha+})\mathbf{D}_\Psi(\mathbf{I}^e \otimes \mathbf{P}^p_{\alpha+})\mathbf{v}_{ij} = \mathbf{0}$$

unless $i = -$ and $j = +$, in which case

$$(\mathbf{I}^e \otimes \mathbf{P}^p_{\alpha+})\mathbf{D}_\Psi(\mathbf{I}^e \otimes \mathbf{P}^p_{\alpha+})\mathbf{v}_{-+} = \frac{1}{2}\mathbf{v}_{-+}$$

(8.41) $$\begin{aligned}\mathrm{Tr}[\mathbf{D}_\Psi(\mathbf{I}^e \otimes \mathbf{P}^p_{\alpha+})] &= \sum_{ij} \langle\, \mathbf{v}_{ij}|\mathbf{D}_\Psi(\mathbf{I}^e \otimes \mathbf{P}^p_{\alpha+})\mathbf{v}_{ij}\,\rangle \\ &= \frac{1}{2}\end{aligned}$$

From (8.40) and (8.41), and the discussion at the end of Section 1.13, we obtain

(8.42) $$\mathbf{D}' = \mathbf{P}^e_{\alpha-} \otimes \mathbf{P}^p_{\alpha+}$$

This result is generalized in Appendix C.

8.9 *Probability, Causality, and Explanation*

The two experiments this chapter deals with, the two-slit experiment discussed in Sections 8.3 and 8.4 and the EPR-type experiment discussed in Sections 8.5–8.8, have a number of things in common. Both give rise to problematic quantum effects, and in each case the problem can be stated in two ways. On the one hand these effects resist causal explanation; on the other they involve probability assignments which cannot be embedded in a classical probability space. However, straightforward analyses of both experiments can be given in terms of generalized probability functions, functions defined not on the subsets of a Kolmogorov event space, but on the subspaces of a Hilbert space. In this section I will argue that such analyses constitute genuine explanations of the effects in question.

This claim is open to an obvious objection. All that accounts in terms of generalized probability functions do, the objection runs, is to deploy the mathematical machinery of quantum theory in another guise. True, it is now evident why Kolmogorov probability theory runs into trouble, but no *explanation* is being offered, either of the interference pattern or of the EPR correlations.

In particular, this objection might be made by someone who shared Salmon's views on scientific explanation. In *Scientific Explanation and the Causal Structure of the World* (1984), Salmon argues that we provide an explanation of a phenomenon by tracing the causal processes that bring it about. And, as he shows by a wealth of corroborative examples, this is just what many explanations do. The consequence of this view, however, is that certain quantum phenomena are simply inexplicable, despite the fact that they are predicted by the best physical theory that we have. Satisfactory causal accounts are available neither of the interference patterns characteristic of the two-slit experiment, nor of the correlations observed in EPR-type experiments. Further, these are not merely gaps in our knowledge, to be repaired at some future date; we have good reason to believe that no such accounts could ever be provided.

Notice that what we lack are accounts of the causal *processes* involved. It seems quite natural to say, for instance, that the event $(S_x^p,+)$ in the electron-positron experiment *causes* the probability of the event $(S_x^e,-)$ to rise to unity, or even to say that it causes that event to happen. Indeed to say so would be in line with the statistical analysis of causation, which says, roughly, that event A causes event B if, within otherwise causally homogeneous ensembles, $p(B|A) > p(B)$. (See Cartwright, 1983, pp. 22–26.) But it is one thing to point to the positron-event $(S_x^p,+)$ as the cause of the electron-event $(S_x^e,-)$; it is another to give an account of the causal process involved. Lacking the latter, on Salmon's view we have no explanation of $(S_x^e,-)$.

Salmon responds to this problem in two ways. One response is to suggest that a future physics may bring a new conception of what constitutes a causal process; the other is to voice "the suspicion that explanations of quantum phenomena may be radically different from explanations of macroscopic phenomena" (p. 253n; see pp. 252–259).

Neither response is very specific. I will offer three comments on them: the first is to agree that accounts of quantum phenomena in terms of quantum probability functions will certainly be different from accounts of macroscopic phenomena, if only because such functions are not classical; the second is to claim that these accounts will, nevertheless, not only be explanations of the phenomena but be explanations of a general type found elsewhere in physics, and which I will call *structural explanations*;* the third is to suggest that any revamped notion of causal processes that a future physics provides will be, at bottom, such an explanation.

The idea of a structural explanation can usefully be approached via an example from special relativity. Suppose we were asked to explain why one particular velocity (in fact the speed of light) is invariant across the set of

* I now find that McMullin (1977) has already used this phrase; he has in mind something closer to Cartwright's *simulacrum* account of explanation (see below) than to my structural explanations.

inertial frames. The answer offered in the last decade of the nineteenth century was to say that measuring rods shrank at high speeds in such a way that a measurement of this velocity in a moving frame always gave the same value as one in a stationary frame. This causal explanation is now seen as seriously misleading; a much better answer would involve sketching the models of space-time which special relativity provides and showing that in these models, for a certain family of pairs of events, not only is their spatial separation x proportional to their temporal separation t, but the quantity x/t is invariant across admissible (that is, inertial) coordinate systems; further, for all such pairs, x/t always has the same value. This answer makes no appeal to causality; rather it points out structural features of the models that special relativity provides. It is, in fact, an example of a structural explanation.

If one believes (as I do) that scientific theories—even those expressed in highly abstract form—provide explanations, then one's account of explanations will be tied to one's account of scientific theories. Consider, for example, the view that an ideal scientific theory should be laid out axiomatically, in the manner of Euclid's geometry, with particular results deducible from general laws, and those in turn deducible from a few fundamental axioms. This axiomatic view of theories ties in naturally with a "covering law" account of explanation of the kind favored by Hempel (1965), who suggested that one event, or set of events, could explain another if the second could be deduced from the first, given the laws of nature. We may contrast this view with the semantic view of theories appealed to in this book. On this view a theory provides a set of models, and ground-level explanation consists in exhibiting relevant features of these mathematical structures.

The term *ground-level* is important. Explanation comes at many levels, as does scientific theorizing. It is the foundational level which concerns us here, since it is at this level that structural explanation occurs. Cartwright (1983), who also distinguishes two levels of explanation, calls them "causal" and "theoretical" (p. 75) and argues convincingly for a *simulacrum* account of the former. She writes, "To explain a phenomenon is to find a model that fits it into the basic framework of the theory" (p. 152). The models she refers to here she calls "simulacra" to emphasize the partial representation of phenomena which they provide. In Section 2.9 I distinguished models of this kind from the mathematical models which, on the semantic view of theories, appear in the exposition of the "basic framework of the theory." It is this second kind of model which is appealed to in a theoretical explanation.

A related distinction, between different kinds of theories, was first made by Einstein, and has been emphasized by Bub (1974, pp. viii, 143) and Demopoulos (1976, p. 721). For these authors, quantum mechanics, like special relativity, is a "principle theory." Such theories may be contrasted with "constructive theories," like the kinetic theory of gases, which show how one theory (such as the phenomenological theory of gases) can be embedded in another (in this case Newtonian mechanics). Principle theories, in contrast, are foundational. They "introduce abstract structural constraints that events are held to satisfy" (Bub, 1974, p. 143). They do so by supplying models which display the structure of a set of events. The four-dimensional manifold postulated by special relativity models the structure of the set of physically localizable events; the Hilbert spaces of quantum mechanics are models of the possibility structure of the set of quantum events. (Here I echo Bub, 1974, and, in particular, Stairs, 1982; see also Stairs, 1984.)

Whenever we appeal to a principle theory to provide a theoretical explanation, I claim, the explanation consists in making explicit the structural features of the models the theory employs. In the same way that we explain the constancy of one particular velocity with respect to all inertial frames by appealing to the structure of Minkowski space-time, we explain paradoxical quantum-mechanical effects by showing, first of all, how Hilbert spaces provide natural models for probabilistic theories (as in Chapters 3 and 4), and, second, what the consequences of accepting these models are (as in the present chapter).

A theory of the kind Salmon looks forward to, which brings with it a new conception of causality, will also, presumably, be a principle theory. And should we identify certain processes as causal in this new theory, and appeal to them within scientific explanations, it seems likely that these explanations will effectively be structural explanations; that is to say, in providing them we will isolate a particular class of elements and relations within the representations the theory provides.

9

Measurement

In the last three chapters we have seen the pairs (A,Δ) treated variously as properties of systems, as propositions in a quantum logic, and as quantum events. The last interpretation seems the most promising: as we saw, talk of the properties of quantum systems is problematic, and talk of the propositions of a quantum logic is uninstructive unless these propositions are themselves interpreted.

But these pairs were originally introduced as *experimental questions,* to which the theory assigned probabilities and to which individual experiments gave the answers yes or no. In Chapter 2 the question (A,Δ) was glossed as, "Will the measurement of observable A yield a result in the set Δ of the reals?" During the course of this chapter I will clarify the relation between quantum events and experimental questions, but the main topic addressed is the measurement process itself and the account of it available in quantum theory: can the theory tell us what goes on when "a measurement of A yields a result in the set Δ"? As a preliminary, I discuss a principle which has often been taken to imply a constraint on possible measurements, namely, the uncertainty principle.

9.1 *Three Principles of Limitation*

In this section I distinguish three principles of quantum mechanics, each of which derives from the existence of incompatible, mutually transformable observables (see Section 3.8). There is no uniform nomenclature for these principles; I will refer to them as the *dispersion principle,* the *support principle,* and the *indeterminacy principle.* The first two we have already met in Section 6.1, but both can be set out more precisely, using the vocabulary of quantum logic. Each of the three principles takes a particularly strong form when we deal with the Fourier-connected observables, position (Q) and momentum (P), for a particle constrained to move in one dimension. Recall that both these observables have a continuous spectrum.

The dispersion principle:

(9.1a) There is no quantum state which maps the totality of quantum events into $\{1,0\}$.

(9.1b) If, for a state **D**, $p_D(P,\Delta) = 1$, where Δ is a bounded subset of the reals, then $p_D(Q,\Gamma) < 1$, for every bounded subset Γ of the reals.

The general principle (9.1a) follows from Gleason's theorem (alternatively, from Kochen and Specker's theorem); (9.1b) follows from a theorem proved by Busch and Lahti (1985, pp. 66–67).

The *support* of a state, with respect to a given observable, is, intuitively, the set which contains just the values of that observable to which the state assigns nonzero probability. More formally,

(9.2) (A,Δ) is said to be the *support* of **D** with respect to A [we write: $s_A(\mathbf{D}) = (A,\Delta)$] if $p_D(A,\Delta) = 1$ and if, for each (A,Γ) such that $p_D(A,\Gamma) = 1$, $\Delta \subseteq \Gamma$.

Quantum-logically, the event which is the support of **D** with respect to A is the lowest A-event in the lattice of events which is assigned probability 1 by **D**.

The support principle:

(9.3a) If A and B are incompatible observables, then there is a pure state **D** whose supports with respect to A and B are not both atoms of the lattice of quantum events.

(9.3b) If the support of **D** with respect to Q is (Q,Δ), where Δ is any bounded subset of the reals, then the support of **D** with respect to P is $(P,\mathbb{R})$, and conversely (Gibbins, 1981a; Busch and Lahti, 1985). ($\mathbb{R}$ is the whole real line.)

Apropos of (9.3a), it is typically the case that operators **A** and **B** representing incompatible observables share no eigenvectors; in that case, there is *no* pure state **D** whose supports with respect to A and B are both atomic. The support principle entails the dispersion principle.

A few preliminaries are in order before we can formulate the principle of indeterminacy. Consider an ensemble of systems, all in the same state.

Unless this state is an eigenstate of the observable A, measurements of A will not yield the same value for each member of the ensemble, but a series of different values, each occurring with a certain frequency. These values scatter round a mean, the *expectation value* $\langle A \rangle$ of observable A. In the case when $\mathbf{A}$ admits eigenvectors we obtain $\langle A \rangle$, as in Section 2.4, by weighting each of the different eigenvalues by the probability of its occurrence. Thus, in this case,

$$\text{(9.4a)} \qquad \langle A \rangle = \sum_i p_i a_i$$

When $\mathbf{A}$ has a continuous spectrum we write, for an ensemble in the state $\Psi(x)$,

$$\text{(9.4b)} \qquad \langle A \rangle = \int_{-\infty}^{\infty} \Psi^* \mathbf{A} \Psi \, dx$$

Note that the value of $\langle A \rangle$ depends on the state of the system. If, for example, the state of an ensemble of spin-$\frac{1}{2}$ particles is $\mathbf{z}_+$, then

$$\langle S_x \rangle = \frac{1}{2}\left(+\frac{1}{2}\right) + \frac{1}{2}\left(-\frac{1}{2}\right) = 0$$

Thus the average value of S_x is zero. As we saw in Chapter 4,

$$p_{z+}(S_\phi, +\tfrac{1}{2}) = \cos^2 \frac{1}{2}\phi$$

and so

$$\begin{aligned} \langle S_\phi \rangle &= \left(+\frac{1}{2}\right) \cos^2 \frac{1}{2}\phi + \left(-\frac{1}{2}\right) \sin^2 \frac{1}{2}\phi \\ &= \frac{1}{2}\left(\cos^2 \frac{1}{2}\phi - \sin^2 \frac{1}{2}\phi\right) \\ &= \frac{1}{2}\cos\phi \end{aligned}$$

(S_ϕ is the component of spin in a direction at an angle ϕ to the z-axis.)

Any given measurement of the observable may differ (and in the examples above, does differ) from the mean. Writing s_x for the actual value obtained in a particular experiment to measure the x-component of spin, we see that

$$s_x - \langle S_x \rangle = \pm\frac{1}{2}$$

The mean value of the *square* of these deviations from the mean is given by

$$\langle (s_x - \langle S_x \rangle)^2 \rangle = \frac{1}{4}$$

(We take the squares in order that the differences between the observed values and the mean should effectively be regarded as positive.) Now we define the *variance*, $\mathcal{V}_{\mathrm{D}}(S_x) = \Delta S_x$, of S_x in state **D** as the square root of this mean square deviation:

$$(\Delta S_x)^2 = \langle (s_x - \langle S_x \rangle)^2 \rangle$$

Thus, for the system in state $\mathbf{z}_+$ (in other words, such that $\mathbf{D} = \mathbf{P}_{z+}$),

$$\Delta S_x = \frac{1}{2}$$

Similarly, $\Delta S_y = \frac{1}{2}$, whereas $\Delta S_z = 0$, since every measurement of S_z yields the same answer. In general, let a be the result of a measurement of the observable A. Then,

$$(\Delta A)^2 = \langle (a - \langle A \rangle)^2 \rangle \tag{9.5}$$

ΔA is sometimes called the *uncertainty* of A. Given the state of the system, ΔA can be calculated by an extension of the method used for $\langle A \rangle$. For example, for the system in the $\mathbf{z}_+$ state:

$$\text{either} \quad s_\phi - \langle S_\phi \rangle = \frac{1}{2} - \frac{1}{2}\cos\phi \quad \left(\text{with probability } \cos^2\frac{1}{2}\phi\right)$$

$$\text{or} \quad s_\phi - \langle S_\phi \rangle = -\frac{1}{2} - \frac{1}{2}\cos\phi \quad \left(\text{with probability } \sin^2\frac{1}{2}\phi\right)$$

And so

$$\langle (s_\phi - \langle S_\phi \rangle)^2 \rangle = \cos^2\frac{1}{2}\phi\left(\frac{1}{2} - \frac{1}{2}\cos\phi\right)^2 + \sin^2\frac{1}{2}\phi\left(-\frac{1}{2} - \frac{1}{2}\cos\phi\right)^2$$

$$= \frac{1}{4}\left[\cos^2\frac{1}{2}\phi(1 - \cos\phi)^2 + \sin^2\frac{1}{2}\phi(1 + \cos\phi)^2\right]$$

$$= \frac{1}{4}\left[1 - 2\cos\phi\left(\cos^2\frac{1}{2}\phi - \sin^2\frac{1}{2}\phi\right) + \cos^2\phi\right]$$

$$= \frac{1}{4}(1 - \cos^2\phi)$$

$$= \frac{1}{4}\sin^2\phi$$

It follows that

$$\Delta S_\phi = \frac{1}{2}\sin\phi$$

Now let **A** and **B** be two Hermitian operators on a Hilbert space. We define their *commutator* [**A**,**B**] as follows:

$$[\mathbf{A},\mathbf{B}] \underset{\text{df}}{=} \mathbf{AB} - \mathbf{BA} = \mathbf{C}$$

Note that **C** is itself an operator (though not, in general, Hermitian); for example, we saw in Section 1.7 that $[\mathbf{S}_x,\mathbf{S}_y] = i\mathbf{S}_z$. It turns out that the uncertainties in two observables A and B are related to the mean value of their commutator. In fact, the product of the uncertainties in A and B is never less than half the (absolute value of the) mean value of [**A**,**B**] (Jordan, 1969, pp. 84–85).

The principle of indeterminacy:

(9.6a) There exist observables A and B such that $[\mathbf{A},\mathbf{B}] = \mathbf{C} \neq 0$ and, for all observables A and B, $\Delta A \cdot \Delta B \geq \frac{1}{2}|\langle C \rangle|$.

It is important to emphasize that all three quantities involved, ΔA, ΔB, and $\langle C \rangle$, are state-dependent.

In our special case, that of the spin-$\frac{1}{2}$ particle in state $\mathbf{z}_+$, we saw that

$$\Delta S_x = \Delta S_y = \frac{1}{2}$$

and so

$$(\Delta S_x)(\Delta S_y) = \frac{1}{4}$$

Now $\mathbf{S}_x\mathbf{S}_y - \mathbf{S}_y\mathbf{S}_x = i\mathbf{S}_z$, and, since every measurement of S_z on a system in state $\mathbf{z}_+$ yields $+\frac{1}{2}$, it follows that

$$\langle iS_z \rangle = \frac{1}{2}i$$

Hence, in conformity with the principle, we have*

$$\frac{1}{2}|\langle[\mathbf{S}_x,\mathbf{S}_y]\rangle| = \frac{1}{4} = (\Delta S_x)(\Delta S_y)$$

All the values of spin used in this example are in natural units, that is, they are multiples of Planck's constant, $\hbar$. In the next paragraph, $\hbar$ has not been "suppressed" in this way.

Consider the position and momentum observables Q and P, represented by the operators x and $-i\hbar\partial/\partial x$ on the space of square-integrable functions $\Psi(x)$ (see Section 1.11).

For any function $\Psi(x)$ we have

$$\mathbf{QP}\Psi(x) = x\left[-i\hbar\,\frac{\partial\Psi(x)}{\partial x}\right]$$

But

$$\begin{aligned}\mathbf{PQ}\Psi(x) &= -i\hbar\,\frac{\partial[x\Psi(x)]}{\partial x}\\ &= -i\hbar x\,\frac{\partial\Psi(x)}{\partial x} - i\hbar\Psi(x)\frac{\partial x}{\partial x}\\ &= -\,i\hbar x\,\frac{\partial\Psi(x)}{\partial x} - i\hbar\Psi(x)\end{aligned}$$

Clearly,

$$(\mathbf{PQ} - \mathbf{QP})\Psi(x) = -i\hbar\Psi(x)$$

and so

$$[\mathbf{P},\mathbf{Q}] = -i\hbar$$

* By a slight abuse of notation, we use "$\langle[\mathbf{S}_x,\mathbf{S}_y]\rangle$" to signify the expectation value of the observable represented by the operator $[\mathbf{S}_x,\mathbf{S}_y]$.

Thus the product of the uncertainties in P and Q is given by,

$$(9.6b) \qquad (\Delta P)(\Delta Q) \geq \frac{1}{2}\hbar$$

We see that, if for a certain state we can obtain a very small uncertainty in the predictions made about momentum measurements, this will be accompanied by a correspondingly large uncertainty in those we make about position measurements, and vice versa. The product of these uncertainties never falls below a certain value.

P and **Q** are incompatible operators with continuous spectra. They are nontypical in that there is *no* state for which the product of their uncertainties lies below a certain (nonzero) value. However, whenever one of a pair of observables A and B admits eigenvectors, then the product $\Delta A \cdot \Delta B$ can be made as small as we wish by a judicious choice of state. For, if a_i is an eigenvalue of **A**, and $\mathbf{v}_i$ the corresponding eigenvector, then when the system is in the state $\mathbf{v}_i$, $\Delta A = 0$, and so, for any observable B, $\Delta A \cdot \Delta B = 0$. For example, given an ensemble in the state $\mathbf{x}_+$,

$$\Delta S_x = 0 \qquad \Delta S_y = \frac{1}{2}$$

Note that this does not violate the indeterminacy principle, since $[\mathbf{S}_x, \mathbf{S}_y] = i\mathbf{S}_z$, and, for the state $\mathbf{x}_+$, $\langle S_z \rangle = 0$. Thus, in general, the indeterminacy principle does not tell us that the product of the variances associated with incompatible observables has a least value greater than zero. (For a careful discussion of this, see Beltrametti and Cassinelli, 1981, pp. 24–26.)

9.2 *Indeterminacy and Measurement*

Of the three principles discussed in the last section, the principle of indeterminacy has received the most attention. Indeed, Busch and Lahti (1985, p. 68) suggest that the support principle was not enunciated, and distinguished from the indeterminacy principle, until Ludwig did so in 1954. Since both principles rest on the same fact—namely, the existence of mutually transformable incompatible operators in quantum theory—one may wonder why it's important to distinguish them. The reason is that there has been considerable conflict, not to say muddle, over the significance to be attached to the quantities ΔA which appear in the indeterminacy principle.

ΔA is defined as the variance $\mathcal{V}_\mathbf{D}(A)$ in measurements of A conducted on an ensemble of particles in state **D**. For some writers (Popper 1982, pp.

53–54, and Margenau, 1950, p. 375, for example), this is the *only* significance to be attached to it. We may call this the *statistical* reading of ΔA, in contrast with the *ontic* reading and the reading under which it expresses a *limitation on measurement.* (Note also that there is a fourfold classification proposed by McMullin and reported by Jammer, 1974, p. 79; see below.)

The ontic reading is more often used than mentioned. Very few writers are as explicit as Davies (1984, p. 8):

> It must not be supposed that the quantum uncertainty is somehow purely the result of an attempt to effect a measurement—a sort of unavoidable clumsiness in probing delicate systems. The uncertainty is inherent in the microsystem—it is there all the time whether or not we actually choose to measure it.

Gibbins (1981a) offers some other examples. More typical is Bohr, who oscillates between an implicit reliance on the ontic reading and an explicit adherence to a reading in terms of constraints on measurements. Thus, in his account of a thought-experiment involving a single slit in a diaphragm, he writes (1949, pp. 213–214):

> Consequently the description of the state involves a certain latitude Δp in the momentum component of the particle and, in the case of a diaphragm with a shutter, an additional latitude ΔE of the kinetic energy.
>
> Since a measure for the latitude Δq in location of the particle in the plane of the diaphragm is given by the radius a of the hole, and since $\theta = 1/\sigma a$, we get . . . just $\Delta p \approx \theta p \approx h/\Delta q$ in accordance with the indeterminacy relation . . .

As Popper (1982, p. 53n38a) has pointed out, Bohr's analysis of thought-experiments like this one is remarkable for its reliance on classical models. In the example above, σ is the wave number of the "train of plane waves" associated with the particle, and the "latitudes" Bohr speaks of are readily identifiable as features of these waves. The passage continues,

> . . . Due to the limited extension of the wave-field at the place of the slit, the component of the wave-number parallel to the plane of the diaphragm will involve a latitude $\Delta\sigma = 1/a = 1/\Delta q$.

However, five pages earlier, Bohr has introduced the indeterminacy principle rather differently

> The commutation rule imposes a reciprocal limitation on the fixation of two conjugate parameters q and p expressed by the relation
>
> $$\Delta q \cdot \Delta p \approx h$$
>
> where Δq and Δp are suitably defined latitudes in the determination of these variables. (p. 209)

Here the latitudes are not in the quantities themselves, but in their "determination"; Bohr is explicitly endorsing Heisenberg's view that the indeterminacy principle expresses a limitation on measurement.

This interpretation of the principle was for many years the dominant one. In Robertson's words (1929, p. 163),

> The principle, as formulated by Heisenberg for two conjugate quantum-mechanical variables, states that the accuracy with which two such variables can be measured simultaneously is subject to the restriction that the product of the uncertainties in the two measurements is at least of order h.

It was Robertson who first derived the indeterminacy principle in the general form in which we now have it, so that it applies to any pair of observables representable in the same Hilbert space. The quotation above is from his preamble to the derivation; the uncertainties are clearly identified with the limits of accuracy obtainable in simultaneous measurements of these observables. Yet, half a dozen lines into the derivation itself, we find Robertson writing,

> The "uncertainty" ΔA in the value A is then defined, in accordance with statistical usage, as the root mean square of the deviation of A from [the] mean. (P. 163)

No account is given of why these uncertainties "defined in accordance with statistical usage" should be identified with the accuracy to which a single measurement can be carried out. Indeed, there seem to be two distinct principles under discussion. The principle that Robertson announced his intention of deriving (*Heisenberg's principle,* as we may call it) places limits on simultaneous measurements. The principle that he in fact derived (the indeterminacy principle) places limits on predictions.

These two principles may well be related, but before we can enquire into that we need to know whether Heisenberg's principle is actually true. Is it the case (1) that there are limits on the accuracy to which noncommuting observables can be simultaneously measured, and (2) that the product of these uncertainties has a lowest value of the order of Planck's constant, so that, formally at least, Heisenberg's principle resembles the indeterminacy principle?

Now (1) may be true, but (2) false. For example, it may be the case, as von Neumann (1932, p. 230) suggested, that "simultaneous measurements [of incompatible observables] are, in general, not possible." I will return to his arguments for this in the next section. But, given his conclusion, it is a bit surprising to find him, eight pages later, presenting and endorsing Heisenberg's arguments to illustrate why simultaneous measurements of P and Q cannot be performed "with arbitrarily high accuracy" (p. 238). Surely, given von Neumann's own conclusions, the reason they cannot be performed with arbitrarily high accuracy is that they cannot be performed at all.

Be that as it may, let us look at Heisenberg's arguments. These are plausibility arguments, the best-known of which (and the one used by von Neumann) involves "Heisenberg's microscope" (1927, p. 174; von Neumann, 1932, pp. 239–247). This is an idealized instrument similar in principle to an optical microscope, but which uses radiations of short wavelengths, like γ-rays, to form images of very small particles. If a small particle were in the field of view of the microscope (see Figure 9.1) then it would be observed if a photon (that is, a γ-ray particle) struck it and were deflected upward into the aperture of the microscope.

We can estimate the coordinate of position of the particle under observation by finding the position of the image formed by the instrument. Let θ be the angle subtended at the aperture of the instrument by the particle. Then, writing Δx for the uncertainty in our measurement of the x-coordinate of position and λ for the wavelength of the radiation, we get

$$\Delta x \sim \frac{\lambda}{\theta}$$

Now, when the photon strikes the particle, a certain amount of momentum is transferred to the particle by the collision; thus any estimate we make of the particle's momentum will have to allow for this. By our conservation laws, we expect the momentum transferred to the particle to be equal and opposite to the change of momentum of the photon. The trouble is, we don't know exactly how much this is. If we knew the path followed by the photon

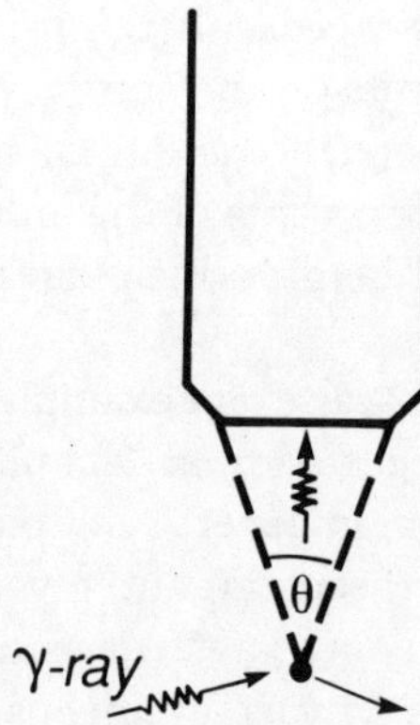

Figure 9.1 Heisenberg's microscope.

through the microscope, then it would be easy to evaluate it, but we don't know exactly where in the aperture the photon enters the instrument. In fact, making θ large (in order to obtain a high resolution) has the effect of increasing the uncertainty Δp in our estimate of momentum. We have

$$\Delta p \sim \frac{h\theta}{\lambda}$$

and so

$$\Delta x \cdot \Delta p \sim h$$

The product of these uncertainties is of the order of Planck's constant, as Heisenberg's principle suggests.

But does this example indeed illustrate what I have called Heisenberg's principle? In the first place, it says nothing about simultaneous measurements. It shows that the price of obtaining a sharp value of, say, position is that we transfer an imprecisely known amount of momentum to the particle, thus rendering any *previous* estimate of its momentum inaccurate. (This is McMullin's fourth reading of the uncertainty relation; see Jammer, 1974, p. 79.) Second, it's not clear what the significance is of the fact that the two quantities are, in the technical sense, incompatible. The general lesson to be drawn from it is that any measurement may involve a disturbance of the object we are looking at, and that, because these disturbances cannot be made small compared with the quantities to be measured, we cannot idealize them away, as we do in classical physics.

To take stock, an ontic reading of the indeterminacy relation relies on the partial picture of quantum effects supplied by the wave model. As Gibbins (1981a, pp. 123–125) points out, if any principle governing the localization of a system in Q-space and P-space emerges from the theory itself, it is not the indeterminacy principle but the support principle. Likewise, Heisenberg's arguments, which became part of the folklore of quantum theory, offer slender grounds for reading the indeterminacy principle as a principle which limits the accuracy with which incompatible observables can be simultaneously measured. Grounds for suggesting that it does *not* do so are provided by the fact, remarked on in Section 9.1, that for many pairs, A and B, of incompatible observables, there are states such that the product $\Delta A \cdot \Delta B$ is zero. It would be peculiar, but not I suppose wholly incredible, if the very feasibility of certain (double) measurement processes were dependent on the states of the systems under test.

Whether, as von Neumann claimed, there are independent reasons for thinking that incompatible observables are not commeasurable is another matter. Various authors have suggested otherwise; in fact Margenau, both on his own and later in collaboration with Park, proposed a number of experiments whereby values for position and momentum could be obtained simultaneously with no more limitation of accuracy than one might expect if they were measured individually (Margenau, 1950, p. 376; Park and Margenau, 1968, 1971). These proposals, however, have not gone unchallenged (see Busch and Lahti, 1984).

I return to the question of simultaneous measurability in the next section; I suggest there that, where it is forbidden, it is forbidden by the support principle. Again, it is this principle, rather than the indeterminacy principle, which summarizes fundamental features of the theory.

Some recent work by Busch and Lahti (1985) offers an interesting footnote to this section. They point out that, in orthodox quantum mechanics, no joint probability measures exist on the set of pairs of Q-events and P-events. That is, no probability function exists that maps all conjunctions of Q-events and P-events into [0,1] and that reduces to the usual quantum-mechanical assignments of probabilities to Q-events when the P-event is the certain event $(P,\mathbb{R})$, and vice versa (see Beltrametti and Cassinelli, 1981, pp. 23–24). However, it is possible to define "unsharp" position and momentum operators with respect to which such measures are well-defined (Davies, 1976). The operators are the usual $\mathbf{Q}$ and $\mathbf{P}$ operators on L^2, modified by functions f and g to become the operators $\mathbf{Q}_f$ and $\mathbf{P}_g$. (I omit the technical details of the modifications.) The modifiers f and g are probability density functions with mean values equal to zero and variances Δf and Δg; they are designed to represent the fact that position and momentum measurements are not sharp, that is, not localized at a point on the real number line. An "uncertainty" relation now holds between Δf and Δg; we have

$$\Delta f \cdot \Delta g \geq \frac{\hbar}{2}$$

The significance Busch and Lahti attach to this result depends on an assumption which is intuitively plausible, but hard to justify conclusively: that joint probability distributions for two observables exist if and only if the two observables are simultaneously measurable. If this is true, then the "unsharp" observables Q_f and P_g are simultaneously measurable, whereas Q and P are not. But "in order to speak of simultaneous values (X,Y) of position and momentum, one has to pay the price—that not both values may be sharply defined" (1985, p. 73).

9.3 *Projection Postulates*

Von Neumann (1932, pp. 223–230) gave a general proof that two incompatible observables are not simultaneously measurable with arbitrarily high precision. A simplified version of this proof in four steps can be given for the case when both observables have discrete spectra and there is no degeneracy.

(1) Assume that a particular experiment to measure the value of observable A for a system gives result a. Then a second measurement of A performed on the system immediately after the first will yield the same result.

(2) Immediately prior to the second measurement the result a has probability 1; thus the first experiment leaves the system in an eigenstate $\mathbf{v}_a$ of **A** (with eigenvalue a).

(3) Simultaneous precise measurements of observables A and B would therefore leave the system in a state which was both an eigenvector $\mathbf{v}_a$ of **A** and an eigenvector $\mathbf{v}_b$ of **B**.

Assume that **A** and **B** are incompatible. There are two cases: (a) **A** and **B** have no eigenvectors in common, and (b) **A** and **B** share one or more eigenvectors.

(4a) If **A** and **B** share no eigenvectors, then no state is an eigenvector of both **A** and **B**. Hence no simultaneous precise measurements of A and B can take place.

(4b) No incompatible operators **A** and **B** share all their eigenvectors; thus there would be values of the observables A and B which could never be obtained in any putative joint measurement process. Such a process should therefore not properly be called a "measurement process"; rather the kind of measurement available in case (4b) would be like the measure of time provided by a stopped clock, which is correct twice a day.

Note that the principle appealed to in step (4) is the support principle.

The first of the four steps is the one most often challenged. Von Neumann sought to justify it by appealing to experiments by Compton and Simon on "Compton scattering" (von Neumann, 1932, pp. 223–230), but whether these experiments in fact offer much in the way of support for it is doubtful (see, for example, van Fraassen, 1974a, p. 297). I will discuss the Compton and Simon experiments in the next section; in the meantime I will enlist an experiment suggested by Heitler (1949, p. 190) to give step (1) some plausibility (see also Margenau, 1950, p. 3).

Suppose we pass electrons through a small hole in a diaphragm and then allow them to hit a screen some distance away. Because diffraction occurs (to use the vocabulary of the wave model), the probability distribution for the electron will be spread out over a large area of the screen. Nonetheless we can record the spot where any individual electron strikes the screen. If we now replace the screen by two thin photographic plates, placed together and parallel to each other, the electron will go through both, and the mark where the electron strikes the second will be very close to the mark where it struck the first. What we have here are two consecutive experiments, both of which measure the position of the electron in a plane perpendicular to the axis of the experiment. The second yields the same result as the first, as step (1) requires. Of course, this second experiment must be "immediately after" the first; that is, between the two measurements the system's state must neither be changed discontinuously, by interactions with other devices, nor must it evolve significantly according to Schrödinger's equation. In the example given, the further apart the plates are, the further apart the two marks may be, because diffraction occurs again after the first impact.

One of the problems with step (1), however, is that some measurements —perhaps most measurements—do not allow a second look at the system; the electron, photon, or whatever is effectively annihilated by the measurement process. Additionally, Landau and Peierls (1931) suggested that, among experiments which allow repetition, we can find, and distinguish between, those which yield the same result the second time as the first and those which do not (see Jammer, 1974, p. 487n). Following Pauli (1933), we call the former "experiments of the first kind." These considerations restrict the scope of von Neumann's proof. They show that incompatible observables are not measurable to arbitrarily high precision by measurements of the first kind. Thus, although von Neumann's result is consistent with the stronger claim, that no possible measurement could do the job, Margenau (1950, pp. 360–364) could accept the proof and still maintain that simultaneous measurability of incompatibles is feasible. Note, however, that a proof of the strong claim, resting on a particular account of the measurement process, has been offered by van Fraassen (1974a, pp. 301–303).

Let us turn to step (2) of the argument, or rather its analogue for the case of an observable with a continuous spectrum, like position. In the experiment described just now, prior to striking the screen the electron behaves like a wave; its probability distribution is spread out in space. The event of its striking the screen is often called "the collapse of the wave packet." It is sometimes described as a change in the properties of the electron—from being spread out in space the electron becomes localized in a small region—and sometimes as a passage from potentiality to actuality—of all the possible events associated with small areas of the screen, just one is actualized. Von Neumann postulates that this collapse (however regarded) is accompanied by a change in the state of the electron: the state changes in such a way that a repetition of the experiment will with certainty yield the same result as before. Margenau (1950) baptized this postulate the *projection postulate,* and it is now generally referred to by that name. We can revert to the case of an observable with a discrete spectrum to see a particularly simple instance of the postulate.

Let us assume that there is no degeneracy and that the result of the first measurement of observable A is a_i. Such an experiment is a *maximal* measurement of A. If the original state is a pure state $\mathbf{v}$, then the projection postulate requires that the transformation

$$\mathbf{v} \xrightarrow{(A,a_i)} \mathbf{v}_i \qquad [\text{equivalently,} \quad \mathbf{P}_{\mathbf{v}} \xrightarrow{(A,a_i)} \mathbf{P}_{\mathbf{v}_i}]$$

takes place, where $\mathbf{v}_i$ is the eigenvector with eigenvalue a_i.

In this maximal case, (A,a_i) is the support of $\mathbf{v}_i$ with respect to A (see Section 9.1). Von Neumann's demand, that in all cases a repetition of an experiment will yield the same result as before, can be put in terms of a *support requirement,* as follows. Assume that a measurement of A localizes the value of A within the Borel set Δ of the reals; we require that the resulting state of the system have support (A,Δ) with respect to A. I will generalize the term *projection postulate* to refer to any rule governing the state transitions induced by measurement which satisfies this requirement.

Effectively, von Neumann's (generalized) projection postulate was that after a measurement of A had localized the value of A within Δ, the projection operator $\mathbf{P}^{\mathbf{A}}_{\Delta}$ from the spectral decomposition of $\mathbf{A}$ would serve as the state description for the system (von Neumann, 1932, p. 218; his specific example involves a discrete spectrum with degeneracy). I write "serve as" because only in the case when $\mathbf{P}^{\mathbf{A}}_{\Delta}$ projects onto a ray (which is to say, when the measurement is maximal) is it of trace one, and hence a density operator. When it projects onto a subspace of higher but finite dimensionality, we can normalize it so that the transformation becomes

$$(9.7) \qquad \mathbf{D} \xrightarrow{(A,\Delta)} \mathbf{D}' = \frac{\mathbf{P}^{\mathbf{A}}_{\Delta}}{\mathrm{Tr}\mathbf{P}^{\mathbf{A}}_{\Delta}}$$

In the infinitely dimensional case—and so in any case where $\mathbf{A}$ has a continuous spectrum—$\mathbf{P}^{\mathbf{A}}_{\Delta}$ cannot be normalized in this way; Bub (1979, pp. 73–74) suggests that in this case it would be consistent with von Neumann's ideas to use the operator $\mathbf{P}^{\mathbf{A}}_{\Delta}$ to give the *relative* probabilities of outcomes of future experiments.

Although this projection postulate meets the support requirement, it nevertheless yields counterintuitive results. Consider, for example, a particle in an initial state which assigns the probabilities $p_1(y)$ shown at the left side of

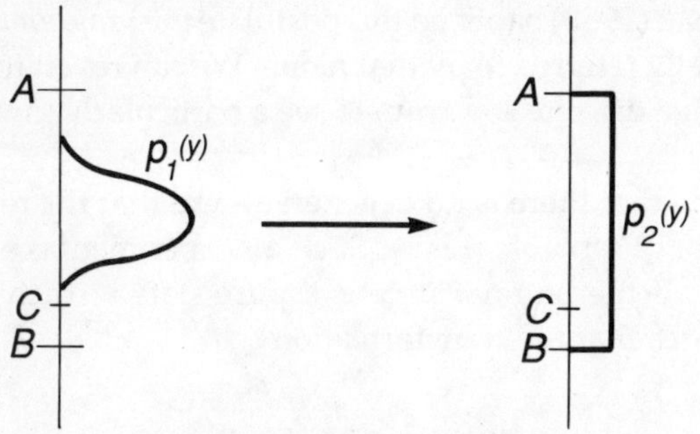

Figure 9.2 Probability transition according to the von Neumann projection postulate.

Figure 9.2 to measurements of position along the y-axis. Assume further that a first coarse measurement of y locates the particle within the region AB. Then, according to the von Neumann projection postulate, if a second, more refined measurement is made, the probabilities would be given by $p_2(y)$, shown at the right of the figure, rather than by $p_1(y)$ again. Note in particular that, whereas there was initially virtually zero probability of detecting the particle at point C, after the first measurement has localized it within AB there is as high a probability of finding it at C as at anywhere else in the region.

Now this is not inconceivable. Quantum mechanics teaches us so often that the implausible happens that the unlikely becomes as likely as not. Nonetheless, it is an odd feature of the von Neumann postulate that the state of the system after a measurement is wholly independent of its initial state, and in 1951 an alternative postulate was suggested. This takes the form

$$\text{(9.8)} \qquad \mathbf{D} \xrightarrow{(A,\Delta)} \mathbf{D}' = \frac{\mathbf{P}^A_\Delta \mathbf{D} \mathbf{P}^A_\Delta}{\mathrm{Tr}(\mathbf{P}^A_\Delta \mathbf{D})}$$

According to this postulate, $\mathbf{D}'$ is dependent on the initial state $\mathbf{D}$, and nevertheless has support (A,Δ) with respect to A.

The form of (9.8) is familiar; it is the Lüders rule we met in Chapter 8. There it appeared as a conditionalization rule for nonclassical probability spaces, but Lüders (1951) first proposed it as an alternative to von Neumann's projection postulate, that is, as a rule governing the changes of state induced by measurements. In Section 8.2 we saw why it was a natural generalization of the classical conditionalization rule. As a projection postulate it is characterized by the following features. (Teller, 1983, pp. 415–418, provides a valuable discussion of them.)

Let A and B be compatible observables.

(a) According to the rule, if a measurement of A is followed successively by a measurement of B and a second measurement of A, then the two values of A will coincide.

(b) Assume we prepare two ensembles of systems in state D. One ensemble is just subjected to a B-measurement; the other is subjected to an A-measurement followed by a B-measurement. Then, according to the rule, the relative frequencies of the various B-outcomes will be the same for both ensembles.

These results can be shown by using the arguments used in the proofs of (8.8) and (8.32), respectively. The support requirement appears as a special case of (a), either by setting $A = B$ and assuming that flip-flop results do not occur, or by setting $B = I$ (the trivial "measurement" which locates the value of every observable within $\mathbb{R}$).

Stairs (1982, pp. 426–427) has shown that when the premeasurement state is a pure state, then the Lüders rule is the only possible projection rule for which (a) holds. As he points out, this means that this rule is the projection postulate that best captures the classical ideal of a nondisturbing measurement; in the quantum case it is the rule of minimal disturbance. Note also that, if the transformation of states by measurement is governed by a rule which guarantees, first, that (a) and (b) both hold and, second, that measurement preserves the convex structure of the set of states (see Section 5.4), then the rule in question must be the Lüders rule.

9.4 *Measurement and Conditionalization*

In Chapter 8 the Lüders rule appeared as the natural extension of classical conditionalization to the set of quantum events; in the last section it was shown to be the projection postulate which most nearly approached a classical account of measurement. In this section I will show how these two uses of the rule may be brought together. For brevity I will use the term "quantum event" sometimes to refer to a particular kind of event—as in "the event (A,Δ)"—and sometimes to refer to a specific occurrence of that event; context will disambiguate between the type and the token.

Von Neumann's views on measurement, though not of course his choice of projection postulate, suggest a natural account of these events. On this account, a quantum event (A,Δ) involves the localization of the observable A within the set Δ of the reals. The event is realized by an interaction between a quantum system and a macroscopic apparatus. This interaction may be one which we would call a measurement, but it need not be. For example, assume that we seek to bring about a localization of the y-coordinate of position of a particle within a small region Δ. We may either use a photographic plate and wait until one particle from an ensemble strikes the region Δ of the plate, or we may use a diaphragm with a small aperture in it and wait until a particle is detected on the far side of the diaphragm. In each case the quantum event (y,Δ) has taken place, and the probability that it would occur is no different in the photographic plate experiment than in the other.

But unless the photographic plate is very thin (as in the Heitler thought-experiment described in Section 9.3), the particle will not pass through it but will be absorbed; to use Pauli's terminology, the experiment will not be a measurement of the first kind, and the projection postulate will not apply. Thus not all quantum events are events on which we can conditionalize.

On the other hand, we can and do conditionalize on the event (y,Δ) occurring in the diaphragm experiment, witness the discussion of the two-slit experiment in Section 8.4. However, we may be justifiably reluctant to call what occurs in the experiment a measurement. Certainly the diaphragm alone does not measure the position of the particle; only when an additional detection device is placed on the far side of the diaphragm will we know that a particle was ever around being "measured." As Margenau has emphasized, in the absence of such a detector, the most we can say is that *if* a particle passed through the diaphragm, *then* at the diaphragm its y-coordinate was localized within Δ. Thus not all quantum events are measurements.

For Margenau (1936, 1963) there is a crucial distinction between measurements and preparations. Measurements yield a value for a particular observable, while preparations produce an ensemble of particles in the same state. According to Margenau, it was a defect of von Neumann's analysis that it confused the two; the projection postulate suggested that an ideal measurement on a system would not only yield a precise value for an observable, but would also project that system's state into the corresponding eigenstate of that observable.

It is a virtue of the "quantum event" interpretation of the theory—about which more will be said in Chapter 10—that it allows some reconciliation of these views. The phrase "the localization of the observable A within Δ" conceals an ambiguity that is fruitful rather than fatal. Quantum events may be measurements; they may also, via conditionalization, serve as preparations. On the one hand, the observable may be being measured and the result found to lie within Δ; on the other, the system may be being prepared in a state **D** with support (A,Δ) with respect to A. In a type-1 measurement both would happen together, but there may in fact be no such events. In their absence, could any quantum event serve both as a measurement and as a preparation?

Surprisingly, the answer is yes. As we saw in Section 8.8, if we have a coupled system of the kind used in EPR-type experiments, then an event associated with one subsystem may be both a measurement of an observable for that subsystem and an event which projects the other system into an eigenstate of that observable. The Compton-Simon experiment to which von Neumann (1932, p. 212) appealed for evidence in support of the projection postulate is similar in kind.

> In this experiment light was scattered by electrons and the scattering process was controlled in such a way that the scattered light and the scattered electrons were subsequently intercepted, and their energy and momentum measured.

Given the initial trajectories of a photon and an electron,

> the measurement of the path of the light quanta of the electron after collision suffices to determine the position of the central line of the collision. The Compton-Simons [*sic*] experiment now shows that these two observations give the same result. (P. 213)

The two observations need not occur simultaneously; if they do not, we can infer the result of the second from the result of the first. Prior to the first observation, we could only make statistical predictions about the second, whereas after the first one has been made, the second is "already determined causally [sic] and uniquely" (p. 213).

As an argument for the projection postulate, this has recently come under heavy fire. Van Fraassen (1974a, p. 297), for example, writes,

> Upon what slender support dogma may be founded! In the experiment described, measurements are made *directly* on two objects . . . which have interacted and then separated again. The observables *directly* measured are ones which have become correlated by the interaction . . . And on the basis of this, an inference is made about what would happen if a single experiment could be immediately repeated on the same object!

Indeed, one wonders why von Neumann chose this particular experiment for his purposes. Einstein, in contrast, was content to illustrate the projection postulate by two polarizers P_1 and P_2; if their axes of polarization are parallel, then any photon passing the first will also pass the second (Einstein, in correspondence with Margenau; see Jammer, 1974, p. 228).

One motivation was von Neumann's desire to use the Compton-Simon experiment to make a further point. The experiment shows that, contrary to a suggestion made by Bohr, Kramers, and Slater (1924; see Jammer, 1966, pp. 183–188), the principles of conservation of energy and momentum hold in individual cases and are not merely statistical laws. As von Neumann (1932, p. 213) pointed out, this implies that the quantum world lies somewhere between a purely statistical world and a wholly determined world; for him the projection postulate was an expression of this intermediate "degree of causality." With hindsight, we can reread von Neumann's argument as an argument not for his version of the projection postulate, but for the Lüders rule viewed as a rule of probability conditionalization. Both rules indicate where, within a statistical theory, deterministic correlations may obtain.

That said, in the remainder of this chapter I will leave aside the connection between conditionalization and measurement, and look solely at the latter. In particular, I postpone a discussion of Teller's views until Section 10.1.

9.5 *The Measurement Problem and Schrödinger's Cat*

By the projection postulate, wrote von Neumann (1932, p. 217), "we have then answered the question as to what happens in the measurement of a quantity. To be sure, the 'how' remains unexplained for the present." And, fifty years later, this second question is still with us.

On the "orthodox view" of measurement, as von Neumann's account has come to be called, a system's state can evolve in two different ways. It can change continuously through time: we may have, in accordance with the Schrödinger equation,

$$\text{(9.9)} \qquad \mathbf{D}_0 \rightarrow \mathbf{D}_t = \mathbf{U}_t\mathbf{D}_0\mathbf{U}_t^{-1}$$

where $\mathbf{U}_t$ is a unitary operator. It may also change discontinuously in accordance with the Lüders rule:

$$\text{(9.10)} \qquad \mathbf{D}_0 \rightarrow \mathbf{D}' = \frac{\mathbf{P}_\Delta^A\mathbf{D}_0\mathbf{P}_\Delta^A}{\mathrm{Tr}(\mathbf{P}_\Delta^A\mathbf{D}_0)}$$

as a result of the quantum event (A,Δ). The "quantum event" interpretation of quantum mechanics I propose in Chapter 10 accepts this "strange dualism" (Wigner, 1963, p. 7) within quantum theory; however, many theorists have found it unacceptable. In particular, one may ask what it is that physically distinguishes the kinds of interactions governed by Schrödinger's equation from those in which discontinuous changes (allegedly) occur.

The latter kind of state transition is, of course, not only discontinuous but often nonunique. Assume, for example, that a system is in a pure state $\mathbf{v}$ which is a superposition of eigenvectors $\{\mathbf{v}_i\}$ of some observable represented by $\mathbf{A}$: $\mathbf{v} = \Sigma_i c_i \mathbf{v}_i$. Then a maximal measurement of A will yield, as a special case of (9.10),

$$\text{(9.10*)} \qquad \mathbf{v} \rightarrow \mathbf{v}_i \quad \text{with probability} \quad |c_i|^2$$

and a transition to any one of the $\mathbf{v}_i$ for which $c_i \neq 0$ has a nonzero probability of occurrence.

As this shows, the problem of the projection postulate is just one element of another, larger problem confronting quantum theory, the problem of measurement. What account can quantum mechanics offer of the statistically governed but individually undetermined events characteristic of measurement processes? The problem has two aspects. First, whatever theoretical account we give, the processes it describes may have more than one possible outcome. Second, this account, though couched in quantum theoretical terms, must include some treatment of the classical measuring device.

Apropos of the second point, Schrödinger (1935, pp. 156–157) has pointed out that we are led to bizarre conclusions if we try to apply the quantum-mechanical formalism to a macroscopic object. He instances the case of a radioactive atom and a detector. An alpha-particle within a radioactive nucleus evolves into a superposition of states, so that as time goes on there is an increasing probability of its being detected outside the nucleus. (It "tunnels through" the potential barrier which the nucleus provides; Bohm, 1951, pp. 240–242.) Schrödinger (1935, pp. 156–157) writes colloquially of the state being "blurred":

> The state of a radioactive nucleus is presumably blurred in such a degree and fashion that neither the instant of decay nor the direction in which the emitted α-particle leaves the nucleus is well-established. Inside the nucleus, blurring doesn't bother us. The emerging particle is described, if one wants to explain intuitively, as a spherical wave that continuously emanates in all directions from the nucleus and that impinges continuously on a surrounding luminescent screen over its full expanse.

But while we may accept this "blurred" picture of the microscopic system, we cannot accept a similar picture of the macroscopic measurement apparatus. Schrödinger continues,

> The screen however does not show a more or less constant uniform surface glow, but rather lights up at *one* spot—or, to honor the truth, it lights up now here, now there, for it is impossible to do the experiment with only a single radioactive atom.

And, as a further illustration, he introduces the legendary creature who now appears in every philosophical bestiary, Schrödinger's cat.*

> One can even set up quite ridiculous cases. A cat is penned up in a steel chamber, along with the following diabolic device (which must be secured against direct interference by the cat); in a Geiger counter there is a tiny bit of radioactive substance, *so* small, that *perhaps* in the course of one hour one of the atoms decays, but also, with equal probability, perhaps none; if it happens, the counter tube discharges and through a relay releases a hammer which shatters a small flask of hydrocyanic

* Tierliebhaber (1939) discusses the relationship of this animal to Buridan's ass.

acid. If one has left this entire system to itself for one hour, one would say that the cat still lives *if* meanwhile no atom has decayed. The first atomic decay would have poisoned it. The ψ-function of the entire system would express this by having in it the living and the dead cat (pardon the expression) mixed or smeared out in equal parts.

As a specification of indicator states of a measurement apparatus, "cat alive" and "cat dead" may seem a trifle *outré*. But, as the previous paragraph makes clear, Schrödinger's point is that, however these indicator states are chosen, no superposition of them can exist, since they are states of a classical measuring apparatus.

With Schrödinger's cat in mind, let us review the measurement problem. We are looking for an account of a particular kind of process, whereby a system *S* interacts with a measurement apparatus *M*; during the interaction *M* evolves to a state indicating a value of some observable *A* associated with *S*. We may call such an account an "internal account" of the measurement process if the evolution is governed by Schrödinger's equation.

For simplicity let us consider an observable *A* with a discrete spectrum $\{a_1, a_2, \ldots\}$. Then the account must satisfy the following requirements.

(9.11a) *M* must have a set $\{\mathbf{u}_0, \mathbf{u}_1, \mathbf{u}_2 \ldots\}$ of possible states; $\mathbf{u}_0$ is the ground state of the apparatus, and $\mathbf{u}_1, \mathbf{u}_2, \ldots$ correspond to the outcomes of the measurement (pointer readings) associated with values $a_1, a_2, \ldots$ of *A*. Since *M* is classical, the indicator states $\{\mathbf{u}_0, \mathbf{u}_1, \mathbf{u}_2, \ldots\}$ must be pairwise orthogonal, and no (nontrivial) superposition of these states can be a state of *M*.

(9.11b) As a result of a measurement of *A*, the state of *M* must evolve from $\mathbf{u}_0$ to one of $\mathbf{u}_1, \mathbf{u}_2, \ldots$.

(9.11c) The probability that the transition $\mathbf{u}_0 \rightarrow \mathbf{u}_1$ takes place must equal the probability assigned to (A, a_i) by the state $\mathbf{v}$ of the system *S*.

The projection postulate appears as a further requirement, independent of requirements (9.11a–c).

(9.11d) Whenever the evolution takes *M* to state $\mathbf{u}_i$, then it takes *S* to the eigenstate $\mathbf{v}_i$ of $\mathbf{A}$ which has eigenvalue a_i.

From (9.11c) it follows that, if *S* is in the eigenstate $\mathbf{v}_i$ of $\mathbf{A}$ which has eigenvalue a_i, then *M* must evolve to $\mathbf{u}_i$ during a measurement of *A* on S. In general (9.11b) and (9.11c) require that at the end of the measurement process M be in a state $\mathbf{u}_i$ with probability $p_\mathbf{v}(A,a_i)$. Let $p_i = p_\mathbf{v}(A,a_i)$; then the general requirement can be expressed by saying that, after the measurement, M must be in the mixed state $\mathbf{D}^M = \Sigma_i p_i \mathbf{P}_i^M$ (where $\mathbf{P}_i^M$ projects onto $\mathbf{u}_i$). *Prima facie* this does not violate (9.11a) since, in contrast to superpositions, mixtures of classical states are perfectly respectable.

Along these lines Heisenberg (1958, p. 53) wrote that

> The probability function [of quantum mechanics] combines objective and subjective elements . . . In ideal cases the subjective element . . . may be practically negligible as compared with the objective one. The physicists then speak of a "pure case."

Although in this passage Heisenberg doesn't use the term, we may add that, conversely, a mixture is a probability function within which a subjective element, "our incomplete knowledge of the world," may be represented. Any measurement process, says Heisenberg (p. 54), produces an interplay between these two elements:

> After the interaction has taken place, the probability function contains the objective element of tendency and the subjective element of incomplete knowledge, even if it has been in a "pure case" before.

In other words, during the measurement process the apparatus evolves into a mixture of indicator states; of these one will be actualized, but which one we cannot predict.

Heisenberg shows how the state of the classical measurement apparatus can be described in quantum-mechanical terms. The question now is, can we give a quantum-theoretical account of the process he describes? In particular, how can this process start with S in a pure state $\mathbf{v}$ and with M in the pure state $\mathbf{u}_0$, finish with M in the mixed state $\Sigma_i p_i \mathbf{P}_i^M$, and yet be governed by Schrödinger's equation?

9.6 *Jauch's Model of the Measurement Process*

An account of such a process was given by J. M. Jauch (1968, chap. VI. 9). On his account, while the measurement is being performed the system S and the measurement apparatus M form a coupled system $S + M$, whose states are represented in a tensor-product space as follows.

Assume that the observable being measured is representable by the operator $\mathbf{A}$ on $\mathcal{H}^S$, and that there are just two values of the observable, eigenvalues of the eigenvectors $\mathbf{v}_+$ and $\mathbf{v}_-$ of $\mathbf{A}$. The measurement device is then assumed to have (at least) three mutually orthogonal possible states, a ground state and two indicator states. Let $\mathbf{u}_0$ be the state before any measurement takes place (the ground state), $\mathbf{u}_+$ the state when the device registers a positive value for A, and $\mathbf{u}_-$ the state when it registers a negative value for A. We assume that the quantum-mechanical formalism can be applied to M, and that these three states are representable by vectors $\mathbf{u}_0$, $\mathbf{u}_1$, and $\mathbf{u}_2$, respectively, in a Hilbert space $\mathcal{H}^M$. No assumption is made that superpositions of $\mathbf{u}_0$, $\mathbf{u}_1$, and $\mathbf{u}_2$ are also possible states of M.

We represent the states of the coupled system $S+M$ in the tensor-product space $\mathcal{H}^S \otimes \mathcal{H}^M$. Assume that, before the measurement begins, the system S is in the pure state $\mathbf{v}$, where $\mathbf{v} = c_+\mathbf{v}_+ + c_-\mathbf{v}_-$, and that M is in the state $\mathbf{u}_0$; then the original state of $S+M$ will be $\mathbf{\Psi}_0 = \mathbf{v} \otimes \mathbf{u}_0$. During the course of the measurement interaction this state will evolve continuously, according to Schrödinger's equation. Accordingly, at the end of the interaction, $S+M$ will again be in a pure state $\mathbf{\Psi} \in \mathcal{H}^S \otimes \mathcal{H}^M$, where $\mathbf{\Psi} = \mathbf{U}\mathbf{\Psi}_0$, and $\mathbf{U}$ is some unitary operator on $\mathcal{H}^S \otimes \mathcal{H}^M$. $\mathbf{U}$ must obey the following constraints: when $\mathbf{v} = \mathbf{v}_+$ (that is, when $c_- = 0$), we require that $\mathbf{\Psi} = \mathbf{\Psi}_+ = \mathbf{v}_+ \otimes \mathbf{u}_+$; when $\mathbf{v} = \mathbf{v}_-$ (that is, when $c_+ = 0$), we require that $\mathbf{\Psi} = \mathbf{\Psi}_- = \mathbf{v}_- \otimes \mathbf{u}_-$.

In each of these two cases $\mathbf{U}$ takes $\mathbf{\Psi}_0$ into a state of $S+M$ reducible into a pure state of S and the corresponding pure state of M. By the linearity of $\mathbf{U}$ we obtain, for the general case,

$$\mathbf{\Psi} = c_+\mathbf{\Psi}_+ + c_-\mathbf{\Psi}_-$$

However, this state, although a pure state of $S+M$, is in general not reducible to pure states of S and of M (see Section 5.8). In fact, using the density operator notation, we have, for the state of the composite system,

$$\mathbf{P}_\Psi = \mathbf{D}^S \otimes \mathbf{D}^M$$

where

$$\mathbf{D}^S = |c_+|^2\mathbf{P}^S_+ + |c_-|^2\mathbf{P}^S_-$$

and

$$\mathbf{D}^M = |c_+|^2\mathbf{P}^M_+ + |c_-|^2\mathbf{P}^M_-$$

The operators $\mathbf{P}^S_+$, $\mathbf{P}^S_-$, $\mathbf{P}^M_+$, $\mathbf{P}^M_-$ project onto rays in $\mathcal{H}^S$ and $\mathcal{H}^M$ containing, respectively, $\mathbf{v}_+$, $\mathbf{v}_-$, $\mathbf{u}_+$, $\mathbf{u}_-$.

This seems to give precisely what we want. The measurement process evolves according to Schrödinger's equation, but the final state of the measurement device is a weighted sum of the indicator states. These weights are exactly the probabilities which quantum theory assigns to the corresponding outcomes (see Section 2.4).

Moreover, as Jauch points out, we can also show that indicator states are correlated with final states of S. For assume that we carry out a measurement $\mathbf{P}^S_+ \otimes \mathbf{P}^M_-$ on the composite system in the state $\mathbf{\Psi}$. That is, we test for the joint event $[(A,+);(A^M,-)]$, where A^M is the act of observing M. In this case,

$$\begin{aligned}(\mathbf{P}^S_+ \otimes \mathbf{P}^M_-)\mathbf{\Psi} &= (\mathbf{P}^S_+ \otimes \mathbf{P}^M_-)[c_+(\mathbf{v}_+ \otimes \mathbf{u}_+) + c_-(\mathbf{v}_- \otimes \mathbf{u}_-)] \\ &= c_+(\mathbf{v}_+ \otimes \mathbf{0}) + c_-(\mathbf{0} \otimes \mathbf{u}_-) \\ &= \mathbf{0}\end{aligned}$$

($\mathbf{0}$ is here the zero vector in $\mathcal{H}^S \otimes \mathcal{H}^M$.) It follows that

$$\langle \mathbf{\Psi} | (\mathbf{P}^S_+ \otimes \mathbf{P}^M_-)\mathbf{\Psi} \rangle = 0$$

and the joint event has zero probability of occurrence.

The consistency of any further measurements with the one that has been carried out—whether these further measurements are conducted on S or on M—is thus assured; the projection postulate has appeared within the analysis as an added bonus.

Alas, elegant as the treatment is, as an account of the transition from the possible to the actual it won't do. The interpretation of mixed states which motivates it cannot be applied to the mixtures which appear within it. What we would like to say, when we speak of the measurement device being in a mixture of $\mathbf{P}^M_+$ and $\mathbf{P}^M_-$, is that it actually *is* in one of these pure states but we don't know which; in other words we would like to use the ignorance interpretation of mixtures. But, as we saw in Section 5.8, this interpretation cannot be used for those mixtures which arise from a reduction of a pure state in a tensor-product space. (This argument is due to Feyerabend, 1962.)

For, to return to our example, the mixed state of S after the measurement interaction has taken place is given by $|c_+|^2\mathbf{P}^S_+ + |c_-|^2\mathbf{P}^S_-$ and that of M by $|c_+|^2\mathbf{P}^M_+ + |c_-|^2\mathbf{P}^M_-$. On the ignorance interpretation of mixtures, this means that the system is actually either in the state $\mathbf{v}_+$ or $\mathbf{v}_-$, and that M is actually in the correlated state $\mathbf{u}_+$ or $\mathbf{u}_-$. The state of the composite system $S+M$ is then either $\mathbf{v}_+ \otimes \mathbf{u}_+$ or $\mathbf{v}_- \otimes \mathbf{u}_-$, each of these having a certain probability. But this means that $S+M$ is in a mixture, contrary to our claim that it is in the superposition $\mathbf{\Psi}$. It is crucial to the analysis that the final state of $S+M$ is indeed pure; if it is not, then the evolution of the composite system has not accorded with Schrödinger's equation, and no internal account of the measurement process has been given.

The move to an analysis of the composite system in terms of a tensor-product space has not, therefore, done what was hoped of it; the "collapse of the wave packet" remains as anomalous as ever.

9.7 A Problem for Internal Accounts of Measurement

As was pointed out in Section 9.5, the measurement problem remains a problem whether or not measurement interactions are required to conform to the projection postulate (9.11d). The problem is crucially one of describing in quantum-mechanical terms an evolution of the state of the apparatus M (or of the combined system $S+M$) which conforms to requirements (9.11a–c). A promising candidate was presented in the last section, and was shown to fail. In this section I will show that there is good reason to believe that no internal account of such a process can be given.

Requirement (9.11a) stipulates that all the admissible states of M, $\{\mathbf{u}_0, \mathbf{u}_1, \mathbf{u}_2, \ldots\}$, must be pairwise orthogonal, so that M will behave classically. If this requirement is accepted, there are then two reasons for demanding that a corresponding requirement should hold for $S+M$.

In the first place, if being a classical system is a matter of scale, then the classical nature of M will impose itself on any system of which M is a subcomponent. Second, it seems plausible to require that the only admissible states $\mathbf{D}$ of $S+M$ be those which reduce into admissible states of S and of M. Now nontrivial superpositions of admissible states of M are prohibited; it also seems justifiable to allow, as mixed states of M, only those mixtures which can be interpreted classically, that is, only those which can be given an ignorance interpretation. As we saw in Section 9.6, this would rule out as states of M all nontrivial mixed states arising through reduction of a pure state of $S+M$. The only admissible pure states of $S+M$ would then have the form $\mathbf{v} \otimes \mathbf{u}_i$ (where $\mathbf{v} \in \mathcal{H}^S$ and $\mathbf{u}_i$ is an indicator state or the ground state of M). If this is so, then any two admissible pure states of $S+M$, $\mathbf{v} \otimes \mathbf{u}_i$ and $\mathbf{v}' \otimes \mathbf{u}_j$, where $i \neq j$, will inherit the orthogonality of $\mathbf{u}_i$ and $\mathbf{u}_j$. The admissible pure states of $S+M$ will fall within a set of pairwise orthogonal subspaces of $\mathcal{H}^S \otimes \mathcal{H}^M$, indexed by the admissible pure states of M.

This restriction on the pure states of $S+M$ implies that no evolution of the state of $S+M$ which is governed by the Schrödinger equation can ever involve a transition of the state of M from its ground state to one of its indicator states. More precisely, let $\mathbf{\Psi}_i = \mathbf{v} \otimes \mathbf{u}_i$ and $\mathbf{\Psi}_j = \mathbf{v}' \otimes \mathbf{u}_j$ be two orthogonal admissible pure states of $S+M$; then, although there exists a unitary operator $\mathbf{U}$ on $\mathcal{H}^S \otimes \mathcal{H}^M$ such that $\mathbf{U}\mathbf{\Psi}_i = \mathbf{\Psi}_j$, this operator is not a member of a *continuous* one-parameter group of unitary operators mapping admissible pure states of $S+M$ into each other. That is, if $\mathbf{\Psi}$ is to be restricted to the set of admissible pure states, we cannot write $i(d\mathbf{\Psi}/dt) = \mathbf{H\Psi}$, as this would require $\mathbf{\Psi}$ to pass through the "no-man's-land" between admissible pure states.

Since an internal account of the measurement process is, by definition, one that conforms to Schrödinger's equation, it would seem that no internal account conforming to (9.11a) can be given.

A way out is suggested by Beltrametti and Cassinelli (1981, chap. 8) and independently by Wan (1980). Beltrametti and Cassinelli's strategy is to distinguish between the mathematical account of the time-evolution of the state vector and the interpretation of this as the evolution of a particular kind of state. On their account of the measurement process, the state vector $\mathbf{\Psi}$ of $S + M$ evolves according to the Schrödinger equation. However, only when $\mathbf{\Psi}$ has the form $\mathbf{v} \otimes \mathbf{u}_i$ (where $\mathbf{v} \in \mathcal{H}^S$ and $\mathbf{u}_i$ is an indicator state of M) does $\mathbf{\Psi}$ represent a pure state; when it does not, it is interpreted as a (classical) mixture of such states.

Before assessing this account, let us see how quantum theory treats situations in which not every normalized vector in the relevant Hilbert space can represent a pure state of a system.

A rule forbidding us to form a pure state by the superposition of other pure states is called a *superselection rule.* Such a rule restricts pure states to those representable by vectors in orthogonal subspaces $L_o, L_1, \ldots$ of the Hilbert space $\mathcal{H}$ for the system; $L_0, L_1, \ldots$ are known as the *superselection subspaces* (sometimes the *coherent subspaces*) of $\mathcal{H}$. In the presence of superselection rules, not every Hermitian operator on the space can represent an observable (see Jordan, 1969, sec. 28; Beltrametti and Cassinelli, 1981, chap. 5). In fact a Hermitian operator $\mathbf{A}$ on $\mathcal{H}$ can represent an observable only if each superselection subspace L_i of $\mathcal{H}$ *reduces* $\mathbf{A}$—in other words, only if $\mathbf{A\Psi} \in L_i$ whenever $\mathbf{\Psi} \in L_i$. This condition holds if and only if every projector in the spectral decomposition of $\mathbf{A}$ projects onto a subspace of some superselection subspace L_i of $\mathcal{H}$. It follows that, in the presence of superselection rules, (1) any function of an observable A is reduced by every superselection subspace, and (2) every projector $\mathbf{P}_E$ representing a quantum event E projects onto a subspace of some superselection subspace (or is the sum of such projectors); hence $\mathbf{P}_E$ is also reduced by every superselection subspace.

Now consider a normalized vector $\mathbf{\Psi}$ which is a nontrivial superposition of two normalized vectors $\mathbf{\Psi}_1$ and $\mathbf{\Psi}_2$ in distinct superselection subspaces L_1 and L_2 of $\mathcal{H}$: $\mathbf{\Psi} = c_1\mathbf{\Psi}_1 + c_2\mathbf{\Psi}_2$. Note that $\mathbf{\Psi}_1 \perp \mathbf{\Psi}_2$, and $|c_1|^2 + |c_2|^2 = 1$. Let $\mathbf{P}_\Psi$ be the projector onto the ray containing $\mathbf{\Psi}$, and $\mathbf{P}_1$ and $\mathbf{P}_2$ the projectors onto the rays containing $\mathbf{\Psi}_1$ and $\mathbf{\Psi}_2$, respectively.

In the absence of superselection rules the superposition $\mathbf{\Psi} = c_1\mathbf{\Psi}_1 + c_2\mathbf{\Psi}_2$ would not be statistically equivalent to the mixture $\mathbf{D} = |c_1|^2\mathbf{P}_1 + |c_2|^2\mathbf{P}_2$.

That is, there would be a quantum event E for which $p_\Psi(E) \neq p_D(E)$. For let E be represented by the projector $\mathbf{P}_E$ on $\mathcal{H}$. Then $p_D(E) = \mathrm{Tr}(\mathbf{P}_E\mathbf{D})$; using an orthonormal basis which includes $\mathbf{\Psi}_1$ and $\mathbf{\Psi}_2$, we obtain

$$\begin{aligned} p_D(E) &= \langle \mathbf{\Psi}_1 | \mathbf{P}_E \mathbf{D} \mathbf{\Psi}_1 \rangle + \langle \mathbf{\Psi}_2 | \mathbf{P}_E \mathbf{D} \mathbf{\Psi}_2 \rangle \\ &= |c_1|^2 \langle \mathbf{\Psi}_1 | \mathbf{P}_E \mathbf{\Psi}_1 \rangle + |c_2|^2 \langle \mathbf{\Psi}_2 | \mathbf{P}_E \mathbf{\Psi}_2 \rangle \end{aligned}$$

On the other hand,

$$\begin{aligned} p_\Psi(E) &= \mathrm{Tr}(\mathbf{P}_E \mathbf{P}_\Psi) = \langle \mathbf{\Psi} | \mathbf{P}_E \mathbf{\Psi} \rangle \\ &= \langle c_1\mathbf{\Psi}_1 + c_2\mathbf{\Psi}_2 | \mathbf{P}_E(c_1\mathbf{\Psi}_1 + c_2\mathbf{\Psi}_2) \rangle \\ &= |c_1|^2 \langle \mathbf{\Psi}_1 | \mathbf{P}_E \mathbf{\Psi}_1 \rangle + |c_2|^2 \langle \mathbf{\Psi}_2 | \mathbf{P}_E \mathbf{\Psi}_2 \rangle \\ &\quad + c_1^* c_2 \langle \mathbf{\Psi}_1 | \mathbf{P}_E \mathbf{\Psi}_2 \rangle + c_2^* c_1 \langle \mathbf{\Psi}_2 | \mathbf{P}_E \mathbf{\Psi}_1 \rangle \end{aligned}$$

In the presence of superselection rules, however, the cross terms vanish—because (a) L_1 and L_2 both reduce $\mathbf{P}_E$, and (b) L_1 and L_2 are mutually orthogonal—and we obtain

$$p_\Psi(E) = |c_1|^2 \langle \mathbf{\Psi}_1 | \mathbf{P}_E \mathbf{\Psi}_1 \rangle + |c_2|^2 \langle \mathbf{\Psi}_2 | \mathbf{P}_E \mathbf{\Psi}_2 \rangle = p_D(E)$$

We see that, in the presence of superselection rules, $\mathbf{\Psi}$ and $\mathbf{D}$ are statistically equivalent. (Recall, in this connection, the discussion in Section 3.9.) Thus although, in accordance with the superselection rule, $\mathbf{\Psi}$ may not represent a pure state of the system, we may use it to represent a mixture; $\mathbf{D}$ and $\mathbf{\Psi}$ become two mathematically equivalent ways to represent the same state.

Let us now return to Beltrametti and Cassinelli's account of the measurement process. They too argue that $S + M$ inherits the superselection rules characteristic of M, and that the superselection subspaces of $\mathcal{H}^{S+M}$ are $\mathcal{H}^S \otimes L_0^M$, $\mathcal{H}^S \otimes L_1^M$, and so on, where $L_0^M, L_1^M, \ldots$ are the rays in $\mathcal{H}^M$ containing the indicator states $\mathbf{u}_0, \mathbf{u}_1, \ldots$ of M (Beltrametti and Cassinelli, 1981, p. 84, though their argument to this conclusion is not the same as the one given here).

As in Section 9.6, we consider the case when the admissible pure states of M are $\mathbf{u}_0$, $\mathbf{u}_+$, and $\mathbf{u}_-$, and $\mathbf{u}_+$ and $\mathbf{u}_-$ correspond to the two values of an observable A associated with eigenstates $\mathbf{v}_+$ and $\mathbf{v}_-$ of S, respectively. We take the initial state of $S + M$ to be $\mathbf{\Psi}_0 = \mathbf{v} \otimes \mathbf{u}_0$, where $\mathbf{v} = c_+\mathbf{v}_+ + c_-\mathbf{v}_-$. Like Jauch, Beltrametti and Cassinelli suggest that $\mathbf{\Psi}_0$ evolves during the measurement process in accordance with the Schrödinger equation, so that

$$\mathbf{U\Psi}_0 = \mathbf{\Psi} = c_+\mathbf{\Psi}_+ + c_-\mathbf{\Psi}_-$$

where $\mathbf{\Psi}_+ = \mathbf{v}_+ \otimes \mathbf{u}_+$ and $\mathbf{\Psi}_- = \mathbf{v}_- \otimes \mathbf{u}_-$. *Contra* Jauch, however, they do not assume that the vector $\mathbf{\Psi}$ must represent a pure state of $S+M$. If neither $c_+ = 0$ nor $c_- = 0$, then $\mathbf{\Psi}$ does not lie within a superselection subspace of $\mathcal{H}^{S+M}$. When it does not, Beltrametti and Cassinelli interpret it as a classical mixed state. That is, they regard it as a mixture of $\mathbf{\Psi}_+$ and $\mathbf{\Psi}_-$, and interpret this mixture according to the ignorance interpretation. The pure state $\mathbf{\Psi}_+$ (respectively, $\mathbf{\Psi}_-$) is assigned probability $|c_+|^2$ (respectively, $|c_-|^2$). Thus in the course of a measurement the objective probabilities built into the state $\mathbf{v}$ of S evolve into the subjective probabilities associated with a classical mixture of states $\mathbf{\Psi}_+$ and $\mathbf{\Psi}_-$ of $S+M$ in accordance with (9.11c). Each component of this mixture reduces to pure states of S and of M ($\mathbf{\Psi}_+$ to $\mathbf{v}_+$ and $\mathbf{u}_+$, and $\mathbf{\Psi}_-$ to $\mathbf{v}_-$ and $\mathbf{u}_-$) so that the projection postulate is also satisfied.

This offers a neat resolution of the measurement problem, which evades the snag on which Jauch's proposal was shipwrecked. But it does so at considerable cost. As van Fraassen has pointed out to me (pers. com., November 1986), it faces a difficulty exactly analogous to that raised earlier in this section for all internal accounts of measurement.

Consider the operator $\mathbf{U}$ that maps $\mathbf{\Psi}_0$ into $\mathbf{\Psi}$. Since $\mathbf{\Psi}_0 \in \mathcal{H}^S \otimes L_0^M$ but $\mathbf{\Psi} \notin \mathcal{H}^S \otimes L_0^M$, the superselection subspaces of $\mathcal{H}^{S+M}$ do not reduce $\mathbf{U}$. Hence $\mathbf{U}$ can be neither an observable for $S+M$, nor a function of one. But, on the Schrödinger picture of the evolution of states, $\mathbf{U} = \mathbf{e}^{-i\mathbf{H}t}$, where $\mathbf{H}$ is the infinitesimal generator of the group $\{\mathbf{U}_t\}$ (see Section 2.7), and is also the operator corresponding to the total energy of the system. For all purely quantum systems, $\mathbf{H}$ is taken to represent an observable quantity; when superselection rules apply to quantum systems, $\mathbf{H}$, like every other operator representing an observable, is reduced by the superselection subspaces of the system (Jordan, 1969, sec. 32). In other words, in order for Beltrametti and Cassinelli's account of the measurement interaction to succeed, we must postulate that, when we deal with a macroscopic system, *either* the infinitesimal generator of the evolution group does not represent the energy of the system, *or* the energy is not an observable for the system.

Wan (1980, p. 980) acknowledges this problem, and points in the direction of a couple of responses, but neither of these seems promising. On the one hand he instances other theories (Dirac's Hamiltonian formulation of general relativity, the Gupta-Bleuler formulation of quantum electrodynamics) in which it seems inappropriate to regard $\mathbf{H}$ as the energy observable; on the other he points out that, if the measurement apparatus is treated as an infinite system, as it is in some other accounts of the measurement process, then "the total energy of an infinitely large system is not something having an obvious meaning which can be taken for granted."

But notice, first of all, that these examples only address the issue of whether $\mathbf{H}$ should represent the *energy* of the system; they do not touch the basic question of whether **H** should represent an *observable.* Second, both responses lose sight of the original project, which was not to establish where quantum theory is inadequate, but to show that a consistent, if schematic, account of measurement can be given within the formalism of the theory. Within orthodox quantum theory, the proposal that **H** does not represent the energy observable is entirely ad hoc; it has no independent motivation, examples from sundry field theories notwithstanding. And the second suggestion, that the measurement system be idealized as an infinite system, raises as many problems as it solves. To take one example, due to van Fraassen (see Hughes and van Fraassen, forthcoming), why should it be a permissible idealization to regard Schrödinger's cat (which contains about 10^{24} particles) as an infinite system, if we may not regard a pot of liquid helium, which is equally macroscopic but yet exhibits quantum behavior, in the same way?

9.8 *Three Accounts of Measurement*

In Chapter 10 I will suggest that, if it is seen as a problem within quantum mechanics, the measurement problem is insoluble. In the remainder of this chapter I will give thumbnail sketches of three different accounts of measurement; each of them, I will argue, while philosophically interesting, is finally unacceptable.

I have contrasted internal accounts of the measurement process with the dualist position presented by von Neumann. From what was said in Section 9.7, it seems that in order to give an internal account, we must drop the requirement that all the permissible pure states of *M* are mutually orthogonal. But having done so, we then need to explain why the behavior of this system seems to be classical. Two of the accounts of measurement I will look at reject the requirement but give different explanations of the apparently classical behavior of *M*; the third is a dualist account of a rather remarkable kind.

THE DANERI-LOINGER-PROSPERI THEORY

The most sober of the three accounts is offered by Daneri, Loinger, and Prosperi (1962). It may seem odd that I portray them as showing why a macroscopic system merely seems to behave classically, since they write that

> In order that objective meaning may be attributed to the macro-states of large bodies, it is of course necessary that . . . states incompatible with the macroscopic observables be actually impossible. (P. 298; Wheeler and Zurek, 1983, p. 658)

It sounds as though, like Beltrametti and Cassinelli, they are going to rule out superpositions of indicator states as possible pure states of $S + M$. (Here I am stretching previous usage by using "indicator states" to refer not merely to states of M but to those states of $S + M$ which would be admissible on a wholly classical picture.) However, this is not what they do. Rather, they show that, because $S + M$ is a very large system, the pure states into which it evolves *behave* like mixtures. Starting from the fact that a measuring instrument is a system of many particles and with correspondingly many degrees of freedom, they argue from thermodynamical considerations that, when such a system is in a superposition of indicator states, the interference terms characteristic of superpositions effectively cancel out (pp. 301/661 and 305/665). As a result, a superposition will be statistically indistinguishable from a mixture with respect to all relevant observables. If we measure the macroscopic system $S + M$ (call it "I") by using another macroscopic system ("II"), then

> A statistical operator . . . for the system I which corresponds to a pure state described by a superposition of vectors belonging to different [macroscopic states] is equivalent, so far as the macroscopic observables on II are concerned, to a statistical operator which is a mixture of the above macroscopic states. (Pp. 314/674)

This resembles the move made by Beltrametti and Cassinelli (see Section 9.7). On both approaches, the state to which $S + M$ evolves, and which is given mathematically by a linear superposition, is shown to be indistinguishable from one given by the weighted sum of projection operators. The difference is this. Beltrametti and Cassinelli suggest that the state in question is a mixed state, Daneri, Loinger and Prosperi that it is pure; however, according to the latter this pure state is statistically indistinguishable from a mixture. But, unless we think that a state-function refers essentially to an ensemble of systems, statistical indistinguishability is not enough. What Daneri, Loinger, and Prosperi conclude is that an ensemble of macroscopic quantum systems will behave like an ensemble of classical systems. As Cartwright (1983, pp. 169–171) has pointed out, however, what we need is an account within which individual systems exhibit classical behavior; if a superposition of indicator states does not represent a classically permissible pure state, then Daneri, Loinger, and Prosperi have failed to provide us with one (see also Bub, 1968; Putnam, 1965).

In brief, their account does not produce the final state we want; Beltrametti and Cassinelli, on the other hand, show us the desired state, but in doing so they make it unattainable.

THE MANY-WORLDS INTERPRETATION

Arguably the most fantastic of interpretations of quantum theory, certainly the one most beloved by writers of fantasy, is the *many-worlds interpretation* (MWI). Here I will follow de Witt (1970) in presenting the interpretation as a resolution of the problem of measurement; however, I should mention that for other advocates of the interpretation, Everett (1957) and Wheeler (1957), its main attraction was that it offered "a reformulation of quantum theory in a form believed suitable for application to general relativity" (Everett, 1957, p. 141).*

On this interpretation a measurement interaction occasions a splitting of this world into a large number of copies of itself. When the measurement leaves $S + M$ in a superposition, each of the indicator states represented in the superposition is the state of $S + M$ in at least one of the worlds. $S + M$ seems to behave classically because the observer is multiply cloned, together with the system; no clone has access to any world other than her own; hence only one of the indicator states presents itself to any one clone, while the others present themselves to counterpart observers in other worlds. Schrödinger's cat, predicted by the theory to be in a superposition of live and dead states, is alive in some worlds, dead in others.

Since quantum systems are continually interacting with one another, every world continually divides into different branches; each of these branches is a fully realized world, which in turn divides into other possible worlds, and so on. To quote de Witt,

> This universe is constantly splitting into a stupendous number of branches, all resulting from the measurementlike interactions between its myriads of components. Moreover, every quantum transition taking place on every star, in every galaxy, in every corner of the universe is splitting our local world into myriads of copies of itself. (De Witt, 1970, p. 161; page references are to de Witt and Graham, 1973)

Without irony—well, perhaps not wholly without irony—this can be described as a wonderfully extravagant and poetic vision of the cosmos; here imagination is bodying forth the forms of things not only unknown but unknowable. But bold metaphysical speculation of this kind can be subjected to various types of criticism. To impose a distinctly procrustean taxonomy, (1) the internal consistency of MWI can be challenged; (2) its philosophical coherence can be doubted; (3) one can object to the lack of fit between MWI and other physical theories; or (4) one can criticize it on general methodological grounds. Criticisms of all these kinds have been leveled at the many-worlds interpretation.

To consider an internal criticism first: after any interaction, so the account runs, the world "branches" so that the interaction yields a number of possible worlds, or rather, as Everett emphasizes, a number of worlds all equally

* As J. P. Jarrett has pointed out to me, not all proponents of the "relative state" approach (Everett's term) accept the many-worlds interpretation of it; see, for example, Geroch (1984). I discuss MWI from a slightly different perspective (and with greater charity) in Section 10.4.

"actual." This branching is determined by the states of the systems involved. Now a feature of Everett's presentation is that, in an interaction, the state of one system is specified with respect to the other; indeed, Everett (1957) called the interpretation the "'Relative State' Formulation of Quantum Mechanics." However, this specification of states is not symmetrical. (This follows from an argument due to Cartwright, 1974.) In other words, the set of possible worlds reachable from the perspective of one participant in an interaction will not mesh with the set reachable from the perspective of the other. There is thus no specifiable set of worlds into which the preinteraction world divides.

Nice examples of criticisms of the second type are given by Healey (1984, pp. 591–593), who spends several pages outlining the "antinomies" to which MWI has been thought to give rise; with one exception, which I discuss below, I will not rehearse them here. (Healey also discusses the problem of space-time structure and the modal realist version of MWI; see below.)

A criticism of the third kind has been voiced by Earman (1986, p. 224):

> What has rarely been explored is the implication for space-time structure of taking [MWI] seriously. To make sure that the different branches cannot interact even in principle they must be made to lie on sheets of space-time that are topologically disconnected after measurement, implying a splitting of space-time something like that illustrated [in Figure 9.3]. I do not balk at giving up the notion, held sacred until now, that space-time is a Hausdorff manifold. But I do balk at trying to invent a causal mechanism by which a measurement of the spin of an electron causes a global bifurcation of space-time.

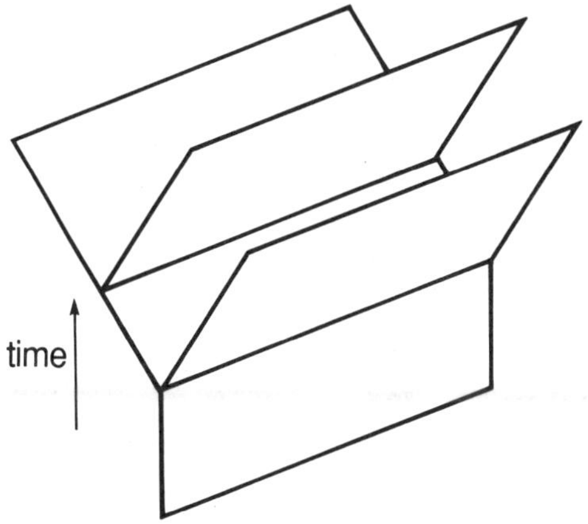

Figure 9.3 Splitting of space-time (from Earman, 1986, p. 225).

No doubt the many-worlds theorist would reject the demand for a *causal* explanation, but, if he does, he needs to say what alternative he has up his sleeve. Lacking one, he is open to the fourth kind of objection.

That is, even if advocates of MWI can respond to criticisms of the first two kinds, one is led by Earman's objection to doubt on general grounds whether the speculative metaphysics they offer provides a genuine answer to a physical problem. In particular, I would question whether what has been produced is anything more than a semantic model for probability statements associated with the measurement process. In the last twenty years philosophers have offered illuminating analyses of a great number of modal concepts in terms of "possible worlds." (See Loux, 1979, for a careful introduction to the literature.) To take a couple of trivial examples, a logically *necessary* statement is analyzed as a statement that is true in all possible worlds, whereas a *contingent* statement is one that is true in some worlds but not in others. Now probability is itself a modal concept (van Fraassen, 1980, chap. 6, calls it "The New Modality of Science") and it too has been analyzed in terms of possible worlds (Bigelow, 1976; Giere, 1976). The suspicion that this kind of conceptual analysis is all that the many-worlds interpretation supplies is strengthened by de Witt's claim (1970, p. 161) that *"the mathematical formalism of the quantum theory is capable of yielding its own interpretation"* (emphasis in the original).

But perhaps the many-worlds theorist could accept the description of his enterprise as one of providing a semantic analysis of the probability statements of quantum theory and claim nonetheless that it was true that each measurement interaction resulted in a division of the world into multiple copies of itself. Our possible-world analyses of modal concepts, he might say, are not merely formal; on our best metaphysical picture of the universe, this world is one of many equally real worlds. David Lewis (1986, p. 3) writes,

> Why believe in a plurality of worlds?—Because the hypothesis is serviceable, and that is a reason to think that it is true. The familiar analysis of necessity as truth in all possible worlds was only the beginning. In the last two decades philosophers have offered a great many more analyses that make reference to possible worlds, or to possible individuals that inhabit possible worlds. I find that record most impressive. I think it is clear that talk of *possibilia* has clarified questions in many parts of the philosophy of logic, of mind, of language, and of science—not to mention metaphysics itself. Even those who officially scoff often cannot resist the temptation to help themselves unabashedly to this useful way of speaking.

Lewis is not here discussing the many-worlds interpretation of quantum theory (nor does he elsewhere in the book I have just quoted from). And he readily acknowledges that many will find the ontological price of his modal realism too much to pay for the theoretical benefits it brings (p. 5). Let us assume, however, that we are willing to make the purchase on the many-worlds theorist's behalf. This still won't give the theorist what he needs. Consider the fact that, on Lewis's account, although all possible worlds are equally real, for us only this world is the actual world. In the grand metaphysical scheme of things, from the perspective of the Almighty, actuality may only function as an indexical marker on the set of worlds (like "here" and "present" across the set of points in space and time; pp. 92–94), but for each observer there is only one actual world, the one which she inhabits. Compare Everett's insistence that "*all* elements of a superposition (all 'branches') are 'actual,' none are more 'real' than the rest" (Everett, 1957, p. 146n). This, it might be said, is a purely verbal difference: Everett uses "actual" and "real" synonymously, where Lewis would use only "real." But what, on Everett's account, has become of the world which is actual in Lewis's? If there is no such privileged world, then something odd happens to our conception of probability. For if *all* (relevant) events with nonzero probability are realized in some world or other, then are not all those events certain of occurrence? (This was pointed out by Healey, 1984, p. 593.) And if I wager on what the outcome of a measurement will be, will it not pay "me" to place my bet on whatever outcome is quoted at the highest odds, without regard to the probabilities involved? We cannot just say, for example, that there are three times as many worlds, and hence three times the total payoff, corresponding to an event A, which has probability $\frac{3}{4}$, as there are corresponding to event B, which has probability $\frac{1}{4}$, since no principle of individuation distinguishes one A-world from another. (Before an epidemic of long-odds betting is upon us, however, I should add that even the National Security Council would be hard put to divert funds from my Swiss bank account in one world to its counterpart in another.)

These levities aside, we may ask what new understanding of the measurement process MWI gives us. After a measurement each observer will inhabit a world (for her the actual world) in which a particular result of the measurement has occurred. And the "total lack of effect of one branch on another also implies that no observer will ever be aware of any 'splitting' process" (Everett, 1957, p. 147n). What is this observer to say about the physical process which has just occurred? From where she stands, the wave packet has collapsed no less mysteriously, albeit no more so, than before.

We are still left with the dualism that the interpretation sought to eradicate. As de Witt (1970, pp. 164–165) himself remarks, the many-worlds interpretation of quantum mechanics "leads to experimental predictions identical with the (dualist) Copenhagen view." The difference is that any transition not governed by Schrödinger's equation is now accompanied by an ontological cloudburst beside which the original modest dualism of von Neumann looks unremarkable, if not pusillanimous.

WIGNER'S FRIEND

It is time to make the acquaintance of Wigner's friend. Wigner's account, the last account of measurement I will discuss here, is a dualist account; measurement produces a discontinuous change of state of the measured object (Wigner, 1961). The radical difference between this and a more orthodox view is that, to qualify as a measurement, an interaction must involve a conscious observer. Note that this is not just an account of why the system $S + M$ seems to behave classically; it is not merely that the conscious observer can register information only in a certain (classical) way. The event of registration is not merely passive; it is this event which brings about the projection of the system's state into an eigenstate of the observable measured. Wigner, a dualist with respect to the mind-body problem, sees the measurement process as an example of mind-body interaction.

He illustrates his view with an example. As the system S he takes a radiation field whose wave function "will tell us with what probability we shall see a flash if we put our eyes at certain points, with what probability it will leave a dark spot on a photographic plate if this is placed at certain positions" (Wigner, 1961, pp. 173–174; page references are to Wigner, 1967). The system S is represented as having two eigenstates $\mathbf{v}_1$ and $\mathbf{v}_2$ which give probabilities 1 and 0, respectively, to the occurrence of the flash. Thus, if the initial state of S is some superposition $\mathbf{v}$ of $\mathbf{v}_1$ and $\mathbf{v}_2$, then, on the orthodox view, the registration of the flash, whether at the observer's eye or the photographic plate, will cause the wave packet to collapse. On the other hand, if the radiation field interacts with a quantum system M, such as an atom, then the evolution of the joint system $S + M$ is governed by the Schrödinger equation and the resulting state will be a superposition $\mathbf{\Psi} = c_1(\mathbf{v}_1 \otimes \mathbf{u}_1) + c_2(\mathbf{v}_2 \otimes \mathbf{u}_2)$ of the kind we saw in section 9.5. (Here $\mathbf{u}_1$ and $\mathbf{u}_2$ are states of the atom.) As we saw there, this is inconsistent with the state of $S + M$ being either $\mathbf{v}_1 \otimes \mathbf{u}_1$ or $\mathbf{v}_2 \otimes \mathbf{u}_2$. Nevertheless, if an observer O now performs a measurement on the system M, this will project M into an eigenstate ($\mathbf{u}_1$, say). Since the systems are correlated, S will also be projected into $\mathbf{v}_1$, and the information received by the observer O will be equivalent to the registration of a flash. (The consistency of direct and indirect measurements is discussed further in Section 10.4.)

Wigner now considers the situation when the system S is observed by a friend. Wigner can find out about the system by asking her whether or not she has observed the flash. In doing so Wigner puts himself in the position of the observer O and his friend in the position of the system M. His "measurement" consists in asking her whether she has seen a flash. But, Wigner continues (pp. 179–180), after completing the whole experiment he can ask his friend, "What did you feel about the flash before I asked you?" If he does so, she will reply, "I told you already, I did (did not) see a flash." Short of giving himself a solipsistically privileged position, Wigner must accept that this report is indeed true, and hence that the interaction between S and his friend has already induced the collapse of the wave packet. The friend and the atom are therefore radically different kinds of systems, and (to quote Wigner, p. 180), "It follows that the being with a consciousness must have a different role in quantum mechanics than the inanimate measuring device, the atom considered above."

Stated in this way the conclusion is true but misleading. It has been shown that an atom behaves differently from a conscious observer. However, it has not been shown that the crucial difference is the consciousness of the observer. His friend is not merely a single atom which (who?) happens to be equipped with consciousness; though the event labeled as "seeing a flash" may have been triggered by an interaction involving one specific molecule in his friend's retina, his friend is a highly complex organism of macroscopic dimensions. What Wigner has done is to emphasize the fact, familiar to every dualist, that measurements, even of quantum systems, are to be described in classical terms—where this means simply that statements about measurement results are bivalent, either true or false. He has also claimed that the place where the discontinuity between the quantum and the classical worlds is located is in the distinction between a conscious observer and an inanimate measuring device. But this claim his argument by no means proves.

I do not wish to underestimate the difficulty for the dualist in specifying where the quantum/classical cut is to be made, and I will return to the topic in section 10.4. The strength of Wigner's proposal is that it points to a difference in kind, the distinction between the mental and the physical, to explain the discontinuity. But is this difference as clear-cut as Wigner assumes? The weakness of his account is that it relies on a dubious theory of mind and body, ironically the very theory which Wigner hoped to bolster by his argument. If, *contra* Wigner, we accept a materialist theory of mind (of whatever stripe), then Wigner's location of the cut between the quantum and the classical worlds no longer looks so precise; it becomes another distinction based on the size and complexity of a measurement system.

10

An Interpretation of Quantum Theory

Part One of this book gave an abstract summary of a physical theory; Part Two has asked, what must the world be like if this theory accurately describes it? In this final chapter I offer a tentative answer to this question. In Section 10.2 I present an interpretation of the theory which I call the "quantum event interpretation"; in Section 3 I compare it with a version of the Copenhagen interpretation; and lastly, in Sections 10.4 and 10.5, I discuss the relation between the quantum world and the classical, macroscopic world.

Prior to this, however, I consider the implications, some might say the hazards, of working with an account of the theory that is as abstract as the one presented in the first half of the book.

10.1 *Abstraction and Interpretation*

To a physicist the "theory" outlined in Part One would be very meager fare. I have already quoted Cartwright's comment (1983, p. 135) on such accounts: "One may know all of this and not know any quantum mechanics." (See Section 2.8.) For example, the treatment of spin in Chapter 4 never alluded to its physical significance; I never mentioned the fact that spin contributes to the magnetic moment of a system and that, in consequence, the Hamiltonian for the system will contain a term depending on its spin and the magnetic field in which it is placed.

Indeed, in at least one regard, my discussion of spin has flagrantly oversimplified matters. I have written as though the measurement of any component of spin of a free electron presented no difficulties. This is not the case. In 1929 Bohr showed that no Stern-Gerlach apparatus could perform such a measurement, owing to the masking effect produced by the interaction between the electron's charge and the magnetic field used to measure the spin component (see Mott and Massey, 1965, p. 215). In this respect a free electron behaves differently from the electrically neutral atoms experimented on by Stern and Gerlach. Bohr also claimed that measurements of the electron's spin components were, for conceptual reasons, impossible (Rosenfeld, 1971, in Cohen and Stachel, 1979, p. 694). However, in the 1950s Crane devised a technique for performing such measurements which evaded the problems of the Stern-Gerlach approach, and since then proton-proton pairs have been used by Lameti-Rachti and Mittig in experiments to show that Bell's inequality is violated. (See Clauser and Shimony, 1978, pp. 1917–1918; d'Espagnat, 1979.) There is also no masking problem when the spin of a neutron is measured (see Leggett, 1986, p. 39). Thus spin components are indeed measurable, though not as easily as I have suggested.

To return to the threatened criticism, that my account has been too abstract, the obvious response is to say that the aim of Part One was precisely that of showing the abstract conceptual structure of the theory. Philosophers of science may rashly tend to equate such abstract structures with the whole of a theory, and thereby be led to mistakes of assessment, but that is another matter. For example, the rejection of the wave picture urged in Section 8.3 may possibly be a mistake of this kind; although at the abstract level the picture is unhelpful, perhaps it is indispensable for pragmatic reasons when physical applications of the theory are at issue. It may be so. Nonetheless, although discussions of these applications would be needed to flesh out an abstract, skeletal account of the theory and give it breath, all these applications will involve a common set of mathematical models, and these abstract structures repay investigation.

A separate question is whether or not the significant features of these structures are being correctly identified. Here I am thinking in particular of the importance attributed, both in Chapter 8 and in the remainder of this chapter, to quantum conditionalization. In contrast, Teller (1983, p. 428) suggests that the Lüders rule is simply a "fortuitous approximation," an approximation because actual processes do not localize the state in precisely the sharp way that the rule suggests, and fortuitous because "there can be no uniform way, no formula which even in principle could be fixed in advance for turning the approximation into exact statements."

I agree on both counts; how then can I resist Teller's conclusion that

> If the projection postulate is a fortuitous approximation, we have no reason to think that it gives even an approximate description of some one specific process which might then stand in need of interpretation. (P. 428)

Teller's paradigm example of a fortuitous approximation is Hooke's law. This law, that strain is proportional to stress (less esoterically, that the deformation of a material object is proportional to the load applied to it) is approximately true of all kinds of materials in all sorts of configurations, from steel wires to foam rubber mattresses. For Teller it is a *fortuitous* approximation because there is no uniform way to correct it to allow for the individual idiosyncracies of the materials involved. In this way, he suggests, it differs from the *uniform* approximation afforded by, for example, the pendulum law: $T = 2\pi\sqrt{l/g}$. We know wherein the approximation of the pendulum law exists; its derivation involves the approximation that, for small θ, $\theta = \sin\theta$. Hence there is a clear-cut way in which it is correctable. Hooke's law, on the other hand, is just a pragmatically useful approximation, roughly true for many materials below their elastic limit (Noakes, 1957, pp. 141–142). Of the latter we can agree with Teller that (1) it is an approximately true law for which no uniform method of approximation exists, and (2) it describes no single and theoretically significant process.

However, there is little reason to think that, in general, (1) entails (2). Consider the ideal gas law, $pV = nRT$. This is only approximately true for real gases. The models supplied by the kinetic theory of gases, within which this law can be derived, represent molecules as point systems, undergoing perfectly elastic collisions, and exerting forces on each other only during these collisions. Molecules of real gases are not like that. In fact, so many different idealizations are involved in the theory that there is no uniform way to correct the ideal gas law. True, judicious choices of a and b make van der Waals' law, $[p + (a/V^2)](V - b) = nRT$, more nearly true for many gases, but near the critical point it too goes astray, and whence are a and b to be derived? (See Noakes, 1957, p. 375.) Nevertheless, the absence of a systematic mode of correction would hardly justify our dubbing the ideal gas law a *fortuitous* approximation, unless that term were shorn of its pejorative implications and became merely a term of art.

The question of a uniform mode of correction is essentially subordinate to another: are we dealing with an idealization within the models that the theory supplies, or with an empirical approximation with no theoretical support? Teller (1983, p. 428) writes that "virtually all descriptions of actual processes *idealize* or *approximate*," but he does not thereafter distinguish between the two. The Lüders rule, I suggest, like the ideal gas law, appears as an idealization, Hooke's law as an empirical approximation.

Still, Teller could disagree; he could accept the distinction I have just made and nevertheless claim that his arguments justify his placing the Lüders rule and Hooke's law in the same basket. He points out that the final projected state that the Lüders rule predicts for the system depends on its initial state. Now, during the measurement process the system's state will be continuously evolving in accordance with Schrödinger's equation. If the system also suffers a discontinuous change of state given by the Lüders rule, then, because the "initial state" is continuously changing, the result of this projection will depend on the time at which it occurs. But there is no theoretical reason to locate the projection at any one time in the measurement process rather than another: "No formulation of the projection postulate tells us exactly at which point to apply it" (Teller, 1983, p. 425). Hence, Teller could continue, there is no warrant for thinking of the postulate as giving an idealization of a physical process.

This is a powerful argument, but it draws its strength, I think, from the fact that Teller looks at the projection postulate solely in terms of its relation to the measurement process. As I pointed out in Sections 9.4 and 9.5, the question of the projection postulate is conceptually separable from the main problem of measurement. Considered just as a constraint on accounts of measurement, the postulate is a seemingly arbitrary stipulation which lacks obvious links with the rest of quantum theory. On the other hand, if we view the Lüders rule as Bub suggests, as the rule of conditionalization appropriate to quantum event structures, we see it in a different light. As the quantum analogue of the classical conditionalization rule, it is built into the non-Boolean event structures around which quantum theory is constructed.

I acknowledge that the Lüders rule differs from the ideal gas law in an important respect. The deviations of real gases from the ideal gas law have explanations (the finite size of actual molecules, their mutual attraction, and so on); further, these explanations also tell us, in general terms, why van der Waals' equation is an improvement. In contrast, we have no decent account of when and why the Lüders rule is a less than adequate idealization. But my reaction to this is not to revise my view of the Lüders rule, but to say that quantum mechanics still faces a major empirical and conceptual task, that of sorting out the relation of quantum systems to the classical, macroscopic world. Take, for example, the simple case of an electron striking a diaphragm with a hole in it (as in Section 8.3). We need to know what it is about the physical structure of a real diaphragm that makes the wave function of an electron passing through it differ from the ideal localized wave function predicted by the Lüders rule. But these gaps in our knowledge do not make the rule a fortuitous approximation; the idealizations it relies on are those assumed by quantum theory itself.

This fact, however, that there is no systematic way to explain deviations from the Lüders rule, prompts a return to the question of the value of abstract theory, since it hints at a deeper issue than the particular problems I have looked at so far.

Duhem (1906) thought that what are often called "fundamental" physical theories (Maxwell's theory of the electromagnetic field, for instance) did no more than provide a formal unification of a wide range of phenomena.

He endorses the view that "a physical theory . . . is an abstract system whose aim is to *summarize* and *classify logically* a group of experimental laws" (p. 7). And he quotes approvingly Hertz's dictum that "Maxwell's theory is the system of Maxwell's equations" (p. 80). Whether or not he is right about Maxwell's theory, Duhem's description accurately fits the version of quantum mechanics given here. This yokes together a disparate group of phenomena in a purely formal way. The analogies between these phenomena, one might think, do no more than allow a unified mathematical treatment of diverse aspects of nature; no further significance attaches to them.

Certainly, the deployment of abstract analogies is part of the physicist's repertoire. For example, in his *Lectures on Physics* Feynman introduces the idea at an early stage, in his discussion of damped harmonic oscillations, by displaying the pair of equations (Feynman, Leighton, and Sands, 1965, vol. 1, p. 25-8):

$$m\frac{d^2x}{dt^2} + \gamma m\frac{dx}{dt} + kx = F \tag{10.1}$$

$$L\frac{d^2q}{dt^2} + R\frac{dq}{dt} + \frac{q}{C} = V \tag{10.2}$$

Equation (10.1) describes the mechanical motion of a mass m on the end of a spring, under the influence of a varying force F; Equation (10.2), the electrical oscillation set up in a circuit by a varying voltage V. The formal correspondence between the two is evident. Any solution for one becomes a solution for the other when corresponding terms are substituted for each other (V for F, $1/C$ for k, and so on). For Duhem, however, this is where the correspondence ends; we simply have two disparate sets of phenomena each of which can be modeled (mathematically) in the same way. There is no more to be said.

Here our views differ. And the greater the number of fields that could be modeled in the same way, and the more heterogeneous they were, the more significant I would find it. But significant in what sense? To go back to the example, it is clearly not the case that the same physical processes are at work in the two types of oscillation.

The formal nature of the correspondence tells us that any underlying commonality between the two exists at the most abstract, conceptual level, and is to be found by examining the form of the mathematical equations in which the analogy between the two is expressed. These equations are second-order differential equations in x and q, respectively. Implicit in the use of these equations is the assumption that both position (x) and charge (q) are continuous, and continuously differentiable, quantities. If similar differential equations appeared throughout our fundamental physical theories, then the implication would be that all physical quantities were continuous in nature. This would then be a significant element within our metaphysical picture of the world. In fact we no longer believe in the continuity of electric charge, and so Equation (10.2) is in this respect misleading: charge is a discrete, not a continuous quantity. The equation is a pragmatically useful approximation, not a part of our foundational theory. (Recall the discussion of Hooke's law.) That, I suggest, is the salient difference in significance between the modeling of oscillations given by the two equations (particularly the latter) and the models furnished by our abstract account of quantum theory.

My point is this. Even if—or especially if—we accept Duhem's account of physical theories, it is nevertheless worthwhile to examine the models a theory employs, to see what metaphysical picture is implicit in them. This is precisely what goes on when we look to Hilbert spaces in order to find a categorial framework within which to interpret quantum theory. To this end, the more abstract the presentation of the theory the better.

To seek such a categorial framework is the reverse of a process Duhem elsewhere condemns, whereby physical theories are assessed in the light of prior metaphysical commitments; instead, we are asking the theory to provide our metaphysics. Nonetheless, a resolute Duhemian skeptic might insist that the search for a categorial framework was not a useful philosophical occupation. This itself, however, would betray a certain metaphysical commitment, albeit one expressed in antimetaphysical terms. There seems no *a priori* reason to think that the search should be either fruitless or uninteresting. And should the skeptic persist—so weak is the power of rational argument to persuade—one could only say, "It was not you for whom Part Two of this book was written."

10.2 *Properties and Latencies: The Quantum Event Interpretation*

In this section I will outline a possible interpretation of quantum mechanics, which I will call the *quantum event interpretation.* That is, I will propose a categorial framework whose elements find representation in the Hilbert-space models the theory displays.

The categorial framework I will outline can be compared to that found within classical mechanics, where we see, first of all, a distinction between a *system* and its *attributes* (or *properties*), and, second, a fully *causal* account of processes. Analogues of all these elements appear within the quantum event interpretation of quantum theory.

The concept of a *system* I have taken for granted; presupposed by the representation supplied by the theory is the assumption that parts of the world are, for the purposes of theory, isolable. However, this presupposition is very much an idealization; indeed it is challenged by the theory itself. In quantum theory, coupled systems are more than the sum of their parts, witness the behavior of the coupled systems used in EPR experiments. To isolate a section of this world is to say that its couplings to other systems have become so attenuated that we may disregard them. This said, the notion of a system will not be further examined.*

The classical notion of a property is inappropriate to quantum theory, as was seen in Chapter 6. Nor is much interpretive work done by retaining this notion within a quantum-logical framework, for the reasons given in Section 7.9. Heisenberg and Margenau have both suggested that quantum theory requires instead a concept that recognizes the inherently probabilistic nature of the quantum world. Heisenberg (1958, p. 53) talked of "tendencies" and suggested that these resembled the "potentia" of Aristotelian science. This particular analogy is very remote; instead, I am adopting the term "latency" suggested by Margenau (1954).

The properties of classical systems were summarized by its state. Given the state we could predict the values which ideal measurements of observables would reveal. The latencies of quantum physics are also represented by the state—here the state vector. These latencies assign probabilities to measurement outcomes. We term these measurement outcomes *quantum events* and no longer treat them as corresponding to possible properties of the quantum system. A quantum measurement should be regarded neither as revealing a property of the system nor as creating that property, for the simple reason that quantum systems do not have properties. Rather, the measurement involves the realization of a particular quantum event from the Boolean algebra of such events associated with the measurement apparatus. And, although only one Boolean algebra of events can be selected at a time, the latency represented by the state vector determines probabilities for a whole orthoalgebra of events.

The so-called wave-particle duality of quantum systems, shorn of its mechanistic associations, fits naturally within this interpretation. For, as Born pointed out, the "waves" which the wave-particle account portrays as spreading through space are "probability waves"; the square of the amplitude of the wave at any point in space gives the probability of finding the "particle" there. Similarly, to ascribe a latency to a system with respect to its

* But see Teller (1989). And, in addition, Ned Hall has pointed out to me the problems raised by the Pauli exclusion principle.

position is just to say that there is an extended region of space within which there is a nonzero probability of finding it. The wave formalism offers a convenient mathematical representation of this latency, for not only can the mathematics of wave effects, like interference and diffraction, be expressed in terms of the addition of vectors (that is, their linear superposition; see Feynman, Leighton, and Sands, 1965, vol. 1, chap. 29-5), but the converse also holds. Clearly, this mathematical equivalence is independent of the fact that vectors can represent probability assignments; hence the propriety of talking of the "interference effects" obtained in, for example, the two-slit experiment. In contrast, "particle" effects typically occur when position is localized; in other words, when a quantum event occurs, latency is actualized and the "wave packet" collapses.

Thus the quantum event interpretation offers both an abstraction and a generalization of the thesis of wave-particle duality; on the one hand, it severs the thesis from its classical nineteenth-century antecedents, and, on the other, it accommodates all quantum observables, not merely position and momentum.

The sense in which a *latency* is a natural probabilistic generalization of a *property* can be made more precise. Although the exact ontological status of a property (greenness, for example) may be questioned, one thing is not in dispute (Staniland, 1972). If we say of a billiard ball that it is green, then our statement entails that, if viewed under normal conditions, it will have a certain appearance; simply put, that it will appear green. In classical physics, the ascription of a property to an object entails the truth of various conditionals of the form, "If an (ideal) measurement of A is made, then the result will lie within Δ." I will call such a conditional a "measurement conditional" and write it as $MA \rightarrow (A,\Delta)$. (A,Δ) is, as usual, the event that an A-measuring device gives a result within Δ.

A complete description of a classical system would give us all its properties, so that every measurement conditional would be assigned "True" or "False."* (This description is familiar from Chapter 2.) In contrast, the ascription of a latency to a quantum system entails the truth or falsity of a host of conditionals of the form:

$$MA \rightarrow [p(A,\Delta) = x]$$

Such *quantum measurement conditionals* also carry reference to a set of events (A,Δ), but this set, as we have seen, has a radically non-Boolean structure; it has the structure of the set of subspaces of a Hilbert space. The

* I am relying here on an intuitive account of the truth-conditions for conditionals.

result is that we can never find a probability function p such that, for every event (A,Δ), either $p(A,\Delta) = 1$ or $p(A,\Delta) = 0$. That is to say, these latencies can never be reduced to properties.

The pure states of quantum mechanics give complete descriptions in the following sense. (1) A pure state assigns to each quantum measurement conditional a value "True" or "False," and (2) the probabilities occurring in these conditionals are not just epistemic probabilities, but objective propensities. We can regard the description as complete with respect to latencies, rather than to properties. In the case of a mixed state, the answer is not so clear-cut. If the mixture can be given an ignorance interpretation, then it does not give a complete description since (2) fails; if an ignorance interpretation is ruled out, then, on this interpretation, there is no reason to think that the description that a mixture provides is less than complete. Of course, quantum theory is not complete in Jarrett's sense of the word (see Section 8.6); one could argue, however, that it *is* complete in Einstein's sense after all (see Section 6.2): whenever the probability of an event (A,Δ) is one, then there is a state specified by the theory whose support with respect to A is a subset of Δ, and only when the system is in that, or one of those, states can one predict the value of A with certainty without disturbing the system.

How does the latency of a system change? In two ways, which exactly match the two modes of evolution of the state function, as von Neumann depicted them. Latencies, like state vectors, can change continuously or discontinuously. The first type of change is not causally problematic. The second is. In the first place, it is stochastic; since the event which induces it is not in general determined by the state, but has just a nonzero probability of occurrence, it differs in at least one respect from a classical cause. Second, it may be nonlocal; the kind of transition which (on the account given in Section 8.8) characterizes EPR experiments is an example.

I don't want to underestimate this last problem; a discussion by Shimony (1986, pp. 193–196) shows just how severe it is. Assume that, in an EPR-type experiment, the measurements performed on two systems a and b are simultaneous in the laboratory frame of reference; call the events associated with these measurements E_a and E_b, respectively. Then the special theory of relativity (STR) tells us that there is a frame of reference $\mathcal{F}_a$ in which E_a precedes E_b and another frame $\mathcal{F}_b$ in which E_b precedes E_a. But, on the interpretation I am offering, this means that within $\mathcal{F}_a$ the event E_a occasions a projection of the state of b to a new state (with support E_b) prior to the event E_b. Within $\mathcal{F}_b$, on the other hand, this projection is produced, if at all, by the event E_b itself, and E_b also occasions a change of state of a.

There is no outright inconsistency here; however, the occurrence or nonoccurrence of a change of latency becomes frame-relative, and this certainly offends the spirit, if not the letter, of STR.

Indeed, at this point I can hear the objection that the interpretation offered has just too many unpalatable features. On the one hand, so the criticism runs, nonlocal conditionalization might be acceptable as a convenient mathematical way to summarize the correlations associated with coupled systems; on the other, the suggestion that there is a new ontological category called "latency" seems fairly inoffensive. But when it transpires that (1) these physical significant latencies can be changed by nonlocal actions, and that (2) these alleged changes are not relativistically invariant, that is just too much to swallow.

Not much can be said, I fear, to sweeten this particular pill, but perhaps we can say more on behalf of the individual ingredients which together prove so distasteful. To reiterate what was said in Section 10.1, in seeking an interpretation of a theory we start from Duhem's thesis that a theory provides an abstract summary and logical classification of a group of experimental laws. However, that is only where we start. Though our final convictions may be instrumentalist, we are setting these attitudes aside for the time being and asking, what sort of world could be represented by the mathematical models the theory provides? Further, if we are not instrumentalists, we may hope that this way of proceeding sidesteps Duhem's argument that, since "explanations" are formulated only with respect to a set of prior metaphysical assumptions, to think that theories provide explanations is misguided. We perform this sidestep by looking *within the theory* for the categorial framework it suggests, and which is to be appealed to in explanations.

Within quantum mechanics we find, in a word, probabilities. However, the probability functions the theory uses cannot be regarded as weighted sums of dispersion-free probability functions — that is, as weighted sums of property ascriptions; quantum theory is irreducibly probabilistic. Rejecting properties from our categorial framework, we replace them with their probabilistic analogues, latencies. But why replace them with anything? Why grant ontological status to these remote and shadowy quasi-attributes? A specific argument for doing so will be offered in the next section; meanwhile, here are some general considerations.

We invoke latencies for much the same reasons that, in the macroscopic world, we invoke properties. Attempts to give a purely phenomenalistic account of properties notoriously failed (see, for example, Hirst, 1967); a property ascription is more than the logical product of a set of conditionals of the kind, "If I were looking at object X now, under normal conditions of illumination, then I would be having sensations of greenness." Similarly for latencies; these too license infinitely many subjunctive conditionals (of which a proper subset are quantum measurement conditionals), but, for much the same reasons, are not reducible to them.

What then of the projection postulate? This too emerges from the nonclassical nature of the probability spaces we deal with. Regarded not just as a postulate applying (occasionally) to the measurement process, but as the quantum version of conditionalization, it provides explanations of the otherwise inexplicable. In Section 8.9 I called these explanations "structural" but, if conditionalization is seen as a change in the latencies of a system, they also acquire an ontological foundation.

It turns out that there is a price to be paid. Some of the conditionalizations which figure in these explanations are nonlocal: latencies may be affected by action at a distance. Even though stochastic Einstein-locality is respected, the price may seem too high. The interpretation may still violate too many intuitions. But so may quantum theory. And, like Isabella on a different occasion, the fierce defender of intuitions may have got his priorities wrong. After all, what's so hot about intuitions? Aren't these the folks who gave us Bell's inequality? Duhem would have had little truck with them.

10.3 The Copenhagen Interpretation

The quantum event interpretation should be distanced from the "Copenhagen agnosticism" van Fraassen (1985) advocates "with respect to what happens to measurable physical magnitudes when they are not being measured." Bohr's expression of this agnosticism was discussed in Section 7.9. There we also saw how it could be set out in algebraic terms. In the same vein, van Fraassen and others offer a "Copenhagen approach" to quantum-mechanical probabilities. On this approach, the fact that there is no simple Kolmogorov model of probabilities involving incompatible observables A, B, and C does not mean that we must jettison classical probability theory; it is a result of the fact that such observables are not jointly measurable. The apparent departures from Kolmogorov probability theory that we find in quantum mechanics occur because quantum probabilities are all conditional probabilities; $p(A,\Delta)$ should be read as, "the probability that a result within Δ will be found, conditional on an A-measurement being made." We obtain a perfectly good Kolmogorov probability space for incompatible observables A, B, and C, so the story runs, by partitioning a classical probability space Ω into three mutually exclusive sets of events, corresponding to measurements of A, B, and C, each of which forms a Boolean algebra.

Assume for the sake of argument that each of A, B, and C has two values, and call them $\{a_1,a_2\}$, $\{b_1,b_2\}$, $\{c_1,c_2\}$, respectively. Then a finer six-way partition $\{a_1,a_2,b_1,b_2,c_1,c_2\}$ of Ω is available, and quantum probabilities appear according to the recipe (for observable A, in this example):

$$p(A,a_1) = p_K(a_1|a_1 \cup a_2)$$

where p_K is a Kolmogorov probability function defined on Ω.

In this formula the term $a_1 \cup a_2$ represents the event that a measurement of A takes place. With a slight abuse of notation we can write

$$p_K(a_1|a_1 \cup a_2) = p_K(a_1|MA)$$

Note that the event $a_1 \cup a_2$ is not identified with the events $b_1 \cup b_2$ and $c_1 \cup c_2$, as it would be in the construction of an orthoalgebra of quantum events (see Section 8.1). On the contrary, these three events are mutually exclusive.

The example may be generalized. That is, given any generalized probability function p defined on an orthoalgebra $\mathcal{A}$, the probabilities p assigns to members of $\mathcal{A}$ may be reproduced as classical conditional probabilities on a Kolmogorov probability space as follows. Consider the family $\{\mathcal{B}_i\}$ of maximal Boolean subalgebras of $\mathcal{A}$. We embed these algebras individually in a Kolmogorov probability space in such a way that their maxima are mutually exclusive and jointly exhaustive: $I_i \cap I_j = 0$ when $i \neq j$, and $\cup_i I_i = \Omega$. $\{I_i\}$ is thus a partition of Ω, and if p_K is any classical probability function on Ω, then $\Sigma_i p_K(I_i) = 1$. To reproduce the probabilities assigned by p to members of $\mathcal{A}$, we stipulate that, for any event e in $\mathcal{B}_i$,

$$p_K(e|I_i) = p(e)$$

Such a probability function p_K always exists, but since the assignments $p_K(I_i)$ are arbitrary (though they must all be nonzero), p_K is not uniquely defined by p.

To summarize. The Copenhagen view of quantum theory and the quantum event view differ significantly in their treatment of probabilities. Whereas on the quantum event view probabilities in quantum mechanics are assigned by generalized probability functions to members of an orthoalgebra $\mathcal{A}$ of events, on the Copenhagen view the underlying probability space is classical. This classical space is coarsely partitioned, each member of the partition being the event that a particular measurement occurs, and each corresponding to a maximal Boolean subalgebra of $\mathcal{A}$. Probabilities are assigned to events in this classical space by a Kolmogorov probability function, and quantum-mechanical probabilities now appear as conditional probabilities, each conditional on some event in the coarse partition.

From the point of view of the quantum event interpretation, this construction is not only formally respectable, but in some circumstances physically significant. Assume, for example, that we are dealing with an experiment, like the Aspect experiment described in Section 8.6, in which there is a probability $p_e(MB)$ that a B-measurement will be performed, and so on; p_e is of course a Kolmogorov probability function. Assume further that the state of the system assigns probability q to some event (A,a_i) according to the usual algorithm, by specifying a generalized probability function on the set of quantum events. We can now construct a Kolmogorov space in the way prescribed, on which the function p_e yields an "absolute probability" for the result a_i, for example, according to the formula

$$p_e(a_i) = p_e(MA) \cdot q$$

On the quantum event interpretation the equation holds because (1) the state makes the conditional $MA \rightarrow [p(A,a_i) = q]$ true, and (2) MA has probability $p_e(MA)$. On the Copenhagen interpretation we obtain the same equation, since

$$q = p_e(a_i|MA) = \frac{p_e(a_i)}{p_e(MA)}$$

In the light of this one may ask, what does the quantum event interpretation achieve that a Copenhagen interpretation does not? What is gained by the appeal to arcane nonclassical algebraic structures, let alone by the invocation of dubiously metaphysical "latencies"?

The same question was raised at the end of Section 10.2, and I can now amplify the answer given there. One specific achievement is the ability to talk of the probability of one quantum event conditional on another. On the quantum event interpretation, to ask what the probability is that a measurement of A will yield result a_i, given that an event (B,b_j) has occurred, is to ask, for what value of x is the statement $MA \rightarrow (p[(A,a_i)|(B,b_j)] = x)$ true? Since p is a generalized probability function (GPF) defined on the set of subspaces of a Hilbert space, the conditional probability $p[(A,a_i)|(B,b_j)]$ is given straightforwardly by the Lüders rule. Chapter 8 demonstrated just how fruitful the application of this rule can be. In contrast, on the Copenhagen approach we have no ready means of dealing with sequences of events; $p_K(a_i|b_j)$ will always be zero if A and B are incompatible.

More generally and fundamentally, the Copenhagen approach offers no account at all of the relations between incompatible observables. There are probability functions p_K, definable on the Kolmogorov space Ω constructed according to the Copenhagen prescription, which do not generate quantum-mechanical probabilities. To return to our earlier example involving observables *A, B,* and *C*, a perfectly respectable classical probability measure on the partition $\{a_1, a_2, b_1, b_2, c_1, c_2\}$ assigns to each of a_1, b_1, and c_1 the value $\frac{4}{15}$, and to each of a_2, b_2, and c_2 the value $\frac{1}{15}$. This would yield the quantum probabilities

$$p(A,a_1) = p(B,b_1) = p(C,c_1) = \frac{4}{5} \qquad p(A,a_2) = p(B,b_2) = p(C,c_2) = \frac{1}{5}$$

Yet if *A, B,* and *C* are the familiar components of spin, S_x, S_y, and S_z, respectively, no quantum-mechanical state assigns probability $\frac{4}{5}$ to the positive value of each observable. (To be precise, no quantum state simultaneously assigns to all three events probabilities greater than $1/2 + \sqrt{3}/6 = 0.786$.)

The Copenhagen interpretation offers no reason why such assignments are ruled out. In rewriting the probabilities assigned by any GPF to elements of an orthoalgebra as conditional probabilities defined on a classical probability space, it takes no account of the fact that quantum mechanics uses orthoalgebras which have a very rich structure; each is isomorphic to the set of subspaces of some Hilbert space.

Not only does the quantum event interpretation regard that fact as central, a partial explanation of it has already been offered which leads naturally to the concept of latency.

The ascription of a particular latency to a system assigns probabilities to the values of a family of observables. With this in mind, consider the analysis of spin in Chapter 4. The question that chapter asks is, what are the results of assuming that the probabilities associated with a particular family of observables are constrained in ways suggested by "natural" symmetries —the isotropy of space, for example? The answer is that *only* if all the observables in the family can in some sense be regarded as components of a vector is a model of the set of events available which uses the full representational capacity of a Hilbert space; a condition must be put on the probabilities associated with the component observables, analogous to those obtaining when we deal with classical vector quantities. Equations (4.10) and (4.11) give equivalent statements of the required condition.

My suggestion is that we think of this intricately related set of probabilities as determined by some one feature of the system, and give the name "latency" to this feature. Again, latencies appear as the probabilistic analogues of properties. In classical mechanics a vector property, that is, a particular value of a vector quantity like momentum, determines the values of all components of that quantity. Analogously, in quantum theory, the latency associated with, say, spin determines the probabilities assigned to the values of all its component observables.

10.4 The Priority of the Classical World

The quantum event interpretation has this in common with the Copenhagen interpretation: both assume a classical world which is in some sense prior to the quantum world. But the kind of conceptual priority granted to the classical world needs to be spelled out with some care.

First, there is the question of specificity. Bohr, in particular, thought that any statement about quantum systems acquired meaning only in the context of a particular experimental procedure (see, for example, Bohr, 1949, pp. 218, 222). The quantum event interpretation, on the other hand, suggests that quantum theory carries with it an implicit reference, not to particular procedures, but to a set of events which are associated with classical devices of some kind or other, and with respect to which latencies are defined.

The second question is the content of the term "classical." I have already (Section 8.3) criticized Bohr's insistence that physicists must restrict themselves to the concepts bequeathed to us by late-nineteenth-century physics. The kind of conceptual priority assumed by the quantum event interpretation is of a more abstract, structural kind. It allows for the possibility of quantum concepts which lack direct analogues in classical physics. What it takes from classical physics is the bare concept of an observable which can take different values.

At the risk of repetition, I will spell out what this entails. The quantum events to which the theory assigns probabilities are all of the form (A,Δ); all events involve reference to some observable A and, if A is an observable, then every pair (A,Δ) represents an event—though this may be the null event even when Δ is not the empty set, as in the case of the electron-event $(S_x,[1,2])$. As we saw in Section 7.5, the classical concept of an observable thus imposes considerable structure on the set of events; this set is divided into Boolean algebras, each associated with an observable. Any measurement apparatus is associated with some observable A. When $\mathbf{A}$, the operator that represents A, has a discrete spectrum, an ideal measurement apparatus would discriminate between all the distinct quantum events associated with A, but when $\mathbf{A}$ has a continuous spectrum this is, of course, impossible. Whether our apparatus is sensitive or insensitive, however, it is a classical device in two linked senses. First, the events it registers will form a Boolean algebra, and so the statements describing these events will allow bivalent truth-assignments. Second, its indicator states are classical states, and can be thought of as a partial list of its properties. This second feature is in fact entailed by the first.

We see that, although the latencies of quantum theory are latencies with respect to a set of events with a thoroughly non-Boolean structure, nevertheless the set of events realizable at any given juncture—namely, the set of events associated with any experimental situation—will form a Boolean algebra. While the contribution of quantum theory is to show that the set of all events, together with the states that assign them probabilities, can be represented in a Hilbert space, the first requirement of this representation is that it respects the classical structure of the set of events associated with a given observable. This is the sense in which, on the quantum event interpretation, the classical world is conceptually prior to the quantum world.

Implicit in quantum theory is a reference to a classical world. But where is the boundary to be drawn? And what is the relation between the worlds? Wigner, as we saw in Section 9.8, located the boundary at the level of consciousness; the only classical device was a conscious observer. But this is undesirable on two grounds, (1) that it is too subjective for our tastes, and (2) that it relies on a dubious distinction between mind and body. In contrast, the original Copenhagen interpretation assumed a self-evident distinction between the quantum and the classical worlds. This, however, is unhelpful to those to whom the grounds for such a distinction do not immediately reveal themselves. Quantum systems, we may say, are smaller than macrosystems: an electron is paradigmatically the kind of system treated in quantum theory, a piece of polaroid plus a photographic plate can act as a classical measuring device. But is there a number N such that all systems of N particles are microsystems, whereas all systems of $N + 1$ particles are macrosystems? That sounds implausible.

One of Everett's aims, in his "relative state" formulation of quantum mechanics (see Section 9.8), was to present the theory in such a way that this "cut" between the quantum and the classical worlds disappears. Quantum theory, on this account, would be a global theory; it would not be conceptually improper—as it is on the Copenhagen interpretation—to talk of the "universal wave function" (Everett, 1973). In implementing this program, the "relative state" formulation ran into a difficulty (see the appendix to Shimony, 1986): if the "branching" of the universe was to correspond properly to the (apparent) collapse of the wave packet, then, contrary to quantum mechanics, there had to be one preferred basis in which the states of measurement systems were represented. Certain systems, in other words, could not be properly accommodated within the theory; the "cut" which

Everett sought to eliminate did not disappear after all, and the problem of the relation of the classical world to the quantum world was still with us.

Everett's interpretation provokes the question whether we can talk meaningfully, as he thought we could, about the "universal wave function." If, as I have claimed, a reference to a classical world is implicit in quantum mechanics, does this mean that this kind of talk is conceptually confused?

It does not. I have argued that a quantum-mechanical state represents, at least in part, dispositions to behave in certain ways in interactions with certain classical systems. These dispositions do not go away if the interactions are not realized; and even if, in our present universe, these dispositions *cannot* be realized, we can still speak counterfactually about what would happen were our universe to be embedded in another. It is thus not incoherent to suggest that the universe has a quantum-mechanical state which is unfolding as it should, even though there is (by definition) no external material agency available to scrutinize it.

However, before arriving at a wave function for the universe, we need to obtain wave functions for its components—including those which, as measurement devices, furnish the classical world within which the latencies of, say, an electron are realized. This confronts us with the measurement problem in its abstract form: if a particular set of quantum events is defined by reference to the classical behavior of a given system, can we give a quantum-mechanical account of that system?

10.5 *Quantum Theory and the Classical Horizon*

The question is this: if a system could function as a measuring device, need this rule out the possibility of describing it in quantum-mechanical terms? (I am here speaking of the kind of description a Laplacean supermind might furnish; we cannot give a fully quantum-mechanical description of a large molecule, but that's our problem.) What are the consequences, we may ask, of allowing the boundary between the quantum and the classical worlds to float, so that it can be drawn and redrawn wherever we will, above a certain point? In order to proffer a quantum-mechanical description of a measurement device, may we not just redraw the classical horizon so that the system now falls below it?

Quantum theory may require that we divide the world into two. Does it forbid us from making the location of the line a matter of convention, so that a particular system may lie now on one side of it, now on the other? The claim that it does not, I will call the thesis of the *conventionality of the classical horizon.*

Let us see how this thesis bears on the analysis of measurement. Assume that a measuring system M interacts with a quantum system S and that we describe this interaction as a measurement by M of the observable A for S. Then, according to the quantum event interpretation, the quantum event E_i occurs, where $E_i = (A, a_i)$, for some a_i. Thus, when we describe M classically, E_i occurs.

What happens if we now describe M quantum-mechanically, as, according to the conventionality thesis, we may? We now portray $S + M$ as evolving according to the Schrödinger equation; no quantum event occurs unless $S + M$ interacts with a new measurement system M^* which lies above the new classical horizon and measures the value of some new observable, either for M or for $S + M$. Nonetheless, von Neumann (1932, pp. 436–442) provides an argument to show that there is a sense in which the two ways of regarding M are equivalent.

Using the notation of Section 9.6, we assume that A has two values, and that the eigenvectors of $\mathbf{A}$ in $\mathcal{H}^S$ are $\mathbf{v}_+$ and $\mathbf{v}_-$. The states of M are $\mathbf{u}_0$ (the ground state) and the two indicator states $\mathbf{u}_+$ and $\mathbf{u}_-$. When we represent M quantum-mechanically, $\mathbf{u}_0$, $\mathbf{u}_+$, and $\mathbf{u}_-$ become orthogonal vectors in $\mathcal{H}^M$. Prior to the interaction with M, let the initial state of S be $\mathbf{v} = c_+\mathbf{v}_+ + c_-\mathbf{v}_-$; we assume M to be in its ground state. Then, if we regard M classically, quantum theory suggests that the event $E_+ = (A, +)$ will occur with probability $|c_+|^2$; conditionalization on E_+ projects the state of S into $\mathbf{v}_+$.

Let us now regard M as a quantum system. Consider the observable A^M for system M whose eigenvectors (in $\mathcal{H}^M$) are $\mathbf{u}_0$, $\mathbf{u}_+$, and $\mathbf{u}_-$, with eigenvalues 0, +1, and −1, respectively. If we apply the Schrödinger equation to the interaction between S and M, we obtain

$$\mathbf{v} \otimes \mathbf{u}_0 = \mathbf{\Psi}_0 \rightarrow \mathbf{\Psi}_t$$

Assume that, when $S + M$ is in state $\mathbf{\Psi}_t$, a measurement of A is performed on S, and a measurement of A^M on M. It was shown in Section 9.6 that the results of these two measurements will be correlated. Hence to measure $A \otimes A^M$ on $S + M$ it suffices to measure A^M on M.

If we now "observe" M with apparatus M^*—that is, if we measure A^M for M—it turns out that, when $S + M$ is in state $\mathbf{\Psi}_t$, the event $E^*_+ = (A^M, +)$ has probability $|c_+|^2$. Conditionalization on E^*_+ projects the state of M into $\mathbf{u}_+$ and also, via the correlation of S and M, projects the state of S into $\mathbf{v}_+$.

Thus whether we think of the measurement of A as being done directly or at one remove, the probability of obtaining the value $(A, +)$ is the same, and, in either case, conditionalization on the associated event projects the state of S into $\mathbf{v}_+$.

Despite this reassurance, we still face a problem. Assume that we use M^* to observe M, and that we obtain the result $(A^M,+)$. We are here regarding M not as a classical measuring device but as a quantum system. The question is, in this situation does the event E_+ occur or not? It seems that, by deciding to draw the classical horizon below M rather than above it, we can bring about the event E_+; in other words, it seems that a conventional choice of horizon has an ontological consequence. *Prima facie,* this seems to bode ill for the conventionalist thesis.

In fact, as this analysis shows, it is the conventionalist thesis that creates the measurement problem. Note that only the least contentious aspect of the quantum event interpretation—the claim that the registration of a value by a measurement device can be called an event—is invoked in the generation of this problem. If, additionally, the projection postulate is accepted, then a further problem appears: does the state of S change to $\mathbf{v}_+$ as a result of the interaction with M or not?

One strategy open to the conventionalist is this. He may say that when S interacts with M the quantum event $(A,+)$ occurs, leaving M with the property corresponding to the positive value of A (call this property A^+). To say this is to describe M in classical terms. This does not rule out the possibility of describing it quantum-theoretically, he may continue, but if we do so we forgo two things. We can no longer speak of a quantum event occurring, since that would involve reference to a classical system, nor can we speak of M as having a property. However, this means neither that no quantum event has taken place, nor that M does not in fact have a property; it is rather that quantum mechanics only allows us to speak of latencies. When M^* "looks at" M, we can describe that interaction classically: M^* tells us what property M has; we may also describe it quantum-mechanically, as the occurrence of the event $(A^M,+)$. These two modes of description are, again, two alternative ways to describe M.

There are two things to be said about this suggestion. The first is that it does not entirely dissolve the problem; it shifts it to a new location. It breaks the "property-eigenvector link" usually assumed to hold of measuring systems. We describe M classically as having the property A^+, or we describe it quantum-mechanically as being in the eigenstate $\mathbf{u}_+$; the assumption is usually made that M has the property A^+ if and only if it is in the indicator state $\mathbf{u}_+$. On the suggested analysis, the conditional holds in one direction only: if M is in the state $\mathbf{u}_+$ then it has the property A^+. However, it may also have the property A^+ even when it is in the mixed state $\mathbf{D}^M = |c_+|^2\mathbf{P}^M_+ + |c_-|^2\mathbf{P}^M_-$ as a result of its interaction with S (see Section 9.6).

Second, although the suggestion allows us to deal with properties, it will not work for the projection postulate. Whereas we can say without inconsistency that M has the property A^+ when it is in the mixed state $\mathbf{D}^M$, we cannot say that S is both in the pure state $\mathbf{v}_+$ and in the mixed state $\mathbf{D}^S = |c_+|^2\mathbf{P}^S_+ + |c_-|^2\mathbf{P}^S_-$.

The strategy, together with the two corollaries just mentioned, moves us very close to van Fraassen's "modal interpretation" of quantum theory. Van Fraassen (1974a, pp. 300–301) presents in the formal mode what I have put in ontological terms:

> We distinguish two kinds of statements—state attributions and value attributions . . . The state of the system describes what is possibly the case about values of observables; what is actual is only possible relative to the state and is not deducible from it.

Van Fraassen is happy to reject the projection postulate (p. 299) and, although he does not write in quite these terms, the severing of the property-eigenvector link appears as a small price to pay for allowing a measurement device to be given both a classical and a quantum-theoretic description.

Ingenious though this interpretation is, I do not think it is right. I say this with some reluctance, since, as we shall see, it solves a number of intractable problems. My reservation stems in part from a belief in the explanatory value of the Lüders rule (which in one guise acts as a projection postulate), and in part from a belief that van Fraassen's partial rejection of the property-eigenvector link does not go far enough. I consider even a partial identification of classical properties of a macroscopic system with quantum states of that system to be problematic.

For the question one cannot avoid is, are nontrivial superpositions of these quantum states also admissible pure states of the measurement device? If so, then they are pure states in a wholly Pickwickian sense, since no observable distinguishes them from the corresponding mixtures of indicator states. If not, if the set of admissible pure states is restricted to the indicator states, then the account runs into the difficulty described in Section 9.7: this restriction on the set of admissible quantum states is incompatible with the application to the system of Schrödinger's equation, and hence with treating it as a quantum system. This is not to say that classical systems admit no quantum-mechanical description, just that, to the extent that an indicator state is a classical property, it is implausible to treat it as a quantum state.*

Von Neumann's consistency proof, in my view, has little to do with measurement or with the question of the classical horizon. If the system $M + S$ evolves according to the Schrödinger equation, then the states $\mathbf{u}_0$, $\mathbf{u}_+$, and $\mathbf{u}_-$ of M cannot be regarded as classical indicator states of M, and so M cannot function as a measurement apparatus in the way the proof suggests.

* See also Leggett (1986). This paper came to my attention too late to be discussed here.

What the proof shows is the possibility of a quantum amplification device or relay.

The mere rejection of a particular identification of classical states with quantum states does nothing, however, to resolve the crucial and persistent question we are left with: what is the conceptual relation between the quantum world and the classical world? This is the touchstone, pyx, assay, ordeal, the High Noon, the Big Enchilada for all interpretations of quantum theory.

Let us approach the question from the classical side, and ask: are there in the actual world systems which behave like classical systems? To reiterate a point made earlier, I am not asking whether there are systems whose behavior is governed by the laws of nineteenth-century physics. The question is: are there systems to which we can consistently ascribe properties, the set of which forms a Boolean algebra? If we permit ourselves the kind of idealization appropriate to any physical theory, the answer is clearly yes. Call these C-systems. It turns out that there are very small systems whose behavior with respect to certain C-systems differs markedly from that of other C-systems. The most complete specification of the state of one of these small systems that we can obtain assigns probabilities to events associated with properties of the C-systems with which it interacts. Call these Q-systems.

Are Q-systems and C-systems different in kind? Our best theory tells us that C-systems are made up of a great number of interacting Q-systems. Further, our theory of Q-systems includes an account of what happens when a number of Q-systems together form a larger system, and this account has received experimental confirmation. We are led to postulate six theses.

(1) A C-system behaves like a large composite Q-system.

(2) Differences between Q-systems and C-systems are to be attributed to the complexity of the latter.

(3) With an increase of complexity of a Q-system classical behavior emerges.

(4) Some systems large enough to be regarded as C-systems behave as follows: in an interaction between one of these and a Q-system *S*, classical properties of the C-system may be associated with pure states of *S*.

(5) When this occurs, these properties of the C-system are realized probabilistically by the interaction.

(6) Together with the realization of a particular property of the C-system, there comes a localization of the state of *S*. (Conditionalization occurs.)

With the exception of (6), I do not take these theses to be particularly controversial. Nonetheless, they are sometimes challenged, as will appear.

The first thesis effectively restates the conventionality of the classical horizon. The others suggest that the differences between quantum and classical behavior which the complexity of a C-system brings about are of two kinds. (a) A description of a C-system in terms of properties is available which is not available in the case of a "pure" Q-system (thesis 3). (b) The mode of interaction between a Q-system and a C-system differs from that between two Q-systems, at least in the way it is described (theses 4, 5, 6).

From (a) it appears that, with an increase of complexity of a system, classical properties appear as emergent properties (and this phrase should perhaps be read as "emergent *properties*"), supervenient on the quantum states. (To say that A-states are supervenient on B-states is just to say that a difference between A-states always involves a difference between B-states.) However, these classical properties need not be associated with particular quantum states; formally, the Boolean algebra of classical properties need not be embeddable in the Hilbert space which provides the quantum description of the system. The facts summarized in (b) are familiar to all students of the measurement problem.

I have no explanation of the differences between C-systems and Q-systems. Theses (1)–(6) constitute a list of the problems such an account would have to resolve; to use Kant's nice phrase, the account itself remains "set as a task." And it's not clear what such an account would look like. Whereas one might look to an analysis like the one provided by Daneri, Loinger, and Prosperi (see Section 9.8) for an account of (3) consistent with (1) and (2), it is hard to see how (4)–(6) could be dealt with. In particular, what are we to say about (6), that is, about the way in which the emergence of properties in a classical system can "force" probabilistic and discontinuous changes on a Q-system coupled to it?

Nor is this problem confined to the quantum event interpretation. Although these theses have been formulated against the background of this interpretation, the problem they pose is the common sticking point for nearly all interpretations of quantum mechanics. One way to evade it is to reject (1) and (2) and to treat the quantum/classical distinction as both sharp and self-evident. This is done, albeit in very different ways, by both Bohr and Wigner. As we saw earlier, another alternative is to adopt a modal interpretation like van Fraassen's. He evades (2) by making no distinction between C-systems and Q-systems, and he denies (3) and (6). Value attributions to Q-systems are permissible; properties are not regarded as supervenient on quantum states. Rather they are underdetermined by them: a given quantum state delimits what is possible, specification of properties tells us what is actual. Theses (4) and (5) hold, in appropriately amended versions. Yet another suggestion, recently made by Bub, is that to describe a system as a C-system is to make the idealization that it consists of an infinite number of Q-systems. In the case of an infinite system, he argues, superselection rules come into play, giving rise to the classical behavior characteristic of C-systems. (This brief summary does not do justice to Bub's argument; see Bub, 1987.) Bub's account is compatible with the thesis of the conventionality of the classical horizon; its location depends on the point at which the idealization is made. Like van Fraassen's, however, this account falls foul of the difficulty raised in Section 9.7: if classical properties are associated with superselection subspaces, then it is not clear that an evolution of one into another can take place that is consistent with quantum theory.

The rejection of these alternatives does nothing to solve the problem. However, not only do I have no explanatory account which encompasses theses (1)–(6), I also think that there is something very odd about requiring quantum theory to provide one. The oddity can be explained in this way.

According to (the quantum event interpretation of) quantum theory, a "pure" Q-system is describable in terms of latencies with respect to a classical horizon. That is to say, it is a system which interacts with certain C-systems in specific, probabilistic ways. We have reason to think that an increase in complexity of a system gives us an alternative way to describe it; we can describe it as having classical properties, that is, as a C-system. We may also hope to explain why these properties emerge. But note, to say that the system behaves like a C-system is to say that it is the sort of system in which probabilistic behavior may be induced by interactions with Q-systems. And this is where we came in.

What else is there to say? I suggest that quantum theory can no more be called on to answer the question of why such probabilistic behavior occurs than the theory of geometrical optics can be required to explain why light travels in straight lines. Indeed, it is not clear what sort of explanation is being demanded; in each case the *explanandum* is the given from which the theory starts. As Chapters 3 and 4 showed, the Hilbert-space models which quantum theory uses are ideal for representing the probabilistic behavior of systems with respect to certain families of events. Given any specific piece of quantum behavior, quantum mechanics will happily provide us with a model within which it can be fitted. Is it also required to justify the use of these models? If "to justify" here means more than "to show that they save the phenomena," and what is required is some deeper analysis warranting their use, then it cannot do so.

This argument is not intended to provide "a tranquilizing philosophy, . . . a gentle pillow for the true believer from which he cannot easily be aroused" (Einstein, letter to Schrödinger, May 1928, on the Copenhagen interpretation; quoted in Bub, 1974, p. 46). It is an argument which claims that the scope of quantum theory is limited by its own structure.

Landau and Lifschitz (1977, p. 3) write,

> Thus quantum mechanics occupies a very unusual place among physical theories: it contains classical mechanics as a limiting case, yet at the same time it requires this limiting case for its own formulation.

I suggest that the explanation of how this can be so, how we can use the limiting cases of quantum theory in order to formulate the theory, cannot be given within the theory itself. It will have to await the arrival of a new physical theory, a theory which is not formulated against a classical horizon in the way that quantum mechanics is.

Can there be such a theory?

Probably.

APPENDIX A

Gleason's Theorem

Gleason's theorem is of fundamental importance, not only for the theory of Hilbert spaces, but for the interpretation of quantum mechanics. Though the original proof, published in 1957, was mathematically very difficult, in 1984 an "elementary proof" of the theorem was given by Cooke, Keane, and Moran (whom I shall refer to collectively as "CKM"), and it is reproduced below. For the amateur mathematician, even this proof is arduous enough. To ease the reader's task I have added a commentary consisting partly of explanations of unfamiliar terms, but mostly of answers to the questions I asked myself as I worked through the proof. These questions were of two kinds: "Why is this move being made here?" and "How does this follow?" I assume a familiarity with Section 5.6 of the text, and with the vocabulary and notation of set theory (see, for example, Monk, 1969).CKM also use one theorem from topology which I quote but do not explain. The theorem guarantees the existence of the limit of certain sequences; the reader will have to take it on trust, but in context the intuitive content of its conclusion will be clear.

I have not altered the symbols used by CKM to make them conform to those used in the text and in my commentary, but since the symbols in the proof are all defined on first use, this should cause no problems; the reader need only be aware that such differences exist.

An Elementary Proof of Gleason's Theorem
by Roger Cooke, Michael Keane, and William Moran

The following proof is reproduced from the *Mathematical Proceedings of the Cambridge Philosophical Society* 98 (1985), pp. 117–128.

Abstract

Gleason's theorem characterizes the totally additive measures on the closed subspaces of a separable real or complex Hilbert space of dimension greater than two. This paper presents an elementary proof of Gleason's theorem which is accessible to undergraduates having completed a first course in real analysis.

Introduction

Let H be a separable Hilbert space over the real or complex field. A (normalized) *state* on H is a function assigning to H the value 1, assigning to each closed subspace of H a number in the unit interval, and satisfying the following additivity property: If any given subspace is written as an orthogonal sum of a finite or countable number of subspaces, then the value of the state on the given subspace is equal to the sum of the values of the state on the summands. States should be thought of as 'quantum mechanical probability measures'; they play an essential role in the quantum mechanical formalism. For an exposition of these ideas we refer to Mackey (1963).

Examples of normalized states are obtained by considering positive self-adjoint trace class operators with trace 1 on H. Such operators correspond to preparation procedures in quantum mechanics. If A is such an operator, then it is easy to see that we can define a state by associating to each one dimensional subspace generated by a unit vector $x \in H$ the inner product $\langle Ax,x \rangle$ and extending to subspaces of dimension greater than one by countable additivity. States of this type are called *regular states.*

In his course on the mathematical foundations of quantum mechanics Mackey (1963) proposed the following problem: determine the set of states on an arbitrary real or complex Hilbert space. This problem was solved by Gleason (1957) and the principal result, known as Gleason's theorem, states that every state on a real or complex Hilbert space of dimension greater than two is regular. Gleason's proof uses the representation theory of $O(3)$, and relies on an intricate continuity argument. Because of the role which Gleason's theorem plays in the foundations of quantum mechanics, there have been several attempts to simplify its proof. Using elementary methods, Bell (1966) proved a special case of the theorem, namely, that there exist no states on the closed subspaces of a Hilbert space of dimension greater than two taking only the values zero and one. Kochen and Specker (1967) proved a similar result for states restricted to a finite number of closed subspaces. Piron (1976) produced an elementary proof of Gleason's theorem for the special case that the state is *extreme* (i.e. assigns the value 1 to some one dimensional subspace).

In this article we give an elementary proof of Gleason's theorem in full generality. Although this proof is longer than Gleason's proof, we believe that it contributes to the intuitive understanding of the underlying reasons for the validity of the theorem. The structure of the argument is as follows. In § 1 we show that it is enough to handle the case $H = \mathbb{R}^3$. This was part of Gleason's original argument, and is well understood; the essential difficulty of the proof is the treatment of the case $H = \mathbb{R}^3$. For this purpose it is convenient to study a certain class of real-valued functions on the unit sphere of $\mathbb{R}^3$, called frame functions. §§ 2 and 3 are devoted to an exposition of the properties of frame functions and the statement of the theorem in the case of $\mathbb{R}^3$ in terms of frame functions. § 3 also contains two 'warm-up theorems' whose contents were essentially known to 19th century mathematicians. Coupled with a basic lemma in § 4 (essentially due to Gleason and Piron), they yield a new proof for the extreme case, which is given in § 5. In § 6 we show that a weak form of continuity in the general case follows from the result of § 5, and in § 7 we treat the general case. The proofs in §§ 2–7 are accessible to undergraduates who have completed a first course in real analysis.

1. *Reduction to $H = \mathbb{R}^3$*

Let H be a real or complex separable Hilbert space, and let L be the set of closed subspaces of H. If $A \in L$, and $B \in L$, then we write $A \perp B$ if A and B are orthogonal. For $A_i \in L$, $i \in I$, $\overline{\bigvee_{i \in I} A_i}$ denotes the smallest closed subspace containing A_i for all $i \in I$. If x is a vector in H, then $\bar{x}$ denotes the one dimensional subspace generated by x.

Definition. A function $p: L \to [0,1]$ is called a *state* if for all sequences $\{A_i\}_{i=1}^{\alpha}$, $A_i \in L$, $i = 1 \ldots$; with $A_i \perp A_j$, for $i \neq j$:

$$p\left(\overline{\bigvee_{i=1}^{\alpha} A_i}\right) = \sum_{i=1}^{\alpha} p(A_i).$$

Definition. p is called *regular* if there exists a self-adjoint trace class operator A on H such that for all unit vectors $x \in H$

$$p(\bar{x}) = \langle Ax, x \rangle.$$

Lemma. *The following statements are equivalent:*
(i) *p is regular.*
(ii) *There is a symmetric continuous bilinear form B on H such that*

$$p(\bar{x}) = B(x,x).$$

Moreover, both A and B are uniquely determined in this way by p.

Proof. See Halmos (1957, §§ 2 and 3). ▮

LEMMA. *If the restriction of p to every two-dimensional subspace of H is regular, then p is regular (the restriction need not be normalized).*

Proof. For each two-dimensional subspace E of H we can find a symmetric continuous bilinear form B_E such that $B_E(x,x) = p(\bar{x})$ $(x \in E,\ \|x\| = 1)$. For $\|x\| = \|y\| = 1$, choose a two-dimensional subspace $E(x,y)$ containing x and y and define

$$B(x,y) = B_E(x,y).$$

It is straightforward to check that B can be uniquely extended to a symmetric continuous bilinear form on H, and that $p(\bar{x}) = B(x,x)$ $(\|x\| = 1)$. ▮

We shall call a closed real-linear subspace of H *completely real* if the inner product on this real linear subspace takes only real values.

LEMMA. *If p is a state on a two-dimensional complex Hilbert space H, and if p is regular on every completely real subspace, then p is regular.*

Proof. We first show that there is a one-dimensional subspace $\bar{x}$ such that $p(\bar{x})$ is maximal. Put

$$M = \sup_{x \in H} p(\bar{x}).$$

Choose a sequence $x_n \in H$ such that $\lim_{n\to\infty} p(\bar{x}_n) = M$. By passing to a subsequence, assume $\lim_{n\to\infty} x_n = x$. Clearly there exist θ_n such that $\langle e^{i\theta_n} x_n, x\rangle$ is real and nonnegative, and passing again to a subsequence, we may assume that $\lim_{n\to\infty}\theta_n = \theta$. By continuity of the scalar product, the limit $\langle e^{i\theta}x, x\rangle = e^{i\theta}\|x\|^2$ is also real, and hence $e^{i\theta} = 1$. Thus $\lim_{n\to\infty} e^{i\theta_n}x_n = x$, and for each n the vectors x and $e^{i\theta_n}x_n$ are in the same completely real subspace. By uniform equicontinuity of regular states it follows that $p(\bar{x}) = M$.

Now for any $y \in H$ there exists θ such that $\langle x, e^{i\theta}y\rangle$ is real; hence $p(\overline{e^{i\theta}y})$ $(= p(\bar{y}))$ is equal to

$$M(\langle x,e^{i\theta}y\rangle)^2 + (1-M)(1-(\langle x,e^{i\theta}y\rangle)^2)$$
$$= M|\langle x,y\rangle|^2 + (1-M)(1-|\langle x,y\rangle|^2),$$

and p is therefore regular. ▮

THEOREM. *If every state on $\mathbb{R}^3$ is regular, then every state on a real or complex separable Hilbert space H of dimension greater than two is regular.*

Proof. Every state on H necessarily induces a continuous symmetric bilinear form on every completely real three-dimensional subspace, and every completely real two-dimensional subspace can be embedded in a completely real three-dimensional subspace. It follows that the restriction of a state on H to any two-dimensional completely real subspace is regular, and from the above lemmata it follows that every state on H is regular. ∎

2. *Frame Functions*

In this section, we define frame functions, collect some of their properties, and give examples. Denote by S the unit sphere of a fixed three-dimensional real Hilbert space. If s and s' are elements (i.e. vectors) of S, the angle between s and s' is designated by $\theta(s,s')$. If $\theta(s,s') = \pi/2$, we write $s \perp s'$.

Definition. A *frame* is an ordered triple (p,q,r) of elements of S such that $p \perp q$, $p \perp r$ and $q \perp r$.

Given a frame (p,q,r), each point in S (and in the vector space) can be uniquely expressed as $xp + yq + zr$, with $x,y,z \in \mathbb{R}$. We call (x,y,z) the frame coordinates of the point with respect to the given frame.

Definition. A *frame function* is a function $f\colon S \to \mathbb{R}$ such that the sum

$$f(p) + f(q) + f(r)$$

has the same value for each frame (p,q,r). This value, called the *weight* of f, will be denoted by $w(f)$.

The following obvious properties of frame functions will be useful in the sequel.

(P_1) *The set of frame functions is a vector space, and*

$$w(\alpha f) = \alpha w(f),$$

$$w(f+g) = w(f) + w(g) \qquad (\alpha \in \mathbb{R},\ f,\ g \text{ frame functions}).$$

(P_2) *If f is a frame function, $f(-s) = f(s)$ $\quad (s \in S)$.*

(P_3) *If f is a frame function, and if $s,t,s',t' \in S$ all lie on the same great circle and $s \perp t$, $s' \perp t'$, then*

$$f(s) + f(t) = f(s') + f(t').$$

To illustrate the use of P_3 we prove:

(P_4) *Let f be a frame function with* $\sup f(s) = M < \infty$ *and* $\inf f(s) = m > -\infty$. *Let $\xi > 0$ and let $s \in S$* with $f(s) > M - \xi$. *Then there is $t \in S$ with $s \perp t$ and $f(t) < m + \xi$.*

Proof. Given s with $f(s) > M - \xi$, choose $\delta > 0$ such that $f(s) > M - \xi + \delta$, and t' such that $f(t') < m + \delta$. Then s and t' determine a great circle on S, and if t, s' are chosen on this great circle with $s \perp t$, $s' \perp t'$, P_3 yields:

$$f(t) = f(s') + f(t') - f(s) < M + m + \delta - (M - \xi + \delta) = m + \xi. \blacksquare$$

Next we give examples of frame functions. Obviously, constants are frame functions. If we fix a vector $p_0 \in S$, then for any frame (p,q,r) the frame coordinates of p_0 with respect to (p,q,r) are given by:

$$(\cos\theta(p_0,p), \cos\theta(p_0,q), \cos\theta(p_0,r)),$$

and the sum of the squares of these three numbers is one since $p_0 \in S$. Hence

$$f(s) = \cos^2\theta(p_0,s)$$

is a frame function, with $w(f) = 1$. Next, fix a frame (p_0,q_0,r_0) and a triple (α,β,γ) of real numbers. Let (x_0,y_0,z_0) denote the frame coordinates of a point $s \in S$ with respect to (p_0,q_0,r_0). By the above and by P_1,

$$f(s) = \alpha x_0^2 + \beta y_0^2 + \gamma z_0^2 \qquad (*)$$

is a frame function, with $w(f) = \alpha + \beta + \gamma$. Now recall that if Q is any quadratic form on our Hilbert space, then there exists a frame (p_0,q_0,r_0) and a triple (α,β,γ) of real numbers such that the restriction of Q to S is given by (*). Hence we have proved the following result:

PROPOSITION. *Let A be a linear operator from the given three dimensional Hilbert space to itself, and let*

$$Q(s) = \langle s,As\rangle$$

be the quadratic form associated with A. Then the restriction of Q to S is a frame function whose weight is the trace of A.

Note that p_0,q_0,r_0 are eigenvectors of $\frac{1}{2}(A + A^T)$ with respective eigenvalues α, β, γ.

Our last example shows that frame functions can be wildly discontinuous. Let $\psi:\mathbb{R} \to \mathbb{R}$ be any map such that $\psi(x + y) = \psi(x) + \psi(y)$ for all $x,y \in \mathbb{R}$. Then if f is a frame function, so is $\psi(f)$, and ψ can be chosen to have arbitrary values on a basis of $\mathbb{R}$ over $\mathbb{Q}$. Of course Cauchy's classical theorem on functional equations tells us that if ψ is bounded on an interval, then $\psi(x) = cx$ for some constant c. This example shows that the restriction to bounded frame functions in the following theorem is essential.

3. *Statement of Gleason's Theorem*

We now state the result to be proved.

GLEASON'S THEOREM. *Let f be a bounded frame function. Define*

$$M = \sup f(s)$$

$$m = \inf f(s)$$

$$\alpha = w(f) - M - m.$$

Then there exists a frame (p,q,r) such that if the frame coordinates with respect to (p,q,r) of $s \in S$ are (x,y,z),

$$f(s) = Mx^2 + \alpha y^2 + mz^2$$

for all $s \in S$.

In particular, the proposition of § 2 provides all bounded frame functions. We remark that the above representation implies that $m \leq \alpha \leq M$; if $m < \alpha < M$, then the frame (p,q,r) is unique up to change of sign; if $m \leq \alpha < M$ then p is unique up to change of sign, and similarly for $m < \alpha \leq M$.

In order to clarify the idea behind our proof of the above result, we now state and prove a theorem which might be called an 'abelianized' version of Gleason's theorem. Its content was essentially known to 19th century mathematicians.

'WARM-UP' THEOREM I. *Let $f\colon [0,1] \to \mathbb{R}$ be a bounded function such that for all $a,b,c \in [0,1]$ with $a + b + c = 1$, $f(a) + f(b) + f(c)$ has the same value $\tilde{w} = w(f)$. Then $f(a) = (\tilde{w} - 3f(0))a + f(0)$* for all $a \in [0,1]$.

Proof. By subtracting a constant, we may assume $f(0) = 0$. Now take $c = 0$, $b = 1 - a$ to obtain

$$f(a) = \tilde{w} - f(1 - a),$$

and then set $c = 1 - (a + b)$ to obtain

$$f(a) + f(b) = \tilde{w} - f(1 - (a + b)) = f(a + b)$$

for all $a,b,a+b \in [0,1]$. This implies immediately that

$$f(a) = \tilde{\omega} a$$

for all rational a, and for general $a \in [0,1]$ and $n \geq 1$ with $na \leq 1$ we have

$$f(na) = nf(a).$$

Hence as a tends to 0, $f(a)$ must tend to 0 because f is bounded, and thus

$$\lim_{a \to 0} f(a+b) = f(b)$$

for all $b \in [0,1]$. Thus $f(a) = \tilde{\omega} a$ for all $a \in [0,1]$. ▌

The above formulation was chosen in order to make the analogy with Gleason's theorem clear. Actually, we shall use the following modified version in our proof.

'WARM-UP' THEOREM II. *Let C be a finite or countable subset of* (0,1). *Let* $f\colon [0,1]\backslash C \to \mathbb{R}$ *be a function such that*

(1) $f(0) = 0$.
(2) *If* $a, b \in [0,1]\backslash C$ *and* $a < b$, *then* $f(a) \leq f(b)$.
(3) *If* $a, b, c \in [0,1]\backslash C$ *and* $a + b + c = 1$, *then* $f(a) + f(b) + f(c) = 1$.

Then $f(a) = a$ *for all* $a \in [0,1]\backslash C$.

Proof. The set

$$\tilde{C} = \{rc\colon c \in C,\ r \text{ rational}\} \cup \{r(1-c)\colon c \in C,\ r \text{ rational}\}$$

is at most countable, so that there exists a point $a_0 \in (0,1)$ with $a_0 \notin \tilde{C}$. Now if r is a rational number such that $ra_0 \in [0,1]$, then neither ra_0 nor $1 - ra_0$ belong to C, since $a_0 \notin \tilde{C}$. As in the proof above, we conclude that

$$f(ra_0) + f(r'a_0) = f((r+r')a_0)$$

for rational r, r' with ra_0, $r'a_0$, $(r+r')a_0 \in [0,1]$, and hence

$$f(ra_0) = rf(a_0)$$

for rational r with $ra_0 \in [0,1]$. It now follows from (2) that $f(a) = a$ for all $a \in [0,1]\backslash C$. ▌

4. The Basic Lemma

In this paragraph, we prove a basic lemma to be used in the following two sections. We fix a vector $p \in S$, to be thought of as the north pole, and use the following notation.

$$N = \{s \in S: \theta(p,s) \leq \pi/2\} = \text{'northern hemisphere'},$$

$$E = \{s \in S: s \perp p\} = \text{'equator'}.$$

For each $s \in N$, set

$$l(s) = \cos^2\theta(p,s) = \text{'latitude' of } s,$$

and define for $0 \leq l \leq 1$:

$$L_l = \{s \in N: l(s) = l\} = \text{'}l\text{th parallel'}.$$

Thus $L_1 = \{p\}$ and $L_0 = E$.

For $s \in N\backslash\{p\}$, there is a unique vector $s^\perp \in N$ such that $s \perp s^\perp$ and $l(s) + l(s^\perp) = 1$ ($s^\perp$ is the 'coldest' vector orthogonal to s). The great half circle D_s defined by

$$D_s = \{t \in N: t \perp s^\perp\} \qquad (s \in N\backslash\{p\})$$

will be called the *descent* through s; it is the great circle through s which has s as its northernmost point. (For $e \in E$, $D_e = E$). We can now state the basic lemma:

BASIC LEMMA. *Let f be a frame function such that*

(1) $f(p) = \sup_{s\in S} f(s)$, and
(2) $f(e)$ *has the same value for all* $e \in E$.

Then if $s \in N\backslash\{p\}$ and if $s' \in D_s$

$$f(s) \geq f(s').$$

Proof. Set $f(p) = M$. Property P_4 implies that

$$f(e) = m = \inf_{s\in S} f(s) \qquad (e \in E).$$

Let $s \in N\backslash\{p\}$ and $s' \in D_s$. Choose $t, t' \in D_s$ with $s \perp t$, and $s' \perp t'$. By property P_3,

$$f(s) + f(t) = f(s') + f(t').$$

And using the fact that $t \in E$ we obtain

$$f(s) - f(s') = f(t') - f(t) = f(t') - m \geq 0. \blacksquare$$

Later on we shall need an

APPROXIMATE VERSION OF THE BASIC LEMMA. *Let f be a frame function and $\xi > 0$ such that*

(1) $f(p) > \sup_{s \in S} f(s) - \xi$, and
(2) $f(e)$ *has the same value for all* $e \in E$.

Then if $s \in N \backslash \{p\}$ *and if* $s' \in D_s$, $f(s) > f(s') - \xi$.

Proof. As above, property P_4 yields

$$f(e) < m + \xi \qquad (e \in E),$$

and with exactly the same choices of t and t':

$$f(s) - f(s') = f(t') - f(t) > f(t') - m - \xi \geq -\xi. \blacksquare$$

5. *Simple Frame Functions*

In this paragraph, we show that Gleason's theorem is true under two additional hypotheses on frame functions. We begin with a geometric lemma due to Piron (1976).

GEOMETRIC LEMMA. *Let* $s, t \in N \backslash \{p\}$ *such that* $l(s) > l(t)$. *Then there exist* $n \geq 1$ *and* $s_0, \ldots, s_n \in N \backslash \{p\}$ *such that* $s_0 = s$, $s_n = t$, *and for each* $1 \leq i \leq n$:

$$s_i \in D_{s_{i-1}}.$$

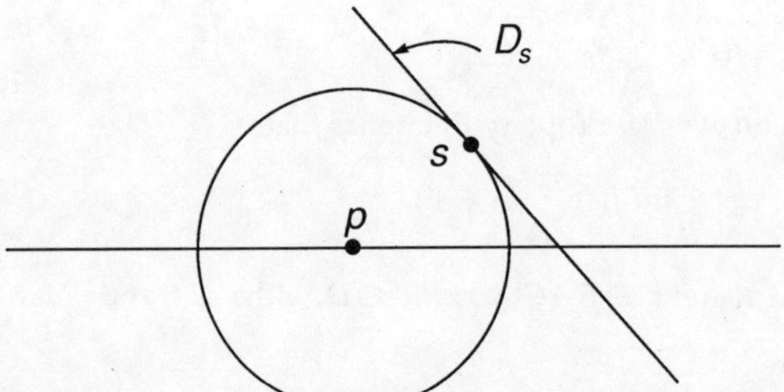

Figure A1.1

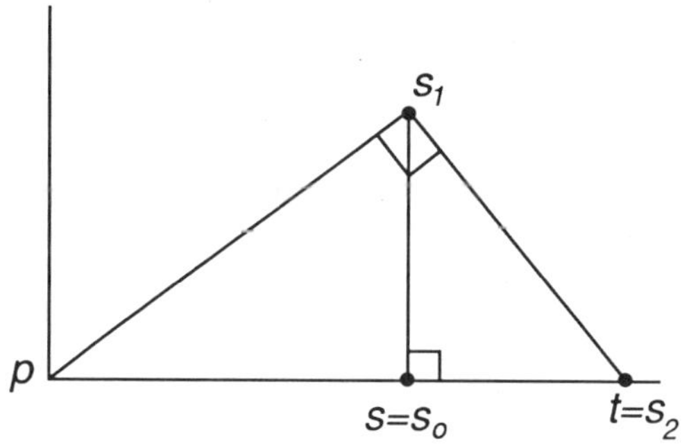

Figure A1.2

Proof. To facilitate the calculations, we transfer this problem to the plane tangent to S at p by projecting each point of N onto this plane from the origin (center of the sphere S). Points of the same latitude on S are projected onto circles centered at p, and the descent through s becomes the straight line through s tangent to the latitude circle at s (see Figure A1.1). In the simplest case, s and t lie on a ray from the origin. In this case we may choose $n = 2$ and pick s_1 as in Figure A1.2. Now fix $s_0 = s = (x,0)$ (in $\mathbb{R}^2$ coordinates) and $n \geq 1$. Choose $s_1 \; . \; . \; . \; s_n$ successively such that $s_i \in D_{s_{i-1}}$ and such that the angle between s_i and s_{i+1} in the plane is π/n (see Figure A1.3). Then s_n has coordinates $(-y,0)$ and we wish to show that $y - x \to 0$ as $n \to \infty$. Let d_k be the distance of s_k from the origin. Then $d_0 = x$ and $d_n = y$. For each i we have

$$d_{i+1}/d_i = 1/\cos(\pi/n),$$

and hence

$$1 \leq y/x = d_n/d_0 = \prod_{i=1}^{n} \frac{d_i}{d_{i-1}} = \frac{1}{(\cos\pi/n)^n} \leq \frac{1}{(1-\pi^2/2n^2)^n},$$

which approaches 1 as n tends to infinity. The lemma is proved. ∎

We now come to the main result of this section.

THEOREM. *Let f be a frame function such that for some point $p \in S$*

(1) $f(p) = M := \sup_{s \in S} f(s)$,
(2) *$f(e)$ takes the constant value m for all $e \in E$.*

Then $f(s) = m + (M - m)\cos^2\theta(s,p)$, for all $s \in S$.

Proof. By property P_4, $m = \inf_{s \in S} f(s)$, so that if $M = m$ the theorem is true. If $M \neq m$, then we may assume that $m = 0$ and $M = 1$ (replace f by

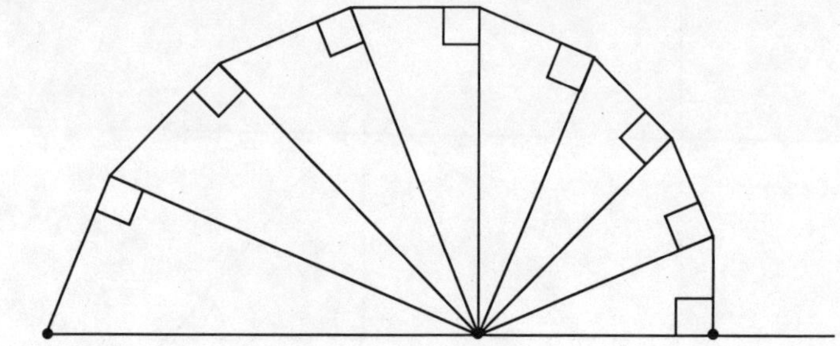

Figure A1.3

$(1/(M-m))(f-m))$. Let $s,t \in N\backslash\{p\}$ with $l(s) > l(t)$. Then by the geometric lemma and the basic lemma of the preceding section, we have

$$f(s) \geq f(t).$$

For each $l \in [0,1]$, define:

$$\bar{f}(l) = \sup\{f(s): s \in N,\ l(s) = l\},$$
$$\underline{f}(l) = \inf\{f(s): s \in N,\ l(s) = l\}.$$

Then $\bar{f}(1) = \underline{f}(1) = 1$, $\bar{f}(0) = \underline{f}(0) = 0$, and if $l, l' \in [0,1]$ with $l < l'$, it follows from the above that

$$\bar{f}(l) \leq \underline{f}(l').$$

Hence the set $C := \{l : \bar{f}(l) > \underline{f}(l)\}$ is at most countable, as

$$\sum_{l \in C} (\bar{f}(l) - \underline{f}(l)) \leq 1.$$

For $l \in [0,1]\backslash C$, define

$$f(l) = \bar{f}(l) = \underline{f}(l).$$

If $l, l', l'' \in [0,1]$ with $l + l' + l'' = 1$, then there exists a frame (q,q',q'') with $l(q) = l$, $l(q') = l'$, $l(q'') = l''$. That is, the function f satisfies the hypotheses of Warm-up Theorem II, and we conclude that

$$f(l) = l \quad \text{for} \quad l \in [0,1]\backslash C.$$

But this implies that $C = \varnothing$, so that for each $s \in N$,

$$f(s) = f(l(s)) = l(s) = \cos^2\theta(s,p).$$

The theorem now follows from property P_2. ∎

6. *Extremal Values*

In this section we use the results of the preceding section to show that bounded frame functions attain their extremal values. Let f be a bounded frame function,

$$M = \sup_{s \in S} f(s),$$

and choose a sequence $p_n \in S$, $n \geq 1$, such that $\lim_{n\to\infty} f(p_n) = M$. Since S is compact, we may assume by passing to a subsequence that p_n converges, and we set

$$p = \lim_{n\to\infty} p_n.$$

Assume also $p_n \in N$ for all n. Our goal is to show that $f(p) = M$.

STEP 1. *Changing coordinates*

For each n, we would like to look at p_n as the north pole, instead of p. We do this as follows. Choose and fix a point $e_0 \in E$ and let C_0 denote the great circle segment from p to e_0. Let $\rho_n : S \to S$ be the rigid motion of S which takes p to p_n and some point, say c_n, on C_0 to p. Obviously

$$\lim_{n\to\infty} c_n = p.$$

Now define the sequence g_n of frame functions by setting

$$g_n(s) = f(\rho_n s) \qquad (s \in S).$$

We note the following properties:

(1) $\lim_{n\to\infty} g_n(p) = M$.
(2) $M = \sup_{s \in S} g_n(s)$ and $m = \inf_{s \in S} f(s) = \inf_{s \in S} g_n(s)$ for each $n \geq 1$.
(3) $g_n(c_n) = f(p)$ for each $n \geq 1$.

Step 2. *Symmetrization*

Denote by $\hat{p}: S \to S$ the right-hand rotation by 90° of S around the pole p. For each $n \geq 1$, set

$$h_n(s) = g_n(s) + g_n(\hat{p}s) \qquad (s \in S).$$

The sequence h_n of frame functions (P_1) has the following properties:

(1) $\sup_{s\in S} h_n \leq 2M$ for all $n \geq 1$.
(2) $\inf_{s\in S} h_n \geq 2m$ for all $n \geq 1$.
(3) $\lim_{n\to\infty} h_n(p) = 2M$.
(4) Each h_n is constant on E (by P_3).
(5) $h_n(c_n) \leq M + f(p)$ for all $n \geq 1$.

Step 3. *Limit*

We consider each h_n as a point in the product space

$$[2m, 2M]^S.$$

Under the product topology, this space is compact, so that the sequence h_n has an accumulation point, which we denote by h. Then:

(1) $h(p) = 2M = \sup_{s\in S} h(s)$.
(2) h is constant on E.
(3) h is a frame function, since the frame functions form a closed subset of $[2m, 2M]^S$.

By the theorem of § 5, h is continuous (and has a special form, which does not interest us here).

Step 4. $f(p) = M$

Choose $\epsilon > 0$, and choose $c \in C_0$ such that $h(c) > 2M - \epsilon$. Applying the approximate version of the basic lemma to h_n and noting that we can reach c from c_n in two steps (easiest case of the geometric lemma) for sufficiently large n, we obtain

$$h_n(c_n) > h_n(c) - 2\delta_n$$

with $\delta_n > 2M - h_n(p) \to 0$ as $n \to \infty$. Now choose a subsequence $n_j \to \infty$ such that

$$\lim_{j\to\infty} h_{n_j}(c) > 2M - \epsilon.$$

It then follows that (step 2, 5)

$$M + f(p) \geq \liminf_{j\to\infty} h_{n_j}(c_{n_j}) \geq \lim_{j\to\infty} (h_{n_j}(c) - 2\delta_n) > 2M - \epsilon,$$

so that $f(p) > M - \epsilon$. Hence we have proved:

THEOREM. *Bounded frame functions attain their extremal values.*

7. *The General Case*

We now prove the theorem stated in § 3. Choose $p \in S$ such that $f(p) = M$, and $r \in S$, $r \perp p$, such that $f(r) = m$. This is possible because of P_4 and the theorem of §6. Choose q orthogonal to p and r, and set $f(q) = \alpha$. We may assume that $m < \alpha < M$ since otherwise the result of §4 applies to f or $-f$ and the proof is finished. As in §6 we let $\hat{p}$, $\hat{q}$, $\hat{r}$ denote the 90° right-hand rotations about p, q, and r.

We shall now use the theorem of § 5 to obtain information concerning f. It is sufficient to know that f belongs to the space of quadratic frame functions. Taking p as the north pole, the function

$$f(s) + f(\hat{p}s)$$

takes the constant value $m + \alpha$ on the equator, and attains its supremum $2M$ at p. Letting

$$g(s) = M \cos^2\theta(s,p) + m \cos^2\theta(s,r) + \alpha \cos^2\theta(s,q),$$

we have from § 4

$$\begin{aligned} f(s) + f(\hat{p}s) &= 2M \cos^2\theta(s,p) + (m + \alpha)(1 - \cos^2\theta(s,p)) \qquad (*) \\ &= g(s) + g(\hat{p}s), \\ f(s) + f(\hat{r}s) &= g(s) + g(\hat{r}s) \end{aligned}$$

(the second equation follows by analogous reasoning, since $-f$ is a frame function taking its supremum $-m$ at r).

Now let (x,y,z) denote the (p,q,r)-frame coordinates of $s \in S$.

Claim. (*a*) If either $x = y$, $x = z$, or $y = z$, then $f(s) = g(s)$;
(*b*) If either $x = -y$, $x = -z$, $y = -z$, then $f(s) = g(s)$.

Proof of claim. (*a*) Note that $\hat{r}(x,y,z) = (-y,x,z)$; $\hat{p}(x,y,z) = (x, -z,y)$. Applying these operations in succession, one verifies:

$$\hat{p}\hat{p}\hat{r}(x,x,z) = (-x, -x, -z),$$
$$\hat{p}\hat{r}\hat{r}(x,z,z) = (-x, -z, -z),$$
$$\hat{r}\hat{p}\hat{p}\hat{p}\hat{r}(x,y,x) = (-x, -y, -x).$$

Suppose $s = (x,x,z)$. Since $f(s) = f(-s)$, $g(s) = g(-s)$ (by property P_2), we conclude from (*):

$$f(s) + f(\hat{r}s) = g(s) + g(\hat{r}s),$$
$$f(\hat{r}s) + f(\hat{p}\hat{r}s) = g(\hat{r}s) + g(\hat{p}\hat{r}s),$$
$$f(\hat{p}\hat{r}s) + f(\hat{p}\hat{p}\hat{r}s) = g(\hat{p}\hat{r}s) + g(\hat{p}\hat{p}\hat{r}s);$$

subtracting the second equation from the sum of the first and third, we conclude that $f(s) = g(s)$. The other two cases under (*a*) are proved similarly.

(*b*) Suppose $s = (x,-x,z)$; then $\hat{r}(x,-x,z) = (x,x,z)$, which lies on the great circle $x = y$. From (*a*) we know that $f(\hat{r}s) = g(\hat{r}s)$, and from (*) we conclude that also $f(s) = g(s)$. The other two cases in (*b*) are proved similarly, and the claim is proved.

Now define $h := g - f$. h is clearly a frame function, and the claim implies that $h(p) = h(q) = h(r) = 0$, so that the weight of h is zero. We also know that h is zero on the six great circles $x = \pm y$, $x = \pm z$, $y = \pm z$. The proof is completed by showing that h is identically zero. Assume that h is not identically zero; then by §5 we may put

$$M' := \sup h = h(p'),$$
$$m' := \inf h = h(r'),$$
$$\alpha' := h(q'); \qquad q' \perp r', \quad q' \perp p'.$$

The argument is broken into four steps.

(i) $M' = -m'$: Assume that $m' > -M'$. Then $\alpha' < 0$, and by P_3, α' is the maximal value of h on the great circle orthogonal to p'. However, the great circle $x = y$ must intersect the former great circle in at least two points, and at these two points h must take the value zero. Considering $-h$, we derive a contradiction from the assumption $m' < -M'$ by the same argument.

(ii) $\alpha' = 0$: This follows immediately from (i) and the fact that h has weight zero.

(iii) $h(x',x',z') = M'(x'^2 - z'^2)$, where (x',y',z') denote the (p',q',r')-frame coordinates. Using the previous two steps, this follows from the claim, upon substituting h for f and $M'(x'^2 - z'^2)$ for g.

(iv) On the great circle $x' = y'$, h takes the value zero at exactly the following four points: (x',x',x'), $(x',x',-x')$, $(-x',-x',x')$ and $(-x',-x',-x')$.

The great circles $x = y$, $x = z$ and $y = z$ intersect in the two points: (x,x,x) and $(-x,-x,-x)$. As h is zero on these great circles, we see that the great circle $x' = y'$ must pass through the points (x,x,x) and $(-x,-x,-x)$, since otherwise there would be six points on $x' = y'$ at which h takes the value zero. The great circles $x = -y$ and $x = -z$ intersect at $(x,-x,-x)$ and $(-x,x,x)$. $x' = y'$ must also intersect these points, since otherwise it would intersect $x = -y$ and $x = -z$ at four points, making six points at which h would take the value zero on $x' = y'$. However, there is only one great circle, passing through the four points (x,x,x), $(-x,-x,-x)$, $(x,-x,-x)$ and $(-x,x,x)$, namely $y = z$. It follows that $y = z$ and $x' = y'$ describe the same great circle, and therefore h must take the value zero at all points of $x' = y'$. This contradicts step (iv) and the theorem is proved. ▌

Commentary on the CKM Proof

Commentary on §1

The goal of this section is the theorem appearing at the end of it. The strategy of the proof is this: Assume that every state on $\mathbb{R}^3$ is regular. Consider a Hilbert space $\mathcal{H}$ on which a state p is defined. Then the restriction of p to any completely real three-dimensional subspace $L(3)$ of $\mathcal{H}$ is a state p_L on $L(3)$. By our assumption p_L is regular. The restriction of p_L to any two-dimensional subspace $L(2)$ of $L(3)$ is therefore a regular state on $L(2)$. $L(2)$ is, of course, also completely real.

Thus, under the assumption, the restriction of p to any completely real two-dimensional subspace of $\mathcal{H}$ is regular. But we can also show:

(1) If p_C is a state on a two-dimensional complex space $\mathbb{C}^2$ and p_C is regular on every completely real subspace of $\mathbb{C}^2$, then p_C is regular (lemma 2).

(2) If the restriction p_C of p to every two-dimensional (complex) subspace of $\mathcal{H}$ is regular, then p is regular (lemma 3).

The theorem follows.

Further notes. A *bilinear form* on $\mathcal{H}$ is a function B mapping pairs $(\mathbf{x},\mathbf{y})$ of vectors into (complex) numbers, such that, for all $\mathbf{x}$, $\mathbf{y} \in \mathcal{H}$, $c \in \mathbb{C}$,

$$B(\mathbf{x},\mathbf{y}+\mathbf{z}) = B(\mathbf{x},\mathbf{y}) + B(\mathbf{x},\mathbf{z})$$

$$B(\mathbf{x}+\mathbf{z},\mathbf{y}) = B(\mathbf{x},\mathbf{y}) + B(\mathbf{z},\mathbf{y})$$

$$B(c\mathbf{x},\mathbf{y}) = cB(\mathbf{x},\mathbf{y})$$

$$B(\mathbf{x},c\mathbf{y}) = c^*B(\mathbf{x},\mathbf{y})$$

B is *symmetric* if, for all $\mathbf{x},\mathbf{y} \in \mathcal{H}$,

$$B(\mathbf{x},\mathbf{y}) = [B(\mathbf{y},\mathbf{x})]^*$$

The restriction of B to pairs of vectors of the form $(\mathbf{x},\mathbf{x})$ yields a *quadratic form* Q (see §2), such that

$$Q(\mathbf{x}) = B(\mathbf{x},\mathbf{x})$$

It turns out that a bilinear form B is completely determined by its quadratic form Q (Halmos, 1957, p. 13). Note also that B is symmetric if and only if Q is real.

The proof of the first lemma is given in Halmos (1957) §§22–24. The move from regular states to bilinear forms achieves three things. First, we need bilinear (rather than quadratic) forms in the proof of Lemma 2. Secondly, regular states are already seen to be continuous functions (Lemma 3). Third, the constraint on states is put in terms of a function on the vectors within the space, rather than an operator on that space. Thus when we claim that the restriction of p_L to $L(2)$ inherits the regularity of p_L on $L(3)$ (see above), there is no problem of the kind that might arise were the regularity of the states just defined in terms of an operator on $L(3)$.

A closed real-linear subspace of $\mathcal{H}$ forms a vector space over the field of the reals (see Section 1.9).

Lemma 3 is the hardest of the three. It contains two arguments, the first of which is a continuity argument to show that, under the assumptions of the lemma, there is a vector $\mathbf{x}$ such that $p(\bar{\mathbf{x}})$ is the supremum of p. (For the definition of supremum, see Section 7.3.) The argument uses a topological fact about *compact* sets (see Kelley, 1955, p. 135): any infinite sequence $\{x_n\}$ of elements of a compact set X contains a converging subsequence $\{x_{n_j}\}$ which converges to a point x in X (Kelley, 1955, p. 136). This property of compact sets is appealed to again (twice) in §6; I will refer to it as the *accumulation point property*, since x is called an *accumulation point in* X.

CKM consider a sequence $\{\mathbf{x}_n\}$ of normalized vectors such that $p(\overline{\mathbf{x}_n}) \to M$. Since the unit sphere S of $\mathcal{H}$ is compact, there is an accumulation point $\mathbf{x}$ in S such that some subsequence $\{\mathbf{x}_{n_j}\}$ of $\{\mathbf{x}_n\}$ converges to $\mathbf{x}$, and, of course, $p(\overline{\mathbf{x}_{n_j}}) \to M$. (From now on it is this subsequence which is referred to as $\{\mathbf{x}_n\}$.) A further move takes us to a sequence $\{e^{i\theta_n}\mathbf{x}_n\}$ of vectors in S such that, for each n, the vectors $\mathbf{x}$ and $e^{i\theta_n}\mathbf{x}_n$ are in the same completely real subspace. (This uses the fact that, for any complex number c, there exists an angle θ such that $ce^{i\theta} = a$, where a is real and $a^2 = |c|^2$; see Section 1.5.) The assumption of the lemma can then come into play, together with the fact that every regular state p is continuous (see Lemma 1). This continuity ensures that $p(\overline{\mathbf{x}}) = \lim p(\overline{e^{i\theta_n}\mathbf{x}_n})$. Since, for each n, $\overline{\mathbf{x}_n} = \overline{e^{i\theta_n}\mathbf{x}_n}$, we obtain

$$p(\overline{\lim \mathbf{x}_n}) = p(\overline{\mathbf{x}}) = \lim p(\overline{\mathbf{x}}_n) = M$$

In the second argument CKM show that, for an arbitrary vector $\mathbf{y}$, $p(\mathbf{y})$ is given by an expression involving just $\mathbf{y}$, $\mathbf{x}$, and M. The vectors $\mathbf{x}$ and $\mathbf{y}$ are assumed to be normalized, and, although the main result does not depend on it, so is p: that is, CKM assume that $p(\mathcal{H}) = 1$; hence, for any $\mathbf{x}^\perp$ orthogonal to $\mathbf{x}$, $p(\mathbf{x}^\perp) = 1 - M$. For any angle θ, since $e^{i\theta}$ is a scalar, $\overline{\mathbf{y}}$ contains $e^{i\theta}\mathbf{y}$. We choose θ so that $\langle \mathbf{x}|e^{i\theta}\mathbf{y}\rangle$ is real; then within the two-dimensional complex space $\mathcal{H}$, there is a completely real two-dimensional space $\mathcal{H}_R$ containing both $\mathbf{x}$ and $e^{i\theta}\mathbf{y}$. Let $\mathbf{x}^\perp$ be a normalized vector in $\mathcal{H}_R$ orthogonal to $\mathbf{x}$; then there exist real numbers b_1 and b_2 such that $b_1^2 + b_2^2 = 1$ and $e^{i\theta}\mathbf{y} = b_1\mathbf{x} + b_2\mathbf{x}^\perp$. Note that $b_1 = \langle \mathbf{x}|e^{i\theta}\mathbf{y}\rangle$ and $b_2 = \langle \mathbf{x}^\perp|e^{i\theta}\mathbf{y}\rangle$. The restriction of p to $\mathcal{H}_R$ is again a normalized state, and by the assumption of the lemma there is a self-adjoint trace-class operator $\mathbf{A}$ on $\mathcal{H}_R$ such that, for all normalized $\mathbf{v}$ in $\mathcal{H}_R$, $p(\overline{\mathbf{v}}) = \langle \mathbf{A}\mathbf{v}|\mathbf{v}\rangle$. Furthermore, we can show that, since $\mathbf{A}$ is a trace-class operator on $\mathcal{H}_R$ and $\langle \mathbf{A}\mathbf{v}|\mathbf{v}\rangle$ is at a maximum when $\mathbf{v} = \mathbf{x}$, $\mathbf{x}$ is an eigenvector of $\mathbf{A}$. Since $\mathcal{H}_R$ is two-dimensional and $\mathbf{A}$ is self-adjoint, $\mathbf{x}^\perp$ is also an eigenvector of $\mathbf{A}$. For any normalized eigenvector $\mathbf{v}$ of $\mathbf{A}$ with corresponding eigenvalue a, we have $\langle \mathbf{A}\mathbf{v}|\mathbf{v}\rangle = a$; hence the eigenvalues of $\mathbf{A}$ corresponding to $\mathbf{x}$ and $\mathbf{x}^\perp$ are, respectively, M and $1 - M$.

As Cooke has pointed out to me (pers. com., May 1988), the neatest way to obtain the result of the lemma is now to use the remark following equation (*) in §2. To see this, consult the commentary on §2 and consider the frame $\{\mathbf{x},\mathbf{x}^\perp\}$ in the two-dimensional space $\mathcal{H}_R$. The coordinates of $e^{i\theta}\mathbf{y}$ with respect to this frame are $\langle \mathbf{x}|e^{i\theta}\mathbf{y}\rangle$ and $\langle \mathbf{x}^\perp|e^{i\theta}\mathbf{y}\rangle$, respectively, and, as we have noted, $\langle \mathbf{x}|e^{i\theta}\mathbf{y}\rangle^2 + \langle \mathbf{x}^\perp|e^{i\theta}\mathbf{y}\rangle^2 = 1$. By plugging in these coordinates and the eigenvalues of $\mathbf{A}$ into the (two-dimensional version of) equation (‡) of the commentary on §2, we get:

$$\begin{aligned} p(\bar{\mathbf{y}}) = p(\overline{e^{i\theta}\mathbf{y}}) &= \langle \mathbf{A}e^{i\theta}\mathbf{y}|e^{i\theta}\mathbf{y}\rangle \\ &= M(\langle \mathbf{x}|e^{i\theta}\mathbf{y}\rangle^2) + (1-M)(\langle \mathbf{x}^{\perp}|e^{i\theta}\mathbf{y}\rangle^2) \\ &= M(\langle \mathbf{x}|e^{i\theta}\mathbf{y}\rangle^2) + (1-M)(1-\langle \mathbf{x}|e^{i\theta}\mathbf{y}\rangle^2) \\ &= M|\langle \mathbf{x}|\mathbf{y}\rangle|^2 + (1-M)(1-|\langle \mathbf{x}|\mathbf{y}\rangle|^2) \end{aligned}$$

This expression defines a continuous real-valued quadratic form $Q(\mathbf{y})$ on $\mathcal{H}$, and hence a symmetric continuous bilinear form $B(\mathbf{y},\mathbf{z})$, and so the lemma is proved.

Commentary on §2

The injunction after the equation marked (*) may well tax the resources of memory. The result can be quickly shown for quadratic forms on $\mathbb{R}^3$, as follows.

To each quadratic form Q on $\mathbb{R}^3$ there corresponds a unique symmetric bilinear form B on $\mathbb{R}^3$, such that $B(\mathbf{x},\mathbf{y}) = B(\mathbf{y},\mathbf{x})$, and a symmetric operator $\mathbf{A}$ on $\mathbb{R}^3$ such that, for all $\mathbf{s} \in \mathbb{R}^3$,

$$Q(\mathbf{s}) = B(\mathbf{s},\mathbf{s}) = \langle \mathbf{s}|\mathbf{A}\mathbf{s}\rangle$$

(Halmos, 1957, §24; the properties of symmetric operators on a real space resemble those of Hermitian operators on a complex space: see Section 1.2). Now let $(\mathbf{p},\mathbf{q},\mathbf{r})$ be an arbitrary basis for $\mathbb{R}^3$. Then for any $\mathbf{s} \in S$ there are x,y,z such that $\mathbf{s} = x\mathbf{p} + y\mathbf{q} + z\mathbf{r}$. Hence

$$\begin{aligned} Q(\mathbf{s}) = \langle \mathbf{s}|\mathbf{A}\mathbf{s}\rangle &= \langle x\mathbf{p} + y\mathbf{q} + z\mathbf{r}|\mathbf{A}(x\mathbf{p} + y\mathbf{q} + z\mathbf{r})\rangle \\ &= x^2\langle \mathbf{p}|\mathbf{A}\mathbf{p}\rangle + y^2\langle \mathbf{q}|\mathbf{A}\mathbf{q}\rangle + z^2\langle \mathbf{r}|\mathbf{A}\mathbf{r}\rangle \\ &\quad + xy(\langle \mathbf{p}|\mathbf{A}\mathbf{q}\rangle + \langle \mathbf{q}|\mathbf{A}\mathbf{p}\rangle) + yz(\langle \mathbf{q}|\mathbf{A}\mathbf{r}\rangle + \langle \mathbf{r}|\mathbf{A}\mathbf{q}\rangle) \\ &\quad + zx(\langle \mathbf{r}|\mathbf{A}\mathbf{p}\rangle + \langle \mathbf{p}|\mathbf{A}\mathbf{r}\rangle) \end{aligned}$$

Now choose $\mathbf{p}_0$, $\mathbf{q}_0$, $\mathbf{r}_0$ to be a set of orthonormal eigenvectors of $\mathbf{A}$; we know that such a basis exists because $\mathbf{A}$ is symmetric (see Sections 1.2 and 1.14). The cross terms in the expression above now vanish and we obtain:

$$Q(\mathbf{s}) = \langle \mathbf{s}|\mathbf{A}\mathbf{s}\rangle = \alpha x^2 + \beta y^2 + \gamma z^2 \qquad (\ddagger)$$

where α, β, γ are the eigenvalues of $\mathbf{A}$. Further,

$$w(Q) = \alpha + \beta + \gamma = \mathrm{Tr}(\mathbf{A})$$

In the proposition at the end of the section, CKM treat a more general case, since **A** is not necessarily symmetric. To extend the above proof to the general case, we need to consider the symmetric operator $\frac{1}{2}(\mathbf{A} + \mathbf{A}^T)$ (see Fano, 1971, p. 68).

Further notes. (1) Property P_4 plays a large part in what follows; note that it yields an *in*equality: $f(\mathbf{t}) < m + \xi$.

(2) Compare the frame function $f(\mathbf{s}) = \cos^2\theta(p_0, s)$ with equation (4.4).

Commentary on §3

To recognize the theorem given by CKM at the beginning of this section as Gleason's theorem, note that (1) every state p on $\mathbb{R}^3$ is a bounded frame function; we must also show (2) that from the conclusion of the CKM theorem it follows that there is a symmetric operator **A** on $\mathbb{R}^3$ such that, for every $\mathbf{s} \in S$, $p(\bar{\mathbf{s}}) = f(\mathbf{s}) = \langle \mathbf{As}|\mathbf{s}\rangle$. (Recall that $\bar{\mathbf{s}}$ is the ray containing **s**.) (2) is the converse of the proposition of §2. Proof by construction: Let $\mathbf{A} = M\mathbf{P}_p + \alpha\mathbf{P}_q + m\mathbf{P}_r$, where $\mathbf{P}_p$, $\mathbf{P}_q$, $\mathbf{P}_r$ project onto $\bar{\mathbf{p}}$, $\bar{\mathbf{q}}$, $\bar{\mathbf{r}}$, respectively. If the coordinates of **s** with respect to (**p**,**q**,**r**) are (x,y,z), then, since $\langle \mathbf{s}|\mathbf{P}_p\mathbf{s}\rangle = |\mathbf{P}_p\mathbf{s}|^2 = x^2$ (and similarly for **q** and **r**), we obtain

$$\langle \mathbf{s}|\mathbf{As}\rangle = Mx^2 + \alpha y^2 + mz^2 = f(\mathbf{s})$$

as required.

The implicit quantifications in the proof of "warm-up" theorem I may give trouble. Throughout this theorem we are considering a fixed (although arbitrary) f with the property $f(a) + f(b) + f(c) = \overline{w}$ for all triples (a,b,c) such that $a + b + c = 1$. We take an arbitrary a and obtain $f(a) = \overline{w} - f(1 - a)$, by considering a as part of the triple $(a, 1 - a, 0)$. This holds for *all* $a \in [0,1]$, and is applied to $(a + b)$ to obtain

$$\text{(A1.1)} \qquad f(a) + f(b) = f(a + b)$$

for all a, b, $a + b \in [0,1]$. By extending (A1.1) we obtain, for any integer n $(na \leq 1)$, $nf(a) = f(na)$. Whence, for $a = \frac{1}{n}$, $f(a) = \frac{1}{n}\overline{w}$. Applying (A1.1) again, for any integer m $(m < n)$, we obtain $f\left(\frac{m}{n}\right) = \frac{m}{n}\overline{w}$; in other words, $f(a) = \overline{w}a$ for all rational a.

We obtain the final conclusion of "warm-up" theorem II as follows. From (1) and (2) f is bounded from below, and, for $a_0 \in [0,1] - C$ (in CKM notation, $a_0 \in [0,1]\backslash C$),

$$\lim_{a_0 \to 0} f(a_0) = 0 = f(0)$$

From (1) and (3) f is bounded from above, and, using (2), we obtain

$$\lim_{a_0 \to 1} f(a_0) = \sup f(a_0) = 1 \tag{A1.2}$$

But now assume that, for some a_0, $f(a_0) \neq a_0$. Then for a sequence $r_0, r_1, r_2 \ldots$ such that $r_i a_0 \to 1$, we have

$$\lim_{i \to \infty} f(r_i a_0) = \lim_{i \to \infty} r_i f(a_0) \neq 1$$

This violates (A1.2) above; hence, for all $a_0 \in [0,1] - C$, $f(a_0) = a_0$.

Commentary on §4

Figure A1.4 illustrates the two lemmata of this section.

Commentary on §5

The geometric lemma, together with the basic lemma of §4, shows that, given premises (1) and (2) of the basic lemma,

$$\text{if} \quad l(s) > l(s') \quad \text{then} \quad f(s) \geq f(s')$$

The geometric lemma itself shows that from any point s in N one can reach another of lower latitude via a sequence of descents, starting with the

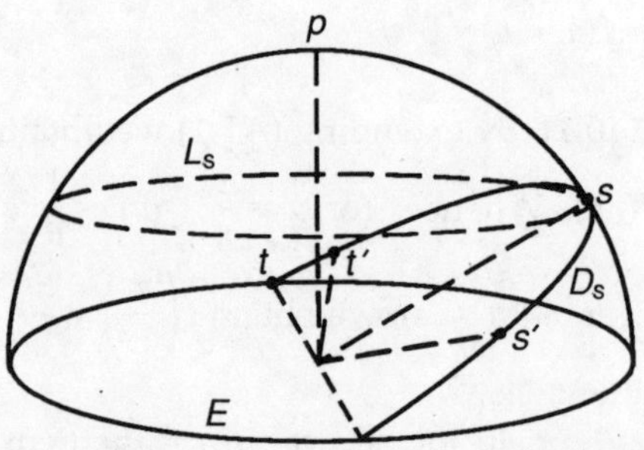

Figure A1.4

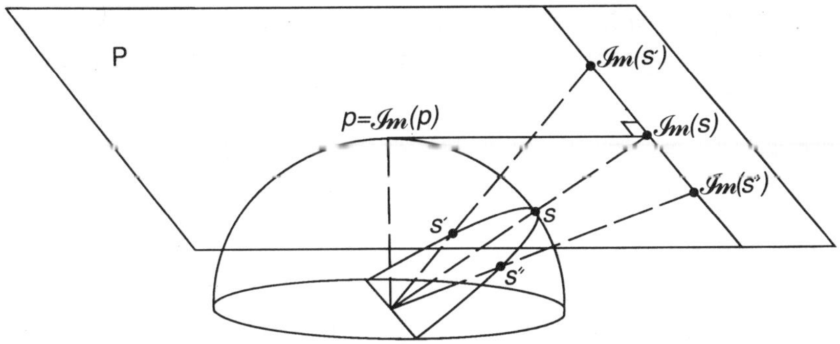

Figure A1.5 Projection of N onto the tangent plane P.

descent through s. The method of proof employs projective geometry: the strategy is to map each point s in N onto the tangent plane P to S at p, so that the image of s [Im(s)] is the point on the plane P where the extended radius through s meets the plane (see Figure A1.5). The result is as though the hemisphere N had been stretched out to an infinite plane. Although distances on N are not preserved under the transformation, various relations carry over; thus, if s_1 and s_2 are equidistant from p, then their images are equidistant from Im(p), and, if $l(s_1) > l(s_2)$, then Im(s_2) is further from Im(p) than is Im(s_1). Also, if s_1 and s_2 are on the same line of longitude on N, then Im(s_1), Im(s_2), and Im(p) are collinear.

Any great circle on S lies in a plane through the center of S, and this plane will cut P in a straight line. It follows that the descent D_s through s is mapped onto a straight line Im(D_s) in P, and Im(D_s) is tangent to the image of the circle of latitude through s. The problem of finding a sequence of descents on N becomes a problem of finding a sequence of straight lines on P.

From now on, like CKM, I will talk of points, such as p and s_0, on P, rather than of their images Im(p) and Im(s_0).

We take s, t such that $l(s) > l(t)$. Stage (1) of the proof deals with the case when s and t have the same longitude. For the general case CKM then construct what I will call an *n-polygon* (which actually has $n + 1$ sides) to show a sequence of descents starting from s_0 and ending on s_n, where s_0 and s_n are 180° of longitude apart. Now, given arbitrary s and t [$l(s) > l(t)$], any n-polygon starting from s and moving in the direction of t will intersect the line pt: call the point of intersection $t_{(n)}$. The next step of the CKM proof shows that, by making n big enough, we can obtain $l(t_{(n)}) > l(t)$. The required sequence of descents takes us round this n-polygon from s to $t_{(n)}$ and then, using the maneuver of Stage (1), from $t_{(n)}$ to t.

Three points in the theorem deserve comment.

(1) To show that $\Sigma_C[\bar{f}(l) - \underline{f}(l)] \leq 1$, note that, for $l < l'$, $\bar{f}(l) \leq \underline{f}(l')$, so that, as we move up to p from the equator, the differences $\bar{f}(l) - \underline{f}(l)$ will add up. But, by hypothesis, $f(p) = 1$, and so the sum of these differences is no greater than 1.

(2) The existence of the frame $(\mathbf{q},\mathbf{q}',\mathbf{q}'')$ may be seen as follows. Let $(\mathbf{q}_0,\mathbf{q}_0',\mathbf{q}_0'')$ be an arbitrary frame. For any θ, θ', θ'' such that $\cos^2\theta + \cos^2\theta' + \cos^2\theta'' = 1$, we can construct a normalized vector $\mathbf{p}_0$ with coordinates $(\cos\theta, \cos\theta', \cos\theta'')$ with respect to $(\mathbf{q}_0, \mathbf{q}_0', \mathbf{q}_0'')$. We now choose $\theta = l$, $\theta' = l'$, $\theta'' = l''$, construct $\mathbf{p}_0$, and rotate $(\mathbf{q}_0, \mathbf{q}_0', \mathbf{q}_0'')$ within S to make $\mathbf{p}_0$ coincide with $\mathbf{p}$ (the N-pole of S). This rotation transforms $(\mathbf{q}_0, \mathbf{q}_0', \mathbf{q}_0'')$ to the required frame $(\mathbf{q},\mathbf{q}',\mathbf{q}'')$.

(3) To show that $C = \emptyset$, assume that $l' \in C$; then, for $l \in [0,l') - C$, we have

$$\lim_{l \to l'} f(l) = l'$$

and, for $l \in (l',1] - C$,

$$\lim_{l \to l'} f(l) = l'$$

Whence $l' \leq \underline{f}(l') \leq \bar{f}(l') \leq l'$, and so $\bar{f}(l') - \underline{f}(l') = 0$, *contra* hypothesis.

Commentary on §6

At this stage it is useful to compare the theorem of §5 with the statement of Gleason's theorem in §3. The premises of the §5 theorem are stronger than the premises of Gleason's theorem: they impose both (1) an *extreme-value* requirement and (2) a *symmetry* condition. The extreme-value requirement not only requires that f be bounded ($\sup f(s) = M$, $\inf f(s) = m$), but also that there exist a point p on S such that $f(p) = M$ and a (set of) points for which $f(s) = m$. Symmetry requires that for *all* $s \perp p$ (that is, for $s \in E$), $f(s) = m$.

§6 shows that the extreme-value requirement holds for any bounded frame function f; it also introduces a technique for symmetrization which is used again in §7. Note, however, that in general f does not satisfy the symmetry condition.

The conclusion of the §5 theorem is a special case of the conclusion of the §3 version of Gleason's theorem; if the function f is expressed in terms of coordinates (x,y,z) with respect to the frame $(\mathbf{p},\mathbf{q},\mathbf{r})$ ($\mathbf{q}$, $\mathbf{r} \in E$), it appears as:

$$f(s) = m + (M - m)\cos^2\theta(s,p)$$
$$= M\cos^2\theta(s,p) + m[1 - \cos^2\theta(s,p)]$$
$$= Mx^2 + m(y^2 + z^2)$$

Note that this is symmetrical about $\bar{\mathbf{p}}$.

§6 has a preamble and four steps. To prove that a bounded frame function f attains its extremal values we use the same strategy as in lemma 3 of §2; we consider a sequence of points $p_n \in S$ such that $\lim_{n\to\infty} f(p_n) = M$. Since S is compact, the accumulation point property tells us that (if we pass to a subsequence $\{p_n\}$) there is a point p such that $p = \lim_{n\to\infty} (p_n)$. These limits must be shown to match, as it were, so that $f(\lim_{n\to\infty} p_n) = f(p) = \lim_{n\to\infty} f(p_n)$. This is a continuity requirement. It would be violated if, for example, $f(p)$ dropped discontinuously to the value $M - \xi$ at p.

The trick is to use f and the original sequence p_n of points to define a frame function h that satisfies the premises of the §5 theorem (steps 1, 2, and 3); any function which satisfies these premises is known to be continuous. At p the function h has value $2M$; we then show (step 4) that, for any $\epsilon > 0$, $M + f(p) > 2M - \epsilon$. It follows that $f(p) = M$.

Step 1. This takes the original function f and, so to speak, drags it around on the surface of the sphere; we obtain a sequence g_n of functions, each just like f but dislocated over the sphere's surface. Each dislocation is equivalent to a rigid motion of the sphere that carries the function f with it, and that takes the N-pole p to the point p_n; thus the sequence g_n is in one-to-one correspondence with the sequence p_n. A *rigid motion* of S is a rotation of S. Obviously the angular separation of points of S is invariant under rigid motions. Any rotation can be specified by its effect on two points in $N - E$. We define ρ_n by selecting c_n on c_0 such that $\theta(p,c_n) = \theta(p,p_n)$; ρ_n is then the rotation that takes p to p_n and c_n to p. We define

$$g_n(s) = f(\rho_n s)$$

Step 2. Symmetrization of the functions g_n yields a sequence h_n of functions. This symmetrization (1) allows h_n to satisfy the premises of the approximate version of the basic lemma (see step 4) and (2) allows h to satisfy the premises of the §5 theorem (see step 3).

Step 3. The existence of the function h is now proved by the accumulation point property. The space $[2m,2M]^S$ is the set of functions from S into the closed subset $[2m,2M]$ of the reals; this set is compact, and so, by passing to a subsequence of h_n, we obtain the limit h. CKM's emphasis here on the

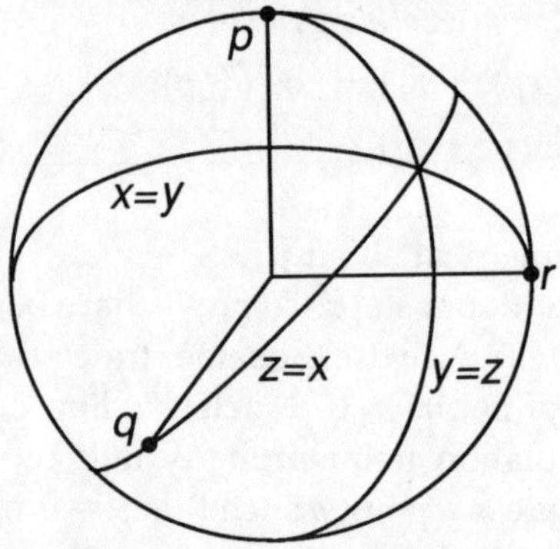

Figure A1.6 Great circles on S.

product topology is important, since there are other topologies under which the space $[2m,2M]^S$ is not compact (see Kelley, 1955, pp. 217–218).

Step 4. The existence of this function h allows the final move to be made in the chain of inequalities that yields the desired result.

Commentary on §7

We now know that any bounded frame function f satisfies the extreme-value requirement, and we have a technique for using f to define a function f_{sym} which fulfills the symmetry condition of the §5 theorem: we write $f_{sym}(s) = f(s) + f(\hat{p}s)$ (§6, step 2). By the §5 theorem we also know the form of f_{sym} [§7, Equation (*)].

In §7 f is compared with a quadratic frame function g which has the same extreme values, M and m, and the same weight, $M + m + \alpha$, as does f. We see first that $g_{sym} = f_{sym}$, and then that $g(s) = f(s)$ for points on selected great circles [claims (a) and (b): see Figure A1.6]. Lastly, the function $h = g - f$ is shown to be zero, not merely for points on these great circles, but over all S. Hence any bounded frame function is a quadratic frame function, and Gleason's theorem is proved.

Further notes. Step (iii) in showing that $g - f = 0$ is an elegant move whereby claim (a) is made on behalf of h and the quadratic frame function $M'(x'^2 - z'^2)$; this quadratic frame function is constructed from the extreme values of h as was g from the extreme values of f.

APPENDIX B

The Lüders Rule

In Section 8.2 it was shown that, if subspaces P and Q are compatible, then the Lüders rule yields classical conditionalization; in other words, if we conditionalize according to the rule, then

$$\mathbb{P}(P|Q) = \frac{p(P \cap Q)}{p(Q)}$$

for any generalized probability function (GPF) p on $S(\mathcal{H})$. It follows that, when $P \subseteq Q$ (and hence $P \cap Q = P$), according to the Lüders rule:

$$\mathbb{P}(P|Q) = \frac{p(P)}{p(Q)} = q(P)$$

The Lüders rule thus renormalizes the probabilities assigned to all $P \subseteq Q$, so that $q(Q) = 1$. We now show that the rule specifies the *only* GPF on $S(\mathcal{H})$ which does this.

In this proof, $\mathbf{Q}$ denotes both a subspace and the projector onto it, and $\mathbf{Q}^{\perp}$ denotes both the orthocomplement of $\mathbf{Q}$ and the corresponding projector. We write $\overline{\mathbf{v}}$ for the ray containing a normalized vector $\mathbf{v}$.

Note first that, for any density operator $\mathbf{D}$, the operator $\mathbf{QDQ}$ is a trace-class operator [see (5.6)], and hence the operator

$$\frac{\mathbf{QDQ}}{\mathrm{Tr}(\mathbf{QDQ})}$$

appearing in the Lüders rule is a density operator [see (5.7)].

Now let q be any GPF on $S(\mathcal{H})$ which yields the renormalization described above. We know that (1) since any GPF is additive over orthogonal subspaces, q is completely defined by the probabilities it assigns to the rays of $\mathcal{H}$; (2) by Gleason's theorem, q can be represented by a density operator $\mathbf{D}_q$ on $\mathcal{H}$, so that, for any ray $\overline{\mathbf{v}}$, $q(\overline{\mathbf{v}}) = \langle \mathbf{v} | \mathbf{D}_q \mathbf{v} \rangle$; (3) if, for some GPF q, represented by $\mathbf{D}_q$, $q(\mathbf{Q}) = 1$, then, for all $\mathbf{v} \in \mathbf{Q}^{\perp}$, $q(\overline{\mathbf{v}}) = 0 = \langle \mathbf{v} | \mathbf{D}_q \mathbf{v} \rangle$; since $\mathbf{D}_q$ is a (weighted) sum of projection operators, it follows that $\mathbf{D}_q \mathbf{v} = \mathbf{0}$ for all $\mathbf{v} \in \mathbf{Q}^{\perp}$.

Now let $\overline{\mathbf{v}}$ be an arbitrary ray in $\mathcal{H}$. Then

$$
\begin{aligned}
q(\overline{\mathbf{v}}) &= \langle \mathbf{v} | \mathbf{D}_q \mathbf{v} \rangle \\
&= \langle \mathbf{Qv} + \mathbf{Q}^{\perp}\mathbf{v} | \mathbf{D}_q(\mathbf{Qv} + \mathbf{Q}^{\perp}\mathbf{v}) \rangle \\
&= \langle \mathbf{Qv} + \mathbf{Q}^{\perp}\mathbf{v} | \mathbf{D}_q \mathbf{Qv} \rangle && \text{[(3), above]} \\
&= \langle \mathbf{D}_q(\mathbf{Qv} + \mathbf{Q}^{\perp}\mathbf{v}) | \mathbf{Qv} \rangle && \text{[Hermiticity]} \\
&= \langle \mathbf{D}_q \mathbf{Qv} | \mathbf{Qv} \rangle && \text{[(3), above]} \\
&= \langle \mathbf{Qv} | \mathbf{D}_q \mathbf{Qv} \rangle && \text{[Hermiticity]}
\end{aligned}
$$

Now $\mathbf{Qv}$ lies within $\mathbf{Q}$, and so $\mathbf{Qv} = c\mathbf{x}$ for some scalar c and normalized vector $\mathbf{x}$ in $\mathbf{Q}$. Thus we obtain

$$q(\overline{\mathbf{v}}) = |c|^2 \langle \mathbf{x} | \mathbf{D}_q \mathbf{x} \rangle = |c|^2 q(\overline{\mathbf{x}})$$

We see that any GPF q on $S(\mathcal{H})$ such that $q(\mathbf{Q}) = 1$ is completely specified by the values which it assigns to the rays within $\mathbf{Q}$. Hence, given any GPF p, there is a unique GPF q on $S(\mathcal{H})$ such that, for all $\mathbf{P} \subseteq \mathbf{Q}$,

$$q(\mathbf{P}) = \frac{p(\mathbf{P})}{p(\mathbf{Q})}$$

In turn, q is uniquely represented by the density operator $\mathbf{D}_q$.

But the operator

$$\frac{\mathbf{QDQ}}{\mathrm{Tr}(\mathbf{QDQ})}$$

appearing in the Lüders rule is a density operator. It follows that

$$\mathbf{D}_q = \frac{\mathbf{QDQ}}{\mathrm{Tr}(\mathbf{QDQ})}$$

Thus the Lüders rule gives the unique GPF q with the property that, for all $\mathbf{P} \subseteq \mathbf{Q}$,

$$q(\mathbf{P}) = \frac{p(\mathbf{P})}{p(\mathbf{Q})}$$

APPENDIX C

Coupled Systems and Conditionalization

At the end of Section 8.8, it was shown that, when an electron-positron pair is prepared in the singlet spin state, Lüders-rule conditionalization on the event $(S^p_\alpha, +)$, associated with the positron, projects the state of the electron into the pure state $\mathbf{P}^e_{\alpha-}$; further, that this state indeed yields the quantum-theoretic probabilities for measurements of spin on the electron, given that a measurement of S_α on the positron has yielded the result $+$.

Here I generalize this result, by taking a coupled system in an arbitrary initial state $\mathbf{D}$ and looking at the effect of conditionalizing on an event associated with one of its components. I use the notation of the last part of Section 8.2, and the proof is an extension of the one which appears there.

Consider a coupled system with components a and b, whose states are representable in a Hilbert space $\mathcal{H}^a \otimes \mathcal{H}^b$. Assume that a measurement of A^b is conducted on system b, and let A^a be an observable associated with system a. We can then form a classical probability space partitioned by the conjunctions $(\mathbf{P}^a \cdot \mathbf{P}^b)$ of A^a-events and A^b-events. Since this space is classical, conditionalization on the event $\mathbf{P}^b$ (the result of the measurement of A^b) will yield conditional probabilities for the A^a-events given by the classical rule:

$$\mathbb{P}(\mathbf{P}^a|\mathbf{P}^b) = \frac{p(\mathbf{P}^a \cdot \mathbf{P}^b)}{p(\mathbf{P}^b)}$$

But A^a was an arbitrarily chosen a-observable, and so this rule holds for all a-events $\mathbf{P}^a$.

Note that the probabilities appearing in the expression on the right of this equation are given by the statistical algorithm of quantum mechanics, if we know the initial state of the composite system. For if this system has been prepared in a quantum state $\mathbf{D}_1$, which reduces to states $\mathbf{D}^a_1$ and $\mathbf{D}^b_1$ of the components, we then have

$$p(\mathbf{P}^a \cdot \mathbf{P}^b) = \mathrm{Tr}[\mathbf{D}_1(\mathbf{P}^a \otimes \mathbf{P}^b)]$$

$$p(\mathbf{P}^b) = \mathrm{Tr}[\mathbf{D}_1(\mathbf{I}^a \otimes \mathbf{P}^b)] = \mathrm{Tr}(\mathbf{D}_1^b \mathbf{P}^b) \qquad [(5.27)]$$

According to the Lüders rule, conditionalization on the event $\mathbf{P}^b$ yields the state $\mathbf{D}_2$ of the composite system, where

$$\mathbf{D}_2 = \frac{(\mathbf{I}^a \otimes \mathbf{P}^b)\mathbf{D}_1(\mathbf{I}^a \otimes \mathbf{P}^b)}{\mathrm{Tr}[\mathbf{D}_1(\mathbf{I}^a \otimes \mathbf{P}^b)]}$$

We write $\mathbf{D}_2^a$ and $\mathbf{D}_2^b$ for the reduced states of the components.

We now show that

$$\mathbb{P}(\mathbf{P}^a|\mathbf{P}^b) = \mathrm{Tr}(\mathbf{D}_2^a \mathbf{P}^a)$$

for an arbitrary a-event $\mathbf{P}^a$; in other words, that the conditional probabilities for all a-events are as though $\mathbf{P}^b$ projects the state of system a to $\mathbf{D}_2^a$.

$$\mathrm{Tr}(\mathbf{D}_2^a \mathbf{P}^a) = \mathrm{Tr}[\mathbf{D}_2(\mathbf{P}^a \otimes \mathbf{I}^b)] \qquad [(5.27)]$$

$$= \frac{\mathrm{Tr}[(\mathbf{I}^a \otimes \mathbf{P}^b)\mathbf{D}_1(\mathbf{I}^a \otimes \mathbf{P}^b)(\mathbf{P}^a \otimes \mathbf{I}^b)]}{\mathrm{Tr}[\mathbf{D}_1(\mathbf{I}^a \otimes \mathbf{P}^b)]}$$

$$= \frac{\mathrm{Tr}[\mathbf{D}_1(\mathbf{P}^a \otimes \mathbf{P}^b)]}{\mathrm{Tr}[\mathbf{D}_1(\mathbf{I}^a \otimes \mathbf{P}^b)]} \qquad \text{[by (5.6), idempotence, and operator multiplication on } \mathcal{H}^a \otimes \mathcal{H}^b\text{]}$$

$$= \frac{p(\mathbf{P}^a \cdot \mathbf{P}^b)}{p(\mathbf{P}^b)}$$

References

Accardi, L., and A. Fedullo, 1982. "On the Statistical Meaning of Complex Numbers in Quantum Mechanics." *Lettere al Nuovo Cimento* 34:161–172.

Aristotle. 1984. *The Complete Works of Aristotle,* 2 vols. Ed. J. Barnes. Princeton, N.J.: Princeton University Press.

Aspect, A. 1976. "Proposed Experiment to Test the Non-Separability of Quantum Mechanics." *Physical Review* D 14:1944–1951. Reprinted in Wheeler and Zurek (1983), pp. 435–442.

Asquith, P. D., and R. N. Giere, eds. 1980. *PSA 1980,* vol. 1. East Lansing, Mich.: Philosophy of Science Association.

——— 1981. *PSA 1980,* vol. 2. East Lansing, Mich.: Philosophy of Science Association.

Asquith, P. D., and T. Nickles, eds. 1982. *PSA 1982,* vol. 1. East Lansing, Mich.: Philosophy of Science Association.

Ballentine, L. E. 1970. "The Statistical Interpretation of Quantum Mechanics." *Reviews of Modern Physics* 42:358–381.

——— 1972. "Einstein's Interpretation of Quantum Mechanics." *American Journal of Physics* 40:1763–1771.

Belinfante, F. J. 1973. *A Survey of Hidden Variable Theories.* Oxford: Pergamon Press.

Bell, J. L., and A. D. Slomson. 1969. *Models and Ultraproducts: An Introduction.* Amsterdam: North Holland.

Bell, J. S. 1964. "On the Einstein-Podolsky-Rosen Paradox." *Physics* 1:195–200. Reprinted in Wheeler and Zurek (1983), pp. 403–408.

——— 1966. "On the Problem of Hidden Variables in Quantum Mechanics." *Review of Modern Physics* 38:447–452.

Beltrametti, E. G., and G. Cassinelli. 1981. *The Logic of Quantum Mechanics.* Reading, Mass: Addison Wesley.

Beltrametti, E.G., and B. C. van Fraassen, eds. 1981. *Current Issues in Quantum Logic.* New York: Plenum Press.

Bigelow, J. C. 1976. "Possible Worlds Foundations for Probability." *Journal of Philosophical Logic* 5:299–320.

Birkhoff, G., and J. von Neumann. 1936. "The Logic of Quantum Mechanics." *Annals of Mathematics* 37:823–843. Reprinted in Hooker (1975), pp. 1–26.

Blanché, R. 1962. *Axiomatics.* Trans. G. B. Keene. London: Routledge and Kegan Paul.

Bohm, D. 1951. *Quantum Theory.* Englewood Cliffs, N.J.: Prentice Hall.

——— 1957. *Causality and Chance in Modern Physics.* London: Routledge and Kegan Paul.

Bohr, N. 1934. *Atomic Theory and the Description of Nature.* Cambridge: Cambridge University Press.

——— 1935a. "Can Quantum-Mechanical Description of Reality Be Considered Complete?" *Physical Review* 48:696–702. Reprinted in Wheeler and Zurek (1983), pp. 145–151.

——— 1935b. "Quantum Mechanics and Physical Reality." *Nature* 12:65. Reprinted in Wheeler and Zurek (1983), p. 144.

——— 1949. "Discussion with Einstein on Epistemological Problems in Atomic Physics." In Schilpp (1949), pp. 200–241. Reprinted in Wheeler and Zurek (1983), pp. 9–49.

Bohr, N., H. A. Kramers, and J. C. Slater. 1924. "Über die Quantentheorie der Strahlung." *Zeitschrift für Physik* 24:69–87.

Born, M. 1926a. "Zur Quantenmechanik der Stossvergänge." *Zeitschrift für Physik* 37:863–867. Trans. in Wheeler and Zurek (1983), pp. 52–55.

——— 1926b. "Quantenmechanik der Stossvergänge." *Zeitschrift für Physik* 38:803–827.

Bub, J. 1968. "The Daneri-Loinger-Prosperi Quantum Theory of Measurement." *Il Nuovo Cimento* 57B:503–520.

——— 1974. *The Interpretation of Quantum Mechanics.* Dordrecht, Holland: Reidel.

——— 1975. "Popper's Propensity Interpretation of Probability and Quantum Mechanics." In Maxwell and Anderson (1975), pp. 416–429.

——— 1977. "Von Neumann's Projection Postulate as a Possibility Conditionalization Rule in Quantum Mechanics." *Journal of Philosophical Logic* 6:381–390.

——— 1979. "The Measurement Problem of Quantum Mechanics." *Problems in the Philosophy of Physics* (72d Corso). Bologna: Società Italiana di Fisica.

——— 1987. "How to Solve the Measurement Problem of Quantum Mechanics." Paper delivered at the VIIIth International Congress of Logic, Methodology and Philosophy of Science, in Moscow, 1987. College Park, Md.: University of Maryland, mimeo.

Busch, P., and P. Lahti. 1984. "On Various Joint Measurements of Position and Momentum Observables." *Physical Review* D 29:1634–1646.

——— 1985. "A Note on Quantum Theory, Complementarity and Uncertainty." *Philosophy of Science* 52:64–77.

Carnap, R. 1974. *An Introduction to the Philosophy of Science.* Ed. M. Gardner. New York: Basic Books.

Cartwright, N. 1974. "Van Fraassen's Modal Model of Quantum Mechanics." *Philosophy of Science* 41:199–202.

——— 1983, *How the Laws of Physics Lie,* Oxford: Clarendon Press, 1983.

Clauser, J. F., M. A. Horne, A. Shimony, and R. A. Holt. 1969. "Proposed Experiment to Test Hidden Variable Theories." *Physical Review Letters* 23:880–883.

Clauser, J. F., and A. Shimony. 1978. "Bell's Theorem: Experimental Tests and Implications." *Reports on Progress in Physics* 41:1881–1927.

Cohen, R. S., C. A. Hooker, A. C. Michalos, and J. W. van Ezra, eds. 1976. *PSA 1974. Boston Studies in the Philosophy of Science,* vol. 32. Dordrecht, Holland: Reidel.

Cohen, R. S., and J. J. Stachel, eds. 1979. *Selected Papers of Leon Rosenfeld.* Dordrecht, Holland: Reidel.

Cohen, R. S., and M. W. Wartofsky, eds. 1969. *Boston Studies in the Philosophy of Science,* vol. 5. Dordrecht, Holland: Reidel.

——— 1974. *Logical and Epistemological Studies in Contemporary Physics. Boston Studies in the Philosophy of Science,* vol. 13. Dordrecht, Holland: Reidel.

Colodny, R. A., ed. 1965. *Beyond the Edge of Certainty.* Englewood Cliffs, N.J.: Prentice Hall.

——— 1972. *Paradigms and Paradoxes: The Philosophical Challenge of the Quantum Domain,* Pittsburgh: University of Pittsburgh Press, 1972.

Cooke, R. M., and J. Hilgevoord. 1981. "A New Approach to Equivalence in Quantum Logic." In Beltrametti and van Fraassen (1981), pp. 101–113.

Cooke, R., M. Keane, and W. Moran. 1985. "An Elementary Proof of Gleason's Theorem." *Mathematical Proceedings of the Cambridge Philosophical Society* 98:117–128.

Cushing, J. T., C. F. Delaney, and G. Gutting, eds. 1984. *Science and Reality: Recent Work in the Philosophy of Science.* Notre Dame, Ind.: University of Notre Dame Press.

Cushing, J. T., and E. McMullin, eds. 1989. *Philosophical Consequences of Quantum Theory.* Notre Dame, Ind: University of Notre Dame Press.

Dalla Chiara, M. L. 1977. "Quantum Logic and Physical Modalities." *Journal of Philosophical Logic* 6:391–404.

——— 1986. "Quantum Logic." In Gabbay and Guenther (1986), vol. 3, pp. 427–469.

Daneri, A., A. Loinger, and G. M. Prosperi. 1962. "Quantum Theory of Measurement and Ergodicity Conditions." *Nuclear Physics* 33:297–319. Reprinted in Wheeler and Zurek (1983), pp. 657–679.

Davies, E. B. 1976. *Quantum Theory and Open Systems.* London: Academic Press.

Davies, P. C. W. 1984. *Quantum Mechanics.* London: Routledge and Kegan Paul.

de Boer, J., E. Dal, and O. Ulfbeck, eds. 1986. *The Lesson of Quantum Theory: Niels Bohr Centennial Symposium, 1985.* Amsterdam: North Holland.

Demopoulos, W. 1976. "What Is the Logical Interpretation of Quantum Mechanics?" In Cohen et al. (1976), pp. 721–728.

D'Espagnat, B. 1979. "The Quantum Theory and Reality." *Scientific American* 241:158–180.

de Witt, B. S. 1970. "Quantum Mechanics and Reality." *Physics Today* 23:30–35. Reprinted in de Witt and Graham (1973), pp. 155–165.

de Witt, B. S., and N. Graham, eds. 1973. *The Many Worlds Interpretation of Quantum Mechanics.* Princeton, N.J.: Princeton University Press.

Dirac, P. A. M. [1930] 1967. *The Principles of Quantum Mechanics,* 4th ed., rev. Oxford: Clarendon Press.

Duhem, P. [1906] 1962. *The Aim and Structure of Physical Theory.* Trans. P. P. Wiener. New York: Athaneum.

Earman, J. 1986. *A Primer on Determinism.* Dordrecht, Holland: Reidel.

Eberhard, P. H. 1977. "Bell's Theorem without Hidden Variables." *Il Nuovo Cimento* 388 (1):75–79.

Eco, U. 1979. *The Role of the Reader,* Bloomington, Ind.: Indiana University Press.

Eddington, A. S. 1935a. "The Theory of Groups." In Eddington (1935b). Reprinted in Newman (1956), vol. 3, pp. 1558–1573.

——— 1935b. *New Pathways in Science.* Cambridge: Cambridge University Press.

Edwards, P., ed. 1967. *The Encyclopedia of Philosophy,* 8 vols. New York: Macmillan.

Ehrenfest, P. 1959. *Collected Scientific Papers.* Ed. M. Klein. Amsterdam: North Holland.

Einstein, A. 1948. "Quantenmechanik und Wirklichkiet." *Dialectica* 2:320–324.

Einstein, A., and P. Ehrenfest. 1922. "Quantentheoretische Bemerkungen zum Experiment von Stern und Gerlach." *Zeitschrift für Physik* 11:31–34. Reprinted in Ehrenfest (1959), pp. 452–455.

Einstein, A., B. Podolsky, and N. Rosen. 1935. "Can Quantum Mechanical Description of Physical Reality Be Considered Complete?" *Physical Review* 47:777–780. Reprinted in Wheeler and Zurek (1983), pp. 138–141.

Everett, H., III. 1957. "'Relative State' Formulation of Quantum Mechanics." *Reviews of Modern Physics* 29:454–462. Reprinted in de Witt and Graham (1973), pp. 141–149, and in Wheeler and Zurek (1983), pp. 315–323.

——— 1973. "The Theory of the Universal Wave Function." In de Witt and Graham (1973), pp. 3–140.

Fano, G. 1971. *Mathematical Methods of Quantum Mechanics.* New York: McGraw Hill.

Fano, U. 1957. "Description of States in Quantum Mechanics by Density Matrix and Operator Techniques." *Reviews of Modern Physics* 29:74–93.

Feyerabend, P. K. (1962), "On the Quantum Theory of Measurement." In Körner (1962), pp. 121–130.

——— 1975. *Against Method.* London: New Left Books.

Feynman, R. P. 1965. *The Character of Physical Law.* Cambridge, Mass.: M.I.T. Press.

Feynman, R. P., R. B. Leighton, and M. Sands. 1965. *The Feynman Lectures on Physics,* 3 vols. Reading, Mass.: Addison Wesley.

Finch, P. D. 1969. "On the Structure of Quantum Logic." *Journal of Symbolic Logic* 34:275–282. Reprinted in Hooker (1975), pp. 415–425.

Fine, A. 1970. "Insolubility of the Quantum Measurement Problem." *Physical Review* 2D:2783–2787.

——— 1972. "Some Conceptual Problems of Quantum Theory." In Colodny (1972), pp. 3–31.

——— 1979. "How to Count Frequencies, a Primer for Quantum Realists." *Synthese* 42:145–154.

——— 1984. "Einstein's Realism." In Cushing, Delaney, and Guttig (1984), pp. 106–133.

Finkelstein, D. 1969. "Matter, Space and Logic." In Cohen and Wartofsky (1969), pp. 199–215.

French, A. P., ed. 1979. *Einstein, A Centenary Volume.* Cambridge, Mass.: Harvard University Press.

Friedman, M., and C. Glymour. 1972. "If Quanta Had Logic." *Journal of Philosophical Logic* 1:16–28.

Friedman, M., and H. Putnam. 1978. "Quantum Logic, Conditional Probability and Interference." *Dialectica* 32:305–315.

Gabbay, D., and F. Guenther. 1986. *Handbook of Philosophical Logic,* 4 vols. Dordrecht, Holland: Reidel.

Geroch, R. 1984. "The Everett Interpretation." *Nous* 18:617–633.

Gibbins, P. 1981a. "A Note on Quantum Logic and the Uncertainty Principle." *Philosophy of Science* 48:122–126.

——— 1981b. "Putnam on the Two-Slit Experiment." *Erkenntnis* 16:235–241.

——— 1987. *Particles and Paradoxes.* Cambridge: Cambridge University Press.

Giere, R. N. 1973. "Objective Single-Case Probabilities and the Foundations of Statistics." In Suppes et al. (1973), pp. 467–483.

——— 1976. "A Laplacean Formal Semantics for Single-Case Propensities." *Journal of Philosophical Logic* 5:321–353.

——— 1979. *Understanding Scientific Reasoning.* New York: Holt, Rinehart, Winston.

Gillespie, D. T. 1970. *A Quantum Mechanics Primer.* Leighton Buzzard, Beds.: International Textbook Company.

Gleason, A. M. 1957. "Measures on the Closed Subspaces of a Hilbert Space." *Journal of Mathematics and Mechanics* 6:885–893.

Gödel, K. 1933. "An Interpretation of the Intuitionistic Sentential Logic." Trans. J. Hintikka and L. Rossi. In Hintikka (1969), pp. 128–129.

Goldstein, H. 1950. *Classical Mechanics.* Reading , Mass.: Addison Wesley.

Good, I. J., ed. 1961. *The Scientist Speculates.* London: Heinemann.

Gudder, S. P. 1970. "On Hidden Variable Theories." *Journal of Mathematical Physics* 11:431–436.

——— 1972. "Partial Algebraic Structures Associated with Orthomodular Posets." *Pacific Journal of Mathematics* 41:712–730.

——— 1973. "Quantum Logics, Physical Space, Position Observables and Symmetry." *Reports on Mathematical Physics* 4:193–202.

——— 1976. "A Generalised Measure and Probability Theory for the Physical Sciences." In Harper and Hooker (1976), pp. 121–141.

Haag, R. 1973. *Boulder Lectures in Theoretical Physics,* vol. 14B. Ed. W. E. Britten. New York: Gordon and Breach.

Hacking, I. 1983. *Representing and Intervening: Introductory Topics in the Philosophy of Science.* Cambridge: Cambridge University Press.

Halmos, P. R. 1957. *Introduction to Hilbert Space and the Theory of Spectral Multiplicity,* 2d ed. New York: Chelsea.

Hanson, N. R. 1967. "Quantum Mechanics, Philosophical Implications of." In Edwards (1967), vol. 7, pp. 41–49.

Hardegree, G. M. 1980. "Micro-States in the Interpretation of Quantum Theory." In Asquith and Giere (1980), pp. 43–54.

Hardegree, G. M., and P. J. Frazer. 1981. "Charting the Labyrinth of Quantum Logics: A Progress Report." In Beltrametti and van Fraassen (1981), pp. 53–76.

Harper, W. L., and C. A. Hooker, eds. 1976. *Foundations and Philosophy of Statistical Theories in the Physical Sciences.* Dordrecht, Holland: Reidel.

Harrison, J. 1983. "Against Quantum Logic." *Analysis* 43:82–85.

Healey, R. 1979. "Quantum Realism: Naïveté Is No Excuse." *Synthese* 42:121–144.

——— 1984. "How Many Worlds?" *Noûs* 18:591–616.

Heisenberg, W. 1927. "Über den anschaulichen Inhalt den quantentheoretischen Kinematik and Mechanik." *Zeitschrift für Physik* 43:172–198. Trans. as "The Physical Content of Quantum Kinematics and Mechanics," in Wheeler and Zurek (1983), pp. 62–84.

——— 1958. *Physics and Philosophy: The Revolution in Modern Science.* New York: Harper and Row.

Heitler, W. 1949. "The Departure from Classical Thought in Modern Physics." In Schilpp (1949), pp. 181–198.

Hellman, G. 1982a. "Einstein and Bell: Tightening the Case for Microphysical Randomness." *Synthese* 53:445–460.

——— 1982b. "Stochastic Einstein Locality and the Bell Theorems." *Synthese* 53:461–504.

——— 1984. "Introduction." *Noûs* 18:557–567.

Hempel, C. G. 1954. "A Logical Appraisal of Operationism." *Scientific Monthly* 79:215–220. Reprinted in Hempel (1965), pp. 123–133.

——— 1965. *Aspects of Scientific Explanation and Other Essays in the Philosophy of Science.* New York: Free Press.

Hintikka, J., ed. 1969. *The Philosophy of Mathematics.* Oxford: Oxford University Press.

Hirst, R. J. 1967. "Phenomenalism." In Edwards (1967), vol. 6, pp. 130–135.

Holdsworth, D. G., and C. A. Hooker. 1983. "A Critical Survey of Quantum Logic." In *Logic in the 20th Century. Scientia* 1983:127–246.

Holland S. S., Jr. 1970. "The Current Interst in Orthomodular Lattices." In *Trends in Lattice Theory.* New York: van Nostrand. Reprinted in Hooker (1975), pp. 437–496.

Hooker, C. A. 1972. "The Nature of Quantum Mechanical Reality: Einstein versus Bohr." In Colodny (1972), pp. 67–302.

Hooker, C. A., ed. 1973. *Contemporary Research in the Foundations and Philosophy of Quantum Theory.* Dordrecht, Holland: Reidel.

——— 1975. *The Logico-Algebraic Approach to Quantum Mechanics,* vol. 1: *Historical Evolution.* Dordrecht, Holland: Reidel.

Hughes, G. E., and M. J. Cresswell. 1968. *An Introduction to Modal Logic.* London: Methuen.

Hughes, R. I. G. 1979. *Systems of Quantum Logic.*Ph.D. diss. Vancouver: University of British Columbia.

——— 1981. "Quantum Logic." *Scientific American* 243:202–213.

——— 1982. "The Logic of Experimental Questions." In Asquith and Nickles (1982), pp. 243–256.

——— 1985a. "Logics Based on Partial Boolean Algebras" [Review Article]. *Journal of Symbolic Logic* 50:558–566.

——— 1985b. "Semantic Alternatives in Partial Boolean Quantum Logic." *Journal of Philosophical Logic* 14:411–446.

Hughes, R. I. G., and B. C. van Fraassen. 1988. "Can the Measurement Problem Be Solved by Superselection Rules?" Forthcoming.

Jammer, M. 1966. *The Conceptual Development of Quantum Mechanics.* New York: McGraw Hill.

——— 1974. *The Philosophy of Quantum Mechanics. The Interpretation of Quantum Mechanics in Historical Perspective.* New York: John Wiley.

Jarrett, J. P. 1984. "On the Physical Significance of the Locality Conditions in the Bell Arguments." *Noûs* 18:569–589.

——— 1989. "Bell's Theorem: A Guide to the Implications." In Cushing and McMullin (1989).

Jauch, J. M. 1968. *Foundations of Quantum Mechanics.* Reading, Mass.: Addison Wesley.

Jauch, J. M., and C. Piron. 1963. "Can Hidden Variables Be Excluded in Quantum Mechanics?" *Helvetica Physica Acta* 38:827–837.

Jeffrey, R. C., ed. 1980. *Studies in Inductive Logic and Probability,* vol. 2. Berkeley, Calif.: University of California Press.

Jordan, T. F. 1969. *Linear Operators for Quantum Mechanics.* New York: John Wiley.

Kadison, R. 1951. "Isometries of Operator Algebras." *Annals of Mathematics* 54:325–338.

Kant, I. [1787] 1929. *Critique of Pure Reason.* Trans. N. Kemp Smith. New York: St. Martin's Press.

——— [1786] 1970. *Metaphysical Foundations of Natural Science.* Trans. J. Ellington. Indianapolis: Bobbs Merrill.

Kelley, J. L. 1955. *General Topology.* New York: van Nostrand.

Kleene, S. C. 1967. *Mathematical Logic.* New York: John Wiley.

Kochen, S. 1978. "The Interpretation of Quantum Mechanics." Address to the Biennial Conference of the Philosophy of Science Association, 1978. Princeton, N.J.: Princeton University, mimeo.

Kochen, S., and E. P. Specker. 1965. "Logical Structures Arising in Quantum Theory." *Symposium on the Theory of Models.* Amsterdam: North Holland. Reprinted in Hooker (1975), pp. 263–276.

——— 1967. "The Problem of Hidden Variables in Quantum Mechanics." *Journal of Mathematics and Mechanics* 17:59–87.

Kolmogorov, A. N. [1933] 1950. *Foundations of the Theory of Probability.* Trans. N. Morrison. New York: Chelsea.

Körner, S., ed. 1962. *Observation and Interpretation in the Philosophy of Physics.* New York: Dover.

Körner, S. 1969. *Fundamental Questions of Philosophy.* Harmondsworth, Middx.: Penguin Books.

Lakatos, I. 1970. "Falsification and the Methodology of Scientific Research Programmes." In Lakatos and Musgrave (1970), pp. 91–196.

Lakatos, I., and A. Musgrave, eds. 1970. *Criticism and the Growth of Knowledge.* Cambridge: Cambridge University Press.

Landau, L. D., and E. M. Lifschitz. 1977. *Quantum Mechanics (Non-Relativistic Theory),* 3d ed. Oxford: Pergamon Press.

Landau, L. D., and R. Peierls. 1931. "Erweiterung des Unbestimmtheitsprinzips für die relativische Quantentheorie." *Zeitschrift für Physik* 69:56–69.

Lang, S. 1972. *Linear Algebra,* 2d ed. Reading, Mass.: Addison Wesley.

Laplace, P. [1814] 1951. *A Philosophical Essay on Probabilities.* Trans. E. W. Truscott and F. L. Emory. New York: Dover.

Leggett, A. J. 1986. "Quantum Mechanics at the Macroscopic Level." In de Boer, Dal, and Ulfbeck (1986), pp. 35–57.

Lewis, D. 1980. "A Subjectivist's Guide to Objective Chance." In Jeffrey (1980), pp. 263–293.

——— 1986. *On the Plurality of Worlds.* Oxford: Blackwell.

Lieb, E. H., B. Simon, and A. S. Wightman, eds. 1976. *Studies in Mathematical Physics: Essays in Honour of Valentine Bargmann.* Princeton, N.J.: Princeton University Press.

Loux, M. J. 1979. *The Possible and the Actual: Readings in the Metaphysics of Modality.* Ithaca: Cornell University Press.

Lüders, G. 1951. "Über die Zustandsänderung durch den Messprozess." *Annalen der Physik* 8:323–328.

Mackey, G. W. 1963. *Mathematical Foundations of Quantum Mechanics.* New York: Benjamin.

MacKinnon, E. 1984. "Semantics and Quantum Logic." In Cushing, Delaney, and Gutting (1984), pp. 173–195.

MacLane, S., and G. Birkhoff. 1979. *Algebra,* 2d ed. New York: Macmillan.

Maczynski, M. J. 1967. "A Remark on Mackey's Axiom System for Quantum Mechanics." *Bulletin de L'Académie Polonaise des Sciences,* Serie des Sciences Mathematiques, Astronomiques et Physiques 15:583–587.

Margenau, H. 1936. "Quantum Mechanical Descriptions." *Physical Review* 49:240–242.

——— 1950. *The Nature of Physical Reality.* New York: McGraw Hill.

——— 1954. "Advantages and Disadvantages of Various Interpretations of the Quantum Theory." *Physics Today* 7:6–13.

——— 1958. "Philosophical Problems Concerning the Meaning of Measurement in Physics." *Philosophy of Science* 25:23–33.

——— 1963. "Measurements in Quantum Mechanics." *Annals of Physics* 23:469–485.

Maxwell, G., and R. M. Anderson, Jr., eds. 1975. *Induction, Probability and Confirmation. Minnesota Studies in Philosophy of Science,* vol. 6. Minneapolis: University of Minnesota Press.

McMullin, E. 1978. "Structural Explanation." *American Philosophical Quarterly* 15:139–147.

Messiah, A. 1958. *Quantum Mechanics,* 2 vols. Vol. 1 trans. G. M. Tenner; vol. 2 trans. J. Potter. New York: John Wiley.

Mielnik, B. 1968. "Geometry of Quantum States." *Communications in Mathematical Physics* 9:55–80.

Mittelstaedt, P. 1981. "Classification of Different Areas of Work Afferent to Quantum Logic." In Beltrametti and van Fraassen (1981), pp. 3–16.

Monk, J. D. 1969. *Introduction to Set Theory.* New York: McGraw Hill.

Morgenbesser, S., ed. 1967. *Philosophy of Science Today.* New York: Basic Books.

Mott, N. F., and H. S. W. Massey. 1965. *The Theory of Atomic Collisions.* Oxford: Clarendon Press. Reprinted in part in Wheeler and Zurek (1983), pp. 701–706.

Nagel, E., P. Suppes, and A. Tarski, eds. 1962. *Logic, Methodology and Philosophy of Science.* Stanford: Stanford University Press.

Newman, J. R., ed. 1956. *The World of Mathematics,* 4 vols. New York: Simon and Schuster.

Noakes, G. R. 1957. *New Intermediate Physics.* London: Macmillan.

Pagels, H. R. 1982. *The Cosmic Code: Quantum Physics as the Language of Nature.* New York: Simon and Schuster.

Park, J. L., and H. Margenau. 1968. "Simultaneous Measurability in Quantum Theory." *International Journal of Theoretical Physics* 1:211–283.

——— 1971. "The Logic of Noncommutability of Quantum Mechanical Operators and Its Empirical Consequences." In Yourgrau and van der Merwe (1971), pp. 37–70.

Pauli, W. 1933. "Die allgemeinen Prinzipien der Wellenmechanik." *Handbuch der Physik* (ed. H. Geiger and K. Scheel), 2d ed., vol. 24, pp. 83–272. Berlin: Springer Verlag.

Penrose, R., and C. J. Isham, eds. 1986. *Quantum Concepts in Space and Time.* Oxford: Clarendon Press.

Petersen, A. 1963. "The Philosophy of Niels Bohr." *Bulletin of the Atomic Scientists,* September 1963, pp. 8–14.

Piron, C. 1972. "Survey of General Quantum Physics." *Foundations of Physics* 2:287–314.

——— 1976. *Foundations of Quantum Physics.* Reading, Mass.: Benjamin.

Popper, K. R. 1959. *The Logic of Scientific Discovery.* London: Hutchinson.

——— 1982. *Quantum Theory and the Schism in Physics.* Totowa, N.J.: Rowan and Littlefield.

PSSC (Physical Sciences Study Committee). 1960. *Physics.* New York: Heath.

Putnam, H. 1962. "What Theories Are Not." In Nagel, Suppes, and Tarski (1962), pp. 240–251.

——— 1965. "A Philosopher Looks at Quantum Mechanics." In Colodny (1965), pp. 75–101.

——— 1969. "Is Logic Empirical?" In Cohen and Wartofsky (1969), pp. 181–241. Reprinted in Hooker (1975), pp. 181–206.

Reichenbach, H. 1944. *Philosophic Foundations of Quantum Mechanics.* Berkeley, Calif.: University of California Press.

——— 1956. *The Direction of Time.* Berkeley, Calif.: University of California Press.

Robertson, H. P. 1929. "The Uncertainty Principle." *Physical Review* 34:163–164. Reprinted in Wheeler and Zurek (1983), pp. 127–128.

Rosenfeld, L. 1971. "Quantum Theory in 1929." In Cohen and Stachel (1979); see also Wheeler and Zurek (1983), pp. 699–700.

Russell, B. 1917. *Mysticism and Logic.* London: Allen and Unwin.

Salmon, W. C. 1984. *Scientific Explanation and the Causal Structure of the World.* Princeton, N.J.: Princeton University Press.

Schilpp, P. A., ed. 1949. *Albert Einstein: Philosopher-Scientist.* La Sale, Ill.: Open Court.

Schrödinger, E. 1935. "Die gegenwärtige Situation in der Quantenmechanik." *Naturwissenschaften* 22:807–812, 823–828, 844–849. Trans. as "The Present Situation in Quantum Mechanics" by J. D. Trimmer, in Wheeler and Zurek (1983), pp. 152–167.

——— 1953. "What Is Matter?" *Scientific American,* September 1953, pp. 52–56.

Shimony, A. 1980. "The Point We Have Reached." *Epistemological Letters,* June 1980.

——— 1981. "Critique of the Papers of Fine and Suppes." In Asquith and Giere (1981), pp. 572–580.

——— 1986. "Events and Processes in the Quantum World." In Penrose and Isham (1986), pp. 182–203.

Sikorsky, R. 1964. *Boolean Algebras,* 2d ed. Berlin: Springer Verlag.

Simon, B. 1976. "Quantum Dynamics: From Automorphism to Hamiltonian." In Lieb, Simon, and Wightman (1976), pp. 327–349.

Skyrms, B. 1980. *Causal Necessity: A Pragmatic Investigation of the Necessity of Laws.* New Haven, Conn.: Yale University Press.

Stairs, A. 1982. "Quantum Logic and the Lüders Rule." *Philosophy of Science* 49:422–436.

——— 1983a. "On the Logic of Pairs of Quantum Systems." *Synthese* 56:47–60.

——— 1983b. "Quantum Logic, Realism and Value Definiteness." *Philosophy of Science* 50:578–602.

——— 1984. "Sailing into the Charybdis: van Fraassen on Bell's Theorem." *Synthese* 61:351–359.

Staniland, H. 1972. *Universals.* New York: Anchor Books.

Stein, H. 1972. "On the Conceptual Structure of Quantum Mechanics." In Colodny (1972), pp. 367–438.

Suppe, F. 1977. "The Search for Philosophic Understanding of Scientific Theories." In *The Structure of Scientific Theories,* ed. F. Suppe, pp. 3–232. Urbana:University of Illinois Press.

Suppes, P. 1966. "The Probabilistic Argument for a Nonclassical Logic in Quantum Mechanics." *Philosophy of Science* 33:14–21.

——— 1967. "What Is a Scientific Theory?" In Morgenbesser (1967), pp. 55–67.

Suppes, P., L. Henken, A. Joja, and G. C. Moisil, eds. 1973. *Logic, Methodology and Philosophy of Science,* vol. 4. Amsterdam: North-Holland.

Swift, A. R., and R. Wright. 1980. "Generalized Stern-Gerlach Experiments and the Observability of Arbitrary Spin Operators." *Journal of Mathematical Physics* 21 (1):77–82.

Taylor, E. F., and J. A. Wheeler. 1963. *Space-Time Physics.* San Francisco: Freeman.

Teller, P. 1979. "Quantum Mechanics and the Nature of Continuous Physical Quantities." *Journal of Philosophy* 76:345–360.

——— 1983. "The Projection Postulate as a Fortuitous Approximation." *Philosophy of Science* 50:413–431.

——— 1989. "Relativity, Relational Holism, and the Bell Inequalities." In Cushing and McMullin (1989).

Tierliebhaber, X. 1939. "Katzen und Affen, Affen und Katzen: die Tiere der Philosophen." *Zeitschrift für Philosophische Zoologie* 1:1–26.

Toulmin, S. 1953. *Philosophy of Science: An Introduction.* London: Hutchinson.

van Fraassen, B. C. 1972. "A Formal Approach to the Philosophy of Science." In Colodny (1972), pp. 303–366.

——— 1974a, "The Einstein-Podolsky-Rosen Paradox." *Synthese* 29:291–309.

——— 1974b, "The Labyrinth of Quantum Logic." In Cohen and Wartofsky (1974), pp. 72–102. Reprinted in Hooker (1975), pp. 577–607.

——— 1980. *The Scientific Image.* Oxford: Clarendon Press.

——— 1981a. "Assumptions and Interpretations of Quantum Logic." In Beltrametti and van Fraassen (1981), pp. 17–31.

——— 1981b. "A Modal Interpretation of Quantum Mechanics." In Beltrametti and van Fraassen (1981), pp. 229–258.

——— 1982. "The Charybdis of Realism: Epistemological Implications of Bell's Inequality." *Synthese* 52:25–38.

——— 1985. "Salmon on Explanation." Contribution to a symposium at the Eastern Division Meeting of the American Philosophical Association, 1985. Princeton, N.J.: Princeton University, mimeo.

von Neumann, J. [1932] 1955. *Mathematical Foundations of Quantum Mechanics.* Trans. R. T. Beyer. Princeton, N.J.: Princeton University Press.

Wan, K.-K. 1980. "Superselection Rules, Quantum Measurement and the Schrödinger's Cat." *Canadian Journal of Physics* 58:976–982.

Weyl, H. 1952. *Symmetry.* Princeton, N.J.: Princeton University Press.

Wheeler, J. A. 1957. "Assessment of Everett's 'Relative State' Formulation of Quantum Theory." *Reviews of Modern Physics* 29:463–465. Reprinted in de Witt and Graham (1973), pp. 151–153.

Wheeler, J. A., and W. H. Zurek, eds. 1983. *Quantum Theory and Measurement.* Princeton, N.J.: Princeton University Press.

Wigner, E. P. 1961. "Remarks on the Mind-Body Question." In Good (1961). Reprinted in Wigner (1967), pp. 171–184.

——— 1963. "The Problem of Measurement." *American Journal of Physics* 31:6–15. Reprinted in Wigner (1967), pp. 153–170, and Wheeler and Zurek (1983), pp. 324–341.

——— 1967. *Symmetries and Reflections.* Bloomington, Ind.: Indiana University Press.

——— 1970. "On Hidden Variables and Quantum Mechanical Probabilities." *American Journal of Physics* 38:1005–1009.

——— 1973. "Epistemological Perspectives in Quantum Theory." In Hooker (1973), pp. 369–385.

Yourgrau, W., and A. van der Merwe, eds. 1971. *Perspectives in Quantum Theory: Essays in Honor of Alfred Landé.* Cambridge, Mass.: M.I.T. Press.

Index